Reaching
the Special
Learner
Through
Music

# Reaching the Special Learner Through Music

Sona D. Nocera

**SILVER BURDETT COMPANY** • Morristown, New Jersey

Glenview, Illinois     Palo Alto     Dallas     Atlanta

# Contents

Library of Congress Catalog Card Number 78-62981      ISBN 0-382-05636-1

Cover: Molly J. Jenkins     Art: Rahn Studio

# Music

Music is a tale told in sounds
Of such infinite reach
All time, all life, all tongues
Are in its speech.
Music is the sound of events
So moving, in its classic or its blue,
The heart nods recognition: "I was there.
And I have felt that, too . . ."

Mary L. O'Neill

# The Role of Music
# in the Education of Special Learners

# The Role of Music in the Education of Special Learners

## The Music Education of Special Learners

The importance of music in the education of children is well established in American schools. All children, including those with handicapping conditions, have a right to a music education in which the *primary goals are aesthetic,* achieved through the development of music concepts and skills commensurate with intellectual and physical abilities. As increasing numbers of children with handicapping conditions are educated in public school classrooms, the preparation of *every teacher* should be focused on developing teaching competencies to meet the needs of *every child.* Unfortunately, in the past, preparation for teaching children with learning problems has generally been neglected in teacher training programs.

Preparing teachers to effectively teach special learners includes the development not only of teaching skills but of attitudes as well. Some teachers will need to come to grips with personal feelings and expectations regarding handicapped individuals. All will need to understand the implications of certain disabling conditions for music learning. Music teachers who intend to achieve music goals in their work with special learners must acquire special teaching techniques and develop skills in selecting and adapting appropriate resource materials.

Education is an ongoing process in the achievement of specific attitudes, concepts, and skills. Teaching is one part of that process, in which an individual (i.e., the teacher) by planning specific strategies based on instructional objectives guides learners in developing those goals. Although there are infinite ways to plan strategies, the general goals of music education are non-negotiable and are the *same* for *all* children.

Music is a multisensory experience. Listening, seeing, moving, and feeling are all important in the music education curriculum, making music a natural discipline through which to develop sensory perception and psychomotor skills. As more children with learning difficulties are identified, educators have come to realize that music education, in addition to being a valuable content area of the curriculum in its own right, can also be an aid in developing basic skills in all children. Children actually *learn to learn* through music activities, since music helps develop skills that are necessary for cognitive, affective, and psychomotor functioning utilized in all areas of the school curriculum. Unlike activities dependent on verbal interaction, music rarely fails to communicate with *every* child. In addition, because of the flexibility and vast resources available in music, a single activity can include children of widely differing abilities. Thus, music enables every intellect to be challenged, no matter how inhibited. Music provides an alternative means through which children who are unable or unwilling to speak can express feelings and ideas.

Music education for special learners should not attempt to replace other teaching methods in developing basic learning skills, but it should *supplement* them by providing a different medium through which they can be reinforced and refined. When music programs derive goals and objectives from basic skills rather than from music, they cease to be music *education.* The foremost goals of the music education curriculum are to develop in children musical understandings and skills that are appropriate to their functioning level. Some have confused the goals of therapy with those of education. Although Carl Rogers and others have given credence to the idea that education can *also* be therapeutic, the goals of such therapies as recreation and music do not include the development of music concepts and skills that contribute to musical understanding. Unlike music education, music therapy is the *functional use* of music to develop *nonmusic goals.* It does not concern itself with music as a content area of the curriculum. Since the music therapist does not teach music, the structure and quality of the music used are not a concern in its selection. For music educators, the selection of music materials is a major consideration, since these materials must clearly illustrate the music concepts to be learned and must be of the highest musical quality in order to withstand manipulation and repetition.

All children need an aesthetic education, and this is most effectively achieved through participation in the arts. For a handicapped child, achievement in music can reaffirm a sense of personal worth as well as improve general educational functioning. It may even expand career options, as musical aptitude and talent are not the exclusive legacy of nonhandicapped individuals in our society. As professionals who are committed to the development of musical potential in *every* child, music educators must find ways in which the handicapped as well as the nonhandicapped can express and develop that potential.

**Special education music** The special education music teacher is a music educator who has been trained to design and implement a program that *simultaneously* combines music and nonmusic goals. At no time do the music goals become subordinate to the nonmusic goals; ideally they are achieved cooperatively. The primary purpose of music education programs for handicapped children (as for all children) is to actively involve the child in meaningful music experiences that will develop music concepts and skills appropriate to individual functioning level. Comprehensive music education training is the prerequisite of a qualified special education music teacher. Just as the music teacher is a musician and educator, the music teacher of special learners is a musician and *special* educator. In both cases, neither musicianship nor teaching effectiveness can be compromised. A special education music teacher must be prepared to be a member of a multidisciplinary team of professionals who coordinate their individual efforts with each child. Such a team might include the school psychologist, psychiatrist, resource teacher, classroom teacher, nurse, health officer, social worker, speech therapist, and any other school staff member directly concerned with the development of children. Communications among team members must be continuous, with problems and progress discussed freely. All must appreciate each other's expertise in his or her respective field when decisions are made concerning a child.

The use of music as one way to foster learning skills need not affect the music goals and objectives of a music education program. In fact, these music goals alone do a great deal to improve perceptual motor functioning, although many teachers are unaware of these "fringe benefits." When a music teacher can recognize deficient skill functioning and deliberately plan music activities that help that functioning while achieving music goals, a new dimension of music teaching emerges. Music teachers are rarely trained to plan for individual differences in this way, which is termed *prescriptive teaching* by general educationists.

One may question whether this approach to music education is the exclusive right of handicapped children. Absolutely not! *All* children must master basic skills before intellectual potential can be realized. The earlier an individual possesses the basic skills for learning, the more effective and challenging education can be. By focusing educational management on learning skills, we seek to discourage typing or labeling children as *impaired, disabled,* or *handicapped.* Labeling has created stigmas and stereotypes that do a great disservice to individuals with disabilities. A disability or an impairment is not necessarily a handicap. Most often, society determines what is a handicap by the way it accepts or rejects certain disabilities and impairments. As educators, we must strive to educate not only those individuals handicapped by society's attitudes, but society itself.

Throughout the years, educators have accepted the labels and classifications of exceptional children given them by other professionals. The medical profession most often labels by etiology, or the cause of the disability. The psychology profession most often labels by the dysfunction itself. Although these terms may be meaningful to *those* professionals, they do not provide much insight that will enhance the *educational* management of

children and, therefore, are not helpful to educators. As a result, teaching is often designed to fit labels rather than individuals. What teachers need to know in order to deal more effectively with all children is a profile of *both* strengths and weaknesses in specific skill areas. IQ scores alone do not provide functional data in this regard; an inventory of basic skill development, on the other hand, will give both the classroom teacher and the music teacher something more concrete on which to base goals for individuals. The Individualized Education Program (IEP), when made available to all teachers, has the potential to coordinate the various curriculum areas in planning goals for special learners.

Specific learning skills are generally grouped into categories such as gross motor, language, auditory, and visual. All learning skills can be dealt with in any music situation, but some are nearly always inherent in every music activity. These fall into the perceptual motor classification, since most music experiences involve sensory perception (i.e., listening, seeing, feeling) combined with motor acts (i.e., singing, playing, moving).

The key role of sensory perception, and hence music education, in the development of the intellect has been recognized for more than two hundred years. The experiments of Itard and Seguin have been the basis of the work of contemporary researchers such as Montessori and Piaget. In music education, the teachings of Carl Orff, Emile Jaques-Dalcroze, and Shinichi Suzuki emphasize sensory development as *the essential readiness factor* for the more complex cognitive tasks in music, such as music reading. Moreover, recent research has pointed out that not all individuals develop sensory functioning according to the same timetable or with equal ease. Traditional educational approaches tended to plan activities geared to the "average" child. Today, few educators are willing to describe what "average" is. A current concern in education is individualizing the curriculum—a direct testimonial to the increasing awareness of individual differences in children. Because early special education classes were often dumping grounds for every child who couldn't function in a classroom geared to the "average," successful teachers of special children learned several decades ago how to individualize their teaching.

Until special education methodology and technology became sufficiently developed, individuals with certain impairments were considered *unteachable,* though not necessarily *uneducable.* Even today, there are those who are unaware that children with cognitive and physical impairments can, *with effective teaching,* learn music concepts and skills, and that music programs for them need not be relegated to a merely recreational or entertainment level. Of course, there have always been dedicated and imaginative music teachers who were unwilling to compromise their professional goals. Fortunately, these individuals accepted the challenge to teach the deaf to sing and to play instruments, the retarded to learn fundamental music skills, and individuals lacking functional hands and fingers to play instruments. Those music educators, who can be found in countries around the world, have led the way in applying special education research to music teaching and have been responsible for this new aspect of music education.

Some of the leading colleges and universities throughout the world are now offering music education degree programs with special education emphasis. Their graduates have been prepared to teach *all* the children in the public schools, and they are a welcome resource to music faculties bewildered by the expanding scope of their profession. Some schools are using the expertise of these special music educators to aid in implementing special music programs aimed at developing basic learning goals. In addition, these educators can function as resource persons for classroom teachers and other professionals who desire to include music activities in their work with special learners. Music departments are finding it a definite advantage to have among their music education staff a teacher who has a basic understanding of the learning styles and needs of special learners, who comprehends the jargon that couches reports about specific children, and who has some common ground on which to meet special education professionals. In view of recent legislation guaranteeing equal educational opportunity for the handicapped, both public schools and colleges need to be equipped with qualified staff who can knowledgeably interpret the implications for music education and assist in implementing music curriculums that comply with this legislation.

## Education for All Handicapped Children Act (P.L. 94-142)—Implications for Music Education

"It is the purpose of the Act to assure that all handicapped children have available to them, within the time periods specified in section 612 (2)(B), a free appropriate public education which emphasizes special education and related services designed to meet their unique needs, to assure that the rights of handicapped children and their parents or guardians are protected, to assist States and localities to provide for the education of all handicapped children, and to assess and assure the effectiveness of efforts to educate handicapped children." (P.L. 94-142)

In November 1975, the passing of this act represented a milestone for human rights while creating panic among the nation's educational system. The recurring theme throughout the document is that handicapped children, like all children, have the right to a free appropriate public education with full educational opportunities. Prior to its passage, more than one half of the eight million handicapped children in the United States were not receiving educational opportunities that would enable them to realize their full potential. At least one million had been excluded from public schools altogether, forcing their parents to seek private education without the assistance

of financial aid or transportation. As a result of studying the problem, Congress concluded that educational research, technology, and teacher training were sufficiently developed to enable state and local educational agencies to provide effective special education programs to meet the needs of handicapped children. Of interest to music educators is the estimate that only about two million handicapped children (out of eight million) are currently receiving *any kind of arts education.* Certainly this situation will need to be rectified if schools are to comply with providing appropriate educational experiences and full educational opportunities for the handicapped as well as the nonhandicapped. Since music education programs are a part of the curriculum for nonhandicapped in virtually all parts of the United States, failure to provide a music education for handicapped children would clearly be discriminatory.

**Mainstreaming**   While P.L. 94-142 does not *mandate* mainstreaming, its message is clear regarding the education of handicapped children in "isolated environments." Although some children may never be able to function totally in a regular classroom, the law seeks to ensure that they are at least brought into the educational mainstream and educated alongside their nonhandicapped peers. The intent is that handicapped individuals should be continually progressing up a ladder of varied educational settings, with each one being less restrictive (or isolated from the mainstream) than the one before.

Special education received its greatest impetus in American public schools during the 1950s. The birth of the "special class era" can almost be dated from a classic study showing the social rejection of below-average learners in the regular classroom. (Johnson, 1950.)[1] Ironically, children with the same learning problems are being moved back to regular classrooms today on the basis of the same social argument. It is important for us as educators to understand that P.L. 94-142 is a human rights issue and that we arrived at mainstreaming for social rather than educational reasons. Indeed, there is no research that proves mainstreaming to be a *superior educational* approach for children with learning difficulties. Mainstreaming came about on the heels of the civil rights legislation of the 1960s and the public demand for equal opportunities for all. No one can argue the potential social value to society as a whole when average children grow up working and playing with children who are different. Perhaps the greatest fruits of current mainstreaming efforts will be that the next generation of adults will not have the stereotyped ideas regarding handicapped individuals that are held by much of the adult population today. It should be emphasized, however, that social attitudes can only be enhanced if the handicapped child can function in the mainstream. If not, other children inevitably develop negative, or at best patronizing, attitudes toward that individual and all the handicapped in general.

It seems too obvious to consider that there is no educational reason why physically disabled children of normal intelligence should not be educated in regular classrooms. They have not been in the past because of architectural barriers rather than educational theory. Another public law (P.L. 93-112, Section 504) now requires public schools to be accessible to the physically disabled. The vast majority of the blind and deaf with average intelligence or better also should be educated in classrooms with unafflicted peers. These individuals will, of course, require the support services of a teacher specially trained to teach them written or spoken language. Special schools that have traditionally educated these individuals have performed an invaluable service in pointing the way regarding technique and materials. The time has come, however, for them to turn back to the public schools those children singularly handicapped by vision, hearing, or mobility in order to concentrate their efforts on those children who are multiply handicapped. Educational research is desperately needed to develop programs to meet the needs of the child who is both deaf and blind, is mentally and physically impaired, or has other combinations of disabling conditions that affect learning style and needs.

When compared with children in "isolated environments," the children who have been successfully mainstreamed have shown better social and academic adjustment. School records indicate that normally intelligent, hearing-impaired children have improved skills in both speaking and understanding language, attributed presumably to day-to-day contact with hearing peers; the sight impaired have shown increased mobility and independence, and children with chronic health and crippling conditions seem to be more tolerant of their limitations and more willing to try alternative activities. Also, when mainstreaming begins at the preprimary level, there is a far better chance for both normal and handicapped children to adjust socially to each other.

Mainstreaming children with serious cognitive or behavior problems places a tremendous responsibility on the classroom teacher. Even with adequate support services (e.g., resource rooms, counseling), the burden of meeting the needs of the special learner falls on this individual. We can hardly expect overwhelming success unless teacher education programs move swiftly to provide more functional preparation for this task. For this reason, one of the top funding priorities of P.L. 94-142 is inservice training of teachers in *all* curriculum areas.

Schools that have hastened to comply with what some administrators erroneously interpreted as mandatory mainstreaming often did so without adequate preplanning, staff development, or support services. Instead of providing equal and appropriate education for their handicapped pupils, they succeeded in demoralizing both them and their unprepared teachers. A child in need of special methods and/or materials cannot be adequately (much less better) educated in a classroom directed by a teacher who has no knowledge of those methods and materials, and who has no one to turn to for assistance. Hopefully, regulations governing funding under P.L. 94-142 will bring a halt to these irresponsible practices. All teachers need to become familiar with the functions and services provided by support systems such as resource rooms; and resource room personnel need to be more familiar with the nonacademic areas of the curriculum, such as the arts, so that they can assist teachers in those areas to cooperate more fully in implementing programs for special learners.

Mainstreamed programs that are floundering or are outright failures are usually characterized by a lack of, or ineffective, support systems and teacher skills. Many teachers lack skills to develop appropriate curriculum and teaching designs for special learners. For example, a teacher trained to teach retarded children understands that the rate of learning for mildly retarded individuals is about three fourths the rate of children with normal intelligence. The teacher who is unaware of this characteristic difference in learning style, or who is unable to design teaching accordingly, blazes ahead, leaving the retarded child to fall by the wayside as the class advances. Although many retarded children lack skills to work independently, the open classroom has sometimes been viewed as a suitable environment for mainstreaming. There is little doubt that, with proper attention to their individual needs, special learners could be successfully mainstreamed into this type of learning environment. However, teachers would need to be both aware of the special needs and capable of continually arranging projects to meet them. Unfortunately, this is not always the case. Whereas a few projects may be designed at the beginning of the year with special learners in mind, all good intentions too often fall prey to majority demands, which increase as the year progresses. In the education of special learners, the open classroom approach is definitely not a way to economize staff, time, or direct teaching.

Perhaps the most devastating result of lack of support systems and teacher skills is the inevitable poor attitude on the part of the teachers. Without teacher enthusiasm, confidence, and cooperation, any program is doomed to failure.

No responsible advocate of mainstreaming ever suggested "wholesale" mainstreaming of special children. Not *every* child is able to function in a mainstreamed situation at any given time. Each child should be evaluated on individual merits as a candidate for mainstreaming *in every aspect of school life,* and this evaluation should be continuous, even after placement. *Mainstreaming should not be an all-or-nothing approach.* If curriculum areas are selected at the academic *and* social levels of the child, there is a reasonable chance for success. For the more severely impaired, mainstreaming may need to be limited to the social aspects of school life until enough skills are mastered to enable success in the curriculum mainstream.

It is quite clear that if mainstreaming is ever to be effective, four things must happen.

**1.** All teachers, *including music teachers,* must have at least minimum competencies in teaching children with learning problems.

**2.** School districts must engage in extensive preplanning activities that include in-service training for staff, hiring qualified special education personnel (including certified teachers in the so-called "special" curriculum areas of music, art, and physical education), acquiring essential materials and facilities where indicated, and conducting responsible evaluation of children who are potential candidates for success in this type of program.

**3.** Teachers in each curriculum area, *including music,* must learn how to implement individualized long-range goals and instructional objectives for special learners through various curriculum areas. (See IEP, pp. 3, 11.)

**4.** All states must follow the example of those that have already revised certification requirements to include special education training for all school professionals at all levels and in all curriculum areas (e.g., teachers, administrators, psychologists). Former New York State Commissioner of Education Ewald B. Nyquist has written: "If school districts send all of their special children back to the regular classrooms without adequate teacher preparation, supportive personnel, and individualized programs and materials, all of the children in the school will suffer." (Nyquist, 1975.)[2]

**The mainstreamed child in music** To consider a handicapped child for successful placement into a regular general or instrumental music class, one must be cognizant of the individual's mental age, motor development, abstracting abilities, attention span, and social development, as well as the level of certain academic skills such as reading and computation. Music education programs designed for the majority make heavy demands on perceptual motor skills, integration and synthesis, symbolization and abstraction, and physical energy. Since the majority of handicapped children are characteristically lacking in many of these skills, particularly in the formative years, music teachers will need to be very aware of individual learning styles and needs in order to plan for their successful participation. The versatility of music activities and the multiple general education benefits that accrue from music education experiences, tend to make the general music class an attractive curriculum area for mainstreaming. However, the placement of special learners must be considered and planned for as carefully in music as placement in the regular classroom. Once music teachers understand the academic and social level of achievement of the mainstreamed child, selecting materials and goals that are equally valid for the special child should pose few serious problems.

Special music educators are trained to design music teaching in ways that enable special learners to improve deficient skill functioning while achieving music goals.

This is truly representative of individualized curriculums but, like those curriculums, requires a great expenditure of time for planning, communicating, adapting materials, and so forth, even for those music teachers who have been specially trained. Mainstreaming of slower-learning children is more difficult for the instrumental teacher than for the general classroom music teacher. The instructional objectives and activities of instrumental music instruction are not as flexible as those of general music instruction. Therefore, it is more difficult to individualize for learners of varying ability levels, especially in group lessons in which everyone is learning the same instrument. Sound educational practice would seem to favor grouping together children of like cognitive and motor abilities when group instrumental instruction is a necessity. Sometimes, the instrumental teacher will find it necessary to depart completely from routine methods and procedures, devising some that are more appropriate to individual learning styles and needs. At other times, however, children with certain impairments can be successfully mainstreamed for instrumental instruction with only a few supplementary lessons, especially in the beginning stages, to ensure that the basic concepts presented in the group lesson have been understood.

As education becomes more concerned with individual differences, music teachers are finding that their roles in the education of special learners extend beyond the music room. In addition to their involvement in multidisciplinary team approaches to identifying and planning programs for special learners, music teachers are recognizing the benefits of more direct contact with the parents of their pupils. Very successful programs of any type are often characterized by parental support and involvement. Parent groups were largely responsible for initiating events that ultimately brought about P.L. 94-142. Many parents report noticing their youngster's positive responses to music at an early age, and they are extremely supportive of music education programs. Special education music teachers can counsel parents as to musical toys, records, and activities that can be useful in the home. When professionals show a sincere interest in helping parents understand and cope with their child's differences, parents can be powerful allies.

Mainstreaming in music should ultimately be decided by the music teacher, who has determined appropriate music goals and objectives in the overall program, understands the nonmusic skills required to successfully achieve those goals, and knows the makeup of groups into which a special learner might be mainstreamed. For example, a retarded child may need to be placed with a group of children much younger in chronological age in order to function commensurately in motor and cognitive skills. This could create social problems, especially with mildly retarded youngsters who may feel that the social content of those music activities is offensive.

Opportunities outside the music class also should be explored for mainstreaming potential. Retarded children who sing very well are often capable of learning songs by rote and can be valuable chorus members. Similarly, slower-learning instrumentalists can often be included in ensembles even if only for certain selections in which they learn their parts by rote or special notation. Children handicapped by behavioral disabilities can also be programmed for both rehearsals and performances in which the activities and length of concentration time are more proportionate to their functioning level. These opportunities often motivate extraordinary efforts in both musical performance and behavior control. School programs, assemblies, and musical productions such as operettas should include opportunities for handicapped as well as nonhandicapped children. Parts can often be adapted to suit individual functioning levels. Even children who are nonverbal or have limited verbal skills can be included with a little ingenuity, and the benefits for the child cannot be measured by any standards. The major consideration is, of course, the needs and abilities of the individual child. Including the handicapped or featuring groups of handicapped children in school programs primarily for public relations or minority representation value is a goal so unworthy of a professional educator that it does not merit discussion.

## Summary

Recent legislation charges all schools with the responsibility of providing suitable learning environments and qualified teachers capable of implementing a music education curriculum for handicapped as well as nonhandicapped learners. Music is a content area of the curriculum that not only strives for the achievement of facts and skills, but provides all children with learning experiences that are basic to learning in other areas of the curriculum as well. Because of its multisensory demands, music contributes to helping children learn how to both process and react to sensory stimulation. Since most music activities are perceptual motor by nature, these abilities are continually being developed in the music class and music lesson.

In order to capitalize on the extra-musical benefits that aid children in developing the skills with which to learn, music educators must be trained to recognize and evaluate basic skill functioning in individuals. However, restricting the goals of music experiences to those that are nonmusic denies special learners the opportunity to demonstrate their musical abilities and to develop musical potentials. If music goals are to be realized, teachers must additionally understand how to select and adapt materials as well as how to plan activities that include special strategies for mainstreamed learners. These competencies are essential if we are to bring special learners into the mainstream of music education in ways that not only guarantee their successful participation, but provide the quality of music education they deserve. While educational mainstreaming is a goal for all handicapped children, music teachers will continue to teach classes of special learners as well as classes into which special learners have been mainstreamed. Both teacher and learner need to demonstrate a level of proficiency equal to the demands of each situation if quality music education programs are to result.

Music education curriculums focus on activities in which children conceptualize through experiencing the elements of music (e.g., melody, rhythm, form, tone color), the styles of music, and uses of music in society. In addition, by relating music elements to other art media, the children learn to integrate and synthesize concepts that are common to all the arts. Finally, through active participation in music, children are guided in analyzing music processes by discovering how the various elements of music are combined in composition. If the foregoing experiences have been amply provided, children are able to make musical judgments based not just on arbitrary personal preference, but on aesthetic rationale as well.

If we believe a music education is a vital part of the general education of all children, then we must more actively advocate music education programs for special learners. This includes providing an equal opportunity aesthetic education through music that offers the same program options that are available to other children (i.e., classroom music instruction, instrumental lessons, performance ensembles). The challenge to the music educator teaching special learners is in ensuring that the music experiences provided are not only appropriate to the individual abilities of that child, but faithful to accepted music education goals for all children as well.

### References/Recommended Reading

*Conference Summary of Public Law 94-142.* U. S. Office of Education, Bureau of Education for the Handicapped, Division of Personnel Preparation, Division of Media Services. Washington, DC: Roy Littlejohn Associates, 1976.

Cruickshank, Wm., Paul, J., and Turnbull, A. *Mainstreaming: A Practical Guide.* Syracuse, NY: Syracuse University Press, 1977.

Dunn, Lloyd, ed. *Exceptional Children in the Schools.* New York: Holt, Rinehart and Winston, 1973.

Fairchild, T. *Mainstreaming Exceptional Children.* Austin, TX: Learning Concepts, 1977.

Ferguson, Marilyn. *The Brain Revolution.* New York: Taplinger, 1973.

Gearhart, B., and Weishahn, M. *The Handicapped Child in the Regular Classroom.* St. Louis: C. V. Mosby, 1976.

Itard, J. *Wild Boy of Aveyron.* New York: Appleton, 1932 (hard cover); Englewood Cliffs, NJ: Prentice-Hall, Inc., 1962 (paperback).

Jaques-Dalcroze, Emile. *Eurhythmics, Art and Education*. 1930. Reprint. New York: Arno Press, 1976.

[1]Johnson, G. O. 1950 (July) "A Study of the Social Position of Mentally Handicapped Children in the Regular Grades." *American Journal of Mental Deficiency*, Vol. 55, No. 1, pp. 60–89.

Kirk, S., ed. *Education of Exceptional Children*. Boston: Houghton Mifflin, 1972.

Molloy, Larry. *Arts and the Handicapped: An Issue of Access*. New York: Educational Facilities Laboratory, 1975.

Nocera, Sona D. *Music and the Handicapped*. Washington, DC: National Committee * Arts for the Handicapped, 1977.

Nordoff, P., and Robbins, C. *Music Therapy in Special Education*. New York: John Day Co., 1971.

[2]Nyquist, Ewald B. *Mainstreaming: Idea and Actuality*. Albany, NY: State Education Department, 1975.

Orem, R. C. *Montessori and the Special Child*. New York: Putnam, 1970.

Rogers, Carl. *Freedom to Learn*. Columbus, OH: Chas. Merrill, 1969.

Schafer, R. Murray. *The Tuning of the World*. New York: Alfred Knopf, 1977.

Seguin, E. *Idiocy and Its Treatment*. 1866. Reprint. Fairfield, NJ: Augustus M. Kelley, Pubs. 1971.

Suzuki, S. *Nurtured by Love: A New Approach to Education*. Translated by Shinichi Suzuki. Hicksville, NY: Exposition Press, 1969.

Telford, C., and Sawrey, J. *The Exceptional Individual*. Englewood Cliffs, NJ: Prentice-Hall, 1967.

Zukerkandl, V. *Sound and Symbol: Man the Musician*. Vol. 2. Translated by Norbert Guterman. Princeton, NJ: Princeton University Press, 1973.

*Additional Resources*

Council for Exceptional Children, 1920 Association Drive, Reston, Virginia 22091. Journals: *Exceptional Children; Teaching Exceptional Children*. Information and publications.

Educational Resources Information Center (ERIC), U.S. Department of Health, Education, and Welfare, National Institute of Education, Washington, D.C. 20202. Library service providing access to a wide variety of special education literature.

Music Educators National Conference, 1902 Association Drive, Reston, Virginia 22091. Journals: *Music Educators Journal, Journal of Research in Music Education*. Special publications: *Music for the Exceptional Child, Music in Special Education*, (originally published as *Music Educators Journal*, April 1972 issue).

National Committee * Arts for the Handicapped, Suite 804, 1701 K Street NW, Washington, D.C. 20006. Bibliographies and selected literature concerning instruction in the arts for handicapped individuals.

State Education Departments. Write to both music education and special education departments for information concerning the music education of special children.

U. S. Department of Health, Education, and Welfare, Bureau of Education for the Handicapped, Office of Education, 400 Maryland Avenue, SW, Washington, D.C. 20202. Information regarding educational and vocational programs; grants and funding; legislation.

# Designing Music Teaching Based on Learning Skills

# Designing Music Teaching Based on Learning Skills

The hazards of labeling, classifying, and pigeonholing have already been discussed. If we are to effectively plan for individual needs in both music and learning skills, it is necessary to be aware of each child's strengths and weaknesses in both these areas. Often, when teachers consult school records to seek out information about a child, they are confronted with test names and scores that are incomprehensible to them. Consequently, they garner information from what they can understand, which is often anecdotal records. While these records may provide some valuable insights into a child's behavior, they do not always give a complete picture of the child's *potential* for learning or the specific learning areas in which difficulties are encountered. The chart provided in the Appendix (*see* p. 272) represents some, but by no means all, of the tests commonly used in school testing programs. It is included solely for the purpose of acquainting the reader with what each instrument tests and the age group for which it is intended. (Detailed descriptions and critical evaluations of tests are found in Buros, O. K. (ed.), *Mental Measurements Yearbook.*[1]) With this information it may be easier for the teacher to decide which test results may be relevant to the information being sought regarding a specific child. The appropriate individual (e.g., school psychologist, resource teacher) can then be consulted for interpretation of the score. It cannot be emphasized strongly enough that test results must be interpreted by those who are trained in this area, as numbers do not always mean what they seem. A trained professional can also give you some insight as to why a particular test was administered (e.g., suspected learning disability) as well as the significance of the scores achieved by a specific individual on the various parts of a test battery. Professionals who are employed by schools to administer diagnostic and achievement tests also have a responsibility to help teachers use the test results to improve their teaching effectiveness. Once those skills in which the child is deficient are known, specific objectives can be formulated to strengthen them. The most effective approach is to work through those skills or strengths that the child already has.

## Prescriptive Teaching

In prescriptive teaching, strengths and weaknesses are first evaluated by clinical testing, teacher assessment, or, ideally, both. Next, long-range goals are formulated, and teaching strategies that will create an optimum learning environment for the child are developed. Each instructional objective is planned to sequentially advance the child to a new level of achievement. Strengths are used as supportive skills to guarantee a degree of success in those activities specifically planned to improve deficient skill functioning. Subsequent activities must be planned to help the child generalize new learning and to facilitate transfer to new situations. After teaching, the results must be evaluated to determine if the child has really made progress toward the goals. If not, the same prescription may be modified, or a new one substituted. This type of goal setting and evaluation for each special learner is specified in Public Law 94-142. Called *Individualized Education Program* (IEP), it requires each school to draw up goals and short-term objectives, at least annually, for each handicapped learner in the school program. To improve deficient skill functioning, a comprehensive plan of progressively challenging goals and objectives must be formulated. In music, continually spontaneous sessions reap only random and spontaneous skills. Although this may be desirable in the beginning stages, a time must come when the child is called upon to develop and generalize these skills. Only when this level is reached does a child become a *learner.* Structure is essential, but there can be freedom within structure. When working toward a goal, it is often a spontaneous response that signals when a new plateau has been reached and the child is ready for a different challenge.

## Goals and Objectives

Successful teaching of special learners in music lies in planning and technique, not in materials *per se.* The formulation of goals and objectives is the first and most important step. The novice teacher invariably begins planning from the activity or materials, rather than the objective. When objective and activity are simultaneously conceived, one has truly reached a high level of sophistication in planning. Similarly, formulating music objectives in relation to learning skills also reflects sophisticated planning, as one must be familiar with basic learning skill development and its relationship to music skill development.

*Goals,* as used here, are long-range achievements described in general statements. They may be *cognitive* or *affective,* need not be stated in behavioral terms, and are understood to take some time for accomplishment. Some music education goals take the entire public school tenure to achieve! Long-range goals are often based on the six experience areas traditionally considered to be essential to the music education curriculum: singing, playing instruments, listening, moving to music, creating, and reading notation. In addition, music education goals largely fall into the psychomotor domain, as we seldom ask children to perceive music (listen, look, feel) without *doing* something as well (sing, play, move).

There are some who advocate formulating long-range goals in behavioral terms (e.g., Regelski, pp. 290–294[3]). However, since handicapped children present a multitude of variables because of physical and/or mental disabilities, it is impossible to generalize behaviorally for any one skill. To illustrate this, consider the following goal as written in behavioral terms.

BY THE END OF THE YEAR, GIVEN ONLY THE TONAL CENTER, EACH CHILD WILL DEMONSTRATE THE ABILITY TO SING ALL FAMILIAR SONGS IN TUNE, WITH PROPER PHRASING, RHYTHM, AND DYNAMICS.

Similar goals are no doubt universally accepted among music educators as attainable by the majority of children in the elementary grades. But consider the problems in achieving this particular goal for the child with a hearing impairment. To begin with, this individual's aural and vocal skills are not likely to be commensurate with those of hearing peers. Therefore, it is probably unrealistic to expect the same level of achievement, and certainly not given the same conditions and time element. Goals for this child are more realistic if they are somewhat general. In addition, special attention may need to be directed toward developing a number of subgoals, many of which hearing peers have been able to develop *without specific instruction*. To reach a general goal, such as the following,

TO DEVELOP THE SINGING VOICE AS AN INSTRUMENT OF MUSICAL EXPRESSION,

the hearing-impaired child may need first to achieve the following subgoals.

THE ABILITY TO
• USE THE SINGING VOICE (as opposed to speaking)
• SING WITH PROPER PITCH *DIRECTION*
• SING WITH PROPER PHRASING
• SING WITH ACCURATE RHYTHM
• SING WITH A RECOGNIZABLE MELODIC LINE

Note that conditions or criteria, or even a time, under which the above goals will be evaluated are intentionally avoided. These will be determined appropriate to individual abilities when instructional objectives are formulated, and these are written in behavioral terms. It is easy to understand why goals that include such statements as "by the end of the year," "each child," and "will demonstrate understanding by" (doing a specific task) are inappropriate for children representing both psychomotor and cognitive abilities that run the gamut from zero to above average at the beginning of instruction. In addition, the functioning level of some handicapped children can improve or degenerate drastically within a short period of time because of a number of physical and/or emotional factors.

Still another reason for leaving the long range goal open-ended may not be so obvious. Many studies were undertaken in the 1960s relative to teacher expectation. Most showed rather dramatically that children have an uncanny tendency to achieve only as well as their teachers expect they will! Let's again consider the hearing-impaired youngster. A goal written in behavioral terms and individualized for this child would necessarily impose preconceived standards based on what the teacher presumed the child could accomplish. Time and again, handicapped as well as normal children have surprised us in achieving an insight or skill that, in the opinion of professionals, was considered too difficult for them. We should take *every* precaution to keep open minds regarding individual potential, taking each day as it comes. Journals are rife with accounts of achievements of handicapped children, some in music, that should have been mentally or physically impossible for them and for which no satisfactory explanation exists.

**Formulating instructional objectives**   Entire books have been written concerning instructional objectives and how to write them. It is not the purpose of this book to develop such skills, as this has been done very competently by other individuals. Neither is it the purpose of this book to provide ready-made plans and objectives. It would indeed be presumptuous to formulate objectives to be used by and for others. If nothing else, writing instructional objectives in behavioral terms has forced teachers to come to grips with the problem of individual differences, and in so doing has actually provided a solution. The reader will find that all essential elements for formulating goals and instructional objectives are contained in the activities in Developmental Learning Skills (pp. 19–110). The teacher has but to select the activity appropriate to the target behaviors desired for the individual(s) concerned.

Both *cognitive* and *affective* learning are essential in the education of children. The issue of affective (feelings and attitudes) versus cognitive (facts and skills) learning in the arts has at times been belabored. The issue really centers around the fact that no one has yet discovered a valid way to measure affective learning. Overzealous commitment to standardized testing may have led us to the point where we no longer trust our eyes to see or our ears to hear! Is a test score really necessary to know that affective learning has taken place when a previously withdrawn child readily enters into group music activities, or an impoverished teenager saves the money earned at odd jobs to buy a recording first heard in music class? Used properly, psychological testing instruments can enhance our sensitivity to human behavior. Used in isolation, they are rarely effective in understanding an individual's behavior.

There are times when affective goals may actually take priority over cognitive ones. This is often true when dealing with children who exhibit serious emotional or social handicaps. Affective behaviors include feelings, attitudes, and values, and are closely related to social skills. These skills are often prerequisite to achieving cognitive goals. Beginning-level social skills, for example, may be directed toward cooperation or consistently completing an activity and progress to the ability to function in both solo and large-group music activities (ego strength, peer group relations). The skillful teacher will continually be building music skills in each individual through a repertoire of increasingly challenging experiences.

**Covert versus overt behaviors** The psychomotor approach to cognitive music learning is generally considered to be the most effective. Individuals learn by active involvement with a musical environment. (For a list of Music Skills, see Appendix, p. 272.) Many complex musical concepts can be experienced through simple singing, playing, and movement activities adapted to individual functioning levels. Those familiar with planning behavioral objectives are aware that cognitive behavior can take two forms: *overt* (obvious, or demonstrated) and *covert* (not obvious, or internalized). In working with special children, serious consideration must be given to the terminal behaviors that are the desired result of cognitive learning.

Overt responses commonly require psychomotor and/or verbal skills. Since many handicapped children lack skills in these areas, alternatives will have to be provided in order for them to demonstrate cognitive learning. An aphasic child, for instance, may be perfectly capable of identifying or labeling music concepts, but not by the common overt responses used by the majority, which involve language. Similarly, a physically disabled child may need an alternative, and perhaps unconventional, method of response. Individuals who are *both* aphasic and physically handicapped will challenge the ingenuity and imagination of the teachers who formulate objectives for them.

The necessity for evaluating achievement by considering terminal behavior in relation to skill level at the beginning of instruction should be obvious in light of the foregoing. In prescriptive teaching, growth becomes the yardstick by which learning is measured.

## Learning Style and Needs

Music goals and objectives can most easily be formulated to correspond with the following general categories of learning skills: *auditory, visual, motor, language,* and *social.* In planning goals and objectives, the individual learning style of each child must be considered. Some children learn best through listening (auditory) while others need to see a visual representation of a concept. Still others have difficulty conceptualizing unless they can experience what is to be learned in some way (kinesthetic, tactile). Some children will need experiences in all modalities in order to learn.

If the development of learning skills is to be included in our target music behaviors, then music goals and objectives must reflect consideration of the relationship of music and learning skills. (See Guide to the Relationship of Music Objectives and Learning Skills, p. 14.) For example, a child who is an out-of-tune singer is found to have deficient auditory perception skills. It can be assumed that skills relative to pitch discrimination are worthy of attention for both the musical and the general development of this child. The specific instructional objectives for this individual should include many opportunities to participate in musical experiences of increasing difficulty that require pitch discrimination. That is, once the ability to discriminate at one level is demonstrated, the next level is attempted. Other classmates may also need to reinforce or develop this same skill. Or they may be developing different skills even though participating in the same activity. This is where planning can get a bit complicated when the group numbers more than ten or twelve and the teacher has yet to learn how to individualize music teaching. In situations where a handicapped child is mainstreamed, the specific abilities and needs of the target child are accommodated in the same fashion when planning each music experience.

## The Relationship of Music Concepts and Learning Skills

Conceptual development in music can be accomplished in many ways. It is sometimes difficult for teachers to realize that concept and skill development do not go hand in hand, particularly for individuals with handicaps. The ability to understand the basic concept may not be at all in proportion to the ability to perform a music skill that demonstrates it. Music concepts can be taught through activities that require very elementary skills just as well as through those in which advanced skills are necessary. Indeed, much of the great music literature that has survived the test of time is characterized by its simplicity. Current music education methodology advocates conceptual development in music through active involvement of the learners, even at the preprimary level. Our ultimate goal in music for all children should be to teach music concepts in ways that will enable children to recognize and identify them (label), perform them at whatever skill level is possible, and finally apply them in a different activity that, ideally, encourages their creative use.

Music is a multisensory experience. It is a unique educational area because all the basic skills are taught simultaneously in music education. Few other curricular areas have the strong appeal that music holds for children. Often children refuse to cooperate in other remedial programs but readily engage in music making, even in clinical settings. It is often through music that the first breakthrough is made—a child makes the first attempt to communicate, cooperate with structure, or relate to others. A period of individual music sessions can frequently provide the groundwork that enables other programs to begin productive work with the child as well. Formulating goals and objectives solely on the basis of learning skills may be a valid approach for the classroom teacher or music therapist who desires to use music functionally to develop nonmusic skills. The music educator, however, has a primary responsibility to *provide each child with a music education commensurate with individual ability*. It is all too easy to get so involved with developing nonmusic skills that one loses sight of the music goals and objectives. To decrease this possibility, it is recommended that music goals and objectives be planned together with related learning skills for each activity. The following chart can be used as a guide.

# GUIDE TO THE RELATIONSHIP OF MUSIC OBJECTIVES AND LEARNING SKILLS

| LEARNING SKILLS | MUSIC OBJECTIVES | DESCRIPTORS |
|---|---|---|
| **AUDITORY PERCEPTION** | | |
| **Sound Awareness** | Sound versus silence | Reacts appropriately to sound and silence; starts and stops on cue, without cue |
| **Sound Localization** | Sound localization | Locates the source of sound with visual clue, without visual clue |
| **Sound Discrimination** | | |
| **Intensity** | **Dynamics:** same/different; loud/soft/medium; crescendo/decrescendo | |
| **Duration** | **Tempo:** same/different; fast/slow/moderate; accelerando/ritardando | |
| | **Meter:** beat/no beat; steady beat; same/different; two pulses, three pulses | |
| | **Rhythm:** long/short; even/uneven; accent/no accent; staccato/legato; ostinato; patterns; rest; beat divided into two, beat divided into three (triplet); syncopation | Identifies, performs, and creatively uses all music elements |
| **Pitch** | **Pitch:** same/different; high/low/middle; interval (3rd, 4th, 5th, octave); chord | |
| | **Melody:** same/different; up/down; step/skip; contour; ostinato; phrase, cadence; major, minor, sequence | |
| **Timbre** | **Tone color:** environmental; animal; vocal; instrumental | |
| **Auditory Figure-Ground** | **Texture:** one sound, two sounds, many sounds; harmony | Remains on part in rounds, partner songs, part songs; instrumental activities |

| LEARNING SKILLS | MUSIC OBJECTIVES | DESCRIPTORS |
|---|---|---|
| **Auditory Memory** | Selected songs and listening repertoire; echo, call-and-response activities, movement | Retains and recalls activities, words to songs, vocal or instrumental parts, movements |
| **Auditory Sequencing** | **Music design:** repetition/contrast; AB (binary), ABA (ternary), rondo, theme and variation, canon; cumulative and sequencing songs, movement and playing activities | Recognizes simple music forms; correctly orders verses in songs, parts in ensembles, movements in dances, pitches in scale, etc. |

## VISUAL PERCEPTION

| LEARNING SKILLS | MUSIC OBJECTIVES | DESCRIPTORS |
|---|---|---|
| **Visual Awareness** | Awareness of visual cues, gestures; symbols | Responds appropriately to visual cues to start, stop; responds to visual symbols |
| **Visual Focus** | Focuses on music score; playing instruments; action songs and games | Locates objects in environment; locates symbols in score; focuses on leader; directs hand to object |
| **Visual Tracking** | Instrumental ensembles; action songs, singing games, dances | Follows beat, dynamics, etc., indicated by conductor; successfully copies or mirrors movements of others; successfully manipulates balls, balloons, etc. |
| **Visual Discrimination** | | |
|   **Color** | **Music score:** notes, symbols, rhythm and melodic patterns; selected instrumental and movement activities | |
|   **Shape** | **Music score:** notes, symbols, rhythm and melodic patterns; numbers, letters, words; selected instrumental and movement activities | |
|   **Size** | **Music score:** notes, symbols, rhythm and melodic patterns | Recognizes, interprets, and uses visual elements of music activities creatively |
|   **Quantity** | **Music score:** notes, symbols, rhythm and melodic patterns | |
|   **Direction** | **Music score:** notes, symbols, rhythm and melodic patterns; melodic contour; bow markings | |
|   **Distance** | **Music score:** notes, symbols, rhythm and melodic patterns; intervals | |
| **Visual Figure-Ground** | Music blueprints; scores | Follows successfully while listening; remains focused on own part; selects important visual elements in pictures, scores |

| LEARNING SKILLS | MUSIC OBJECTIVES | DESCRIPTORS |
|---|---|---|
| **Visual Memory** | Selected song and instrumental scores; movement activities | Visually recognizes same/different, repetition/contrast in score; memorizes words, parts, movements |
| **Visual Sequencing** | **Music design:** AB, ABA, canon, rondo, theme and variation; movement and dramatization | Visually identifies simple music form; correctly orders visuals that represent verses or words in songs, dramatizations, or dances |

## MOTOR SKILLS

| | | |
|---|---|---|
| **Gross Motor** | Body movement activities; playing instruments; conducting | Maintains rhythm and balance in locomotor and nonlocomotor activities; changes body position, level, direction quickly and easily in rhythm; shows consistent preference for sidedness; comprehends directional words; demonstrates awareness of body parts and functions |
| **Fine Motor** | Action songs and games; playing instruments | Coordinates eye and hand movements in action and finger-play songs, manipulating objects and instruments; demonstrates adequate finger strength and separation when playing piano, Melodica, Autoharp, etc.; initiates and maintains grasp when playing instruments; uses wrist rotation and snap as appropriate playing technique for maracas, tambourine, etc. |

## LANGUAGE DEVELOPMENT

| | | |
|---|---|---|
| **Vocalization** | **Vocal sounds:** high/low; up/down; long/short | Imitates or responds with meaningful vocal sounds in call-and-response or echo activities |
| **Verbalization** | Sings with speech sounds | Responds with words in short call-and-response or echo activities; labels; uses two- and three-word sentences |
| **Expressive** | Creates new words/verses to familiar or pupil-composed songs and chants | Uses appropriate vocabulary to label, identify, describe |
| **Receptive** | Action songs; selected poetry; singing games, dances | Comprehends words in poetry, story, or nonsense songs; follows directions in action songs, singing games, and simple dances; interprets poetry |
| **Articulation** | Selected song literature, poetry, and speech chants | Enunciates clearly in both speaking and singing; uses appropriate inflections and rhythms in speaking and singing |

| LEARNING SKILLS | MUSIC OBJECTIVES | DESCRIPTORS |
|---|---|---|
| **SOCIAL SKILLS** | | |
| **Self Concept/Ego** | Sings and plays solo, in ensembles; leads selected activities | Accepts challenges; contributes ideas, skills; evaluates realistically |
| **Cooperation** | Follows directions and cues of others; adheres to meter, rhythm, pitch, words, to best of ability | Shows enthusiasm for music activities; uses materials appropriately |
| **Attention Span** | Follows activity through to completion; sustains interest in continuation and expansion projects | Maintains interest appropriate to mental age |
| **Peer Group Relations** | Singing games, dances, dramatizations; partner, small-group, large-group movement activities and ensemble participation | Successfully participates with others in various-sized groups and activities; demonstrates ability to both lead and follow |
| **Predict Outcomes** | Selected song literature and program music; creative song writing on social themes | Demonstrates ability to foresee consequences of behavior |
| **Value Judgment** | Selected song literature and program music; creative song writing on social themes | Demonstrates values consistent with society |

## Planning the Lesson

Thoughtful planning is essential to effective teaching, even for the experienced teacher. Some individuals are capable of presenting very entertaining sessions by leading the group through a number of activities selected "off the top of their heads." But teaching children specific skills and concepts requires that activities be planned and developed in sequence and progress toward the ultimate long-range goals. In teaching special learners, procedures and organization of the learning environment are crucial and demand planning prior to lesson time.

Many different formats are used in writing out plans and are largely a matter of personal preference. The components of the plan are more important than how they are written down. A good music plan should include the following elements.

**Long-range music goals** Including the long-range goals (as well as daily objectives) on every plan helps keep your planning focused toward those goals. You are less likely to get sidetracked or to lose sight of the ultimate music goals that you are striving for.

**Instructional music objectives** These should describe the target behaviors for *individuals as well as for the group*. When objectives for individuals are different,

this can often be noted by placing the names of specific children in parentheses, with a notation of how the objective differs for them.

**Related learning skills** Learning skills that are prerequisite to achieving the objective should be considered and noted for each activity. In this way you will be reminded of those skills that specific children do not have or need to practice, and when it will be necessary to adapt an activity for them.

**Activities and procedures** List activities in the order you plan to present them, with whatever notes will help you to remember the procedure. The correct sequencing of steps in the procedures is important, because if one is left out, the activity may not be successful and may not even be salvable.

**Materials** Music classes often involve the use of many materials. Failure to organize materials has ruined many a well planned lesson. Whatever format is used for writing plans, it should provide a place where materials are clearly listed and described (e.g., "resonator bells, C, G"). Be sure to gather and prepare materials well in advance of the lesson, keeping them out of sight until ready for use.

**Evaluation** Meaningful evaluation includes two perspectives: (1) the children's response to the activities presented, and (2) your appraisal of the activity in accomplishing the objective and, hence, progress made toward the long-range goals. It is only by considering both of these that any valuable information can be learned when activities are not successful in achieving the objectives. Again, specific notation should be made regarding individual children when appropriate. Some reasons for the children's failure to respond might include materials inappropriate to the level of interest, inappropriate level of difficulty, and failure to understand the objective. Some reasons for teacher ineffectiveness might include not enough preparation, inadequate organization of the learning environment, and inefficient or inaccurate procedure. Most often the difficulty can be found in one of the above. If not, there may be extenuating circumstances (e.g., a fire drill in the middle of an activity), but, generally, these should not be considered until all planning elements have been realistically evaluated.

If planning and evaluations are conscientiously written out for each lesson, the teacher has a permanent record of class achievement as well as the individual progress of special learners.

Upon perusing the various activities presented in Developmental Learning Skills (pp. 19–110), one will, no doubt, be immediately aware of the great overlap of learning skills. In fact, *it is nearly impossible to isolate a single learning skill in designing a music activity.* Remember that the perceptual process operates as a gestalt. The integration of other skills is inevitably required. Probably the most difficult task in designing teaching strategies is evaluating the advantages of using one activity rather than another to develop a specific skill when the skill is required to some degree in both. This is mainly a question of professional judgment, and given training as well as knowledge of the child's abilities, a teacher will endeavor to make the best possible decision. Undoubtedly, some decisions will not produce the desired outcomes. Every teacher learns through experience, but in working with children who have learning difficulties, experimentation is often the name of the game. Once a good technique or activity is found, there is little assurance that it will work with a different child or group, or even the same one another time. Spontaneity, quick thinking, and flexibility will pay off, but only when objectives have been carefully planned. It is *only* when teachers know what they seek in outcomes that they can afford to be creative in procedure! As Mager has so aptly put it, "If you're not sure where you're going, you're liable to end up someplace else—and not even know it." (Mager, vii.[2])

## Summary

At the beginning of the year, or semester, it is necessary to formulate long-range music goals appropriate to each individual special learner. General statements that allow flexibility in reaching the goal are more realistic when planning for children with learning handicaps. Both cognitive and affective goals should be included, as well as music skills and learning skills.

Instructional objectives are short-term minigoals, usually planned sequentially and individualized. They are formulated to develop specific behaviors in both music and learning skills, which will collectively lead to accomplishment of the long range goals. Care should be taken to ensure that each child has skills appropriate to the mode of response expected. Growth should be the single most important factor in evaluating learning.

## References/Recommended Reading

Barsch, Ray. *Achieving Perceptual-Motor Efficiency.* Seattle, WA: Special Child Publications, 1967.

———. *Each to a Different Drummer.* Canoga Park, CA: Ray Barsch Center for Learning, 1974.

[1] Buros, O. K., ed. *Seventh Mental Measurements Yearbook.* 2 vols. Highland Park, NJ: Gryphon Press, 1972.

Cratty, B. *Developmental Sequences of Perceptual-Motor Tasks.* Baldwin, NY: Activity Records, Inc., 1967.

———. *Perceptual-Motor Efficiency in Children.* Philadelphia: Lea and Febiger, 1969.

Frostig, Marianne. *Movement Education, Theory and Practice.* Chicago: Follett Educational Corp., 1970.

Furth, H., and Wachs, H. *Thinking Goes to School.* New York: Oxford University Press, 1975.

Jones, C., and Nunn, N. *The Learning Pyramid: Potential Through Perception.* Columbus, OH: Charles Merrill, 1972.

Landis, B., and Carder, P. *The Eclectic Curriculum in American Music Education: Contributions of Dalcroze, Kodaly, and Orff.* Reston, VA: MENC, 1972.

[2] Mager, Robert. *Preparing Instructional Objectives.* Palo Alto, CA: Fearon, 1962.

Montagu, Ashley. *Touching: The Human Significance of the Skin.* (cloth), New York: Columbia University Press, 1971; (paperback), New York: Harper & Row, 1972.

Peter, Laurence. *Prescriptive Teaching.* New York: McGraw-Hill, 1965.

[3] Regelski, Thomas. *Principles and Problems of Music Education.* Englewood Cliffs, NJ: Prentice-Hall, 1975.

Schmidt, Lloyd. 1976 (Sept.) Music as a Learning Mode. *Music Educators Journal,* Vol. 63, No. 1, pp. 94–97.

Vallett, Robert. *Remediation of Learning Disabilities: A Handbook of Psychoeducational Resource Programs.* Palo Alto, CA: Fearon, 1967.

Zimmerman, Marilyn. *Musical Characteristics of Children.* Reston, VA: MENC, 1971.

# Activities for Developing Music Skills and Learning Skills

# Activities for Developing Music Skills and Learning Skills

It cannot be emphasized strongly enough that the philosophy underlying the activities that follow is that all children, with few exceptions, are capable of learning music. The task for the teacher is to match learning skills, mastered or developing, with a music goal of appropriate difficulty. Because handicapped children are as diverse in musical abilities and learning styles as normal children, any good program must present activities and examples that are *widely* varied in content and skill level. Therefore, the activities presented are not listed in order of difficulty for either music skills or learning skills. Teachers should create their own learning spiral, or curriculum, through selection of activities that reflect consideration of both learning and music skill levels. In this way, the degree of sophistication, as well as depth of musical learning, is *decided by the teacher* for *individuals*. Teachers can design their own learning modules by selecting activities from the various areas (auditory, visual, motor, language, and social) using either a specific learning skill or a music concept as the basic criterion. The activities are not to be considered a complete curriculum. **Their main purpose is to provide examples that meet both the learning skill and the music goal criteria described for each activity.** Hopefully, these will generate new ideas from teachers using them.

Development of music concepts cannot occur without experiencing and perceiving the musical process. The achievement of music goals must begin with a musical response—sing, play, move. Most children will respond naturally to music in one of these ways. The more seriously handicapped the child, the more subtle the response may be (e.g., blinking eyes). At this level our goals should be toward eliciting consistent responses in as many different ways as possible (e.g., sing, play, move). Before concepts can be formed, *perception of music elements* must be mastered. The next step then is to develop musical responses *based on* perception of music elements. Hence, the child is able to match dynamic level, to echo pitch and rhythm patterns, to repeat melodic phrases, and so forth. The highest level of musical achievement is realized when musical response is based on *both* perception and conceptualization of the elements of music. The child now demonstrates through musical performance (including creative responses) the understanding of music concepts (e.g., melodic contour, repetition/contrast, even/uneven rhythm). In practice, this

process becomes cumulative *and* cyclical since all steps are interrelated in the aesthetic experience.

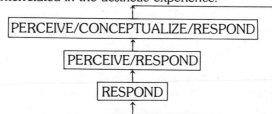

If we are to develop musicality in children, we cannot get stuck on the bottom step. Although children are entertained and can be kept participating at this level, we must continue to move upward, building psychomotor skills, expanding repertoires of skills and activities, and challenging the achievement of increasingly difficult music concepts. Nothing motivates learning as effectively as a sense of accomplishment, and without continuous progress, even retarded children lose interest.

## Using the Goals and Activities

In each section (auditory, visual, motor, language, and social) the long range goals that precede each group of activities are set in a gray screen (see p. 24).

The first column (at the left) lists the type of musical response expected (sing, play, move). Sometimes more than one response is possible and the teacher will have to decide which are appropriate to individual abilities.

In the second column are listed the elements of music to be perceived and/or conceptualized.

In the middle column are activities suggested for each long range goal. Most of these activities can be adapted to a variety of teaching situations and environments (i.e., individual, small group, large group). Some activities are suitable for individual learning centers or small groups that work independent of a teacher.

Letters in the fourth column (A—Auditory, V—Visual, M—Motor, FM—Fine Motor, L—Language, S—Social, T—Tactile) indicate use of the activity for other skills.

The last column (to the right) includes additional suggestions and variations for the activity. (Further activities are available through ''SEE ALSO'' at the end of some groups of activities.)

Listed in the color band below the activity are recommended music and materials to be used. (See p. 286 for index of songs, recordings, poems, and available visuals. Songs, beginning on page 113, are in alphabetical order and all are recorded. Other selections, recorded only, are indicated by ⊙ symbol. Sequencing cards are abbreviated **SC**.)

For many of the activities, the list of materials includes several songs and/or recordings. The teacher will need to review each in order to decide which *most suitably* illustrates the specific music goal and learning skill for the target child. The songs and recorded selections listed will generally serve to achieve the music goals and learning skills described.

As with any worthwhile resource, there are often different objectives that can be realized from one source. Hence, some songs may be listed in many different activities and sections. Repeating songs with different music goals or learning skill goals is helpful when children have difficulty learning songs or words.

In using the activities with music especially selected to best achieve certain goals, the teacher can gain an understanding of why those materials are suitable, thus learning how to select and adapt appropriate materials. The teacher, therefore, is given specific opportunities to select and adapt where the material list indicates "select vocal and instrumental music."

## Song Material

The songs chosen to be included (pp. 113–223) are generally pitched to be comfortably sung by low voices, but many can be transposed to higher keys if appropriate. Some variety of pitch range is represented as well, but high tessituras have been avoided. Certain songs may be more suitable for listening than singing by some children. Singing *to* children is not only enjoyable for them, but is a good way to develop perceptive listening and language skills. Songs for listening can be sung by the teacher (unaccompanied or with simple accompaniment) or played in their recorded versions. Generally, songs selected for this purpose should be those that
• have expressive language or vocal skills beyond the level of the target group, but can be musically and receptively understood by them
• effectively illustrate mood (i.e., humor, seriousness)
• tell a story
Sometimes children can join in on repetitive phrases or refrains.

Piano accompaniments are provided for all songs for which such settings are appropriate. Harmonies indicated by chord symbols do not necessarily agree with harmonies in the written arrangements.

## Recordings

Teachers lacking music reading skills may find the recordings a helpful way to learn songs. The first time a song is presented to the children is often more successful if sung by the teacher without accompaniment, or only the vocal track of the recording is played. Accompaniment can be added later when the melody is more familiar and secure.

Every attempt has been made to keep piano accompaniments and instrumentation simple in order to be least distracting. In the recordings, the intent of the performances is not necessarily to duplicate the exact notation in all cases, but rather to create as powerful a musical experience as possible for children to hear and share. The teacher must bear this fact in mind when comparing the performances on the recordings with the notation in the book.

Attention has also been given to tempo. Some selections are recorded in more than one tempo to enable slower processing children to respond more easily and to provide a practice tempo for learning activities involving motor skills. Some selections have been included to develop perceptive listening skills. These include short musical pieces, environmental sounds, and sound sequences that are coordinated with specific activities.

Many children do not readily respond to recorded music, notably severely retarded, neurologically impaired, and hearing impaired. Although some may physically respond to music that has a strong rhythmic pulse, this response seldom reflects any real comprehension of the music itself. Changes in dynamics, meter, or tempo will generally be completely ignored even when pointed out. Recorded vocal music, such as action songs, is usually ineffective when used with language impaired children unless the teacher provides a visual model to imitate. It would seem that recorded music without visual cues is simply too abstract for children with serious language, cognitive, or auditory (including perceptual) deficiencies. To develop good listening skills in these children, the more basic auditory skills of awareness and discrimination must be developed before recordings can be effective.

The Pick-a-Track recordings enable the teacher to isolate specific musical components of the recordings (e.g., vocal line, echo part, instrumental activity), thereby helping the children focus attention on the auditory goal.

## Visuals

The use of visual and manipulative materials helps to secure both learning and music concepts. Charts and sequencing cards suggested for use in the lesson help to relate sound to symbol, to order auditory information, and in many cases provide alternative response choices. These materials are visually simple (i.e., photographs, line drawings) and they provide a visual reinforcement of many concepts presented in the activities. When appropriate, a portion of a chart can be isolated for special needs simply by covering the other parts. (See p. 288.)

Student activity pads (available from the publisher) encourage the use of visual motor skills such as tracing, drawing, writing, cutting, or pasting, to integrate sensory functioning and symbolization. They are intended to be used flexibly so the teacher may adapt them to individual functioning levels. (See p. 289.)

# AUDITORY PERCEPTION

It is commonly thought that in the normal individual the auditory sense is the only one to function perfectly from the moment of birth, whereas other senses take some time to develop completely. However, unless an individual can make sense out of what is heard, hearing is, for all practical purposes, nonfunctional. Recently, we have come to realize that certain types of brain injury or dysfunction make it difficult, or impossible, for an individual to make sense naturally of the auditory stimuli received by the brain. It should be pointed out that *hearing* and *listening* are not synonymous in the auditory process. Whereas hearing is basically a physiological process, listening is an intellectual one, requiring interpretation, analysis, integration, and evaluation.

Some children have yet to learn that sounds have meaning. The ability to pinpoint the source of a sound and identify its unique characteristics requires that the child be able to focus attention long enough to learn these things. Outside noises and subtle classroom sounds, such as the hum of fluorescent lights and radiator noises, can distract the child who has a problem focusing attention. In addition, the ability to store auditory information and retrieve it in proper sequence is basic to the learning process. Without these skills it is virtually impossible to learn spoken or written language. Without language, one is extremely limited in the ability to communicate with others or to understand the world.

Children with auditory perception problems *may* have *some* of the following characteristics. It is seldom, however, that we would see all these behaviors in one individual.

The inability to
- locate the source of a sound (localization)
- identify specific characteristics of sound (intensity, duration, pitch, timbre)
- relate a sound to its symbol
- repeat what was said without visual clues
- follow directions without visual clues
- recognize when a sound changes
- identify same and different sounds
- distinguish a specific sound from among others (figure-ground)
- recognize or remember previous auditory information (memory)
- correctly order auditory information (sequencing)
- recognize previously learned auditory material when presented in a different medium
- integrate auditory information with other sensory data
- comprehend words in a song

Training in listening and interpreting sound develops auditory perception. It is obvious that music learning depends on one's ability to perceive aurally. Conversely, music training can enhance auditory perception. When planned with specific aural skills in mind, music activities can help a child
- improve the ability to attend to aural stimuli
- interpret both verbal and nonverbal information
- remember auditory learning from one experience to the next
- integrate auditory information with that received through other sensory channels

## Sound discrimination

The characteristics of a sound (i.e.,*intensity, duration, pitch,* and *timbre*) are presented as subdivisions in the activities for developing auditory discrimination skills. (See pp. 24–54.) Music education goals and objectives generate sequential music experiences leading to a thorough understanding of these characteristics and the ways in which they are combined in music composition. Children with auditory perception problems frequently have difficulty in processing speech sounds. It is interesting to note that speech, singing, and music all have the following common elements: tempo, rhythm, pitch, stress (accent), and dynamics. Auditory discrimination skills, then, are equally important for general learning and for music learning.

**Intensity**   Of all music elements, dynamics is most easily comprehended. In the average child it is the first to develop, and we usually find that young children can easily discriminate between loud and soft by the time they enter preschool or kindergarten. With these children our task is mainly to refine their skill to include discrimination of more subtle differences in dynamic levels. Children who lack gross loud-soft discrimination are likely to include the hearing impaired.

**Duration**   Duration is the element in music that deals with time concepts. These are tempo (the speed of the music), meter (the organization of beats, usually into measures), and rhythm (the organization of longer and shorter sounds and silences within a time framework). Rhythm is basic to body function and speech as well as music. Recently, much attention has been focused on biorhythms, and educators, too, are beginning to be concerned with how an individual's natural inner rhythm relates to learning style and needs. Classroom activities (and/or tempo in music) are often paced too fast to enable all learners to grasp the objective.

**Pitch**   Pitch concepts, such as high/low and up/down, are necessary for understanding the melodic structure of music. Seriation and sequencing skills, characteristically lacking in many learning-disabled children, are utilized in understanding scales, modes, and harmonic structure in music. In some countries of the Orient and Africa, languages are tonally based; therefore, pitch discrimination is a prerequisite to speech. The same word spoken with different pitch inflections has multiple meanings. It is often said that there are no tone-deaf individuals in those countries. Whether or not this is true, one can certainly appreciate why a poor sense of pitch would be a handicap in learning the language. The importance of pitch inflection in the English language is probably underestimated until one experiences listening to speech without inflection or with misplaced inflections. It has been reported that, in retrospect, Anne Sullivan regretted she did not train Helen Keller's voice before teaching her to speak. Miss Keller's voice quality was reportedly quite poor and her speech totally lacking in pitch variance, making it difficult to attend to for any length of time. It was a great source of disappointment to Miss Keller herself, who as a young adult took singing lessons in an effort to improve it. In addition to speech and language development, the ability to recognize, identify, and reproduce pitches of varying frequencies is necessary in perceiving and reacting to one's environment.

**Timbre**    Timbre is the ''color'' characteristics of a sound that give it a unique quality. It is the awareness of timbre that allows a person to aurally distinguish a clarinet from an oboe, or a car horn from a train whistle. Without timbre discrimination skills, the environment could be a hostile place in which to live. Again, this is an important skill in the development of speech and language. Comprehending vowel and consonant sounds depends largely on the ability to discriminate differing timbres. When children are screened for auditory discrimination problems, the measures used test for discrimination of *speech* sounds *only*. It is not unusual, however, for children who have been identified as having auditory discrimination problems to perform as well as their peers in nonverbal discrimination tasks. Discrimination of musical sounds involves a more gross discrimination. Often the child's problem will be more obvious in the inability to learn and remember words to songs.

In all discrimination tasks, the lowest level of competency is that of recognition of same and different, followed by identification of specific characteristics and, finally, by integration and synthesis. Discrimination tasks should begin with two greatly contrasting sounds and gradually move to finer discrimination of sound among more dimensions. Subsequent goals should facilitate generalization and transfer.

The long-range goals for auditory discrimination skills are found in all music education curriculums and are equally valid for developing auditory skills for general learning. Each child demonstrates

- the ability to perceive and identify (label) each characteristic of sound
- an understanding of the characteristics of sound through musical performance
- the ability to creatively apply understanding of the characteristics of music

For the child who has difficulty processing sound, auditory learning is facilitated by pairing the auditory stimulus with another sensory mode such as *visual* (pictures, diagrams), *kinesthetic* (body movement), or *tactile* (manipulative materials). At some point, however, these extra auditory clues must be withdrawn lest the child become dependent on them. Since distance is a major factor in auding, it is recommended that the distance between the sound source and the child be increased *gradually* to as much as thirty feet for those activities in which it would be appropriate.

To summarize, auditory perception skills are basic both to general learning skills and to the development of musicianship. Specific auditory skills include awareness, localization, memory, sequencing, and the ability to discriminate the sound characteristics of pitch, duration, intensity, and timbre. Deficiencies in auditory skills frequently cause language and speech difficulties. Music activities not only provide experiences in all auditory skills, but they also motivate increased auditory attention because of the basic appeal of music and the physical involvement of the learners.

**The child demonstrates**
**AWARENESS OF SOUND AND SILENCE**

**AWARENESS**

| sound/ silence | 1. Call attention to sound versus silence by turning sound on and off intermittently. Child indicates by word or gesture when sound is heard and when it is not. | L |
| --- | --- | --- |
| | *record player, tape player, radio* | |

| | | | | |
|---|---|---|---|---|
| **PLAY** | sound/ silence | **2.** Help children explore several instruments on which sustained sounds are produced. Children should experience both starting and stopping sound, indicating each by word or gesture. | **L, M, T** | |
| | | *Autoharp, guitar, cymbal, triangle, piano* | | |
| | sound/ silence | **3.** Teacher produces sound on instruments with natural sustaining properties and allows sound to stop naturally. With eyes covered, children indicate by word or gesture when sound has completely stopped. | **L** | Change location from which sound is produced so all children have an opportunity to be close to the sound source. |
| | | *Autoharp, guitar, cymbal, triangle, piano* | | |
| **SING** | | **4.** All children should be encouraged to make a singing response on "Here I am." Nonverbal children may respond by gesture. | **L** | For a different activity, improvise melodies with familiar tonal patterns. Example: |

*Where is Mar - y?*

*Where is Me - lin - da?*

**The Roll Call Song**

| | | | | |
|---|---|---|---|---|
| **MOVE** | sound/ silence even phrase beat | **5.** Children walk to the beat, stopping at the end of each phrase on the word "stop." | **M** | Substitute other appropriate motor tasks for walking (e.g., clapping). |
| | | | **L** | Children say "stop" when stopping. |
| | | | **M, V** | Substitute ball passing or bouncing for walking. |
| | | | **M** | Sing and move to the song in different tempos. |
| | | | **M** | Incorporate the game "statues" into the activity by freezing in a pose on "stop." |

*Stop and Go ⊙*

| | | | | |
|---|---|---|---|---|
| **MOVE/ PLAY** | sound/ silence beat uneven phrase | **6.** Children move creatively to drumbeat or suitable music, stopping on each pause. | **M** | See Appendix, p. 274, for variations on walking. |
| | | | **S, V** | Substitute ball bouncing or tossing to a partner. |
| | | | **M** | Incorporate the game "statues." |
| | | | **M** | Substitute playing instruments for moving. |
| | | | **M** | Move and play an instrument. |

**A Little Flight Music ("Stop" version)**

| | | |
|---|---|---|
| **locate sound** | **1.** Class or child covers eyes while a ticking metronome is hidden. One child is selected to locate the hidden metronome. | **V**    Beginning efforts may be more successful if hiding place is visually obvious.<br><br>For a different challenge, selected child first declares if the metronome is believed to be *near* by or *far* away. |

*metronome*

| | | |
|---|---|---|
| **locate sound** | **2.** Class covers eyes as four children each take one instrument to different corners in the room. The teacher, or a child, silently signals players when to sound their instrument. Class points to the corner where sound originates. | For a more challenging task:<br>**a.** use instruments of similar timbres;<br>**b.** point to two or more instruments to play at one time.<br><br>**V**    Draw a map of the room layout on the board. Have a volunteer indicate where sound originated. |

*four classroom instruments with different timbres*

| | | |
|---|---|---|
| **locate sound** | **3.** Class sit at desks or in a circle with eyes closed and hands behind backs. Teacher quietly places bells in one child's hands. Child with the bells rings them briefly while class attempts to determine who has the bells. | In beginning activities, class can uncover eyes before child rings bells. |

*wrist bells, or similar instrument*

| | | |
|---|---|---|
| **locate sound** | **4.** Class covers eyes. Teacher or child moves to different locations around the room while playing an instrument. Keeping eyes closed, class follows the moving sound with their fingers. If player walks a discernible route (e.g., to door and back), a volunteer can be asked to recreate the path taken. | A variation can be used with "The Roll Call Song." Each child turns to face the teacher when responding with "here I am."<br><br>**L**    Describe location of sound verbally. |

*small percussion instrument*

| | | |
|---|---|---|
| **locate sound** | **5.** One child is blindfolded; another child is given the instrument. As the player moves about the room, the blindfolded child follows the sound by moving toward it. | |

*small percussion instrument*

*blindfold*

| | | | |
|---|---|---|---|
| loud/soft | 1. Children group naturally loud-sounding instruments on one side of a table, soft on the other. | V | Pictures representing loud and soft can be placed at appropriate sides of the table to help relate sound and symbol. |
| | | L | Make word cards (soft, loud) to place at appropriate sides of the table. |
| | *shakers, rattles having loud and soft properties* | | **Chart:** 3 |
| CREATE  loud/soft | 2. Help children make a sound mobile using materials found around the classroom or home. After assembling, ask children to find all the objects that sound loud when struck and those that sound soft. Experiment with mallets made from different materials (e.g., yarn, rubber, wood) to discover if dynamic level changes. | FM V | Make a chart with pictures of items found to be loud or soft when struck with certain mallets. |
| | | L | Make chart, as above, adding names of the items. |
| | *found sounds, assorted mallets, wire coat hangers, fish line* | | |
| loud/soft | 3. *Room tap.* Select children to explore the room for loud and soft sounds by tapping objects with their mallets. | V, L | Make charts, as above. |
| | *assorted mallets* | | |
| soft | 4. Children indicate by word or gesture the dynamic level heard as soft. | V, L | Use picture or word cards for an alternative response choice. |
| | *Mussorgsky: Ballet of the Unhatched Chicks* ⊙ <br> *Tchaikovsky: Dance of the Sugar Plum Fairy* ⊙ | | **Chart:** 3 |
| loud | 5. Children indicate by word or gesture the dynamic level heard as loud. | V, L | Use picture or word cards, as above. |
| | *Ginastera: Invocation of the Powerful Spirits* ⊙ | | **Chart:** 3 |
| loud/soft | 6. The teacher plays short examples of loud and soft. Children indicate by word or gesture which dynamic level was heard. | V, L | Use picture or word cards, as above. |
| | *piano, Autoharp, drum, or other classroom instruments* | | **Chart:** 3 |
| loud/soft contrasts | 7. Children indicate by word or gesture the loud-soft changes heard in the music. | V, L | Graphics, picture, or word charts can be used for an alternative response choice. |
| | *Bach: Allegro* ⊙ <br> *Handel: Bourrée* ⊙ <br> *Shostakovich: Polka* ⊙ | | **Chart:** 3 |
| crescendo | 8. Children indicate by word or gesture when crescendos are heard in the music. | V, L | Graphics, picture, or word charts can be used for an alternative response choice. |
| | *Grieg: In the Hall of the Mountain King* ⊙ <br> *Mussorgsky: Bydlo* ⊙ | | |

| | | | | |
|---|---|---|---|---|
| decrescendo | **9.** Children indicate by word or gesture when decrescendos are heard in the music. | | V, L | Use visuals, as above. |

*Fauré: Berceuse* ⊙
*McBride: Pony Express* ⊙

| | | | | |
|---|---|---|---|---|
| loud/soft | **10.** Children indicate by word or gesture environmental sounds that are soft, loud, or sometimes soft and sometimes loud. Discuss factors that affect loud and soft, such as distance (i.e., near = loud; far = soft). | | V, L | |

*live or recorded environmental sounds*

Charts: ③ ⑤ ⑥ ⑦
SC: 1 - 9

**The child demonstrates**
# UNDERSTANDING OF SPECIFIC CHARACTERISTICS OF SOUND THROUGH MUSICAL PERFORMANCE

**PERFORM DYNAMICS**

| | | | | |
|---|---|---|---|---|
| SING | soft | **1.** Sing songs for which the appropriate dynamic level is soft throughout. | L | |

**Canoe Round**          **Japanese Rain Song**
**For Health and Strength**  **My Father's House**
**Hush, Little Baby**

| | | | | |
|---|---|---|---|---|
| SING | loud | **2.** Sing songs for which the appropriate dynamic level is loud throughout. | L | |

**The Angel Band**          **Marching to Pretoria**
**The Ants Go Marching**    **Ticky Ticky Tambo**

| | | | | |
|---|---|---|---|---|
| PLAY | loud/soft | **3.** Play an echo game in which the leader plays simple rhythmic patterns at loud or soft dynamic levels. Eventually vary the dynamic level from very soft to very loud. | M | Substitute singing or body sounds. |

*two percussion instruments with similar timbres*

| | | | | |
|---|---|---|---|---|
| PLAY | loud/soft | **4.** In "Charlie Knows How to Beat That Drum," one child is selected to play the drum *on* the beat, playing softly when indicated by the words in the song. | L, M | For children unable to beat both slowly *and* softly, repeat the word "softly" throughout. |

**Charlie Knows How to Beat That Drum**
*drum*

| | | | | |
|---|---|---|---|---|
| SING | loud/soft contrasts | **5.** Sing songs with phrases that are appropriately performed at contrasting dynamic levels. | L | |

**Jack-in-the-Box**          **Three Little Ducks**
**John Jacob Jingelheimer Schmidt**

| | | | | |
|---|---|---|---|---|
| SING | crescendo/ decrescendo | **6.** Sing songs in which crescendo and decrescendo are appropriately included. | M, L | For a movement variation, children stand in a circle, making the circle bigger with crescendos and smaller with decrescendos. |

**Breezes Are Blowing**      **Jack-in-the-Box**
**Chumbara**

## The child demonstrates
## ABILITY TO APPLY UNDERSTANDING OF
## MUSICAL CHARACTERISTICS CREATIVELY

### CREATE DYNAMICS

| CREATE | **1.** Children decide appropriate dynamics for interpreting a short poem or story. | L |
|---|---|---|
| | Rain Sizes (poem) | |
| CREATE/SING/ PLAY/MOVE | **2.** Children interpret dynamics through body movement, graphic representation, drawings, and so forth. | V, M |
| | *select vocal and instrumental music* | |
| CREATE/SING/ PLAY/MOVE | **3.** Children compose songs, instrumental compositions, and movement compositions, reflecting consideration of dynamic level. | M, L |

## The child perceives and identifies
## SPECIFIC CHARACTERISTICS OF SOUND

### TEMPO

| fast/slow | **1.** Help children discover sounds that have a fast pattern and those with patterns that are slow. | V | Use picture charts showing things that move fast and slow. |
|---|---|---|---|
| | | L | Make a word chart listing sounds |
| | *live or recorded environmental sounds* | | **Charts:** 5 6 7 8 9 <br> **SC:** 1 - 9 |
| fast/slow | **2.** Teacher or selected child plays two measures of four beats each, in the same or contrasting tempo. Class determines if both measures were played at the same tempo, or one was slower (faster) than the other. | V | Some children may find it easier to select a graphic choice. For example: <br><br> **(a)** \| \| \| \|     **(b)** \|\|\|\| <br><br> For a greater challenge, rhythmic patterns can be substituted for even beats. |
| | *drum* | | |
| slow | **3.** Children indicate by word or gesture the tempo heard as slow. | V, L | Use pictures, word cards, or graphics for an alternative response choice. |
| | ***Boccherini: Pastorale*** ⊙ <br> ***Mussorgsky: Bydlo*** ⊙ | | **Chart:** 8 |
| fast | **4.** Children indicate by word or gesture the tempo heard as fast. | V, L | Use visuals, as above. |
| | *Handel: Bourrée* ⊙ <br> *McBride: Pony Express* ⊙ <br> *Mussorgsky: Ballet of the Unhatched Chicks* ⊙ <br> *Tchaikovsky: Trepak* ⊙ | | **Charts:** 5 9 10 |

| | | | | |
|---|---|---|---|---|
| changing tempo | 5. Children indicate by word or gesture when and how tempo changes occur in the music. | V, L | Use visuals, as above. |
| | *Bizet: Farandole* ⊙ <br> *Shostakovich: Polka* ⊙ <br> *Stravinsky: Russian Dance* ⊙ <br> *Thomson: Walking Song* ⊙ | | |
| accelerando (faster) | 6. Children indicate by word or gesture that, in the music heard, the tempo gets faster. | V, L | Use visuals, as above. |
| | *Grieg: In the Hall of the Mountain King* ⊙ <br> *Offenbach: "Cancan" Theme* ⊙ <br> *Step Lively (accelerated version)* ⊙ | | Chart: ⑩ |
| ritardando (slower) | 7. Children indicate by word or gesture that, in the music heard, the tempo gets slower. | V, L | Use visuals, as above. |
| | *Fauré: Berceuse* ⊙ <br> *Handel: Minuet and Bourrée* ⊙ | | Chart: ⑩ |

**The child demonstrates**
# UNDERSTANDING OF SPECIFIC CHARACTERISTICS OF SOUND THROUGH MUSICAL PERFORMANCE

## PERFORM TEMPO

| | | | | |
|---|---|---|---|---|
| SING | slow | 1. Sing songs that are appropriately performed in slow tempos. | M, L | Emphasize slow tempo by conducting or moving to the beat. |
| | | Canoe Round     Joe Turner Blues <br> Down, Down     My Father's House <br> For Health and Strength | | |
| SING | fast | 2. Sing songs that are appropriately performed in fast tempos. | M, L | Emphasize fast tempo by conducting or moving to the beat. |
| | | Chumbara     The Man in Blue <br> John Jacob Jingelheimer Schmidt | | |
| PLAY | fast/slow | 3. Select instrumental activities in which playing in fast and slow tempos is experienced. | M, L | Emphasize tempo. |
| | | Japanese Rain Song | | |
| SING/MOVE | | 4. Select materials in which the tempo gets slower (*ritardando*). | M, L | |
| | | Pat-a-Cake     Singing Top | | |
| SING/ PLAY/ MOVE | accelerando/ ritardando | 5. Accompany or move to songs and instrumental music depicting starting and stopping trains. | M, L | |
| | | Chicka Hanka     Train Is A-Coming <br> Down at the Station     When the Train Comes Along | | |

| PLAY | accelerando/ ritardando contrast | **6.** Children take turns matching drumbeat to music with gradual tempo changes; with abrupt tempo changes. | **M** | |
|---|---|---|---|---|
| | | *appropriate improvised or recorded music* | | |
| | | *drum or other suitable percussion instrument* | | |
| MOVE | | **7.** Circle formation, seated on the floor. Prepare for the game by practicing the following movement patterns.<br><br>**Section A:** With right hand, slap left knee two times, right knee two times (4 beats); with right hand, slap left knee four times (4 beats). Do Section A four times.<br><br>**Section B:** With right hand, hit the floor two times; spread arms to side; clap hands together once (4 beats). Do Section B eight times.<br><br>When children can perform the above easily, give one stick to each and slowly talk through both Sections without music. In Section B, sticks are hit on the floor twice, passed to the person on the right with the right hand at the same time a stick is accepted from the person on the left with the left hand. (Passing occurs on the third and fourth beats.) The stick received by the left hand is then transferred to the right hand and the sequence is repeated (eight times in all before Section A begins again). When adding the music, begin with the slower tempo until all are ready to attempt the faster one. | **V, M** | If children are unable to keep up, it is better to stop the recording before the fastest tempo is reached. Practice will increase the length of successful performance as well as speed.<br><br>A variation of the game can be played by passing or bouncing balls from one person to another around the circle on every other beat.<br><br>It is sometimes wiser to have several small circles of six to eight children rather than one large one, particularly in beginning experiences. Position children with known laterality and/or sequencing problems between two others with good skills in those areas. |
| | | *Cotton Eyed Joe (accelerated version)* ⊙<br>*Step Lively (accelerated version)* ⊙<br>*rhythm sticks (one for each player)* | | |
| SING/ MOVE | contrast | **8.** Select materials that involve a tempo change. | **M, L** | |
| | | **Charlie Knows How to Beat That Drum**<br>**Walrus Hunt** | **The Wind Blew East** | |

The child demonstrates
## ABILITY TO APPLY UNDERSTANDING OF MUSICAL CHARACTERISTICS CREATIVELY

**CREATE TEMPO**

| CREATE/ MOVE | | **1.** Children interpret tempo through body movement, graphic representation, drawings, etc. | **V, M** |
|---|---|---|---|
| | | *select appropriate vocal and instrumental music* | |

| CREATE/<br>PLAY | **2.** Children create appropriate accompaniments to familiar songs representing a variety of tempos. | M,<br>L | |
|---|---|---|---|
| | **The Ants Go Marching**<br>**Canoe Round** | **Chumbara**<br>**For Health and Strength** | |
| SING | **3.** Experiment with singing familiar songs at tempos that contrast with those at which they are usually performed. | L | |
| | **The Ants Go Marching**<br>**Canoe Round**<br>**For Health and Strength** | **The Man in Blue**<br>**Ticky Ticky Tambo** | |

## The child perceives and identifies
# SPECIFIC CHARACTERISTICS OF SOUND                                        METER

| steady beat | **1.** Children identify by word or gesture music that has an ongoing steady pulse. | V,<br>L | Use pictures, word cards, or graphics for alternative response choice. |
|---|---|---|---|
| | **Marching to Pretoria**<br>*Bach: Badinere* ⊙<br>*Bizet: March* ⊙<br>*Herbert: March of the Toys* ⊙<br>*Prokofiev: March* ⊙ | | Charts: 4 11 12 |
| no beat | **2.** Children identify by word or gesture music that has no definite pulse. | V,<br>L | Use visuals, as above. |
| | *Searching* ⊙ | | Chart: 12 |
| duple meter | **3.** Children identify by word or gesture music in which beats occur in sets of two. | V,<br>L | Use visuals, as above. |
| | *Fauré: Berceuse* ⊙<br>*German: Morris Dance* ⊙<br>*Grieg: In the Hall of the Mountain King* ⊙<br>*Handel: Bourrée* ⊙<br>*Offenbach: "Cancan" Theme* ⊙<br>*Shostakovich: Polka* ⊙ | | Chart: 13 |
| triple meter | **4.** Children identify by word or gesture music in which beats occur in sets of three. | V,<br>L | Use visuals, as above. |
| | *Bach: Minuet* ⊙<br>*Handel: Minuet* ⊙<br>*Meyerbeer: Waltz* ⊙<br>*Swing High* ⊙ | | Chart: 14 |
| changing meter | **5.** Children identify by word or gesture music in which beats sometimes occur in sets of two, and sometimes in sets of three. | V,<br>L | Use visuals, as above. |
| | *Bartok: Diary of a Fly* ⊙<br>*Enciña: Villancico* ⊙ | | Charts: 13 14 |

## UNDERSTANDING OF SPECIFIC CHARACTERISTICS OF SOUND THROUGH MUSICAL PERFORMANCE

**PERFORM METER**

| | | | | |
|---|---|---|---|---|
| **PLAY** | beat | **1.** Children sustain beat in both duple and triple meters. | **M** | Placing a suspended cymbal to the side of the child's dominant hand will often encourage the child to demonstrate a sense of phrasing in the music.<br><br>Walking or marching can be substituted for playing.<br><br>For a greater challenge, the beat can be altered by means of accelerando, ritardando, or abruptly establishing a new tempo. |
| | | *select familiar and unfamiliar recorded or live music in duple and triple meters*<br><br>*drum, suspended cymbal* | | **Charts:** 13 14 |
| **MOVE** | accent | **2.** Children bounce balls, balloons, or pass bean bags on the accented beat. | **M** | |
| | | **Rolling Along**   *Meyerbeer: Waltz* ☉<br>*Handel: Minuet* ☉   *Swing High* ☉ | | |
| **SING/ PLAY/ MOVE** | duple meter accent tempo | **3.** Children move, clap, conduct, or play basic beat of music with two pulses in a variety of tempos. | **M, L** | |
| | | **Canoe Round**        **Rolling Along**<br>**Chumbara**<br>**Down at the Station**<br>**For Health and Strength**   *German: Morris Dance* ☉<br>**Marching to Pretoria**   *Mussorgsky: Bydlo* ☉<br>**My Father's House**   *Thomson: Walking Song* ☉ | | **Chart:** 13 |
| **SING/ PLAY/ MOVE** | triple meter accent tempo | **4.** Children move, clap, conduct, or play basic beat of music with three pulses in a variety of tempos. | **M, L** | |
| | | **Man on the Flying Trapeze**   *Handel: Minuet* ☉<br>**So Long**   *Meyerbeer: Waltz* ☉<br>**Tra La La La**   *Swing High* ☉ | | **Chart:** 14 |
| **PLAY/ MOVE** | meter | **5.** Children practice strumming movements in preparation for accompanying appropriate songs in duple and triple meters with autoharp or guitar. | **M** | One-chord accompaniments will be more successful in beginning activities.<br><br>See special activities following the songs. |
| | | **Canoe Round**   **Tra La La La**<br>**Roll Over** | | **Charts:** 13 14 |
| **MOVE** | triple meter | **6.** All children should practice the pole rhythm while singing the song, "Tinikling." (See special activities and dance directions following the song.) Only when the pole rhythm is easily performed should the dance be attempted. | **V, M** | |
| | | **Tinikling** | | |

## The child demonstrates
## ABILITY TO APPLY UNDERSTANDING OF MUSICAL CHARACTERISTICS CREATIVELY

**CREATE METER**

| CREATE/ MOVE | **1.** Children interpret meter through body movement, graphic representation, drawings, etc. | V, M | |
|---|---|---|---|
| | *select vocal and instrumental music of varied meters* | | |
| SING/ PLAY/ CREATE | **2.** Children create accompaniments to familiar songs using appropriate beat patterns. | M, L | |
| | **Canoe Round**     **Man on the Flying Trapeze**<br>**Let's Go Walking**     **So Long** | | |
| CREATE | **3.** Children determine appropriate meter for a short poem or chant. | M, L | Simple instruments can accompany the beat. |
| | *select suitable poetry or speech chants* | | |

## The child perceives and identifies
## SPECIFIC CHARACTERISTICS OF SOUND

**RHYTHM**

| long/short | **1.** Help children discover instruments and objects that have naturally sustained sounds (e.g., gong) and those that have naturally short sounding properties (e.g., woodblock). | V<br><br>L | Make a picture chart of findings.<br><br>Make a word chart with names of found instruments. |
|---|---|---|---|
| | *assorted melody and percussion instruments, found sounds* | | |
| long/short | **2.** Help children make a sound mobile from materials found around the classroom or home. After assembling, ask children to find all the objects that produce a sustained sound when struck and those from which sound fades quickly. Experiment with mallets of different materials (e.g., yarn, rubber, wood). | FM<br><br>V<br><br>L | Make a picture chart of findings.<br><br>Make a word chart with names of objects. |
| | *found sounds, assorted mallets,<br>wire coat hanger, fish line* | | **Chart:** 15 |
| long/short | **3.** *Room tap.* Select children to explore the room for long and short sounds. | V, L | Make charts, as above. |
| | *assorted mallets* | | **Chart:** 15 |
| long/short patterns | **4.** The teacher plays pairs of rhythm patterns made up of long and short sounds. Children indicate by word or gesture whether they are the same or different. Example: ⎯⎯ ⎯ ⎯⎯ ⎯ ⎯<br>⎯ ⎯⎯ ⎯⎯ ⎯ ⎯ | | |
| | *drum* | | |
| long/short | **5.** Teacher plays short sequences of either long, sustained tones or short tones. Children identify by word or gesture whether each is made up of long or short tones. | V, L | Use pictures, word cards, or graphics for an alternative response choice. |

|  |  |  |  |  |
|---|---|---|---|---|
|  |  | *piano, Autoharp* |  | Chart: 15 |
| **rhythm pattern** | | **6.** *Somebody's Name Sounds Like This.* Teacher claps the rhythm pattern of children's first names. Children indicate by word or gesture when they recognize the pattern of their name. Note: More than one child may correctly respond to the same pattern. Example: Alexander / Margarita | | When children are very familiar with personal rhythm patterns, play "Rhythm Roll Call" by taking the roll in this way. Last names can be added when ready. |
|  |  | *drum or other percussion instrument* |  | |
| **long/short ostinato** | | **7.** Have children listen for long, sustained sounds as well as short, repeated patterns (e.g., saw, hammer). | V | Find pictures of sounds. |
|  |  |  | L | Make word lists of sounds. |
|  |  |  | V | Make graphic illustrations of sound patterns. Example: telephone / clock ● ● ● ● ● ● ● ● |
|  |  | *live or recorded environmental sounds* |  | Charts: 4 5 6 7 / SC: 1-9 |
| **even rhythm legato/ staccato divided beat** | | **8.** Children identify by word or gesture rhythmic structure as predominantly even; legato/staccato contrasts of selections; subdivided beat ( ). | V, L | Use pictures, word cards, or graphics for alternative choice. |
|  |  | **My Father's House** *Grieg: In the Hall of the Mountain King* ☉ |  | Chart: 11 |
| **uneven rhythm** | | **9.** Children identify by word or gesture rhythmic structure as predominantly uneven; legato/staccato contrasts | V, L | Use visuals, as above. |
|  |  | **Japanese Rain Song**   *Meyerbeer: Waltz* ☉ **My White Mouse** |  | Chart: 11 |
| **melodic rhythm** | | **10.** *Rhythmic Name That Tune.* Teacher or a child taps out the melodic rhythm of a familiar tune. Class tries to identify. | L | Listening themes as well as songs can be used. Play as a team game with one point scored for each correct response. |
|  |  | *drum or percussion instrument (optional)* |  | |

**The child demonstrates**
# UNDERSTANDING OF SPECIFIC CHARACTERISTICS OF SOUND THROUGH MUSICAL PERFORMANCE

### PERFORM RHYTHM

|  |  |  |  |  |
|---|---|---|---|---|
| **PLAY** | **long/short** | **1.** Call attention to long sounds produced by allowing instrument to sound until vibrations stop. Show children how to produce short sounds by stopping the vibrations. | V, M | Find visual examples of long and short in the room. |
|  |  | *any instrument with sustaining properties (e.g., piano, Autoharp, strings, gong, cymbal)* | | |
| **SING/ PLAY/ MOVE** | **even rhythm divided beat** | **2.** Children clap or play subdivided beat for trotting rhythm ( ). | M | |

| | | | | |
|---|---|---|---|---|
| | | **My Little Pony**<br>*drum, woodblock, etc.* | | |
| MOVE | even rhythm | **3.** Clap and/or step the melodic rhythm of selected familiar songs. | M | |
| | | **I Like You**       **My Father's House**<br>**Miss Mary Mack** | | |
| MOVE | uneven rhythm | **4.** Clap and/or step the melodic rhythm of familiar songs. | M | |
| | | **The Best of Buddies   My White Mouse**<br>**John the Rabbit** | | |
| CHANT/<br>MOVE/<br>PLAY | rhythm pattern | **5.** Help each child to chant and clap out the rhythm of his or her first name. Be sure that stressed syllables fall on the accented beats. Example:<br><br>Ma - *ri* - a ♪\| ♩ ♩<br><br>*Jen* - ni - fer ♩♩♩ (3) | M,<br>L | Add last names when individuals are ready.<br><br>Substitute ball bouncing for clapping.<br><br>Step rhythms with feet. |
| | | *drum (optional)* | | |
| PLAY/<br>MOVE | rhythm pattern | **6.** *Rhythm Echoes.* The teacher (or a child) plays or claps a short rhythm pattern for class to repeat. Begin with one-measure phrases and gradually increase length. | M<br><br><br><br>S | When class is ready, remove visual clues by playing patterns from the back of the class or some other location that is out of their sight.<br><br>Pass out instruments to pairs of children and let them take turns being leader and echo.<br><br>Children can echo patterns with their feet or with ball bouncing. |
| | | *drum or other suitable percussion instrument (optional)* | | |
| MOVE | rhythm patterns | **7.** See special activities, following "Somebody's Knocking at Your Door," for making this song a rhythm game. Both even and uneven rhythms should be included. Children's names can be used as well. | M<br><br>V<br><br>L | Make charts with patterns in either graphic or standard notation.<br>Chant patterns. |
| | | **Somebody's Knocking at Your Door** | | |
| MOVE | changing rhythm | **8.** Children respond to changing rhythm patterns with appropriate movement. | M | Begin by pairing verbal directions with change in rhythm (walk, run, skip). Later, withdraw verbal reinforcement. |
| | | **Rig-a-jig-jig     The Wind Blew East**<br>*drum or improvised piano* | | |
| SING/<br>MOVE | syncopation | **9.** Help children locate and clap the syncopated rhythms in familiar songs. | M | |
| | | **Bones**          **The Man in Blue**<br>**Canoe Round**     **What Can Make a Hippopotamus Smile?** | | |
| SING/<br>MOVE/<br>PLAY | ostinato | **10.** Select two or three rhythm patterns from "The Man in Blue" for suitable ostinatos. Select children (or divide the class) to perform while singing. Example: ¢ ♪ ♩♩ ♪ ♩\| | M | |

| | | The Man in Blue | | |
|---|---|---|---|---|
| SING/ PLAY | triplet | **11.** Children clap or play triplet rhythm $(\widehat{\text{♩♩♩}})$ | M, L | |
| | | **Throw It Out the Window** | | |
| SING/ PLAY | rest | **12.** Select songs in which rests help to convey the meaning of the words in the song and/or the character of the music. | L | |
| | | My Little Pony          Stop! Look! Listen! | | |

## The child demonstrates
## ABILITY TO APPLY UNDERSTANDING
## OF MUSICAL CHARACTERISTICS CREATIVELY                    CREATE RHYTHM

| | | | |
|---|---|---|---|
| CREATE/ MOVE | **1.** Children interpret rhythm through body movement, graphic representation, drawing, etc. | V, M | |
| | *select appropriate vocal and instrumental music* | | |
| CREATE/ SING/ PLAY | **2.** Children create accompaniments to familiar songs using appropriate rhythm patterns. | V, M | |
| | **Breezes Are Blowing       The Man in Blue**<br>**Chicka Hanka              Ticky Ticky Tambo**<br>**Japanese Rain Song** | | |
| CREATE/SING/ PLAY/MOVE | **3.** Children select appropriate instruments to accompany songs with contrasting melodic rhythms. | M | |
| | **Rig-a-jig-jig     The Wind Blew East** | | |
| CREATE/MOVE | **4.** Children graphically notate the rhythms of their names using long and short lines. Collect and use as an echo clap activity. Children identify names as they are clapped. | V, M, T | Some children may find it easier to notate with textured or manipulative materials.<br><br>For a different challenge, teacher can copy children's notations on the chalkboard for visual identification.<br><br>Substitute original patterns for names.<br><br>Combine patterns to make a rhythm piece. |
| | *paper, pencil* | | |
| CREATE | **5.** Children graphically notate the melodic rhythm of the first phrase of a familiar tune. Write on the chalkboard or chart for identification. | V, M | |
| | *paper, pencil* | | |
| CREATE/PLAY/ MOVE/CHANT | **6.** Children create rhythm sequences by combining patterns of names, charts, slogans, etc. Play; notate. | V, M, L | Additional concepts may be reviewed by using categories as a basis (cars, foods, etc.). |

| | | | |
|---|---|---|---|
| **PLAY/CREATE** | **7.** *Rhythmic gossip.* Scatter players with their instruments about the room. One child begins a rhythm pattern which is "sent" to another player. This player in turn passes it on to another. When the last player has repeated the "message," class decides if the pattern was performed exactly as initiated. (It is a good idea for the teacher to write down the original pattern for future reference.) The message can be sent in a predetermined order, or each player can call out the name of the player for whom the message is intended. | **M** | |
| | *percussion instruments (one for each participant)* | | |
| **CREATE/MOVE** | **8.** *Rhythmic phrase building.* The teacher begins with a one measure rhythm phrase. The next individual repeats the teacher's pattern and adds another measure of their own. Game progresses with each child repeating the pattern of the individual before them, then adding their own. | **M** | For a more difficult challenge, individuals repeat *all* previous patterns before adding a new one. |

## The child perceives and identifies
## SPECIFIC CHARACTERISTICS OF SOUND                              PITCH

| | | | |
|---|---|---|---|
| **high/low** | **1.** Help children group instruments with high sounds on one side of a table, those with low on the other. | **V** | Make a picture chart of the instruments and the pitch of their sounds. |
| | | **L** | Make a word chart with names of instruments. |
| | *assorted high and low single pitched instruments (e.g., resonator bells, big and little drums)* | | **Charts:** 16 17 18 <br> **SC:** 10 - 12 |
| **high/low** | **2.** Help children discover environmental sounds that have high and low pitches. | **V, L** | Make visuals, as above. |
| | *live or recorded environmental sounds* | | **Charts:** 6 7 <br> **SC:** 1 - 9 |
| **high/low** | **3.** Teacher plays single pitches in high/low contrasts. Children indicate by word or gesture pitches that are the same, higher, or lower. | **V, L** | Make picture, word, or graphic chart for an alternative response choice. <br><br> For a more difficult task, melodies or chords can be substituted for single pitches. |
| | *melody instruments* | | **Charts:** 16 17 18 |
| **high/low** | **4.** Help children make a sound mobile from materials found around the classroom or home. After assembling, ask children to find high and low sounds on the mobile. Experiment with mallets made from different materials to discover if sounds change in pitch. | **FM V** <br><br><br> **L** | Make a chart with pictures of those items found to produce high or low sounds when struck with various mallets. <br><br> Make a word chart, as above. |

38

| | | | | |
|---|---|---|---|---|
| | | *found sounds, assorted mallets, wire coat hanger, fish line* | | |
| | high/low | 5. Two children are each given a bell and stand side by side in front of class. Class covers eyes; players move to different locations in the room playing their bells as they move. Teacher calls out either "high" or "low" and class points to the source of the appropriate sound. | M | If group is small and facilities permit, they can move toward the appropriate sound source. |
| | | *two melodic instruments of contrasting pitches (e.g., bells)* | | |
| | high/low | 6. *Room tap.* Select children to explore the room for high and low pitched sounds. | | Make charts of findings. |
| | | *assorted mallets* | | |
| | high | 7. Children identify by word or gesture predominant pitch level of melody as high. | V, L | Use picture, word, or graphic chart for alternative response choice. |
| | | *Bach: Badinere* ⊙ <br> *Mussorgsky: Ballet of the Unhatched Chicks* ⊙ <br> *Shostakovich: Polka* ⊙ | | Chart: 19 |
| | low | 8. Children identify by word or gesture predominant pitch level of melody as low. | V, L | Use charts, as above. |
| | | *Grieg: In the Hall of the Mountain King* ⊙ <br> *Mussorgsky: Bydlo* ⊙ | | Chart: 19 |
| | high/low contrasts | 9. Children identify by word or gesture pitch contrasts as they occur in music. | V, L | Use charts, as above. |
| | | *Bach: Allegro* ⊙ <br> *Bartok: Jack-in-the-Box* ⊙ <br> *Shostakovich: Polka* ⊙ | | Chart: 19 |
| | register | 10. Children recognize melody of a familiar tune ("Happy Birthday") even though heard fragmented and in different pitch registers. | V, L | Use charts, as above. |
| | | *Stravinsky: Greeting Prelude* ⊙ | | |

**The child demonstrates**
## UNDERSTANDING OF SPECIFIC CHARACTERISTICS OF SOUND THROUGH MUSICAL PERFORMANCE

### PERFORM PITCH

| | | | | |
|---|---|---|---|---|
| SING/ MOVE | high/low | 1. Learn the "Stretching Song," adding appropriate body movement to dramatize "tall" and "small." Call attention to ascending and descending melodic line in relation to the words. | V, M | Use pictures of "tall" and "small." |
| | | **Stretching Song** | | Chart: 21 |
| SING | high/low | 2. Learn the song "My Farm." Encourage the use of high pitched vocal sounds for little animals and low pitched vocal sounds for big animals. | V | Use pictures of big and little animals. |

| | | | | |
|---|---|---|---|---|
| **MOVE** | high/low | **3.** Arrange children in row formation (one behind the other) standing with legs apart. Ball is passed overhead when high tones are heard, between legs when low tones are heard. | V, M, S | |
| | | *instrument with contrasting high and low pitches* | | |
| | | *ball* | | |
| **MOVE** | high/low | **4.** *Pass the Ball.* Circle formation, standing or sitting. An object (shaker, ball, beanbag) is passed *on the beat* beginning in a counterclockwise direction. Teacher or child plays a high or low pitch to signal a change in the way object is passed. Decide before play how passing movements will change when high and low tones are heard. Examples:<br>high (or low) - stop (or change direction)<br>high - pass clockwise<br>low - pass counterclockwise | V M, S | Pitch cues can also signal the manner in which the object is passed (e.g., left or right hand, behind back).<br><br>For a more difficult task, pass more than one object around the circle at one time. |
| | | *instruments with contrasting high and low pitches* | | |
| | | *small shakers, ball, or beanbag* | | |
| **PLAY** | high/low | **5.** The child selected to play the bells may play *ad lib* but should be encouraged to match the high/low pitches of the melody. | M | Place the high bell in a location where players must *reach* to play; low bell where they must *bend down*. |
| | | *resonator bells or xylophone (C and C')* | | |
| | | ***Swing High*** ⊙ | | |
| **SING/ PLAY** | interval (fourth) | **6.** Select one child to play the interval of a fourth (*sol - do*) when it occurs in the music. | M | |
| | | **Jack-in-the-Box** | | |
| | | *bells (G and C)* | | |
| **SING/ PLAY** | interval (minor third) | **7.** For "Train is A - Coming," select two children to play the bells on "Oh yes." Beginning activities may need to be visually cued for success. | V, M | |
| | | **Train Is A-Coming** | | |
| | | *bells (C and E$^\flat$, G and B$^\flat$)* | | |
| **SING/ PLAY** | interval recognition | **8.** *Grab bag game.* Place cards in a bag. Each child chooses a card and then performs (vocally or instrumentally) a musical interval that matches the description on the card. Class identifies what the word on the card is. Note: It may be helpful for the teacher to give the fundamental (or first) pitch for some children for singing responses. | V | Some children may find a graphic representation of interval size easier to interpret than words.<br><br>For a more difficult task, specific intervals can be either notated or indicated by number.<br><br>Procedure can be reversed by playing the interval, then have children identify or notate.<br><br>Play as a team game. |

| | | | | |
|---|---|---|---|---|
| | | *about a dozen cards—on each write either "small," "medium," or "large"* *melody instrument* | | |
| PLAY | register | **9.** Play an echo game in which children echo patterns played by the teacher on the piano in appropriate registers. | M | Before beginning the activity, tune the drum or otherwise explore the pitch of the instruments with the children. |
| | | *two to four drums or other suitable classroom instruments of contrasting pitch ranges* | | |
| SING/ PLAY | high/low up/down | **10.** Children simulate environmental sounds that are high and low or have up and down pitch patterns (e.g., sirens, wind). | M | |
| | | | | Charts: 19 34 |
| PLAY | | **11.** Play an echo game using only two tones. Gradually increase number of tones until melodic phrase results. | M | Instrument keys or bars can be coded with colored tape when single tones are not possible. This activity can be helpful with beginning instrumentalists, using only notes for which they know fingerings. |
| | | *melody instruments (piano, bells, xylophones)* | | |

**The child demonstrates**
## ABILITY TO APPLY UNDERSTANDING OF MUSICAL CHARACTERISTICS CREATIVELY

**CREATE PITCH**

| | | | |
|---|---|---|---|
| CREATE/MOVE | **1.** Children interpret pitch level through appropriate body movement, graphic representation, or drawings. | V, M | |
| | *select suitable vocal and instrumental music* | | |
| CREATE/CHANT | **2.** Children create graphic scores to notate pitch inflection of names, familiar speech phrases, or original chants. Example: I want some ⌢ | V, M | |
| | *paper, pencil* | | |
| CREATE/SING | **3.** Sing the first phrase in call-and-response style. Encourage individual singers to improvise different interval responses to "hello." | | |
| | **Hello!** | | |
| CREATE/MOVE | **4.** Play a pitch game using the song "Charlie Over the Water" (see Special Activities, Auditory, following song). | V, M, L | |
| | **Charlie Over the Water** | | |

| | | | |
|---|---|---|---|
| **up** | **1.** Children indicate by word or gesture recognition of ascending melody line. | V, L | Use picture, word, or graphic chart for nonverbal response choice. |
| | **I Like to Ride the Elevator (first half)**<br>**Pussy Willow**<br>**Upstairs, Downstairs (first half)** | | Chart: 8 |
| **down** | **2.** Children indicate by word or gesture recognition of descending melody line. | V, L | Use visuals, as above. |
| | **Down, Down**    **Jack-in-the-Box**<br>**For Health and Strength** | | Chart: 9 |
| **up/down** | **3.** Children indicate by word or gesture recognition of melodic contour that goes both up and down. | V, L | |
| | **I Like to Ride the Elevator**  **Snowflakes**<br>**I Roll the Ball**  **Upstairs, Downstairs**<br>**My Father's House**  *Bartok: Jack-in-the-Box* ⊙<br>**My Little Pony**  *Hill and Dell* ⊙<br>**Singing Top**<br>**Skippin' and Steppin'** | | Charts: 22 24 |
| **phrase** | **4.** Children indicate by word or gesture recognition of identical melodic phrases. | V, L | Use visuals, as above. |
| | **Candles of Hannukah**  **My Father's House**<br>**Canoe Round**  **My White Mouse**<br>**Halloween Night**  **Train Is A-Coming**<br>**Let's Go Walking**  **Valentine** | | |
| **phrase** | **5.** Children indicate by word or gesture recognition of regular phrases in music. | V, L | Use visuals, as above. |
| | **My Father's House**  *Bach: Badinere* ⊙<br>*Fauré: Berceuse* ⊙<br>*Meyerbeer: Waltz* ⊙<br>*Vivaldi: Allegro* ⊙ | | |
| **contour** | **6.** Children indicate by word or gesture recognition of jagged melody line. | V, L | Use visuals, as above. |
| | **There Was a Crooked Man**<br>*McBride: Pumpkin Eater's Little Fugue* ⊙<br>*Shostakovich: Polka* ⊙<br>*Stravinsky: Greeting Prelude* ⊙ | | Chart: 23 |
| **phrase form** | **7.** Children indicate by word or gesture recognition of contrasting phrases. | V, L | Use visuals, as above. |
| | **Marching to Pretoria** | | |
| **sequence** | **8.** Children indicate by word or gesture recognition of melodic sequence. | V, L | Use visuals, as above. |
| | **Hush, Little Baby** | | |
| **stepwise** | **9.** Children indicate by word or gesture recognition of melodies that progress stepwise and scalewise. | V, L | Use visuals, as above. |

| | | | | |
|---|---|---|---|---|
| | | **I Like to Ride the Elevator** Upstairs, Downstairs **Pussy Willow** | | |
| | step/skip | **10.** Children indicate by word or gesture recognition of a single skip in otherwise stepwise melody. | V, L | Use visuals, as above. |
| | | **For Health and Strength** I Like to Ride the Elevator **Hush, Little Baby** | | |
| | step/skip | **11.** Children indicate by word or gesture recognition of measures in which melody skips, and measures in which melody progresses stepwise. | V, L | Use visuals, as above. |
| | | **False Face** Tra La La La **My Little Pony** | | |
| | minor | **12.** Children indicate by word or gesture recognition of melody in the minor mode. | V, L | Use visuals, as above. |
| | | **Candles of Hannukah** Halloween Night **Canoe Round** Lots of Worms | | |
| | pattern | **13.** Children indicate by word or gesture recognition of melodic patterns. For example: *do mi sol sol fa mi re do* | V, L | Use visuals, as above. For example: |
| | | **My Little Pony** | | |

**The child demonstrates**
## UNDERSTANDING OF SPECIFIC CHARACTERISTICS OF SOUND THROUGH MUSICAL PERFORMANCE

**PERFORM MELODY**

| | | | | |
|---|---|---|---|---|
| SING/ PLAY | up/down scale | **1.** Teach children to play simple scale melodies, emphasizing the upward and downward direction. | M | Arrange bells in step fashion, from low to high. |
| | | | V | Number the bells or keys from lowest to highest. |
| | | | V, L | Make a word chart or graphic score that depicts the melodic direction. |
| | | **Down, Down** Jack-in-the-Box **For Health and Strength** Pussy Willow *bells, xylophone* **Upstairs, Downstairs** | | |
| PLAY | up/down | **2.** Arrange bells vertically from low to high. Teach children to play the bell part in "Skippin' and Steppin'," by calling out "up" or "down" as indicated in the score. | V, M, L | See above. |
| | | **Skippin' and Steppin'** *bells, xylophone (G, B, C, and D); piano* | | Chart: 24 |

| | | | | |
|---|---|---|---|---|
| MOVE | up/down contour | **3.** Direct children in moving scarves or streamers up and down with the melody line. | **V, M** | |

| | | |
|---|---|---|
| | **My Father's House** **Snowflakes**   Hill and Dell ☉  *scarves, streamers* | **Chart:** 22 |

| | | | | |
|---|---|---|---|---|
| SING | melody | **4.** *Crayon Game.* Children cover eyes and hold out one hand, palm up, as teacher passes out the crayons. On signal, class opens eyes and listens as teacher calls for each crayon, one at a time. Child who has crayon called for responds by echoing the melody. Begin with colors that are known. New colors can be introduced one at a time. | **V** | Once children are familiar with the game, they can give away and call for the crayon they received.

For a more difficult task, the melody can be changed with each crayon. |

*Teacher:* Who has the yel - low?
*Child:* I have the yel - low.

| | |
|---|---|
| *four to six crayons (or other small objects) of different colors* | |

| | | | | |
|---|---|---|---|---|
| SING | jagged contour | **5.** Call attention to the crooked, or jagged, melodic contour, as children sing or dramatize "There was a Crooked Man." | **V** | Have children draw a graphic representation of the melody. |

| | |
|---|---|
| **There Was a Crooked Man**   *McBride: Pumpkin Eater's Little Fugue* ☉ | **Chart:** 23 |

| | | | | |
|---|---|---|---|---|
| MOVE | regular phrase | **6.** Children walk to the beat of the music, stopping at the end of each phrase. Call attention to the regular phrasing by noting that exactly the same number of steps are taken from one stop to the next. | **V, M** | Mark distances on the floor with tape.

Make a chart showing regular phrases of 8 beats each. |

| | |
|---|---|
| **A Little Flight Music ("Stop" version)**   *Alley Cat* ☉  *Stop and Go* ☉ | |

| | | | | |
|---|---|---|---|---|
| MOVE | phrase | **7.** Point out the elements in the dance that correspond with the beginning of a new phrase, such as change of direction, new movement, in "Bingo." | **M** | For dance directions, see special activities following the song. |

| | |
|---|---|
| **Bingo** | |

| | | | | |
|---|---|---|---|---|
| MOVE | regular phrase | **8.** Select a familiar song or tune. Partners stand facing each other about five feet apart (or a distance at which the ball can be bounced and passed successfully). The ball is bounced (or passed) to a partner at the end of each phrase in the music. | **V, M, S** | In beginning experiences it may be necessary for the teacher to signal the phrase endings.

This can also be performed in circle formation with a leader in the center who passes, or bounces, one ball to individuals around the circle. |

| | |
|---|---|
| *one ball for each couple*   *Alley Cat* ☉ | |

| | | | | |
|---|---|---|---|---|
| SING | phrase melody | **9.** Select a familiar song, such as "Happy Birthday," that the class knows and can sing very well. Teacher (or child) begins by singing the first phrase; individuals volunteer to supply each of the remaining phrases. | **L** | |

| | | | | |
|---|---|---|---|---|
| SING/ MOVE | phrase | **10.** Select songs in which phrases are easily distinguished. Help children make up appropriate movements for each phrase, keeping movement the same for repeated phrases. | M, L V | Make graphic representations of phrase length. |
| | | **Canoe Round**     **Puppets** **My Father's House**     **Singing Top** | | |
| SING | phrase | **11.** Select call-and-response songs in which individuals respond with melodic phrases. | L | |
| | | **False Face     Two Little Hands** **The Goat** | | |
| PLAY | phrase direction (stepwise) | **12.** Select children to play on the stepwise ascending and descending phrases: (Angels): "The first one lights the fire, . . ." (Beehive): "One, two, three, four, five." | V, M | |
| | | **Five Angels** *bells or xylophone: C, D, E, F, G* **Here's the Beehive** *bells or xylophone: F, G, A, B♭, C'* | | |
| PLAY | phrase direction (skips) | **13.** Select children to play the first and third phrases in "Puppets": "See them dance, so so!" | V, M | |
| | | **Puppets** *bells or xylophone: F, A, C, D* | | |
| MOVE | irregular phrase | **14.** Children walk to the beat, stopping at the pauses. Call attention to places where it is easy to be fooled because phrases are irregular in length. | M | Children can practice clapping first, if necessary. |
| | | **A Little Flight Music ("Stop" version)** | | |

**The child demonstrates**
# ABILITY TO APPLY UNDERSTANDING OF MUSICAL CHARACTERISTICS CREATIVELY

**CREATE MELODY**

| | | | |
|---|---|---|---|
| CREATE/ MOVE | **1.** Children interpret melodic contour through body movement, graphic representation, or drawings. | V, M | |
| | *select vocal and instrumental music* | | |
| CREATE/ PLAY | **2.** Children create appropriate melodic ostinatos to accompany a familiar song. | M | See special activities following song. |
| | **Japanese Rain Song** *melody instruments* | | |
| CREATE/PLAY/ SING/MOVE | **3.** Children write or choose short poems to set to music, to be sung, dramatized, orchestrated, or illustrated. | V, M | |

| | | | | |
|---|---|---|---|---|
| | | *select suitable poetry* | | |
| | | *melody instruments* | | |
| **CREATE/PLAY** | | **4.** *Questions and answers.* Limit the number of pitches used to as many as individual children can successfully handle. This can be as few as two, the pentatonic scale, or a full diatonic scale. Children can be in pairs, or teacher and child can play. One person plays the "question" and the other gives the "answer." Encourage children to vary rhythm and phrase lengths. | **M, S** | |
| | | *melody instruments* | | |
| **CREATE/SING** | | **5.** Select songs in which the melody can be embellished vocally and/or instrumentally. | | |
| | | **Joe Turner Blues**    **My Father's House** | | |
| **CREATE/PLAY** | | **6.** Tape paper *horizontally* to chalkboard or wall. One child is selected to create the score, another to create the melody by playing pitches in high, low, and middle register of a melody instrument. Child creating score places (marks) each tone in an appropriate location on the paper. Paper can be divided into three sections to help in placing high, middle, and low tones. Another child can volunteer to re-create the finished score by performing it. | **V, M** | |
| | | *length of shelf paper, 4' to 5' long* | | |
| | | *melody instrument (bells, xylophone, piano)* | | |
| **CREATE/PLAY** | | **7.** Select children to improvise melodies during the interludes separating the phrases (8 beats) in "Joe Turner Blues." | **V, M** | Activity can also be done with teacher playing traditional blues progression on piano, guitar, or autoharp: C  C  C  C₇   F₇  F₇  C  C   G₇  G₇  C  C (See activities following the song.) |
| | | **Joe Turner Blues** | | |
| | | *bells (or coded xylophone) arranged as a blues scale: C, D, E♭, F, G, A, B♭, C* | | |

## The child perceives and identifies
## SPECIFIC CHARACTERISTICS OF SOUND

**TIMBRE**

| | | | | |
|---|---|---|---|---|
| PLAY | timbre | **1.** Help children group instruments of similar timbres together. | V | Use picture charts showing instruments. |
| | | | L | Make word charts with names of instruments. |
| | | *classroom instruments* | | **Charts:** 16 17 18 |
| | | *shakers with a variety of timbres* | | |

| | | | | |
|---|---|---|---|---|
| **PLAY** | timbre | **2.** *Four Corners Rhapsody.* Divide class into four groups and send each to a corner of the room (each corner having a similar number of sound sources). One group begins by selecting one sound source to be played out of sight of the other groups. Each group attempts to find a sound source among their instruments to match the timbre of the one played by the first group. | **M** | New groups can be formed using like sounds as criteria. |
| | | *classroom instruments and/or found sounds* | | |
| **PLAY** | instrumental timbre | **3.** Four individuals are selected to go to different corners with an instrument. Each plays briefly in turn. Class points to the corner where the instrument with the different timbre is heard. Players switch locations while class hides eyes. Repeat. | **M** | |
| | | *four instruments, three with similar timbre, one different* | | |
| | instrumental timbre | **4.** Children indicate by word or gesture which sound (of three instruments) has a different timbre. | **V** | Help children match sounds to a picture of the instrument used, or the actual instrument. |
| | | | **L** | Substitute word cards for pictures. |
| | | *three instruments, two with similar timbre, one different*<br>**One of These Things** ⊙ | | Charts: ⬛16⬛ ⬛17⬛ ⬛18⬛ |
| | instrumental timbre | **5.** Show two instruments to children, naming each. Play one behind a screen or out of sight. Children try to identify which instrument was played. | | For a more challenging task, increase the number of instruments. |
| | | *two instruments of contrasting timbre* | | Charts: ⬛1⬛ ⬛2⬛ ⬛16⬛⬛17⬛⬛18⬛ |
| | timbre | **6.** Help children describe the sound of the various instruments and shakers. Example: scratchy, rough, tinny. | **L** | Reverse the procedures by asking children to find an instrument to fit your verbal description (smooth, scratchy, etc.). |
| | | | **V** | Make word charts with findings. |
| | | *instruments; shakers with a variety of timbres* | | |
| | environmental timbre | **7.** Children identify by word or gesture familiar environmental sounds. | **V,**<br>**L** | Use picture, word, or graphic charts for alternative response choice. |
| | | *live or recorded environmental sounds* | | Charts: ⬛6⬛ ⬛7⬛<br>SC: ⬛1 - 9⬛ |
| | environmental timbre | **8.** Help children identify *simulated* environmental sounds in songs and instrumental music. | **L,**<br>**V** | Use visuals, as above. |
| | | **Bartok: Diary of a Fly** ⊙<br>**Rimsky-Korsakov: Flight of the Bumblebee** ⊙ | | |
| | vocal timbre | **9.** Children indicate by word or gesture recognition of familiar vocal sounds such as laughing, crying. | **V,**<br>**L** | Use visuals, as above. |
| | | *live or recorded vocal sounds* | | Chart: ⬛25⬛ |

| SING | vocal timbre | 10. *Who Am I?* Children can be seated at desks or in a circle on the floor. Class covers eyes as teacher walks among the group singing the song below. One child is signaled (tap on shoulder) to answer. The child responding may choose to try to trick the class by answering with another child's name. Class must decide if voice is that of person named. | L<br><br>V | To avoid children determining voices on the basis of location, have children scramble positions frequently. A signal, such as a bell, often helps to speed up relocation.<br><br>Game can be adapted to the song "False Face" by providing disguises for the individual responding. |

*Teacher*:  Sing  me, sing  me, sing  me your name.
*Child*:        My  name, my  name, my  name is_____.

| | | **False Face** | | |
|---|---|---|---|---|
| | vocal timbre | 11. Individual children record short solos for class to identify on playback. | L | |
| | | *tape recorder* | | |
| | instrumental timbre | 12. Children indicate by word or gesture when a section of contrasting timbre is heard in the music. | V | Use picture, word, or graphic charts for alternative response choice. |
| | | ***Bizet: Farandole*** ⊙ | | |
| | | 13. Children indicate by word or gesture recognition of a familiar song heard in a different medium (i.e., instrumental). | V | Use visuals, as above. |
| | | **My White Mouse (instrumental version)**<br>**Woodstock's Samba**<br>***McDonald: Children's Symphony*** ⊙<br>***Stravinsky: Greeting Prelude*** ⊙ | | |
| | timbre | 14. Children indicate by word or gesture recognition of sounds electronically produced as contrasted with those sounds produced by instrumental timbres. | V | Use visuals, as above. |
| | | ***Mussorgsky: Ballet of the Unhatched Chicks*** ⊙<br>***Untitled Machine Music*** ⊙ | | |
| | timbre | 15. Help children discover the various timbres that contribute to selected descriptive compositions. | | |
| | | ***Grieg: In the Hall of the Mountain King*** ⊙<br>***Shostakovich: Polka*** ⊙ | | |

**The child demonstrates**
## UNDERSTANDING OF SPECIFIC CHARACTERISTICS OF SOUND THROUGH MUSICAL PERFORMANCE

## PERFORM TIMBRE

| | environmental timbre | 1. Children vocally simulate familiar environmental sounds. | V,<br>M | Use visuals, draw, or find pictures of sounds. |
|---|---|---|---|---|
| | | Bear Hunt<br>**The Wind Blew East**<br>*recorded or live environmental sounds* | | Charts: [4] [6] [7]<br>SC: [1 - 9] |

| | vocal timbre | **2.** Children reproduce vocal timbres associated with laughing, crying, and so forth. | | |
|---|---|---|---|---|
| | | *live or recorded vocal sounds* | | Chart: 25 |
| **MOVE** | timbre | **3.** Children produce a variety of timbres through body percussion in accompanying songs. | M, L | |
| | | **Bear Hunt**    **Somebody's Knocking at Your Door**<br>**Miss Mary Mack**    **The Wind Blew East**<br>**The Snapdragon Song** | | Chart: 31 |
| **PLAY** | timbre | **4.** Teacher and child (or two children) each have identical sets of sound sources. Teacher plays one out of sight of the child. Child echoes using an identical sound source. | M | Begin with gross differences (e.g., triangle, drum). Gradually progress to finer timbre discrimination (e.g., triangle, bells, tambourine).<br><br>Use pictures of sound sources if child is unable to play instruments, or if only one set of sound sources is available. |
| | | | L | Play game as described, with child giving the name of each instrument played. |
| | | | L | Revise game, using one set of instruments played by the child at the verbal description of the teacher (e.g., "Play the instrument that sounds like . . ."). |
| | | *duplicate sets of two to five sound sources with varying timbres (e.g., rhythm instruments, shakers)* | | Charts: 16 17 18 |

**The child demonstrates**
## ABILITY TO APPLY UNDERSTANDING OF MUSICAL CHARACTERISTICS CREATIVELY

### CREATE TIMBRE

| | | | | |
|---|---|---|---|---|
| **CREATE** | | **1.** Pairs, or small groups, of children with portable tape recorders record environmental sounds at suitable locations (e.g., playground, cafeteria, office). On playback, others attempt to identify the sounds. A sound piece can be composed by having the children decide which sounds to include, the order in which to record them, and the duration of play for each. The composite sounds are re-recorded on another machine.<br>Note: This activity could be combined with a field trip to a farm, zoo, factory, etc. | V, M | A multimedia project could result from the activity, including drawings, photographs, posters, models, body movement, pantomime, to accompany the tape composition. |
| | | *portable tape recorders* | | |
| **CREATE/PLAY** | | **2.** Children make a list of environmental sounds and then attempt to simulate them through the use of available instruments. Arrange as a composition. | V, M | Use pictures or word cards for nonverbal children. |

| | | | |
|---|---|---|---|
| | *assorted classroom instruments* | | **Charts:** 6 7 |
| | *found sounds* | | **SC:** 1 - 9 |
| **CREATE/PLAY** | **3.** Help children to make their own instruments to produce specific timbres or environmental sounds. | **V, M** | |
| **CREATE/SING/ PLAY** | **4.** Write or select short poems and stories that describe environmental timbres suitable for interpretation with vocal or instrumental sounds. | **V, M, L** | Creating a score may be helpful for future performance. |
| | Rain Sizes (poem) | | |
| | *select suitable poems or stories* | | |
| **CREATE/PLAY** | **5.** Divide class into small groups. Each group creates a short composition using only familiar found sounds, such as keys, paper, zippers. Be sure class understands the basic elements of composition (form, rhythm, etc.). Limit group working time to no more than ten minutes. Completed pieces are performed out of sight of other class members, who try to guess objects used as instruments. | **V** | Scores can be made for compositions by groups or class. |
| | *found sounds* | | |
| **CREATE/PLAY** | **6.** Children select appropriate instruments to accompany songs that have contrasting sections or phrases. | **M, L** | |
| | **The Angel Band** **Breezes Are Blowing** **Rig-a-jig-jig** | | |
| **CREATE/PLAY/ SING** | **7.** Children select found sounds, body percussion, or instruments to provide appropriate sound effects for accompanying selected songs and rhythm activities. | **V, M** | |
| | Bear Hunt **Bones**     **Halloween Night** **Five Fat Turkeys**   **Walrus Hunt** **The Goat**     **When the Train Comes Along** | | **Chart:** 31 |
| **CREATE** | **8.** Select poems or stories for interpretation that will encourage a variety of vocal timbres. | **L** | |
| | The Bugle-Billed Bazoo (poem) | | |
| | *select suitable poems or stories* | | |
| **CREATE/MOVE** | **9.** Children interpret timbre through body movement, pantomime, drawing, etc. | **V, M** | |
| | *select suitable vocal or instrumental music* | | |
| **CREATE/PLAY** | **10.** Help children create a sound story describing a favorite theme, story, or picture. | **V, M** | Make a score. |
| | *found sounds or classroom instruments* | | **Charts:** 35 36 |

| CREATE/PLAY/<br>SING | 11. Children select appropriate accompanying instruments to simulate the sounds of rain (e.g., finger cymbals, tap drums lightly) in "Japanese Rain Song."<br><br>Note: A koto effect can be produced by plucking autoharp strings. Colored tape can be attached to strings played for a suitable pentatonic (CDEGA) ostinato pattern. An interlude thunder storm could be included to involve more timbres, such as gong, cymbals, deep drum. | V,<br>M,<br>L | |
|---|---|---|---|
| | **Japanese Rain Song**<br>*classroom instruments* | | |
| CREATE | 12. Children select tactile materials to correspond with instrumental timbres. | L,<br>T | Help children to verbally describe their choice. |
| | *select suitable instrumental music*<br><br>*assorted tactile materials (e.g., sandpaper, marble chips, velvet swatch)* | | |

The child demonstrates
## ABILITY TO DISTINGUISH A SPECIFIC SOUND AMONG OTHERS

## FIGURE-GROUND

| environmental<br>sounds | 1. Children identify each of two or more environmental sounds heard simultaneously. | V,<br>L | Use picture, word, or graphic charts for alternative response choice. |
|---|---|---|---|
| | *Environmental sounds* ⊙ | | Charts: 5 6 7<br>SC: 1 - 9 |
| SING/CHANT/<br>MOVE/PLAY | 2. Children remain focused on singing or chanting without being distracted by ongoing beat or ostinato patterns. | M,<br>L | |
| | Bear Hunt    **Charlie Knows How to Beat That Drum**<br>**Breezes Are Blowing**    **Japanese Rain Song** | | |
| SING/  melody<br>CHANT  rhythm | 3. Children remain focused on appropriate part in rounds and fugues. | L | |
| | **Canoe Round**    **For Health and Strength**<br>**Down at the Station**    Speech Fugue | | |
| MOVE/  rhythm<br>CHANT | 4. Children remain focused on appropriate part when two or more rhythm patterns are performed simultaneously. Example: | M,<br>L | Creating suitable speech chants may help the performance of the rhythm pattern for some children. |
| | Tick-y Tick-y Tam - bo<br>Bon - go  Bon - go | | |
| | **Canoe Round**    **Ticky Ticky Tambo**<br>Speech Fugue | | |

| | | | | |
|---|---|---|---|---|
| | **melody** | 5. Children identify two melodic themes played simultaneously. | V, L | Use picture, word, or graphic charts for alternative response choice. |
| | | *Bizet: Farandole* ⊙ | | |
| **MOVE/ CREATE** | **texture** | 6. Select music representing various musical textures. Children move freely about the room grouping themselves in accordance with texture heard in the music (e.g., singly, pairs, threes). | V, M | |
| | | *improvised or recorded music* | | |
| | **instrumental timbre** | 7. Children identify prominently heard familiar instruments in duets, trios, quartets. | V, L | Use pictures or illustrations for alternative response choice. |
| | | *Bach: Allegro* ⊙<br>*Shostakovich: Polka* ⊙<br>*Vivaldi: Allegro* ⊙<br>*Hill and Dell* ⊙ | | Charts: ⟨1⟩⟨2⟩<br>SC: ⟨10 - 12⟩ |
| **SING/ PLAY/ MOVE** | **melody rhythm** | 8. Children reproduce a prominent rhythm or melodic pattern heard in the music. | M | |
| | | **The Man in Blue** | | |
| | | *Grieg: In the Hall of the Mountain King* ⊙<br>*Hill and Dell* ⊙ | | Chart: ⟨22⟩ |
| **SING** | | 9. Children remain focused on appropriate part in easy part and partner songs. | L | |
| | | **So Long** | | |

<br>

## The child retains and recalls
# AUDITORY INFORMATION                    AUDITORY MEMORY

| | | | | |
|---|---|---|---|---|
| **SING/ MOVE/ CHANT** | **rhythm melody** | 1. Ask children to clap repetitive rhythm patterns from familiar songs *before* singing. | V, M | Ask a volunteer to notate the pattern in either standard or graphic notation. |
| | | **The Giant's Shoes**   Speech Fugue<br>**Hello!** | | |
| **SING/ MOVE** | **rhythm** | 2. Learn songs that have a rhythmic clapping pattern as an integral part of the song. | M, L | |
| | | **Bingo**          **Pat-a-Cake**<br>**Chicka Hanka    Way Down Yonder in the Brickyard** | | |
| **SING** | **melody rhythm** | 3. Learn echo songs in which each phrase is immediately repeated. Select student leaders after song is learned well. | L | |
| | | **The Goat**               *Tah-boo* ⊙<br>**I Like You**<br>**Oh, My Aunt Came Back**<br>**Two Little Hands** | | |

| | | | | |
|---|---|---|---|---|
| **SING** | **melody** **rhythm** | **4.** Learn call-and-response songs with individuals taking turns as leaders. | **L,** **S** | Could be done as a partner activity. |
| | | | **M** | For a different challenge, clap parts without singing. |
| | | **False Face**     **The Roll Call Song** **John the Rabbit**    **Train is A-Coming** | | |
| **SING** | | **5.** Sing or play a familiar song (such as "Happy Birthday") for the class leaving out a phrase or singing some notes incorrectly. Children supply missing or corrected phrases. | **L** | |
| | | *select familiar songs* | | |
| **SING** | **melody** **rhythm** **pitch** **beat** | **6.** Select a song the class knows and can sing well. All sing the first phrase out loud and the rest of the song silently until the last phrase, which is also sung out loud. Everyone should arrive at the last word together and on pitch. The beginning phrase can be gradually shortened to only one word, if desired. | **L** | |
| | | **John Jacob Jingelheimer Schmidt** | | |
| **SING** | | **7.** Sing familiar songs in which some phrases are sung silently while others are sung out loud. When children know the song well, try leaving out the words to one line at a time until the entire song is sung silently. Children will stay together better during the silent phrases if accompanying motions are very rhythmic and emphasize the basic beat. Try singing other favorite songs silently, with perhaps the first and last notes sung out loud. | | |
| | | **Cabin in the Wood** | | |
| | **rhythm** | **8.** Write, on the chalkboard or chart, three short rhythm patterns appropriate to the functioning level of the class. After giving the class a few minutes to study, cover patterns while clapping or playing one on the drum. Uncover the patterns and ask children to identify which was played. | **V** | |
| | | *drum* | | |
| | **melody** | **9.** *Name That Tune.* Play or sing melodies, or themes from familiar music, for children to identify. This can also be played as a team game. | | |
| | | *select suitable vocal and instrumental music* | | |
| **SING/** **PLAY** | **melody** **rhythm** | **10.** Select simple familiar songs for children to play by ear on melody instruments. | **V,** **M** | |
| | | **Candles of Hannukah** **I See You** | | |
| | | *melody instruments* | | |

| | | | |
|---|---|---|---|
| **SING/ MOVE** | **11.** Children dramatize a favorite song, story record, or programmatic piece. | **M, L** | |

The Goat
The Old Gray Cat

*Dukas: Sorcerer's Apprentice* ⊙
*MacDowell: Of a Tailor and a Bear* ⊙   Charts: 26 27 28 29

---

**The child arranges**
## AUDITORY INFORMATION IN PROPER SEQUENCE    AUDITORY SEQUENCING

| | | | |
|---|---|---|---|
| **SING/ MOVE** | **1.** Learn songs and rhythmic activities in which the sequence of verses is important to the overall effect of the song. | **V, M, L** | Use picture charts or make cards with verse cues. |

| | | |
|---|---|---|
| Bear Hunt | My White Mouse | |
| Bones | New River Train | |
| Hush, Little Baby | The Old Gray Cat | |
| I Had a Little Overcoat | Walrus Hunt | SC: 21 - 25 |

| | | | |
|---|---|---|---|
| **SING** | **2.** Learn songs in which the verses are *both* sequential and cumulative. | **V, L** | Use visuals, as above. |

I Know an Old Lady
Oh, My Aunt Came Back
The Tree in the Valley   SC: 26 - 31, 17, 19
The Twelve Days of Christmas   SC: 32 - 37, 28

| | | | |
|---|---|---|---|
| **SING/ MOVE** | **3.** Learn simple dances in which movement patterns are sequenced. | **V, M** | Use visuals, as above. |

| | |
|---|---|
| Bingo | Hornpipe Dance ⊙ |
| Step in Time | Step Lively ⊙ |
| Valentine | |

| | | | |
|---|---|---|---|
| **SING/ PLAY** | **4.** Learn instrumental activities in which melodic or rhythm patterns are sequenced. | **V, M** | Use visuals, as above. |

The Man in Blue    Skippin' and Steppin'    Chart: 24

| | | | |
|---|---|---|---|
| **SING/CHANT/ MOVE** | **5.** Learn action songs and other activities in which motor responses are sequenced. | **V, M** | Use visuals, as above. |

Bear Hunt    Cabin in the Wood
Walrus Hunt

| | | | |
|---|---|---|---|
| **SING/MOVE** | **6.** Dramatize sequence of events in a sound story, story song, or programmatic piece. | **V, M, L** | Use visuals, as above. |

Cabin in the Wood
Five Angels

*Dukas: Sorcerer's Apprentice* ⊙    Charts: 26 27 28 29
*MacDowell: Of a Tailor and a Bear* ⊙    SC: 38 - 42

| | | | |
|---|---|---|---|
| | **7.** Children arrange sequence of sounds in the order in which they are heard. | **V, L** | Use picture charts or make cards with cues. |

*Hill and Dell* ⊙    Charts: 1 2
*Environmental sounds* ⊙    SC: 1 - 9  10 - 12

54

# VISUAL PERCEPTION

People are visually oriented beings. Knowledge of our environment is mainly garnered through visually deciphering forms and symbols that convey meanings. As with hearing, the quality of eyesight is not always a factor in a person's ability to *interpret* what is seen. Children with no sight impairment (i.e., 20/20 vision) can fail to develop visual perception skills that are necessary for learning in general and that are particularly crucial for learning how to read and write. (See Specific Learning Disabilities, p. 237.) Just as there is a difference between *hearing* and *listening* in auditory perception (p. 23), so also there is a difference between *looking* and *seeing* in visual perception.

Visual perception is training in seeing and interpreting visual stimuli. Efficient visual functioning normally takes some time to develop, hence the use of oversized and brightly colored visual materials in primary level classrooms. Although the majority of children successfully develop the ability to focus visually and to make fine discriminations in visual materials during the primary years, some will be well into the intermediate grades before these skills are adequately developed for visual learning tasks. Often these children will need special help.

Children who are inefficiently processing visual stimuli may have *some* of the following difficulties.

The inability to
- get meaning from visual clues
- focus on a stationary object
- discriminate characteristic differences in visual stimuli (i.e., color, shape size/quantity, direction/distance)
- perceive individual parts as constituting a whole
- judge distance
- relate symbol to object
- separate foreground from background in a picture
- recognize and remember visual information
- track a moving object with the eyes
- reproduce simple visual patterns
- recognize familiar visual images when reduced or embellished
- direct an extremity to a specific target

Perceiving the visual environment in a meaningful way includes visually recognizing objects, people, and gestures. The ability to analyze and synthesize what is seen is also important. For example, visual analysis is necessary in reading the facial expressions of others. A deficiency in this area could contribute to social problems that are experienced by some children. Closely related to visual analysis is figure-ground discrimination (the ability to visually select relevant stimuli from background material). A problem in this area is manifested in reading music by dysfluency, skipping notes or lines in the music, and frequently losing one's place. Individuals with this problem usually read note by note because they are unable to perceive notes in groups. The same problems are evident

in reading words, but the music page is visually more complex. There are many symbols to contend with and, therefore, many more distractions. Symbols are placed on a staff, making figure-ground discrimination critical. Sometimes music books, especially instrumental method books, have several exercises on one page, making it more difficult to focus on a specific line, measure, or note. *Visual tracking* is following movement with the eyes without turning the head. The music ensemble (e.g., chorus, band, orchestra) is a situation where the ability to shift eyes from music to conductor frequently is required. In action songs, movements must be confined close to the leader's body if head movements are to be discouraged. *Visual sequencing* is similar to auditory sequencing in that it involves the correct ordering of sensory stimuli. In visual activities, the emphasis is usually on left-to-right eye movements to establish that pattern for reading and writing.

Music activities that require coordination of the eyes with the hands (or feet) are more extensively presented in Motor Activities (p. 78). The ability to direct an extremity to either a stationary or a moving target is a precise visual motor skill called *eye-hand coordination*. These activities include those using any manipulative objects such as instruments, balls, hoops, and scarves. The larger the target, the more gross the movement directed toward it. Activities should progress from large target areas to small ones requiring fine motor skills. Instruments and objects that offer relatively easy eye-hand tasks are large drums and cymbals (struck with large beaters), large balls, and hoops. The most challenging tasks are found in accurately playing the triangle, finger cymbals, Autoharp, thumb piano, resonator bells, and keyboard instruments. (See Fine Motor Skills, pp. 77, 92.)

## Visual discrimination

Characteristic differences in visual stimuli include color, shape, size, quantity, direction, and distance.

**Color**  Many children come to school with the ability to discriminate the primary colors (red, yellow, blue) as well as green, black, and white. For children already secure in these, blends and shades can be introduced. Although color discrimination is not usually considered important to visual tasks such as reading and writing, some psychologists are now suggesting that color blindness (lack of color *perception*) may be more common in children than previously thought. If this is true, teachers should use colored paper and inks with greater discrimination. In music class, we often observe that primary level children have difficulty in making a visual transfer from the chalkboard to the printed page, because white on black has now been reversed to black on white. In teaching music symbols, this is frequently noticed when children confuse quarter notes ( ♩ ), which appear white when filled in on the chalkboard, with half notes ( ♩ ) in their books. Wherever visual problems of this nature are suspected, it is wise to make every effort to keep materials as visually consistent as possible (e.g., white background feltboards, posters, black ink on white paper).

**Shape** The basic shapes of triangle, circle, and square are usually introduced first. Diagonal lines and shapes consisting of both curved and straight lines are more difficult to perceive. Recognition of shape is an obvious prerequisite to letter and number recognition, and hence reading and writing both music and words.

**Direction** The ability to discriminate up/down, over/under, right/left, and so forth, in visual stimuli involves spatial orientation. Again, the importance of being able to recognize direction in visual materials is particularly evident in reading and writing skills. In selecting music materials, it is important to make certain that spatial concepts are consistent. Reading or singing songs in which words and melody are spatially opposing can be very confusing to a child who lacks competence in these skills. The following example represents an accurate directional match of words and melody.

— — — — — — — — — — — — — —

*Down, down! Yel-low and brown The leaves are fall-ing o-ver the town.*

From POEMS FOR CHILDREN by Eleanor Farjeon. Copyright 1926, 1954 by Eleanor Farjeon. Reprinted by permission of Harold Ober Associates and J. B. Lippincott Company.

An example of opposing spatial direction is found in the following.

— — — — — — — — — — — — —

*Lon-don Bridge is fall-ing down, fall-ing down, fall-ing down,*

**Size/quantity** Both size and quantity are relative concepts. They are part of a generalization again involving spatial reasoning. Both are important in learning to read words and music as well as in writing skills. Some of these concepts are big/little, fat/thin, long/short, tall/short, more/less, and many/few.

**Distance** Judging distance is more important in music reading than in reading words. Again, spatial relations are crucial in the ability to analyze the distance between lines and spaces, notes on, below, or above the staff, and so forth. The fluent music reader makes these judgments instantaneously and accurately.

As in auditory discrimination tasks, a few general goals can effectively lead to the development of discrimination skills in visual stimuli. Each characteristic is first perceived and labeled, applied in music performance of some kind, and finally utilized creatively in music activities.

## Tactile discrimination

Because concrete and manipulative materials are often necessary for children lacking the most basic visual skills,

tactile experiences will be included in this section. Making a visual activity tactile is often necessary for children with impaired sight. Sighted children will generally progress from concrete materials to illustrations and pictures. Some visuals can be made tactile by covering with glue and spreading with textured materials such as salt, sand, grains, or stone chips. Line drawings and pictures can be outlined with yarn, twine, cord, or a silicone adhesive for a raised effect. Cutouts can be made from sandpaper, corrugated cardboard, fabric, and so forth. Materials that can provide a variety of textures should be used. Tactile characteristics to consider are sticky, soft, hard, coarse, rough, smooth, patterned, and spongy. Raw materials could include wood, tile, glass, Lucite, rubber, plastic, vinyl, sandpaper, tape, cotton, Styrofoam, sponge, and fabrics such as velvet, corduroy, satin, silk, chiffon, and coarse tweed. Raised impressions of paper and pencil activities can be made by placing the paper on top of a piece of window screening with a cardboard backing.

Music activities often demand visual skills combined with motor responses of some kind. Visual motor skills are required to successfully play instruments, engage in body movement activities, read and write music scores, and follow a conductor. Other activities such as card and table games require the visual skills of matching, sorting, memory, and sequencing. Similar activities are often used in individual learning center stations to aid in securing music symbolization and terminology. Similar individual activities can provide valid experiences in visual motor skills. However, one should be cautioned that they are seldom effective in achieving music concepts *without auditory reinforcement of those concepts*. In other words, the goals of paper and pencil activities should be to relate sound and symbol. Stores and catalogues that supply educational materials abound with visual aids that can be used by the skillful teacher to good advantage without losing sight of the music goals.

Although many of the following activities include other perceptual motor skills that may be more obvious, one is reminded that they are presented here as good examples of music experiences in which visual perception *could* be a learning skill focus.

To summarize, visual perception skills are important in many learning tasks, especially those requiring reading and writing. Specific skills include awareness, tracking, figure-ground separation, eye-hand coordination, memory and sequencing, as well as the ability to discriminate the characteristics of color, shape, size, quantity, distance, and direction. Some children lack these skills to such an extent that substitution or pairing of a tactile stimulus may be necessary. Since music is basically an aural art, music concepts cannot effectively be taught through this mode unless continually reinforced with the related sound.

**The child responds
TO VISUAL STIMULI**

| | | | | |
|---|---|---|---|---|
| SING | pitch | 1. Play tone matching games or call-and-response games in which children respond when pointed to. Example: | A, S, T | Touch children who are unable to respond to visual gestures. |

*Teacher:* Your name?
*Child:* Mar - tha.

| | | | | |
|---|---|---|---|---|
| SING/MOVE | | 2. Play singing games in which children indicate their choice of partner or successor by gesture. | A, M, S, T | Touch children who are unable to respond to visual gestures. |

**I Roll the Ball
Rig-a-jig-jig
Valentine
Way Down Yonder in the Brickyard
We're Going Round the Mountain**

| | | | | |
|---|---|---|---|---|
| SING | melody | 3. Sing songs in which pointing to objects or direction can be appropriately included. | A, M, L | |

Bones      *I've Got Two* ⊙
Down, Down      *One of These Things* ⊙
**I Had a Little Turtle
I Like to Ride the Elevator**

| | | | | |
|---|---|---|---|---|
| PLAY | beat rhythm melody form | 4. Learn instrumental activities in which children play on visual cue or gesture from a conductor. | T | Touch children who are unable to respond to visual gestures. |
| | | | A, S | Use gestures that pantomime playing technique, such as shake open palm—tambourine; hit fists on top of each other—woodblock; hit index fingers together—sticks. |

**Japanese Rain Song      Woodstock's Samba
Skippin' and Steppin'**

| | | | | |
|---|---|---|---|---|
| MOVE | beat rhythm | 5. *Gesture game.* One child is selected to be leader. While moving to a drumbeat or suitable music, class responds to gestures of leader that communicate "come," "stop," "go back," "left," etc. | A, L, S | For language experience, leader can hold up word cards. Sign language can be substituted. |

**A Little Flight Music      Marching to Pretoria**

| | | | | |
|---|---|---|---|---|
| SING/MOVE | beat rhythm melody | 6. Learn games and action songs in which gestures communicate the meaning of the words. | A, M, L | See sign language for "My Father's House." |

Bear Hunt      **Oh, My Aunt Came Back
Head, Shoulders      Put Your Hand on Your Shoe
I Had a Little Turtle      Three Little Ducks
I Will Clap My Hands      Two Little Blackbirds
My Father's House      Two Little Hands**

| PLAY | sound/<br>silence | 7. Help children explore string instruments by starting and stopping sound, pointing out the vibrating strings. | T,<br>A | Children with poor visual awareness may need body contact with the instrument to notice vibrations. |
|---|---|---|---|---|

*Autoharp, piano, guitar (any string instrument)*

| SING | melody | 8. Learn songs in which the face and facial expressions are the focus. Provide some disguises for "False Face," such as wig, glasses, mask. | A,<br>S | Children can practice making facial expressions appropriate to the song. A mirror is a good reinforcement. |
|---|---|---|---|---|
| | | | | Visuals of facial expressions can be shown. |
| | | | | Children can draw faces that illustrate happy, sad, mad, etc. |
| | | | FM | Make paper bag masks. |
| | | | T | Close eyes, locate face parts by touch, memory. |

| **False Face** | *I've Got Two* ☉ | | |
|---|---|---|---|
| **Put On a Happy Face** | | Chart: 25 | |

| | dynamics<br>sound/<br>silence | 9. Divide class in two groups. Each group decides on a vocal sound or body sound to be performed on cue. A student conductor visually cues each group when to start and stop, as well as indicate dynamics. | A,<br>S | For a more difficult task, add more groups and more sounds. Other musical elements can be indicated, such as pitch and duration. |
|---|---|---|---|---|

**SEE ALSO**

Auditory Activities
  *Localization: #1 (p. 26)*
  *Identify Dynamics: #3 (p. 27)*
  *Identify Rhythm: #2, #3 (p. 34)*
  *Perform Rhythm: #1 (p. 35)*
  *Identify Pitch: #4, #6 (pp. 38, 39)*

Gross Motor Activities
  *Locomotor: #1 (p. 78)*
  *Body Awareness: #7 (p. 84)*
  *Balance: #1, #2, #3, #4
    (p. 85)*

## The child visually focuses on
## A SPECIFIC OBJECT

# FIGURE-GROUND

| SING | | 1. Select songs that label and identify familiar objects. Have children select, or point out, objects in the songs that are illustrated in the pictures. | A,<br>L | |
|---|---|---|---|---|

| **Five Fat Turkeys** | |
|---|---|
| **Hush, Little Baby** | |
| **I Had a Little Overcoat** | Chart: 33 |
| **I Know an Old Lady** | SC: 21 - 25 |
| **Put Your Hand on Your Shoe** | SC: 26 - 31, 17, 19 |
| **The Tree in the Valley** | SC: 32 - 37, 28 |

| SING | pitch melody | 2. *I See Something.* Devise pitch matching games in which color, size, shape, distance, etc., are used to describe objects. Be sure to give children ample time to study the room before describing an object. Examples: | A, L | Reverse the procedure by providing visual or manipulative materials for children to describe. |
|---|---|---|---|---|

Teacher: I see some-thing that is far a - way.
I see some-thing that is small and round.
I see some - one who is wear-ing green.
Child: Joe is some - one who is wear-ing green.

SC: 43 - 52

| | music notation | 3. Children locate specific notes and other symbols in music. | | Beginning activities may be more successful if the teacher holds up a matching symbol. |
|---|---|---|---|---|

*music books*

| SING | pitch | 4. Children locate individuals whose names are called in "The Roll Call Song" by pointing to them. | A, L | |
|---|---|---|---|---|

**The Roll Call Song**

| | | 5. Children locate a specific instrument from among a group. Begin with two or three choices that are quite dissimilar. Discrimination can be gradually made more difficult by increasing choices and similarity. | L | If instruments are not available, substitute pictures or illustrations. |
|---|---|---|---|---|

Charts: 1 2 16 17 18
SC: 10 - 12

**SEE ALSO**

Auditory Activities
   *Localization: #1, #3* (p. 26)

Gross Motor Activities
   *Body Awareness: #1* (p. 83)
   *Balance: #1, #2, #3, #4*
      (p. 85)

## The child visually tracks A MOVING OBJECT

TRACKING

| SING/ MOVE | beat | 1. Learn singing games in which the eye is challenged to be quicker than the hand. | A, M, L, S, T | See special activities following the song. |
|---|---|---|---|---|

**Button, You Must Wander**

| SING/ MOVE | beat rhythm | 2. Learn singing games in which individuals make up new movements to be immediately mirrored by the group. | A, M, S | See special activities following the songs. |
|---|---|---|---|---|

**I See You    We're Going Round the Mountain**

| | | | | |
|---|---|---|---|---|
| MOVE | beat | **3.** Circle formation: standing or sitting. Children pass object around the circle on the beat in a counterclockwise direction. | A, M, S, T | Small plastic containers filled with pebbles or grains provide an audible beat.<br><br>For a more challenging task, two or three objects can be passed in the same or different directions.<br><br>Increase the challenge by designating some objects to be passed with left hand only, or in a specific direction. Example: blue passes clockwise with left hand; red passes counterclockwise with right hand; or, pass ball with right hand, beanbag with left hand. |
| | | *drum*<br><br>*beanbag, ball, or other suitable object* | | |
| MOVE | beat<br>meter | **4.** Circle formation: standing, arm's length apart. Drummer beats in threes with a strong accent on the first beat in each group. One or two balloons are kept aloft by hitting them on the *accented beat only,* and *only* when a balloon is within arm's reach (feet remain stationary). Suitable music may be added after practice with drumbeat. | A, M, S | |
| | | **So Long**      *Swing High* ⊙<br>**Tra La La La**<br>*drum, balloons* | | |
| MOVE/<br>CREATE | beat<br>rhythm<br>form<br>melody | **5.** Help children create movement and dance sequences that are performed by a leader and mirrored by the class. | A, M, S | See Mirror Dance, p. 228.<br><br>See Appendix, p. 274, for movement suggestions. |
| | | *Alley Cat* ⊙ | | Charts: 30 31 |
| MOVE/<br>CREATE | beat<br>rhythm<br>form | **6.** Help children create movement sequences to suitable music using appropriate manipulative objects. | A, M, T | See Appendix, p. 276, for ball and hoop activities. |
| | | **A Little Flight Music**  *balls, hoops, scarves, etc.*<br>**Put On a Happy Face**<br>**Woodstock's Samba** | | |
| MOVE | beat | **7.** Learn musical games and movement activities involving passing and transferring objects from hand to hand. | A, M, S, T | See Ball Dance, p. 228. |
| | | *balls, sticks, etc.*    *Alley Cat* ⊙ | | |
| SING/<br>MOVE | | **8.** Make up singing games and movement activities involving rolling balls or hoops to a target. | A, M, T, S | Do with a partner. |
| | | **I Roll the Ball**<br>**Rolling Along**<br>*balls, hoops, etc.* | | |

| SING/ MOVE | | 9. Play musical tag games. | A, M, S | See special activities following the song. |
|---|---|---|---|---|

| Charlie Over the Water |
|---|

**SEE ALSO**

| Auditory Activities<br>  *Perform Tempo: #7 (p. 31)* | Gross Motor Activities<br>  *Locomotor: #1 (p. 78)*<br>  *Body Awareness: #10 (p. 83)*<br>  *Reaction/Agility: #4 (p. 87)* |
|---|---|

## The child perceives and identifies
## SPECIFIC VISUAL CHARACTERISTICS                           COLOR

| SING | melody | 1. Sing songs involving colors that the children can identify by word or gesture. | | Beginning level tasks can require children to hold up a color to match the teacher's.<br><br>If colored paper or other objects are not available, children can respond by the color of their clothing. |
|---|---|---|---|---|

| **The Man in Blue**          *One of These Things* ⊙<br>**Miss Mary Mack**<br>**My White Mouse**<br>**The Old Gray Cat**<br>**Two Little Blackbirds**<br>*colored paper or colored objects*                    SC: 43 - 52 |
|---|

**SEE ALSO**

| Auditory Activities<br>  *Perform Melody: #4 (p. 44)* | Language Activities<br>  *Receptive Language: #8 (p. 100)* |
|---|---|

## The child demonstrates
## UNDERSTANDING OF SPECIFIC VISUAL
## CHARACTERISTICS IN MUSIC PERFORMANCE                    COLOR

| PLAY | pitch melody | 1. Color code melody instruments (i.e., bars, keys) to correspond with part to be played. | A, M | Beginning experiences may need to start with a match by coding fingers and/or mallets as well. |
|---|---|---|---|---|
| | | *select music*<br>*colored tape* | | |
| SING/ PLAY | melody rhythm notation | 2. Children musically interpret visuals in which individual parts are indicated by colors. | A, M | Limit beginning experiences to two or three parts. |
| | | *select vocal or instrumental music* | | Chart: 32 |
| | | *appropriate pictures,* | | |

| | | | | |
|---|---|---|---|---|
| PLAY | ostinato melody | 3. Using two different colors, tape positions on fingerboard for melodic ostinatos (e.g., tonic, dominant). | A, M | Some children may need to have appropriate strings coded as well. |
| | | *string instruments (violin, cello, guitar, etc.)* *colored tape* | | |
| PLAY/ CREATE | pitch melody harmony | 4. Color code selected pitches for tone row, chord, ostinato, theme, etc. | A, M | |
| | | *bells, xylophone* *colored tape* | | |
| SING/ PLAY/ MOVE | | 5. Color code picture, word, or graphic charts to indicate dynamics, tempo, meter, rhythm, melody, timbre, etc. | A, M | |
| | | | | Chart: 32 |

**The child demonstrates**
## ABILITY TO APPLY UNDERSTANDING OF VISUAL CHARACTERISTICS CREATIVELY IN MUSICAL EXPERIENCES
## COLOR

| | | | | |
|---|---|---|---|---|
| CREATE/ PLAY/ MOVE | music reading | 1. Children compose a score for found sounds, classroom instruments, or body percussion by scoring each instrument or sound in a different color. | A, M | If traditional notation is not used, the shape and size of all symbols should be the same, if color discrimination is a goal. |
| | | *found sounds, classroom instruments* *paper; crayons or felt-tip pens* | | Chart: 31 |
| CREATE/ PLAY/ MOVE | music reading | 2. Children compose a graphic score using color to represent dynamics, timbre, tempo, etc. | A, M | |
| | | *found sounds, classroom instruments; paper; crayons or felt-tip pens* | | |
| CREATE/ PLAY/ MOVE | music reading rhythm | 3. Children compose scores in which rhythm patterns are color coded. | A, M | |
| | | *paper; crayons or felt-tip pens* | | |
| CREATE/SING/ PLAY/MOVE | | 4. Children interpret colors through instrumental, vocal, movement, drawing, or graphic representation. | M | |

**The child perceives and identifies**
## SPECIFIC VISUAL CHARACTERISTICS
## SHAPE

| | | | | |
|---|---|---|---|---|
| SING | | 1. Children select the shape that is different, as directed by the words of the song. | T | If textured materials are used, they should be the same for identical shapes. |
| | | *shape cut-outs or manipulatives* | | |
| | | ***One of These Things*** ⊙ | | |
| | | | | SC: 43 - 52 |

| | | | | |
|---|---|---|---|---|
| | | **2.** Children group instruments of similar shape together. Example: violin, viola. | **T** | If instruments are not available, pictures can be substituted.<br><br>If textured materials are used, they should be the same for identical shapes. |
| | | *assorted instruments* | | **Charts:** 1 2 16 17 18<br>**SC:** 10 - 12 |
| **PLAY** | | **3.** Children select instruments in the shape of a circle (drum, tambourine, cymbals), triangle (triangle), squares, and rectangles. | **T** | If children have not mastered labels for the various shapes, a matching shape can be shown.<br><br>If textured materials are used, they should be the same for identical shapes.<br><br>Some children may be capable of discussing the relationship of shape to sound in instrument design. |
| | | *assorted classroom instruments* | | **Charts:** 16 17 18<br>**SC:** 43 - 52 |
| **SING** | melody | **4.** Learn songs in which letter and number recognition can be reviewed through the use of appropriate visual and manipulative aids. | **A,**<br>**L** | |
| | | **The Angel Band**  **Letters and Names**<br>**Five Angels**  **The Twelve Days of Christmas**<br>**Here's the Beehive**  **Two Little Blackbirds** | | **SC:** 38 - 42  43 - 52 |
| | **pitch**<br>**melody**<br>**rhythm**<br>**notation** | **5.** Children locate identical phrases, lines and melodic sequences in a musical score. | | |
| | | *select songs from music books or vocal scores* | | |

**SEE ALSO**

Auditory Activities
   *Identify Melody: #13 (p. 39)*
            *(show music)*

Language Activities
   *Receptive Language: #8 (p. 100)*
            *(describe the shape)*

**The child demonstrates**
# UNDERSTANDING OF SPECIFIC VISUAL CHARACTERISTICS IN MUSIC PERFORMANCE

## SHAPE

| | | | | |
|---|---|---|---|---|
| **PLAY** | | **1.** Code groups of instruments for instrumental activities by taping small shapes on them. Teacher conducts by holding up a matching shape when group is to play. | **A,**<br>**M** | Chord tones can be coded similarly on bells or keyboard instruments. |
| | | *select vocal and instrumental music*<br>*assorted classroom instruments* | | |

| | | | | |
|---|---|---|---|---|
| **SING/PLAY/ MOVE** | | **2.** Design instrumental scores using cut-outs or illustrations of instruments as notation. Example:  △ ✂ ▯ ◯ | **M** **T** | When using textured materials, keep texture and shape consistent. |
| | | *select vocal and instrumental music* *assorted classroom instruments* | | |
| | **melody rhythm timbre** | **3.** Help children follow auditory events in a listening experience through the use of teaching aids that visually represent instruments and/or musical characteristics. | **A** | |
| | | *select instrumental music* | | **Charts:** 22 23 24 26 27 28 29 |
| **SING/ PLAY** | **music notation** | **4.** Select short, easy pieces that can be suitably notated with shapes. | **A, M** | |
| | | **5.** Select short, easy pieces that can be suitably notated with letters or numbers. | **A, M** | |
| | | *select vocal and instrumental music* | | |
| **MOVE** | **beat rhythm** | **6.** Children perform locomotor movements, such as walking a specific shape. Beginning experiences will be more successful if shapes are outlined on the floor with masking tape. Later, however, children should walk without the visual reinforcement. | **A, M** | |
| | | *select suitable music* *masking tape* | | |
| **SING/PLAY/ MOVE** | | **7.** Use shapes to make picture, word, or graphic charts and scores to indicate dynamics, tempo, tempo changes, rhythm, melody, timbre, etc. | | |

**SEE ALSO**

Auditory Activities
  *Perform Melody:* #4 (p. 44)
      (substitute shape, letter, or number cut-outs)

---

**The child demonstrates**
**ABILITY TO APPLY UNDERSTANDING OF VISUAL CHARACTERISTICS CREATIVELY IN MUSICAL EXPERIENCES**

**SHAPE**

| | | | | |
|---|---|---|---|---|
| **CREATE** | **melody rhythm dynamics timbre form** | **1.** Using shapes, children design visual representations of auditory events heard in music. | **A, M** | |
| | | *select vocal and instrumental music* *paper, pencil* | | |

| | | | | |
|---|---|---|---|---|
| CREATE/ PLAY | melody rhythm form | 2. Children compose a musical score using shapes to represent themes. Example: ○ △ ○ □ ○ ◇ ○ ▭ | A, M T | Textured materials can be used. |
| | | *paper, pencil* | | |
| CREATE/ SING/ PLAY | melody | 3. Children compose a short piece using numbers or letters to notate melody. | A, M | |
| | | *paper, pencil* | | |
| CREATE/ SING/ PLAY | melody rhythm | 4. Children graphically notate melody and/or rhythm of a familiar tune. | A, M | |
| | | *select vocal and instrumental music paper, pencil* | | |

## The child perceives and identifies
## SPECIFIC VISUAL CHARACTERISTICS                    SIZE

| | | | | |
|---|---|---|---|---|
| | | 1. Children group instruments according to size: big—small; bigger—smaller; biggest—smallest. | | If instruments are not available, substitute pictures. |
| | | *assorted instruments* | | |
| SING | | 2. Children identify the object that is a different size, as directed by words in the song. | A, L | |
| | | *three cut-outs or manipulative objects, one smaller (larger) than the other two* **One of These Things** ⊙ | | |
| PLAY | pitch | 3. Children arrange bells in a scale by sorting individual bells from biggest to smallest. | M, T | For a tactile experience, blindfold the child. |
| | | *bells* | | |
| SING | melody | 4. Teach songs in which the concept of size is included. Children can dramatize or correctly order visuals that illustrate size differences. | A, M, L | |
| | | **Five Fat Turkeys**     **My Farm** <br> **I Had a Little Overcoat**    **Three Little Ducks** <br> **I Know an Old Lady** | | Chart: 33 <br> SC: 13 - 20   21 - 25 <br> 26 - 31, 17, 19 |

## The child demonstrates
## UNDERSTANDING OF SPECIFIC VISUAL CHARACTERISTICS
## IN MUSIC PERFORMANCE                              SIZE

| | | | | |
|---|---|---|---|---|
| SING/ PLAY/ MOVE | music symbolization | 1. Children perform from scores in which music elements are represented by size. Example:    loud ♪     soft ♪ | A, M | |

| | | | |
|---|---|---|---|
| | | *select vocal and instrumental music* | |
| PLAY | music symbolization | **2.** Children perform from scores in which the same symbol is used in different sizes to indicate two different instruments. Example:<br><br>drums ⬤  sticks • | M |
| | | *select vocal and instrumental music*<br>*classroom instruments* | |
| SING/ PLAY/ MOVE | music symbolization form melody | **3.** Design scores in which the themes are represented by different forms of letters or print. Example:<br><br>**A** b **A** c **A** d | |
| | | *paper, pencil* | |
| SING/ PLAY/ MOVE | | **4.** Use size concepts in picture, word, or graphic charts to indicate dynamics, tempo, meter, rhythm, melody, timbre, etc. | |

**SEE ALSO**

Auditory Activities
*Perform Pitch: #1 (p. 39)*

---

**The child demonstrates**
## ABILITY TO APPLY UNDERSTANDING OF VISUAL CHARACTERISTICS CREATIVELY IN MUSICAL EXPERIENCES

**SIZE**

| | |
|---|---|
| SING/ MOVE/ PLAY | **1.** Select appropriate material involving concepts of size for children to interpret in vocal, instrumental, or movement compositions. |
| | *Rain Sizes (poem)* |

**SEE ALSO**

| | |
|---|---|
| Auditory Activities<br>*Create Timbre: #4 (p. 50)* | Gross Motor Activities<br>*Locomotor: #17 (p. 81)* |

---

**The child perceives and identifies**
## SPECIFIC VISUAL CHARACTERISTICS

**QUANTITY**

| | | | |
|---|---|---|---|
| | | **1.** Children group, or point out, instruments with many/few keys or strings. | If instruments are not available, substitute pictures. |
| | | *assorted instruments* | **Charts:** 1 2<br>**SC:** 11 - 12 |
| SING/ MOVE | melody | **2.** Use appropriate visuals and manipulative materials to illustrate counting songs. | A, L |

| | | The Angel Band | New River Train | | |
| | | The Ants Go Marching | Three Little Ducks | | |
| | | Elephant Song | The Twelve Days of Christmas | | |
| | | Five Angels | Two Little Blackbirds | | |
| | | Five Fat Turkeys | | Chart: 33 | |
| | | Here's the Beehive | *I've Got Two* ☉ | SC: 38 - 42  43 - 52 | |

| SING/ PLAY/ MOVE | music notation | **3.** Children locate specific rhythmic and melodic patterns, sequences, etc., in the music. | | | |

*select suitable vocal and instrumental music; music books*

**The child demonstrates**

## UNDERSTANDING OF SPECIFIC VISUAL CHARACTERISTICS IN MUSIC PERFORMANCE

QUANTITY

| PLAY/ MOVE | style dynamics symbolization | **1.** Incorporate the concept many/few to illustrate concerto grosso style. Design a listening cue sheet in which the solo and tutti groups are graphically notated. Example: | A, M | Class can dramatize musicians playing while listening to a record. |
|---|---|---|---|---|

| | | *Bach: Allegro* ☉ | | Charts: 1  2 | |
| | | *Vivaldi: Allegro* ☉ | | SC: 11 - 12 | |

| PLAY | timbre symbolization | **2.** Children perform from musical scores in which the quantity of symbols represents specific instruments. Example:  drum ● tambourine ● ● ● | M | |
|---|---|---|---|---|

| SING/ MOVE | beat melody | **3.** Select counting songs in which children can dramatize quantity concepts. For example, in moving freely to the song, children group themselves in numbers corresponding with numbers mentioned in the song. | A, M, L, S | For a more difficult task, teacher can sing first line of each verse, selecting numbers at random. Use number signs, word cards, or graphic illustration for alternative response choice. |
|---|---|---|---|---|
| | | **New River Train** | | SC: 43 - 52 |

| SING/ MOVE | melody | **4.** Teach songs involving concepts of more (addition) and have children dramatize them. | A, M, L, S | |
|---|---|---|---|---|
| | | **Elephant Song** | | SC: 26 - 31, 17, 19 |
| | | **I Know an Old Lady** | | SC: 43 - 52 |
| | | **The Twelve Days of Christmas** | | |

| SING/ MOVE | melody | **5.** Teach songs involving concepts of less (subtraction) and have children dramatize. | A, M, L, S | |
|---|---|---|---|---|
| | | **I Had a Little Overcoat**   **Three Little Ducks** | | |
| | | **Roll Over**   **Two Little Blackbirds** | | SC: 21 - 25  43 - 52 |

| SING/ PLAY/ MOVE | | **6.** Use quantity concepts in picture, word, or graphic charts to indicate dynamics, tempo, meter, rhythm, melody, timbre, etc. | | |
|---|---|---|---|---|

## ABILITY TO APPLY UNDERSTANDING OF VISUAL CHARACTERISTICS CREATIVELY IN MUSICAL EXPERIENCES

**QUANTITY**

| | | | | |
|---|---|---|---|---|
| | rhythm<br>music<br>notation | **1.** Write two to four rhythm patterns on a chart or the chalkboard in either graphic or standard notation. Include different note values. Teacher or leader claps one of the patterns from the back of the room (out of sight of the class). Children identify the pattern that was clapped. | A | For beginning experiences, use visually contrasting patterns. Example:<br>1. ♫ ♫ ♫ ♫<br>2. ♩    ♩ |
| CREATE/<br>MOVE | rhythm<br>music<br>notation | **2.** Each child creates a rhythm pattern using graphic notation. Teacher collects and writes each on the board, one at a time, for performance. Each child should visually identify own pattern when it appears. | A,<br>M | Rhythm pattern of names can be used. |
| | | *paper, pencil* | | |
| CREATE | rhythm<br>music<br>notation | **3.** Children graphically notate the rhythm of a familiar tune or phrase. | A,<br>M | |
| | | *paper, pencil* | | |
| CREATE/SING/<br>PLAY/MOVE | | **4.** Children compose songs, instrumental, or movement pieces for duos, trios, quartets, etc. | A,<br>M | |
| | | *paper, pencil* | | |

**SEE ALSO**

Auditory Activities
*Create Rhythm: #4, #5, #6 (p. 37)*

## SPECIFIC VISUAL CHARACTERISTICS

**DIRECTION**

| | | | | |
|---|---|---|---|---|
| SING/<br>PLAY/<br>MOVE | melody | **1.** Children visually identify melodies that move up, move down, or stay the same. | A | Pictures or graphic illustrations can be substituted for music. |
| | | *select suitable vocal and instrumental music* | | Charts: 8 9 22 23 24 |
| SING | melody | **2.** Design graphic illustrations of melodic contour of familiar songs. Children match appropriate illustration to corresponding song. | A | |
| | | **Down, Down**     **Upstairs, Downstairs**<br>**There Was a Crooked Man** | | Chart: 23 |
| | melody | **3.** Tape a length of shelf paper horizontally to chalkboard or wall. One child is selected to graphically notate groups of notes, or phrases, representing a variety of melodic contours that are played by the teacher or another child. | A,<br>M | |

melody instrument (bells, xylophone, piano)
shelf paper

| SING | melody | 4. Children recognize a familiar song from a visual illustration of the melodic contour. | A |
|---|---|---|---|
| | | *select appropriate songs* | |

## The child demonstrates
## UNDERSTANDING OF SPECIFIC VISUAL CHARACTERISTICS IN MUSIC PERFORMANCE

DIRECTION

| MOVE/ SING/ CREATE | melody | 1. Children interpret the melodic contour of familiar songs through body movement. | A, M | |
|---|---|---|---|---|
| | | *select suitable vocal and instrumental music* | | **Charts:** 22 23 24 |
| PLAY | melody rhythm | 2. Select familiar songs suitable for designing instrumental scores in which melody and rhythm can be graphically illustrated. | M | |

**Candles of Hannukah**

**SEE ALSO**

Auditory Activities
Perform Pitch: #3, #4
  #5 (use word cues) } (p. 40)
Create Pitch: #2 (p. 41)
Perform Melody: #1, #2, #3 (pp. 43–44)
  #12 (show music) (p. 45)
Create Melody: #6 (p. 46)

Gross Motor Activities
Directionality: #1, #2, #3
(pp. 89–90)

## The child demonstrates
## ABILITY TO APPLY UNDERSTANDING OF SPECIFIC VISUAL CHARACTERISTICS CREATIVELY IN MUSICAL EXPERIENCES

DIRECTION

| | melody | 1. Children draw pictures that appropriately illustrate melodic direction of familiar tunes. | A, M | Some children may need the notation, or "picture," of the melody for reference. |
|---|---|---|---|---|

**Candles of Hannukah**     **Pussy Willow**
**Down, Down**     **Skippin' and Steppin'**
**For Health and Strength**     **Stretching Song**
*paper, pencil, old magazines*

**Chart:** 24

| PLAY/ CREATE | melody | 2. *Play a picture.* Children interpret a picture or graphic illustration with melody instruments. | A, M | |
|---|---|---|---|---|
| | | *select pictures and illustrations of up and down slide whistle, bells, piano, etc.* | | **Charts:** 8 9 22 24 32 |
| PLAY/ CREATE | melody symbolization | 3. Children create a graphic score for bell accompaniment. Use a familiar song with up and/or down melodies. | A, M | |

*select suitable songs;*
*bells; paper, pencil*

| CREATE | melody symbolization | 4. Children graphically notate simple melodic dictation. | A, M | Given the starting note, some children may be able to use standard notation for stepwise melodies. |
|---|---|---|---|---|

*paper, pencil*

| CREATE | melody symbolization | 5. *Visual Name That Tune.* Children create a graphic illustration of the melody of a familiar tune for the class to identify. | A, M | |
|---|---|---|---|---|

*paper, pencil*

**SEE ALSO**

Auditory Activities
 *Create Pitch: #1 (p. 41)*

---

**The child perceives and identifies**
**SPECIFIC VISUAL CHARACTERISTICS**                                    **DISTANCE**

**SEE**

Auditory Activities
 *Localization: #1 (p. 26)*       (near and far)
 *Identify Dynamics: #10 (p. 28)* (near and far)
 *Identify Meter: #1 (p. 32)*     (visual response)
 *Identify Melody: #8 — #11 (pp. 42–43)* (show music)

---

**The child demonstrates**
**UNDERSTANDING OF SPECIFIC VISUAL CHARACTERISTICS**
**IN MUSIC PERFORMANCE**                                                **DISTANCE**

| MOVE/ PLAY | best phrase | 1. Circle formation, seated. A large drum is placed in center of the circle. Teacher or a child plays a series of beats (e.g., 4, 8, or 12) on the piano or other suitable instrument. A child is selected to first listen to the series of beats, then, on the repetition, step on each beat until reaching the drum in the center *on the last beat.* The last beat can be played on the drum by the child. Child must judge how big or small to step in order to cover distance in number of beats allotted. | A, M | Some children may not be able to coordinate playing the drum with the last beat. |
|---|---|---|---|---|

*large, free-standing drum*

| SING/ PLAY/ MOVE | | 2. Use distance in picture, word, graphic, or music charts to indicate dynamics, tempo, rhythm, melody, etc. | | |
|---|---|---|---|---|

SEE ALSO

Auditory Activities
    *Identify Tempo: #2 (p. 29)* (graphic variation)
    *Perform Pitch: #8, (p. 40)*
    *Create Melody: #1, #6 (pp. 45–46)*

**The child demonstrates**
## ABILITY TO APPLY UNDERSTANDING OF SPECIFIC VISUAL CHARACTERISTICS CREATIVELY IN MUSICAL EXPERIENCES

### DISTANCE

| MOVE | tempo<br>beat<br>phrase | 1. Divide class in two groups, with an object placed half way between each group. One child is chosen from one group to declare the exact number of *even* steps it will take to reach the object. (e.g., "I can get there in ___ steps.") The teacher, or another child, accompanies the stepping with a drumbeat. If the object is not reached as declared, the other team tries. If object is reached as declared, the other team can attempt to reach the object in fewer steps. Steps must be even although they can be small or large in size. | A,<br>M,<br>S | For a more difficult task, children may choose to use fancy stepping and irregular beats. |
|---|---|---|---|---|

*large drum or other suitable instrument*

| MOVE/<br>CREATE | beat<br>phrase | 2. *How Far Can You Go?* An even number of beats are played on the drum by the teacher or a child. One child is selected to move (when the beats are repeated) in any fashion (run, walk, skip) as far as possible and still arrive back at the starting place on the last beat. | A,<br>M | For a more difficult task, play uneven meters (e.g., 5, 7). |
|---|---|---|---|---|

*drum*

| PLAY/<br>CREATE | pitch | 3. Children compose an accompaniment to a familiar song using high and low tones. They can notate with letters, numbers, or graphic notation.<br><br>Example:   H  H    H  H<br>            L        L | A,<br>M | |
|---|---|---|---|---|

*pitched instruments*
*paper, pencil*

**The child demonstrates**
## ABILITY TO COORDINATE BODY EXTREMITIES WITH BOTH STATIONARY AND MOVING TARGETS IN MUSIC ACTIVITIES

### EYE—HAND/FOOT COORDINATION

| PLAY | rhythm | 1. Paste a colorful sticker the size of a half dollar on the head of a drum, slightly off-center. Child aims for the sticker when directing hand or beater to the drumhead. | A,<br>M | When child gains proficiency in consistently hitting the sticker, replace with a smaller sticker.<br><br>Other instruments that are struck may be substituted for drum. |
|---|---|---|---|---|

**Charlie Knows How to Beat That Drum**
*drum*
*gummed stickers*

| | | | | |
|---|---|---|---|---|
| PLAY/ SING | texture harmony | **2.** Color code autoharp chords with colored tape. Begin with one-chord songs. | **A, M** | |
| | | *select suitable songs;* *Autoharp; colored tape* | | |
| MOVE | meter accent | **3.** Children roll balls or hoops to a partner or target on accented beats in the music. | **A, M, S** | See Appendix, p. 276, for ball and hoop activities. Substitute balloons for balls. |

**Rolling Along**
*Bach: Badinere* ⊙    *Meyerbeer: Waltz* ⊙
*Handel: Minuet* ⊙    *Swing High* ⊙

**SEE ALSO**

Auditory Activities
  *Identify Dynamics: #2, #3 (p. 27)*
  *Perform Dynamics: #3, #4 (p. 28)*
  *Perform Meter: #1, #2 (p. 33)*
  *Identify Rhythm: #2, #3 (p. 34)*
  *Identify Pitch: #4, #5, #6 (pp. 38–39)*
  *Perform Pitch: #3–#7 (p. 40)*
  *Perform Melody: #2, #8 (pp. 43–44)*
  *Create Timbre: #3, #5, #6, #7, #10, #11 (pp. 50–51)*
  *Memory: #10 (p. 53)*

Gross Motor Activities
  *Body Awareness: #14 (p. 85)*
  *Strength and Energy: #2 (p. 87)*

Fine Motor Activities
  *Wrist Movements: #1 (p. 94)*

---

**The child simultaneously interprets**
## A VARIETY OF VISUAL CHARACTERISTICS IN MUSIC ACTIVITIES

**VISUAL INTEGRATION**

| | | | | |
|---|---|---|---|---|
| SING/ PLAY/ MOVE | | **1.** Children interpret several visual elements, such as color, shape, direction, through vocal, instrumental, and/or movement compositions. | **M, T** | For tactile experiences, textured materials can be used. |
| | | *greeting cards, posters, suitable pictures, etc.* | | **Chart:** 32 |
| | music notation | **2.** In a piece of music, children look for lines or phrases that are alike. | | Beginning experiences should be limited to three lines. |
| | | *music books, vocal or instrumental music* | | |
| SING/ PLAY | music reading | **3.** Teacher writes out the melody of a familiar tune including one or two wrong notes. Children locate obvious mistakes in the notation. | **A** | Beginning efforts should be limited to short, scale songs. |
| | music reading | **4.** Children identify a familiar "mystery tune" from music notation only. | **A** | Begin with short, easy songs. |
| CREATE/ SING/ PLAY/ MOVE | music reading | **5.** Children compose a short piece, notating parts with both form and color codes. Example:<br>red circle—drum   blue circle—tambourine<br>green triangle—triangle | | |

| | | | | |
|---|---|---|---|---|
| | | *classroom instruments; found sounds*<br>*paper and crayons; colored paper* | | |
| | pitch<br>rhythm<br>timbre<br>dynamics | **6.** Children cut out pictures or draw illustrations of sounds heard that show characteristics of pitch, rhythm, timbre, or dynamics. | **A,**<br>**M** | |
| | | *live or recorded environmental sounds; old magazines* | | |
| **SING/**<br>**PLAY/**<br>**MOVE/**<br>**CREATE** | meter<br>rhythm<br>form | **7.** Children interpret visual designs through vocal, instrumental, or movement compositions. | **M** | |
| | | Example:        **Night Song of the Fish** | **T** | Designs can be tactile. |

Christian Morgenstern

Copyright 1963 by Max E. Knight. Reprinted by permission of the University of California Press.

| | | | | |
|---|---|---|---|---|
| | | *select illustrations and designs* | Chart: 32 | |

**SEE ALSO**

Auditory Activities
    *Create Dynamics:  #2 (p. 29)*
    *Create Tempo:  #1 (p. 31)*
    *Create Meter:  #1 (p. 34)*
    *Create Rhythm:  #1, #4, #5 (p. 37)*

*Create Pitch:  #1, #2 (p. 41)*
*Perform Melody:  #1, #2, #12, #13*
        *(show music) (pp. 43–45)*
*Create Melody:  #1, #6 (pp. 45–46)*
*Create Timbre:  #9 (p. 50)*

---

## The child retains and recalls<br>VISUAL INFORMATION                       VISUAL MEMORY

| | | | | |
|---|---|---|---|---|
| **MOVE** | beat<br>rhythm | **1.** Children interpret environmental objects through illustration or body movement. | **M** | |
| | | *live or recorded environmental sounds* | | |
| **MOVE** | rhythm<br>music<br>reading | **2.** Notate in standard or graphic notation two rhythm patterns on the chalkboard. Give class a few seconds to study. Erase and then clap one of the patterns for the class to identify as the first or second as written on the board. | **M** | Number and length of patterns can be increased for a more challenging task.<br><br>After erasing patterns, volunteers can rewrite them, with class deciding if they are the same as the originals.<br><br>For a different challenge, a volunteer can clap the patterns after they are erased. |
| **SING** | melody | **3.** Accompany appropriate songs with visuals to aid children in associating a symbol to its object. | **A,**<br>**M,**<br>**L** | Children can match a picture (or silhouette cut-out) of an object. |

| | | | | |
|---|---|---|---|---|
| | Five Angels<br>Five Fat Turkeys<br>I Had a Little Overcoat<br>I Know an Old Lady<br>Letters and Names<br>My Farm<br>Oh, My Aunt Came Back<br>Three Little Ducks<br>The Tree in the Valley | *I've Got Two* ⊙<br>*One of These Things* ⊙<br><br>Chart: 25<br>SC: 13 - 20  21 - 25<br>26 - 31, 17, 19<br>32 - 37, 28<br>38 - 42 | | |
| CREATE | melody<br>rhythm<br>form | 4. Children illustrate a favorite song or program piece from memory. | A,<br>M | |

## SEE ALSO

Auditory Activities
   *Perform Timbre:* #4 (p. 49)
   *Figure-Ground:* #7 (p. 52)
             (with pictures)
   *Memory:* #8, #9 (notate) (p. 53)
   *Sequencing:* #3, #5 (p. 54)

Gross Motor Activities
   *Locomotor:* #1 (p. 78)
   *Body Awareness:* #10 (p. 84)
   *Memory and Sequencing:* #1, #2,
      #3, #4 (pp. 90–91)
   *Motor Integration:* #5 (p. 91)

Fine Motor Activities
   *Grasp and Release:* #1, #2, #3,
             #4 (p. 92)
   *Finger Strength:* #2, #3, #4, #5
      (p. 93)
   *Combination Fine and Gross Motor:*
     #1 (p. 95)

Language Activities
   *Verbalization:* #3 (p. 101)

## The child arranges
# VISUAL MATERIALS IN PROPER SEQUENCE

# VISUAL SEQUENCING

| | | | | |
|---|---|---|---|---|
| PLAY | scale<br>pitch | 1. Mix up a set of bells and select a child to sort and arrange sequentially until a scale is formed. Beginning experiences may be more successful for some children if the number of bells are limited. White bars (diatonic scale), black bars (pentatonic scale), or both black and white bars (chromatic scale) can be used. | A<br><br>T | For a tactile experience, blindfold the child. |
| | *bells* | | | |
| SING/<br>MOVE | beat<br>rhythm<br>form | 2. Children perform familiar action songs, rhythm games, and dances without visual or verbal clues. | A,<br>M,<br>L | Whenever possible, use instrumental accompaniment only. |
| | | Crocodile Song<br>Here's the Beehive<br>I Had a Little Turtle<br>Miss Mary Mack<br>Oh, My Aunt Came Back | Pat-a-Cake<br>The Shoemaker<br>Three Little Ducks<br><br>*Ballin' the Jack* ⊙ | |

| | | | |
|---|---|---|---|
| **SING/ MOVE** | melody | **3.** Children arrange visuals for songs in which verses are sequenced and/or cumulative. Use a separate visual to illustrate or cue each verse. Have children arrange in order before, during, or after singing the song. | **A, M** |

**The Ants Go Marching**  **Oh, My Aunt Came Back**
**Five Angels**  **The Old Gray Cat**
**I Had a Little Overcoat**  **The Tree in the Valley**
**I Know an Old Lady**  **The Twelve Days of Christmas**

SC: 21 - 25  26 - 31, 17, 19
32 - 37, 28  38 - 42

| | | | |
|---|---|---|---|
| **PLAY** | texture harmony | **4.** Color code chord progressions of three or four chords for appropriate instruments. | **A, M** |

*autoharp, bells, etc.*
*colored tape*

| | | | |
|---|---|---|---|
| **MOVE/ CREATE** | melody rhythm form | **5.** Children interpret favorite songs or program music through movement or illustration without verbal clues. | **A, M** |

*Dukas: Sorcerer's Apprentice* ⊙
*MacDowell: Of a Tailor and a Bear* ⊙

Charts: 26 27 28 29

| | | | |
|---|---|---|---|
| **SING/ MOVE** | melody | **6.** Sing a song in *reverse* sequence, with appropriate visuals and/or actions also in reverse order. | **A, M** |

**Bones**

| | | | |
|---|---|---|---|
| **CREATE** | timbre | **7.** Help children arrange pictures that they have drawn or cut out in a suitable sequence for a sound story. | **A, M** |

*classroom instruments*
*paper, pencil, old magazines*

Charts: 35 36

| | | | |
|---|---|---|---|
| **SING** | melody | **8.** Design a visual illustrating the melodic sequence in a song. | **A** |

**Hush, Little Baby**

**SEE ALSO**

Auditory Activities
    *Memory: #8, #9 (notate) (p. 53)*
    *Sequencing: #3, #5 (p. 54)*

Gross Motor Activities
    *Body Awareness: #10, #11, #13 (pp. 84–85)*
    *Memory and Sequencing: #1, #2, #3, #4 (p. 90)*

Fine Motor Activities
    *Grasp and Release: #1, #2, #3, #4 (p. 92)*
    *Finger Strength: #1, #2, #5, #6 (pp. 93–94)*
    *Wrist Action: #3, #5 (pp. 94–95)*
    *Combination Fine and Gross Motor: #1 (p. 95)*

Many studies have shown a relationship between motor incoordination and learning problems. Kephart, Barsch, Cratty, and others have demonstrated that substantial improvement in motor functioning can be brought about through a systematic program that continues throughout the school career. Certainly one of the greatest contributions music activities can make in basic learning skill development is in the psychomotor area. Singing, playing instruments, and moving to music all require the use of a variety of motor and cognitive functions. The child who is actively engaged in music making is continually improving motor functioning.

Motor activities help develop *kinesthetic perception* (muscle sense), *laterality* (sidedness), and *spatial concepts* (position of the body in space). Many other skills either contribute to or derive from competence in these areas. Children who lack adequate motor skills may

- perform locomotor rhythms in a jerky or an uncoordinated fashion
- be unable to execute locomotor rhythms consisting of more than one basic movement (e.g., skipping)
- be unable to successfully keep their balance when hopping, jumping, stopping quickly, or posturing
- be unaware of body parts and their movements
- be unable to change easily from one motor function to another (agility)
- be unable to use both sides of the body efficiently (laterality)
- be unable to consistently identify right and left (directionality)
- be unable to respond rhythmically with accuracy
- be unable to coordinate eyes and hands to throw, catch, or play instruments successfully (eye-hand coordination)

The sequence of motor development in the normal individual proceeds from head to toe, and from the middle of the body outward. Motor skills are divided into two basic groups: (1) *gross motor*, which develop first and involve the use of large muscles, and (2) *fine motor*, in which the smaller muscles (e.g., hands) are developed to perform more precise motor functions.

## Gross motor skills

Gross motor activity is often described as either *locomotor*, indicating movement from one place to another, or *axial* (nonlocomotor), movement that is executed within the axis of the body, or in place. Music activities that foster the development of large muscles can also provide opportunity for greater overall perceptual-motor development, since listening and looking are of vital importance in music and movement. Many of these activities can be used effectively in movement education programs as well as music education experiences, and

repetition of the skills involved can only benefit the child who has yet to develop them.

Frostig (1970) and Barsch (1974) (see p. 18) have emphasized the importance of teaching children to be aware of their own inner rhythm. There should be some opportunity for children to move without the external influences of beat and/or music in order that they may set their own tempo or pace, especially in beginning activities. However, some children need the structure provided by beat or music to perform motor functions in any coordinated fashion. Additionally, strongly rhythmic and harmonically exciting music is often the catalyst one looks for to motivate a lethargic child to action. For the physically disabled, blind, and severely retarded, something must spark the tremendous effort required to move. Nothing does this as well as music.

It is important to know and remember the following about gross motor skills.

**Body awareness**   Awareness of body parts and their motor function is not always obvious to children who have difficulty integrating sensory skills. Ability to locate and label body parts is not sufficient. Each child must be able to demonstrate understanding and control of movement of those body parts that are capable of being controlled. (See Physical Disabilities, p. 251.)

**Balance / agility**   These skills are closely related, since each depends to some extent on the other. Group and partner activities (e.g., singing games and dances) will help children lacking development in balance and agility, since partners provide physical support when turning, hopping, bending, and so forth. Tempo is also a factor, as fast movements are generally easier than slow ones for undeveloped muscles. Beginning experiences should take these things into consideration.

**Strength / endurance**   Children lacking motor coordination are often lacking physical stamina and energy as well. Endurance for strenuous physical activity needs to be built up gradually. Individual differences must be taken into consideration—what is easy for the physically active child may be strenuous for the child characterized by habitual inactivity.

**Laterality / directionality**   These terms should *not* be used interchangeably. They are quite different abilities. *Laterality* (functional knowledge of left and right sides *of the body*) must be established before *directionality* (functional knowledge of left and right *in space*) can be understood. Since laterality involves internal awareness of the body, it is also related to body awareness. *Lateral dominance* refers to the preferred side of the body and should not be confused with either laterality or directionality. Some children have difficulty integrating motor functions from the two sides of the body. This is often referred to as a *midline* problem. In designing music experiences to encourage cross-lateral movement, activities that require the use of an extremity on one side of the body to do something on the opposite side (without turning the torso) are needed. Clapping to the side, patschen with right hand on left thigh (and vice versa), and crossover steps (one foot crosses the other) are activities in which crossing the midline is required. Directionality skills are required in numerous dances, especially folk and square dances. Excellent sources also are the many singing games that require children to respond to spatial directions such as left, right, over, under.

As with all music activities, body movement requires (in addition to motor skills) integration of a multiplicity of skills. These may include auditory (discrimination, memory, sequencing), visual (spatial relations, memory, sequencing, tracking), language (word comprehension, expression, articulation), and social (peer group interaction, cooperation, following directions). In some cases the music activity may need to be adapted to minimize one skill while another skill may be given equal importance to the target motor function.

Some music games involving motor skills are of the elimination type, requiring children who "miss" to drop out. To avoid a learning environment in which the good get better and the poor get worse, it is advisable to revise these games so that a child who lacks skills may have every opportunity to improve them.

Movement with the handicapped child is particularly important. Since a child's first learning is through the motor area, this is a sensory route that is basic. A thorough understanding of motor development in normal children is necessary if one is to plan effective movement experiences for children with motor dysfunction. Movement activities should help children learn to use space and to explore new space through using different positions and postures. Music activities can motivate the use of muscles that tend to be immobile. In addition, bilateral development is fostered by planning activities that utilize both sides of the body. This is necessary because in some children, handedness is not yet established, and in others (i.e., hemiplegics) one side of the body may be consistently used to avoid use of the weaker side.

Many movement activities are possible with children who have impaired muscle functioning. (See Appendix, p. 277, suggestions for utilizing various body parts.) Activities can be designed by (1) selecting those movements that are within the physical capabilities of individual children and (2) putting them together in a sequence to fit a specific rhythmic or music structure. Generally, it is a good idea to repeat one movement for two to eight beats before moving on to a new one. Consideration of the agility and reaction speeds of the children involved is the most realistic way to arrange the number of repetitions

and the variety of movements in a sequence. A word of caution—most neurologically impaired children have poor balance. If a child lacks protective posturing reflexes (the ability to break a fall with a hand, and so forth), the activity should take place on a soft surface (e.g., rug, mat) and the teacher should be prepared to protect the child from fear and injury if necessary.

It is absolutely essential that the tempo, or speed, of the music is appropriate to the skill level of the children. Teachers who must rely on commercially available recorded materials frequently impose a pace that some children are not able to sustain. Inability to keep up, or physical exhaustion, is enough to discourage even the most enthusiastic participant. Some alternatives need to be considered. One is to give slower reacting children twice as much time to execute a movement (e.g., step to *every other* beat). When movements are in groups of two, these children can perform half as many per measure. Another alternative would be to accompany movement with a drum beat. In beginning activities it is wise to allow individual children to begin moving and then match the beat with their tempo. When children are comfortable with one tempo, the beat can gradually be quickened and presented prior to movement. Recording technology is now sufficiently advanced to enable playback of speech at slower speeds without appreciable pitch distortion. However, such equipment is not yet available for music playback purposes. Slowing down a turntable with variable speed control permits a slight decrease in speed as it lowers the pitch, but beyond a certain point it begins to sound unnatural. Whenever possible (e.g., singing games), the most practical idea is to use the recording to learn the song, if necessary, but perform the game without the record. In this way, you can ensure a tempo that is comfortable for all.

## Fine motor skills

Fine motor skills are the precise movements of the small muscles used in manipulating objects. The majority of the population develop these muscles in the hands, although there are individuals (especially those born without hands) who have developed fine motor skills in the feet to an extraordinary degree.

Fine motor skills include movements such as using the hands to grasp and release, rotate, and transfer objects in each, as well as using fingers and thumb to pull, push, and grasp. In the classroom, all paper and pencil tasks as well as manipulative materials such as scissors, microscopes, and table games require the child to be able to use the hands in these ways. In the music class, finger-play songs and manipulation of instruments are the most obvious activities that require these same skills. However, many activities, including action songs, singing games, and dances, utilize a combination of *both* gross and fine motor skills.

Although some children may be able to perform separate fine motor skills, they lack the ability to perform various sequences of them smoothly. The practice of having children finger an exercise without playing (used by many instrumental teachers) is an excellent technique for helping children develop more coordinated finger movements.

Some physically handicapped children may not be able to develop precise movements in both hands. (For suggestions, refer to the discussion on Physical Disabilities, p. 251.) In assessing fine motor skills, much attention is often given to one-handed operations as contrasted with those in which two hands are used. The importance of developing motor skills on both sides of the body equally has already been discussed. (See Laterality, p. 76.) However, it should be pointed out that the majority of classroom instruments require a second hand only for holding the instrument (e.g., triangle, tone block). If these instruments are supported for the child who is unable to use two hands, the problem is eliminated. The assistance of a helper can be enlisted when playing instruments that require two hands (e.g., Autoharp).

The following represents a classification of specific fine motor movements as they are used in playing simple classroom instruments.

### Grasp/release—palmar

All instruments with handles (e.g., mounted castanets, mounted bells, tone blocks, jingle taps)
Rhythm sticks
Maracas
Triangle with oversize knobs for holding and striking
Sandblocks with oversize knobs for holding and striking
Reed horns
Hand drum
Tambourine

### Grasp/release—thumb and finger (pincer)

Mallets for resonator bells and Orff instruments
Finger cymbals
Standard triangle and beater
Standard sandblocks
Autoharp and guitar picks
Automatic hand castanets
Bows (string instruments)

### Finger strength and separation (push, pull)

Autoharp (push buttons and strum)
Guiro
Kalimba (sansa, thumb piano)
Keyed instruments (song flutes, recorder, Melodica)
All string instruments (including guitar, ukulele)

### Wrist movements (flex, twist, rotate, snap)

Tambourine
Maracas
Cabaza
Instruments with pegs (winding)

To summarize, poor motor skills in children are associated with certain developmental periods, some physical handicaps, and inadequate experiences necessary for their development. Motor skills are classified as either gross or fine. Gross motor is large muscle activity and includes locomotor rhythms, non-locomotor movement, body awareness, balance, agility, strength and endurance, laterality, and directionality. Fine motor skills are those performed by the small muscles of the hands for grasping, releasing, and rotating; and the fingers and thumb for pushing, pulling, and picking up and holding small objects. Music activities that provide motor experiences are body movement, action songs, dramatizations, and playing instruments.

## MOTOR SKILLS
### (Gross Motor)

**The child performs**
**LOCOMOTOR MOVEMENTS TO A STEADY OR RHYTHMIC BEAT (INCLUDING WALKING, MARCHING, RUNNING, ROLLING, CRAWLING, HOPPING, JUMPING, SKIPPING, GALLOPING, AND LEAPING)**

## LOCOMOTOR

| MOVE | beat tempo | 1. Before starting drumbeat, ask individuals to walk briefly. Match drumbeat to individual tempos, having the rest of the class clap or join the child at the same tempo. | A, S | Compare the speed of individual walkers. Who walked faster, slower? |
| | | | V | When children are able to recognize different tempos in walking, ask them to find a partner in the group who is walking at the same tempo |
| | | | | When children can match step with beat, encourage variations on a walk. (See Appendix, p. 274.) |

| | | | | |
|---|---|---|---|---|
| | *drum* | | | |
| MOVE/ SING | beat tempo | **2.** Select suitable instrumental music, songs, or drumbeat to accompany walking in a tempo comfortable to all. | A | Some children may need to step to every *other* beat rather than on each beat. Encourage variations on a walk. (See Appendix, p. 274.) |
| | | **Let's Go Walking**    *Thomson: Walking Song* ⊙ *Alley Cat* ⊙ *Stop and Go* ⊙ | | Chart: 20 |
| MOVE | beat tempo style | **3.** Select music to accompany slow, stately walks or promenades. "Royal capes" (scarves) and "scepters" (sticks) often help to improve posture and style. | A | |
| | | *Bach: Allegro* ⊙ *Handel: Minuet* ⊙ | | |
| MOVE | beat tempo style | **4.** Select drumbeat or music to accompany snappy marches, stepping on every beat. | A | Some children may need to step to every *other* beat. |
| | | *Bizet: March* ⊙    *Prokofiev: March* ⊙ *Herbert: March* ⊙    *Sousa: The Stars and Stripes Forever* ⊙ | | |
| MOVE | beat dynamics style | **5.** Select appropriate music or drumbeat to accompany tiptoeing. | A | |
| | | **My White Mouse** **The Old Gray Cat**    *Grieg: In the Hall of the Mountain King* ⊙ | | |
| MOVE | tempo rhythm | **6.** Select appropriate music or drumbeat to accompany running. | A | |
| | | *Mussorgsky: Ballet of the Unhatched Chicks* ⊙ *Offenbach: "Cancan" Theme* ⊙ *Rimsky-Korsakov: Flight of the Bumblebee* ⊙ *Tchaikovsky: Trepak* ⊙ | | Chart: 20 |
| MOVE | beat rhythm | **7.** Select appropriate music or drumbeat to accompany jumping and hopping. | A | |
| | | *Bartok: Jack-in-the-Box* ⊙ *Handel: Bourrée* ⊙ *McBride: Pony Express* ⊙ *Tchaikovsky: Trepak* ⊙ | | Chart: 20 |
| MOVE | tempo rhythm | **8.** Select appropriate music or drumbeat to accompany galloping and trotting. | A, S | Galloping with a partner is done holding hoops, scarves, or hands of one partner extended backward to join with other partner. |
| | | **My Little Pony**    *McBride: Pony Express* ⊙ | | |
| MOVE | rhythm | **9.** Select appropriate music or drumbeat to accompany skipping. | A | |
| | | *Bach: Badinere* ⊙ | | |
| MOVE/ SING | phrase | **10.** Children take turns rolling to a target or person, then rolling back to starting point, changing direction on phrase endings or repeats. | A | |

| | | | | |
|---|---|---|---|---|
| | | Roll Over (*dramatize*) | | |
| | | Rolling Along      *Cotton Eyed Joe* ⊙ | | |
| MOVE | tempo rhythm | **11.** Select or improvise music descriptive of the movement of familiar animals for children to interpret through body movement. | A, V | Use pictures or illustrations of animals for a nonverbal response choice. See Appendix, p. 275, for special walks. |
| | | *Bartok: Diary of a Fly* ⊙ <br> *Mussorgsky: Ballet of the Unhatched Chicks* ⊙ <br> *Mussorgsky: Bydlo* (oxen) ⊙ <br> *Rimsky-Korsakov: Flight of the Bumblebee* ⊙ | | SC: 13 - 20   26 - 28 / 29 - 31 |
| MOVE/ SING | rhythm form | **12.** Learn singing games that utilize locomotor rhythms. | A, L, S | See special activities following the songs. |
| | | **Charlie Over the Water** <br> **Rig-a-jig-jig** <br> **The Shoemaker** <br> **Valentine** <br> **Way Down Yonder in the Brickyard** | | |
| MOVE | melodic contour rhythm | **13.** Select music that is suggestive of leaping or lunging movements. | A | |
| | | *Bartok: Jack-in-the-Box* ⊙ <br> *Meyerbeer: Waltz* ⊙ <br> *Tchaikovsky: Trepak* ⊙ | | Chart: 21 |
| MOVE SING/ CREATE | tempo beat form rhythm | **14.** Select music for free movement that includes sections with contrasting tempo, rhythms, and melodies. | A | |
| | | **Rig-a-jig-jig** <br> **The Wind Blew East** <br> *Bizet: Farandole* ⊙ <br> *McDonald: Children's Symphony* ⊙ <br> *Stravinsky: Russian Dance* ⊙ <br> *Thomson: Walking Song* ⊙ | | |
| MOVE/ SING/ CREATE | meter | **15.** Select music for free movement in which beats are in groups of two. | A | Help children create movement sequences in groups of two. |
| | | **Canoe Round**   *Fauré: Berceuse* ⊙ <br> *German: Morris Dance* ⊙ <br> *Alley Cat* ⊙ | | Chart: 13 |
| MOVE/ SING/ CREATE | meter | **16.** Select music for free movement in which beats are in groups of three. | A | Help children create movement sequences that occur only on accented beats, or, in groups of three. |
| | | **Man on the Flying Trapeze**   *Handel: Minuet* ⊙ <br> **So Long**   *Swing High* ⊙ | | Chart: 14 |

| MOVE | dynamics | 17. Children interpret dynamic changes in the music through free movement. For example, crescendo—larger movements; decrescendo—smaller movements. | A, V | Beginning experiences can be controlled more easily by substituting a drumbeat and having children hold hands in circle formation that grows bigger or smaller with appropriate dynamics. |
|---|---|---|---|---|
| | | *Grieg: In the Hall of the Mountain King* ⊙ <br> *Mussorgsky: Bydlo* ⊙ | | |
| MOVE | beat tempo | 18. Select music for body movement in which the tempo gradually gets faster or slower. | A | |
| | | *German: Morris Dance* ⊙ <br> *Grieg: In the Hall of the Mountain King* ⊙ | | Chart: 10 |
| MOVE/ CREATE | legato | 19. Select music with legato rhythms to which children move freely. | A | |
| | | *Mussorgsky: Bydlo* ⊙ | | |
| MOVE/ CREATE | staccato | 20. Select music with staccato rhythms to which children more freely. | A | |
| | | *Mussorgsky: Ballet of the Unhatched Chicks* ⊙ <br> *Shostakovich: Polka* ⊙ <br> *Stravinsky: Russian Dance* ⊙ | | |
| MOVE | beat accent | 21. Learn to do a waltz step to suitable music in ¾ meter. | A | See Appendix, p. 275, for steps. |
| | | **Man on the Flying Trapeze**    *Meyerbeer: Waltz* ⊙ <br> **So Long**    *Swing High* ⊙ | | |
| MOVE/ SING/ CREATE | melodic contour | 22. Children interpret melodic contour through body movement. | A | |
| | | **I Like to Ride the Elevator**    *Hill and Dell* ⊙ <br> **Jack-in-the-Box** <br> **Singing Top** <br> **Skippin' and Steppin'** <br> **Snowflakes** <br> **There Was a Crooked Man** | | Charts: 22 23 24 <br> SC: 53 - 60 |
| MOVE/ CREATE | meter rhythm phrase form | 23. Help children create simple dances to suitable music. | A | See Appendix, p. 275, for movement ideas. |
| | | **The Man in Blue** <br> **Woodstock's Samba** <br><br> *German: Morris Dance* ⊙ <br> *Meyerbeer: Waltz* ⊙ <br> *Alley Cat* ⊙ <br> *Cotton Eyed Joe* ⊙ | | Chart: 30 |

**SEE ALSO**

Auditory Activities
    *Awareness: #5, #6 (p. 25)*
    *Perform Melody: #6 (p. 44)*

The child performs
## NONLOCOMOTOR MOVEMENTS
### (INCLUDING ROCKING, SWAYING, BENDING, STRETCHING, SWINGING, TWISTING, AND TWIRLING)

NONLOCOMOTOR

| MOVE | beat tempo accent | 1. Children rock or sway to the beat in either seated or standing position. | A, V, S | Pass balls on the accented beats. |
|---|---|---|---|---|
| | | | A, V | Keep a balloon in the air by hitting only on accented beats. |
| | | | A, S | With a partner, children swing high, then low on alternating strong beats. |

| | | Canoe Round<br>Man on the Flying Trapeze<br>Rolling Along<br>So Long<br>Tra La La La | *Fauré: Berceuse* ⊙<br>*Mussorgsky: Bydlo* ⊙<br>*Swing High* ⊙ | |
|---|---|---|---|---|

| MOVE/ SING | meter beat accent | 2. Partners sit on the floor, legs extended. They join hands and alternately pull each other forward on the strong beats in seesaw fashion. | A, S | Children with good balance can try this activity in a kneeling or squat position. |
|---|---|---|---|---|

| | | So Long<br>Tra La La La | *Handel: Minuet* ⊙<br>*Swing High* ⊙ | |
|---|---|---|---|---|

| MOVE | melody | 3. As children move to the music, encourage them to include stretching with ascending melody lines and bending with descending melody lines. | A | Having the child stand inside a hoop, or masking tape, placed on the floor will help to confine movements to nonlocomotor. |
|---|---|---|---|---|

| | | Singing Top<br>Snowflakes | *Bartok: Jack-in-the-Box* ⊙ | |
|---|---|---|---|---|

| MOVE | beat | 4. Select suitable music for encouraging twisting movements. | A | |
|---|---|---|---|---|

| | | A Little Flight Music<br>The Man in Blue | | Chart: 21 |
|---|---|---|---|---|

| MOVE | | 5. Learn action songs, rhythm games, and rhythm dances that utilize nonlocomotor movements. | A | See special activities following songs. |
|---|---|---|---|---|

| | | Oh, My Aunt Came Back<br>Polynesian Stick Game<br>The Shoemaker (*seated version*)<br>Walrus Hunt | *Hornpipe Dance* (*seated version*) ⊙ | |
|---|---|---|---|---|

| SING/ MOVE | meter melody dynamics form | 6. Select songs suitable for adding nonlocomotor movement. Example:<br><br>"For Health and Strength"<br><br>1st phrase: arms out to sides, palms up<br>2nd phrase: arms forward, palms up<br>3rd phrase: palms together<br>4th phrase: bow head | A, V | See Appendix, p. 276, for movement suggestions. |
|---|---|---|---|---|

| | | Canoe Round<br>Down at the Station<br>For Health and Strength | My Father's House<br>Tra La La La<br>The Wind Blew East | |
|---|---|---|---|---|

| | | | | |
|---|---|---|---|---|
| MOVE/ SING | beat rhythm form | 7. Adapt appropriate dances and singing games for using upper extremities only. | A, L, S | See Appendix, p. 277, for suggested head, arm, and hand movements. |
| | | Bingo<br>Five Angels<br>Jack-in-the-Box<br>The Shoemaker<br>Tinikling<br>We're Going Round the Mountain | *Ballin' the Jack* (seated version) ⊙<br>*Hornpipe Dance* ⊙<br><br>Chart: 31 | |

**SEE ALSO**

Auditory Activities
*Perform Meter: #3, #4, #6 (p. 33)*
*Perform Pitch: #1, #3 (pp. 39–40)*
*Perform Melody: #3, #10 (pp. 44–45)*
*Perform Timbre: #3 (p. 49)*

## The child identifies and uses BODY PARTS EFFICIENTLY

## BODY AWARENESS

| | | | | |
|---|---|---|---|---|
| MOVE/ SING | beat rhythm | 1. Learn action songs in which parts of the body are named and located, including head, eyes, nose, mouth, ears, cheeks, chin, arm, elbow, wrist, hand, finger, shoulders, stomach, hips, thighs, legs, knees, ankles, toes, feet, face, and neck. | A, V, L, S | For a greater challenge, blindfold children so they must locate parts kinesthetically.<br><br>For an abstract task, have one child locate body parts on self while looking in a mirror; on another child or the teacher; on a doll; in a picture. |
| | | Bones<br>Head, Shoulders<br>Put Your Finger in the Air<br>Two Little Hands  *I've Got Two* ⊙ | | |
| MOVE/ SING | beat rhythm | 2. Sing action songs in which lyrics describe movements. | A, L | |
| | | I Roll the Ball  Put Your Hand on Your Shoe<br>I Will Clap My Hands  Stretching Song<br>Open, Shut Them  Two Little Hands<br>Charts: 20 21 | | |
| MOVE | tempo rhythm legato | 3. Select relaxing music appropriate for interpretation through body movement. | A | A rag doll is a good manipulative model of relaxed muscles. |
| | | *Fauré: Berceuse* ⊙ | | |
| MOVE | melody rhythm staccato | 4. Children pretend they are puppets. Call attention to the jerky melody and rhythms that describe the movements of puppets. | V | Children could draw pictures of puppets. |
| | | Puppets  *Bartok: Jack-in-the-Box* ⊙<br>*McBride: Pumpkin Eater's Little Fugue* ⊙<br>*Shostakovich: Polka* ⊙<br>*Stravinsky: Russian Dance* ⊙ | | |
| MOVE | beat meter | 5. Children pretend they are wooden, or tin, soldiers with tense and stiff movements. | A, V | |

*Herbert: March* ⊙
*Prokofiev: March* ⊙

| | | | |
|---|---|---|---|
| **MOVE/ CREATE** | beat rhythm timbre | **6.** As music is played, ask children to move freely. Will movement be relaxed and flowing, or stiff and tense? Discuss musical elements that help create a feeling of tension or relaxation (e.g., short melodic fragments, dissonance). | **A** |

*Ginastera: Invocation of the Powerful Spirits* ⊙
*Mussorgsky: Bydlo* ⊙

| | | | | |
|---|---|---|---|---|
| **MOVE** | sound/ silence beat | **7.** When the music stops, children position their bodies to match those of the model (e.g., skeleton, puppet, picture, individual). | **A, V** | Introduce the activity without music first. Keep postures simple—one arm up, two arms, up, etc. |
| | | | **V** | For a more difficult task, stick figures in various poses can be used. |

*A Little Flight Music ("Stop" version)*

*Stop and Go* ⊙

*paper skeleton or puppet with movable joints pictures*

SC: 53 - 60

| | | | | |
|---|---|---|---|---|
| **MOVE** | sound/ silence beat rhythm | **8.** *Point stopping.* Children move in an appropriate locomotor rhythm. When the music stops, teacher calls out a number from 1 to 6. Children must find a posture in which the appropriate number of body points are touching the floor. For example: "3"—two hands, one foot; two feet, one hand. | **A, V, L** | Some children may need to practice this activity in a confined area first in order to remain focused on the goal. |

*A Little Flight Music ("Stop" version)*

| | | | |
|---|---|---|---|
| **MOVE/ SING/ CREATE** | | **9.** Dramatize songs, poems, and musical stories that describe specific movements. | **A, L, S** |

**Five Angels**    *MacDowell: Of a Tailor and a Bear* ⊙
**The Goat**    Charts: 20 21 28 29
**Snowflakes**    SC: 38 - 42

| | | | | |
|---|---|---|---|---|
| **MOVE/ CREATE** | beat phrase | **10.** *Copycat.* A leader makes up a sequence of movements for the first phrase of the music; group copies the same sequence on the next phrase which is, musically, the same as the first. | **A, V, S** | See Appendix, p. 277, for suggested movements. Beginning efforts will be more successful if the number of different movements is limited to two or three. |

**Two Little Hands**    *Cotton Eyed Joe* ⊙

| | | | |
|---|---|---|---|
| **MOVE/ SING** | beat phrase | **11.** Add movement sequences to like phrases of echo type songs. | **A** |

**The Goat**
**Oh, My Aunt Came Back**    *Tah-boo* ⊙

| | | | |
|---|---|---|---|
| **SING/ MOVE** | beat phrase | **12.** Learn singing games and dances in which movements to be performed are described in the song. | **A, L, S** |

**Step in Time**
**The Shoemaker** *(dance)*    *Ballin' the Jack* ⊙

| MOVE | beat | 13. The teacher or leader performs movements that are mirrored simultaneously by the group. | A, V, S | See Appendix, p. 228, for movement suggestions. |
|---|---|---|---|---|
| | | **I See You**<br>**Oh, My Aunt Came Back**    *Alley Cat* (mirror dance) ⊙ | | |
| MOVE/<br>SING | meter | 14. Children keep balloons in the air by bouncing them off different body parts (e.g., elbows, knees, head) on the strong beats only. | A, V | |
| | | **So Long**        *Handel: Minuet* ⊙<br>**Tra La La La**     *Swing High* ⊙ | | |

<br>

## The child maintains balance
# WHILE MOVING AND STANDING STILL

**BALANCE**

| MOVE | beat | 1. Map out an obstacle course with string, tape, or colored yarn. Children can move along the course to a drumbeat or suitable music. | A, V<br>L, S | For a different challenge, a child can be blindfolded and led through the course by another child, who gives verbal directions (e.g., "to the left," "under"). |
|---|---|---|---|---|
| | | **Marching to Pretoria**    *Sousa: The Stars and Stripes Forever* ⊙ | | |
| MOVE/<br>SING | | 2. When dramatizing appropriate songs, place a piece of string or tape on the floor for balancing. | A, V, S | For "Elephant Song," elephants can assume a pose to hold with the addition of each new elephant. See special activities following song. |
| | | **Elephant Song    Man on the Flying Trapeze** | | |
| MOVE | beat | 3. *Stepping stones.* Tape paper stones or footprints to the floor, appropriately spaced to match children's strides. Children walk to drumbeat or music by stepping from stone to stone. Stops and starts in the beat, or in the music, challenge good balance. | A, V | Cut-out footprints can be labeled or color-coded to indicate stepping foot (left, right) for each. |
| | | *select suitable music for walking or marching*<br><br>*paper stones or footprints* | | |
| MOVE | beat | 4. *Balance beam walk.* Place strips of tape on the floor four inches apart and six to twelve feet in length to simulate a balance beam. Children walk the "beam" in a variety of ways to a drumbeat or suitable music. If children extend their arms out to the side it will help them to balance, especially if walking slowly.<br>    See special activities following the song, "Put On a Happy Face." | A, V | See Appendix, p. 276, for suggested balance beam activities.<br><br>Some children will need a drumbeat matched to *their* tempo for success.<br><br>When children are ready, reduce the width between tape strips to two inches. |
| | | **A Little Flight Music**<br>**Put On a Happy Face**<br>*colored or masking tape (1″ wide)* | | |

| | | | | |
|---|---|---|---|---|
| MOVE | beat<br>sound/<br>silence | **5.** Play a variety of "stop the music" games to drumbeat or suitable music. Children can run, skip, gallop, or walk, stopping as quickly as they can when the music stops. If stops in the music are created by lifting the needle from the record, or improvising on an instrument, be sure some stops are in unexpected places. | A | Incorporate the game "statues," holding positions for five seconds or more. |
| | | **A Little Flight Music ("Stop" version)**<br>*Stop and Go* ⊙ | | Charts: 20 21 |
| MOVE | beat | **6.** Children hold free foot as they hop on the other. Change feet. | A | |
| | | ***Bach: Badinere*** ⊙<br>***Handel: Bourrée*** ⊙<br>***McBride: Pumpkin Eater's Little Fugue*** ⊙<br>***Offenbach: "Cancan" Theme*** ⊙<br>***Tchaikovsky: Trepak*** ⊙ | | |
| MOVE/<br>SING | melodic<br>contour<br>ritardando | **7.** Children dramatize "Singing Top" by beginning with arms stretched overhead, standing on tiptoes. Twirling movements portray the spinning motion of the top. As top winds down, movements become *both* slower and lower until ending in a crouched position. | A,<br>V,<br>L | If children are not familiar with a top, they may need to see and manipulate one before understanding the goals of the activity. |
| | | **Singing Top** | | Chart: 21 |
| MOVE | beat<br>rhythm<br>style | **8.** Teach or help children create dances that include step, hop, and jump combinations. | A,<br>S | See Appendix, p. 274, for suggested steps |
| | | **My White Mouse**<br>**Step in Time** | | Charts: 20 30 |
| MOVE/<br>CREATE | beat<br>rhythm<br>phrase | **9.** Help children create dance step patterns to suitable music in duple and triple meters. | A,<br>V,<br>S | |
| | | **Woodstock's Samba**   *Meyerbeer: Waltz* ⊙<br>*Step Lively* ⊙ | | |

**SEE ALSO**

Gross Motor Activities
    *Locomotor: #2—#9, #11, #13, #18—#21 (pp. 79–81)*
    *Nonlocomotor: #1—#4 (p. 82)*
    *Body Awareness: #8 (p. 84)*
    *Agility: #1, #3 (p. 87)*

The child maintains
# SUFFICIENT MUSCLE STRENGTH AND ENERGY TO COMPLETE MOVEMENT TASKS

**STRENGTH AND ENERGY**

| | | | | |
|---|---|---|---|---|
| MOVE/<br>SING | | **1.** Select singing games and songs to dramatize that utilize strenuous physical movement. | A,<br>L,<br>S | |
| | | **Bingo**      **My Little Pony**<br>**Jack-in-the-Box**      **Step in Time** | | Charts: 20 21 |

| | | | | |
|---|---|---|---|---|
| MOVE/ SING/ CHANT | beat rhythm tempo | **2.** Jump rope to favorite songs or speech chants. | A, V, L | A drumbeat will help maintain steady rhythm and tempo |
| | | **Bingo**       **Miss Mary Mack** <br> **Elephant Song** <br> *rope for jumping* | | |
| MOVE | beat phrase | **3.** Children move freely to strongly rhythmic music or drumbeat. Learn dances that involve strenuous physical movement. | A, S | |
| | | *Bartok: Jack-in-the-Box* ⊙ <br> *Tchaikovsky: Trepak* ⊙ <br> *Step Lively* ⊙ | | |

**SEE ALSO**

Gross Motor Activities
*Locomotor: #10 (p. 79)*

## The child reacts quickly and with ease TO CHANGES IN POSITION OR DIRECTION IN MOVEMENT ACTIVITIES

**REACTION SPEED/AGILITY**

| | | | | |
|---|---|---|---|---|
| MOVE | beat timbre rhythm | **1.** *Directional walk.* Children move (walk, run, skip) to music or drumbeat. When auditory signal is given (e.g., bell), they change direction, level, and/or posture. | A | |
| | | *select suitable instrumental music* | | Charts: [20] [21] |
| MOVE | phrase | **2.** Teach musical tag games, such as "Charlie Over the Water." | A, V, S | See special activities following song. |
| | | **Charlie Over the Water** | | |
| MOVE | beat rhythm form | **3.** Teach singing games and dances in which movement sequences require quick changes in stepping, direction, and position. | A, V, L, S | See special activities following songs. |
| | | **Bingo**      **Tinikling** <br> **Jack-in-the-Box**   **Way Down Yonder in the Brickyard** <br> **Step in Time**    *Step Lively* ⊙ | | |
| MOVE | beat rhythm phrase | **4.** Select suitable instrumental music and singing games in which movements of a leader are mirrored by the group. | A, V, S | |
| | | **Head, Shoulders**      *Cotton Eyed Joe* ⊙ <br> **We're Going Round the Mountain** | | |
| MOVE/ SING | beat tempo form | **5.** Teach activities involving patterned movement. | A, S | |
| | | **Miss Mary Mack** <br> **Polynesian Stick Game** <br> **Tinikling**       *Ballin' the Jack* ⊙ <br> **Walrus Hunt** | | |

| | | | | |
|---|---|---|---|---|
| MOVE/ CREATE | beat rhythm | **6.** Children decide on a movement pattern to be repeated throughout. Example: walk four beats, rest four beats, etc. | A | Activity may need to be introduced using a drumbeat rather than music. |
| | | *improvise, or select suitable recorded music, or drumbeat* | | |
| MOVE/ SING | melody form | **7.** Review "The Twelve Days of Christmas." Assign individuals or groups to respond only on a specific day when it occurs in the song. They may stand, sit, or make up a movement to be repeated each time. | A, L, S | Pass out instruments to be played only on appropriate verse. |
| | | **The Twelve Days of Christmas** | | |
| MOVE | tempo rhythm | **8.** *Movement echoes.* Teacher or child plays short rhythm phrases. Children listen first, then move accordingly. Example: | A, S | Other music concepts, such as dynamics, melodic contour, timbre, can be substituted. |
| | | *drumbeat, or improvised piano* | | |
| MOVE/ SING | beat | **9.** Children number off, one to ten, to correspond with angels in "The Angel Band." As each number is sung, children having that number stand, clap, play instrument, or move in some way. | A | For a more difficult task, have children number off to correspond with the *meter* of a song or recorded selection (e.g., "So Long"). A movement is performed on the assigned beat in each measure. |
| | | **The Angel Band** | | |
| MOVE/ CREATE | rhythm accent phrase | **10.** Play one or two measures of walking or running rhythm, accenting the last note. Children move appropriately to the rhythm and create a motion to do on the last accented beat. Example: | A | Teacher can withhold playing the accented beat for a surprise ending. |
| | | *drumbeat, or improvised piano* | | |

**SEE ALSO**

Auditory Activities
    *Perform Tempo: #7 (p. 31)*
    *Perform Pitch: #4 (p. 40)*

Gross Motor Activities
    *Balance: #1, #8 (pp. 85–86)*
    *Strength and Energy: #2 (p. 87)*

## The child uses
## EXTREMITIES SEPARATELY AND TOGETHER
## ON BOTH SIDES OF THE BODY IN MOVEMENT ACTIVITIES

### LATERALITY

| | | | | |
|---|---|---|---|---|
| MOVE | beat rhythm | **1.** Children climb and descend stairs stepping on *alternate* feet (rather than one step at a time) with a consistent rhythmic gait. | A | |
| | | **Upstairs, Downstairs** | | |
| MOVE/ SING | beat phrase | **2.** Teach movement sequences that are repeated on both sides of the body, bring hands together, or cross the midline. | A | See Appendix, p. 277, for suggestions.<br><br>See special activities following songs. |

| | | | | |
|---|---|---|---|---|
| | | Canoe Round<br>Two Little Blackbirds<br>Two Little Hands | *I've Got Two* ⊙ | |
| MOVE/<br>SING | beat<br>rhythm | **3.** Select singing games and dances in which crossing the midline is a repeated movement pattern. | A,<br>S | See special activities following songs. |
| | | The Ants Go Marching<br>Bingo | Miss Mary Mack<br>The Shoemaker | |
| MOVE/<br>SING | beat<br>rhythm<br>phrase | **4.** Select motor activities in which the extremities on each side of the body are utilized separately. | A,<br>L,<br>S | |
| | | The Ants Go Marching<br>Charlie Knows How to Beat That Drum<br>Here's the Beehive<br>I Had a Little Turtle<br>Put Your Finger in the Air | Put Your Hand on Your Shoe<br>Skippin' and Steppin'<br>Two Little Blackbirds<br>Two Little Hands | |
| MOVE/<br>SING | beat | **5.** Introduce the basic stick pattern after "Polynesian Stick Game" song is thoroughly learned. Limit to bilateral (same side) patterns before introducing sticking that crosses the midline. | A,<br>V,<br>S | See special activities following the song.<br><br>Make up stick patterns to accompany other familiar songs. |
| | | **Polynesian Stick Game** | | |

**SEE ALSO**

Auditory Activities
  *Perform Dynamics:* #4 (p. 28) (use both hands separately and together)
  *Perform Tempo:* #7 (p. 31)
  *Perform Meter:* #1 (p. 33) (use both hands separately and together)
  *Perform Rhythm:* #3, #4 (p. 36)
  *Sequencing:* #3, #5 (p. 54)

Gross Motor Activities
  *Locomotor:* #12 (p. 80)
  *Locomotor:* #21, #23 (p. 81)
  *Nonlocomotor:* #5, #7 (pp. 82–83)
  *Body Awareness:* #10—#14 (pp. 84–85)
  *Balance:* #3, #6 (pp. 85–86)

**The child demonstrates**
## UNDERSTANDING OF SPATIAL RELATIONS IN BODY MOVEMENT ACTIVITIES

# DIRECTIONALITY

| | | | | |
|---|---|---|---|---|
| MOVE/<br>SING | rhythm<br>phrase | **1.** Teach activities in which children are required to respond to directional words including right, left, in, out, forward, back. | A,<br>V,<br>L,<br>S | |
| | | Bear Hunt<br>Jack-in-the-Box<br>Stretching Song<br>Three Little Ducks | *Ballin' the Jack* ⊙<br>*Step Lively* ⊙ | |
| MOVE/<br>SING | melody<br>pitch | **2.** Children dramatize songs about high/low; up/down. | A,<br>L | |
| | | Down, Down<br>I Like to Ride the Elevator | Lots of Worms<br>Upstairs, Downstairs | |

Charts: 8 9 19

| MOVE | sound/ silence | 3. Play *Stop the Music* games to a drum-beat or suitable music. Each time the music stops, teacher (or child) calls out a direction for the class to face (i.e., "left," "right," "back of room," "front of room"). When the music resumes, children can continue in the direction they are facing, or they can move freely. | A, V, L | |
|---|---|---|---|---|
| | | **A Little Flight Music ("Stop" version)** *Stop and Go* ⊙ | | |

**SEE ALSO**

Auditory Activities
*Perform Tempo:* #7 (p. 31)
*Perform Pitch:* #1, #3, #4 (pp. 39–40)
*Perform Melody:* #1, #2, #3 (pp. 43–44)
*Create Melody:* #1 (p. 45)

Visual Activities
*Awareness:* #5 (p. 57)
*Perform Shape:* #6 (p. 64)
*Perform Direction:* #1 (p. 69)
*Create Direction:* #1, #2 (p. 69)

Gross Motor Activities
*Locomotor:* #10, #22 (pp. 79, 81)
*Nonlocomotor:* #3 (p. 82)
*Body Awareness:* #10, #11 (p. 84)
*Balance:* #1 (p. 85) (label obstacles)
*Agility:* #1, #3 ((p. 87)

---

**The child recalls and performs**
# MOTOR SEQUENCES WITHOUT THE AID OF VERBAL OR VISUAL CLUES

**MEMORY AND SEQUENCING**

| MOVE | melody rhythm phrase | 1. Children perform singing games and simple dances without verbal cues or leader. | A, S | Whenever possible, use only instrumental accompaniment. |
|---|---|---|---|---|
| | | **Bingo** **Rig-a-jig-jig** **The Shoemaker** **Step in Time**    *Ballin' the Jack* ⊙ **Valentine**    *Step Lively* ⊙ | | |
| MOVE/ SING | melody beat rhythm phrase | 2. Children perform action songs without verbal cues or leader. | A | Whenever possible, use only instrumental accompaniment. |
| | | **The Ants Go Marching**    **The Snapdragon Song** **Crocodile Song**    **Three Little Ducks** **Here's the Beehive**    **The Tree in the Valley** **Miss Mary Mack**    **Two Little Blackbirds** **Oh, My Aunt Came Back** | | |
| MOVE | beat rhythm phrase form | 3. Children perform rhythm games without verbal or visual cues. | A, V, S | |
| | | **Polynesian Stick Game**    *Alley Cat (ball dance)* ⊙ **Tinikling** | | |

90

| | | | | |
|---|---|---|---|---|
| MOVE | beat<br>rhythm<br>phrase | 4. Children perform traditional dances without cues. | A,<br>S | See Appendix, p. 275, for dance directions (polka, schottische, etc.).<br>Whenever possible, use only instrumental accompaniment. |

*My White Mouse*      *Step in Time*

**SEE ALSO**

Auditory Activities
   *Perform Tempo: #7, #8 (p. 31)*
   *Figure-Ground: #4 (p. 51)*
   *Sequencing: #3 — #6 (p. 54)*

Gross Motor Activities
   *Locomotor: #23 (p. 81)*
   *Body Awareness: #10 (p. 84)*
   *Laterality: #2 (p. 88)*

## The child interprets
## A VARIETY OF SENSORY STIMULI THROUGH BODY MOVEMENT

**MOTOR INTEGRATION**

| | | | | |
|---|---|---|---|---|
| MOVE | rhythm<br>pitch<br>timbre | 1. "Untitled Machine Music" is in three parts, each presented alone and then all are combined. Divide class into three groups, each assigned to listen specifically for the first, second, or third section of the music, and then to decide on body movement to illustrate what was heard. When all three are combined, each group will have to listen carefully to know when to begin their movements. | A,<br>S | Encourage children to create movements that represent pitch and rhythm heard in the music. |

*Untitled Machine Music* ☉

| | | | | |
|---|---|---|---|---|
| MOVE/<br>CREATE | melody<br>rhythm<br>timbre | 2. Children interpret selected program music. | A,<br>S | |

*Dukas: Sorcerer's Apprentice* ☉
*MacDowell: Of a Tailor and a Bear* ☉     Charts: 26 27 28 29

| | | | | |
|---|---|---|---|---|
| MOVE/<br>SING/<br>CREATE | | 3. Children dramatize selected familiar songs. | A,<br>L,<br>S | |

**Five Angels**     **My White Mouse**     Chart: 33
**Five Fat Turkeys**     **The Old Gray Cat**     SC: 38 - 42
**The Goat**     **Three Little Ducks**

| | | | | |
|---|---|---|---|---|
| MOVE/<br>CREATE | rhythm | 4. Children dramatize selected poetry. | A,<br>L,<br>S | |

Cat (poem)                Salvadore Squeak (poem)
The Moose and the Goose (poem)

| | | | | |
|---|---|---|---|---|
| MOVE/<br>CREATE | rhythm | 5. Divide class in groups of four to six each. Assign each group a familiar machine or household appliance to interpret as a group. Some ideas: washing machine, pop-up toaster, trashmasher, typewriter, corn popper, blender. | V,<br>L,<br>S | It is more fun if each group is unaware of the other assignments.<br><br>Some children may want to add sounds to their interpretation.<br><br>Instead of assignment, some groups may want to choose a machine themselves. |

| | | | | |
|---|---|---|---|---|
| MOVE/ CREATE | rhythm pitch timbre | 6. *Create a machine.* One person begins with a simple repetitive movement, usually involving one extremity (while remaining in a stationary place). As other children get ideas, they join *on*, each creating a movement of their own to attach someplace to the structure. Vocal sound effects can be interesting. | V, S | Beginning movements should be simple and not too strenuous, as they may have to be sustained for several minutes. |

### SEE ALSO

Auditory Activities
   *Create Dynamics:* #2, #3 (p. 29)
   *Perform Tempo:* #4, #5 (p. 30)
   *Create Tempo:* #1 (p. 31)
   *Perform Meter:* #3, #4 (p. 33)
   *Create Meter:* #1 (p. 34)
   *Perform Rhythm:* #8 (p. 36)
   *Create Rhythm:* #1 (p. 37)
   *Perform Pitch:* #1 (p. 39)

*Create Pitch:* #1 (p. 41)
*Perform Melody:* #3, #10 (pp. 44–45)
*Create Melody:* #1, #3 (p. 45)
*Perform Timbre:* #3 (p. 49)
*Create Timbre:* #9 (p. 50)
*Figure-Ground:* #6 (p. 52)
*Memory:* #11 (p. 54)

# MOTOR SKILLS
## (Fine Motor)

**The child performs**
**MOTOR TASKS REQUIRING**
**GRASP AND RELEASE MOVEMENTS**

## GRASP AND RELEASE

| | | | | |
|---|---|---|---|---|
| MOVE/ SING | beat rhythm | 1. Teach action songs in which the hands are used in open and clenched positions. | A, L | See special activities following songs. |
| | | **The Ants Go Marching**     **Pat-a-Cake** <br> **Here's the Beehive**     **The Snapdragon Song** <br> **I Will Clap My Hands**     **Stretching Song** (*fine motor version*) <br> **Jack-in-the-Box (variation)**     **Two Little Blackbirds** <br> **Miss Mary Mack**     **Two Little Hands** <br> **Open, Shut Them** | | |
| PLAY/ SING | beat rhythm melody form | 2. Teach instrumental activities in which instruments requiring a palmar grasp are included. | A, L | See special activities following songs. |
| | | **Breezes Are Blowing**     **Woodstock's Samba** <br> **Charlie Knows How to Beat That Drum** | | |
| PLAY/ SING | beat rhythm melody dynamics form | 3. Teach instrumental activities in which instruments requiring a pincer grasp are included | A, L | See special activities following songs. |
| | | **Japanese Rain Song**     **Skippin' and Steppin'** | | |
| MOVE | beat phrase | 4. Teach musical games in which objects are passed, picked up, or transferred from hand to hand. | A, V, S | |
| | | **Polynesian Stick Game** | | |

SEE ALSO

Auditory Activities
  *Perform Tempo:* #7 (p. 31)
  *Create Tempo:* #2 (p. 32)
  *Perform Meter:* #1, #2 (p. 33)
  *Create Meter:* #2 (p. 34)
  *Perform Rhythm:* #2, #10 (pp. 35–36)
  *Create Rhythm:* #2 (p. 37)
  *Perform Pitch:* #4 (p. 40)
  *Create Melody:* #2 (p. 45)
  *Create Timbre:* #2, #3, #5—#7, #11 (pp. 49–51)

Visual Activities
  *Tracking:* #1, #3, #7
  (pp. 59–60)

**The child performs**
# MOTOR TASKS REQUIRING
# FINGER STRENGTH AND SEPARATION

# FINGER STRENGTH

| MOVE/ SING | rhythm beat | 1. Teach finger play songs that require fingers to bend, stretch, curl, flutter, snap, point, etc. | A, L | See special activities following songs. |
|---|---|---|---|---|
| | | Cabin in the Wood    Stretching Song<br>Here's the Beehive    Three Little Ducks<br>I Had a Little Turtle    Two Little Blackbirds<br>The Snapdragon Song    Two Little Hands | | |
| PLAY | melody rhythm beat | 2. Play simple melodies with classroom instruments that are keyed or fingered. | A | |
| | | Candles of Hannukah    Skippin' and Steppin'<br>Down, Down    Upstairs, Downstairs<br>Pussy Willow | | |
| MOVE/ SING/ CREATE | rhythm beat | 3. Children dramatize gross motor skills with finger puppets. | A, L | |
| | | Let's Go Walking    Two Little Blackbirds<br>Rig-a-jig-jig<br>Singing Top    *finger puppets*<br>Snowflakes<br>Stretching Song    *Thomson: Walking Song* ⊙<br>Three Little Ducks | | |
| PLAY/ SING | texture harmony beat | 4. Children accompany familiar one-chord songs with Autoharp or other appropriate instrument. | A, L, S | Some songs may need to be transposed to a suitable key.* |
| | | Breezes Are Blowing    For Health and Strength<br>Candles of Hannukah    * Halloween Night<br>* Canoe Round    Roll Over<br>Chicka Hanka    Train Is A-Coming<br>Five Fat Turkeys | | |
| PLAY/ SING | texture harmony beat | 5. Children accompany familiar two-chord songs with Autoharp. | A, L, S | |

| | | The Angel Band | Hush, Little Baby | | |
| | | Charlie Over the Water | My Farm | | |
| | | Chumbara | There Was a Crooked Man | | |
| | | The Good Morning Song | The Wind Blew East | | |
| PLAY/ SING/ CREATE | | **6.** Children create accompaniments to songs using instruments that require finger strength and separation (e.g., finger cymbals, kalimba, automatic hand castanets). | | A, S | |
| | | *select suitable songs* | | | |

The child performs
## MOTOR TASKS REQUIRING WRIST MOVEMENTS (INCLUDING FLEXING, TWISTING, ROTATING, AND SNAPPING)

## WRIST MOVEMENTS

| MOVE | beat rhythm | **1.** Play an echo-clap game by clapping patterns into the outstretched palms of a partner. When the partner echoes back, both individuals must *rotate* wrists (turn palm the opposite way) to exchange roles. | A, V, S | Sticks can be used when children understand the rotation aspect. |
|---|---|---|---|---|
| PLAY/ SING | beat rhythm | **2.** Select instrumental activities. Use maracas, teaching the children to play with a wrist snap technique, rather than shaking the arm from the elbow to the shoulder. | A, V | Some children may find it easier to begin with one maraca, in the preferred hand. |
| | | **Breezes Are Blowing**   **Woodstock's Samba** *maracas* | | |
| MOVE/ SING | beat rhythm | **3.** Teach action songs that include movements involving flexing, twisting, and rotating the wrists. | A, L | See special activities following songs. |
| | | **The Ants Go Marching**   **The Shoemaker (*seated version*)** **Crocodile Song**   **The Snapdragon Song** **Pat-a-Cake**   **The Tree in the Valley** **Roll Over** | | |
| MOVE/ SING | beat rhythm | **4.** Teach songs suitable for dramatization with hand puppets. | A, V, L | |
| | | **The Ants Go Marching**   **Lots of Worms** **Crocodile Song**   **The Old Gray Cat** **Five Angels**   **Stretching Song** **I Had a Little Turtle**   **Three Little Ducks** **Jack-in-the-Box**   **Two Little Blackbirds** | | |

| PLAY/<br>SING/<br>CREATE | | **5.** Children create accompaniments to songs using instruments that require flexing, twisting, rotating, and snapping the wrists (e.g., maracas, tambourine, triangle, cabaza). | A |
|---|---|---|---|

*select suitable songs*

<br>

## The child performs
## MUSIC ACTIVITIES REQUIRING
## BOTH FINE AND GROSS MOTOR SKILLS

**FINE AND GROSS MOTOR**

| SING/<br>MOVE/<br>PLAY | beat<br>rhythm<br>phrase | **1.** Teach action songs, singing games and dances, in which both fine and gross motor skills are utilized. | A,<br>V,<br>L,<br>S |
|---|---|---|---|

The Ants Go Marching     The Snapdragon Song
Button, You Must Wander     Stretching Song
Five Angels     The Tree in the Valley
Oh, My Aunt Came Back

*Ballin' the Jack* ⊙     Charts: 20 21 30 31

| PLAY | beat<br>rhythm<br>melody<br>form | **2.** Plan activities that utilize a variety of instruments and skills | A,<br>V,<br>S |
|---|---|---|---|

**Japanese Rain Song**     **Woodstock's Samba**

| MOVE | beat<br>rhythm<br>phrase | **3.** Select suitable speech chants, poetry, or stories that can be dramatized using both fine and gross motor movement. | A,<br>V,<br>L,<br>S |
|---|---|---|---|

Bear Hunt     The Moose and the Goose (poem)
Speech Fugue     Salvadore Squeak (poem)
Cat (poem)

| MOVE | timbre<br>texture | **4.** Select suitable recorded music for children to dramatize musicians playing. | A,<br>V,<br>S |
|---|---|---|---|

*Vivaldi: Allegro* ⊙
*Hill and Dell* ⊙

| MOVE | beat | **5.** Children play instruments (or pretend to play) *on* the beat while marching. | A,<br>V,<br>S |
|---|---|---|---|

**Marching to Pretoria**     *Sousa: The Stars and Stripes Forever* ⊙

# LANGUAGE SKILLS

The music education curriculum offers many opportunities to increase language experience and facilitate speech. A differentiation needs to be made between these two skills—language being *what* is said, and speech *how* it is said. Both depend primarily on the auditory skills of discrimination, memory, and sequencing, as well as the ability to physically produce a voiced sound.

**Language** Although language can be a factor in any music activity, song is clearly the most obvious source of language experience in music. Traditionally, music education curriculums were primarily devoted to building a repertoire of song material. More recently, curriculums have treated singing (along with listening, playing instruments, and moving to music) as one way in which basic music concepts can be experienced and, hence, understood.

Language acquisition includes two dimensions: *expressive* (encoding) and *receptive* (decoding). Expressive language is necessary to express one's thoughts through the spoken or written word. Receptive language includes both the ability to understand the spoken word and the ability to comprehend language in written form. Children described as *aphasic* are usually those in whom the developmental process has failed to produce expressive language. Although a significant number of children have difficulties with receptive language, the inability to express oneself through the spoken word is far more common. Since language is the most abstract of all developmental tasks, it is frequently a secondary handicap to conditions that affect cognitive functioning, such as retardation and neurological impairment. The hearing impaired have difficulty developing language because of the physical inability to hear speech sounds accurately. Perceptually handicapped children may have language deficiencies because of their inability to discriminate, remember, and sequence speech sounds.

Children who are language handicapped may
- lack the ability to coordinate breath and vocal mechanisms
- lack vocabulary
- speak in incomplete sentences
- demonstrate inaccurate speech rhythms and inflections
- have poor articulation of speech sounds
- be unable to remember speech sounds
- mix up the syntactical order of words in a sentence
- mix up the order of syllables within a word
- use incorrect word endings or tenses, and make other grammatical errors
- demonstrate language development significantly below the norm

It should be emphasized that while one child seldom exhibits all these problems, a language-handicapped child will *consistently* demonstrate a cluster of them. A word of caution should be made about overreacting to any problem other than failure to develop language at all. Syntactical and grammatical errors, articulation problems, and dysfluency are all considered perfectly normal during certain stages of the developmental process.

If one considers the natural developmental sequence of language in infants, it is apparent that the child spends many months vocalizing before being ready to verbalize meaningful speech sounds. This time is mainly spent learning to listen and attach meaning to sounds that are heard. Gradually the infant begins to experiment with reproducing some of these sounds. It is during this vocalization period that the muscles of the mouth and tongue are conditioned for speech, the breath control increases, and the child learns to reproduce, with accuracy, speech sounds heard. Random vocal sounds eventually develop into sounds characteristic of the pitch and rhythms of the native tongue. It is interesting that the acquisition of the mother tongue follows the same developmental sequence in every country. When children lag in language development, it is wise to keep in mind the importance of the preverbal stage and focus goals on those skills needed to *prepare* for verbalization before attempting specific verbal goals.

Language does not consist *only* of vocabulary. Although vocabulary is certainly a prerequisite to both *receptive* and *expressive* language, a child will never become competent in communication skills without mastering the syntax and grammar of language. Children need many opportunities to use language to express their needs and thoughts, no matter how limited their vocabulary may be. The child who uses one-word statements or responses exclusively must be guided to the next level of expressive communication. Two-word sentences may consist of subject/verb, verb/object, subject/object, or any of these with a modifier. The three-word sentence, which includes subject, verb, *and* object, is usually achieved between the ages of two and three in the average youngster. In language-handicapped children, this milestone in language development will undoubtedly occur much later, perhaps even years after most children have reached it.

Many song collections for children are largely made up of folk songs, which in their authentic versions often are not models of modern English grammar and syntax. Children still in the developmental language stage are unable to recognize these grammatical differences, and it may be wise to change the words to more acceptable forms or look for other material. Similarly, children of ethnic backgrounds should never be given the impression that their speech or language is inferior or incorrect. Linguists have studied the speech and language patterns of certain black American groups, for example, and confirm them to be bona fide dialects. The child who learns English at home that is characterized by speech patterns and word forms that are slightly different will learn, as many Europeans have, when and where each is appropriately used. Our job as educators is to ensure that each child develops language skills for communication with as many people as possible.

Sign language can be used in singing with children who must rely on this medium for language communication. In fact, some songs can become useful action songs when signs are added, and they give a very beautiful visual effect. However, care should be taken to select only songs in which signs can convey adequately the rhythm and meaning of the words without compromising correct grammar, tenses, or word endings. Teachers should also be aware that children who sing and sign will undoubtedly focus more attention on watching the teacher sign than on listening to the teacher's voice. The use of sign language is quite limiting when teaching music concepts and skills. As one would expect, there are very few signs that relate to music terminology (beat, rhythm, melody, and so forth). As sign vocabulary is constantly being revised and expanded to meet the language needs of the deaf in modern society, perhaps we can look forward to more relevant music vocabulary in the near future. It is also worth mentioning that sign language is sometimes used as a teaching aid with *hearing* children in whom neurological or emotional disorders have hindered language and speech development.

**Speech**   Poor speech articulation can be due to physical problems (e.g., teeth and mouth formation, oversized tongue), motor involvement, or auditory perception problems. Vowel sounds are usually secured in the vocalization stage. When consonants are added, speech sounds begin to emerge. The first consonant sounds to develop during infancy are the plosives, such as *b* and *p*, along with *m*, which often is first produced accidentally when the baby vocalizes a vowel with a sucking reflex. High-frequency sounds (e.g., *s, t*) and blends (*sh, ch*) may come as much as a year or two later. The timetable and sequence of development are often quite different for a speech-handicapped child. To avoid confusion, the music teacher must be cognizant of the specific goals and procedures of other professionals working with the child in this area (e.g., speech therapist, classroom teacher). Once it is determined which speech sounds are the focus of attention, music activities can be selected that utilize these same sounds.

Songs with nonsense syllables and foreign language texts are good sources for articulation experiences. However, if children have serious *language deficiencies* in addition to articulation problems, careful consideration should be given to the propriety of using these songs. If children are unable to comprehend that nonsense syllables are speech sounds without meaning or that language sounds differ from country to country, it would seem wise to avoid these materials.

Speech of the deaf is most often characterized by a lack of pitch variance, by improper rhythm, and by misplaced accents. In English, stressed syllables are most often accompanied by a higher voice pitch. Try saying the following, accenting the underlined word. "I know!" "Oh, no." "Oh, oh." In each case, the tendency is for the voice to rise in pitch on the underlined word. Singing helps children discover and extend the pitch range of their voices, but unless this opportunity is afforded to the hearing impaired while they are still young and developing speech, it is unlikely to become part of their natural speech pattern. Experiences in practicing the melodies and rhythms of speech are definitely beneficial for all children and are essential for the hearing-impaired child. The Orff approach to music education, which combines speech, music, and movement, has been very successfully used with speech-handicapped children.

To summarize, language and speech difficulties often accompany other handicapping conditions. Language skills include both the ability to understand language and the ability to use language in expressing thoughts and ideas. Meaningful speech is preceded by a period of vocalization in which the physical and aural aspects of speech are developed. Music activities in general, and singing in particular, offer many excellent opportunities to aid language development and speech articulation in children. Specific goals include vocalization, breath and muscle control, verbalization, receptive language, expressive language, and accuracy of speech rhythms and inflections.

## LANGUAGE SKILLS

| The child demonstrates<br>**ABILITY TO VOCALIZE** | | | | **VOCALIZATION** | |
|---|---|---|---|---|---|
| **SING** | vocalization | 1. Sing songs to the children that include sustained vowel sounds (e.g., *oo, oh, ah*). Encourage children to join in when these sounds occur in the songs. | **A, M** | | Show direction of voice with hand or body. |

| | | | | |
|---|---|---|---|---|
| | | **Halloween Night**<br>**The Wind Blew East** *Tah-boo* ⊙ | | |
| SING | vocalization<br>pitch | 2. Encourage children to imitate familiar sounds in the environment, especially those that slide from low to high, or high to low (e.g., sirens, wind, jet plane). | A,<br>V | Pictures will be helpful in relating sound to object. |
| | | *live or recorded environmental sounds* | | Charts: 5 6 7 19 34<br>SC: 1 - 9 |
| SING | vocalization<br>pitch<br>rhythm | 3. Sing echo-type and call-and-response songs that have short phrases. Encourage children when they make a response that approximates accurate rhythm and pitch inflection. | A | |
| | | **The Ants Go Marching**   **I Like You**<br>**Chicka Hanka**   **John the Rabbit**<br>**The Good Morning Song**   **Train Is A-Coming**<br>**Hello!** | | |
| SING | vocalization<br>pitch<br>timbre | 4. Sing songs that include animal sounds. Encourage *vocal simulation* of actual sounds rather than melodic patterns for each animal. | A,<br>V | Pictures will help to relate sound to animal. |
| | | **My Farm**   **Three Little Ducks** | | SC: 13 - 20<br>29, 30, 31 |
| SING | vocalization<br>pitch<br>timbre<br>rhythm | 5. Sing songs that include environmental sounds. | A,<br>V | Pictures will help to relate sound to object. |
| | | **Chicka Hanka**<br>**Down at the Station**<br>**The Wind Blew East** | | Charts: 5 6 7 34 |
| SING/<br>CREATE | vocalization<br>pitch<br>timbre | 6. Help children create a *vocal* sound story around a favorite theme, story, or picture. | A | Begin by making a list of selected sounds. Theme suggestions:<br>• visit to a construction site<br>• sounds of traffic<br>• sounds of machinery<br>• at the park<br>• trip to a supermarket |
| | | *select pictures and/or stories* | | Charts: 5 6 7 34<br>35 36 |

**The child demonstrates**
**ADEQUATE BREATH AND MUSCLE**
**CONTROL FOR SPEECH**

## BREATH AND MUSCLE CONTROL

| | | | | |
|---|---|---|---|---|
| PLAY | pitch<br>rhythm<br>timbre | 1. Help children make simple wind instruments, such as straw flutes or tissue paper combs. When instruments are made, play echo games producing long and short tones, different pitches. | A,<br>FM | Listen to a recording of a wind instrument, such as "Hill and Dell." Invite a student who plays a wind instrument to give a demonstration. |
| | | *straws, tissue paper, combs, bottles, plastic tubing, etc.* | | |

| | | | | |
|---|---|---|---|---|
| PLAY | pitch<br>rhythm | 2. Child must be able to *easily* produce a tone on a selected simple wind instrument. Experiment with making high and low sounds as well as long and short ones. | A,<br>V | Charts or graphic illustrations can be used to show duration and direction. |
| | | *simple wind instruments (kazoo, slide whistle, melody flute, recorder, reed horn, etc.)*<br><br>*Melodicas, Pianicas* | | Charts: 15 19 |
| PLAY | rhythm | 3. Select an appropriate call-and-response song for which the child may play the response on a suitable wind instrument. | A | If single pitched instrument is not available, holes or keys can be taped down on other instruments to sound appropriate pitch.<br><br>Appropriate keys on Melodicas and Pianicas can be color coded with tape. |
| | | **The Ants Go Marching**    **John the Rabbit**<br>**The Good Morning Song**    **Train Is A-Coming**<br>**Hello!**      *simple wind instruments* | | |
| | rhythm<br>timbre | 4. Play echo games using only mouth sounds (e.g., tongue clicks, lip smacks, pops, hisses). | A | Create rondos or sound stories. |
| SING | duration<br>timbre | 5. Sing songs to the children that include speech sounds, encouraging them to join in when these sounds occur in the songs. | A,<br>V | Some children may be ready for visual reinforcement of letters. |
| | | **Here's the Beehive**    **Tra La La La**<br>**Letters and Names**    **Zippers**<br>**Singing Top** | | |
| SING/<br>MOVE | dynamics | 6. Learn activities in which attention to the dynamic level of specific words, phrases, or verses is important to express the mood. | A | |
| | | **The Ants Go Marching**      **Jack-in-the-Box**<br>Bear Hunt      **John Jacob Jingelheimer Schmidt**<br>**Charlie Knows How to Beat That Drum**   **The Old Gray Cat**<br>**Halloween Night** | | |
| CHANT | dynamics<br>timbre<br>rhythm<br>pitch | 7. Learn songs and chants that include suitable speech ostinatos. | A | |
| | | **Chicka Hanka**    Speech Fugue<br>**Japanese Rain Song** | | |

| The child demonstrates | | | | RECEPTIVE LANGUAGE |
|---|---|---|---|---|
| **COMPREHENSION OF SONG LYRICS** | | | | |
| SING/<br>MOVE | beat<br>rhythm<br>phrase<br>tempo | 1. Learn songs in which short or repeated phrases describe movements. | A,<br>V,<br>M | Pictures or gestures that illustrate movements may be helpful to relate action with word in the beginning. They should be withdrawn as soon as possible. |

99

| | | | | |
|---|---|---|---|---|
| | | **I Will Clap My Hands**<br>**Put Your Finger in the Air**<br>**Put Your Hand on Your Shoe** | | Chart: 31 |
| SING/<br>MOVE | beat<br>rhythm<br>phrase<br>tempo<br>dynamics | **2.** Learn action songs and singing games in which more complex directions are given in the lyrics of the songs. | A,<br>M | |
| | | **Charlie Knows How to Beat That Drum**<br>**Letters and Names**<br>**Open, Shut Them** | **Stretching Song**<br>**Two Little Hands** | |
| SING/<br>MOVE | beat<br>rhythm<br>phrase<br>tempo | **3.** Learn simple dances in which song lyrics describe dance steps. | A,<br>V,<br>M | It may be helpful to provide pictures or models of different steps for beginners. |
| | | **The Shoemaker** (*dance*)<br>**Step in Time**      *Ballin' the Jack* ⊙ | | Charts: 20 21 30 |
| MOVE | | **4.** Children perform activities #1 - #3 above without the help of visual or gesture cues. | A,<br>M | |
| | | *select songs from activities #1 - #3 above* | | |
| SING/<br>MOVE | beat<br>rhythm<br>phrase<br>tempo | **5.** Sing songs in which some words are left out, sung silently, or replaced with actions. | A,<br>V,<br>M | |
| | | **Bingo**      **John Jacob Jingelheimer Schmidt**<br>**Cabin in the Wood** | | |
| SING/<br>MOVE | repetition/<br>contrast<br>form<br>melody | **6.** Sing or listen to songs that tell a story. Ask children to tell the story in their own words. | A<br><br>V | Begin with short songs and gradually increase to songs with several verses.<br><br>Nonverbal children can draw illustrations, respond to appropriate pictures, or dramatize their stories. |
| | | **Five Angels**     **I Had a Little Turtle**<br>**Five Fat Turkeys**   **The Man in Blue**<br>**The Giant's Shoes**   **The Old Gray Cat** | | |
| SING/<br>MOVE | | **7.** Sing or listen to songs with silly or nonsense lyrics. Ask children to explain what makes them ridiculous. | A | |
| | | **The Ants Go Marching**   **Throw It Out the Window**<br>**Crocodile Song**         **What Can Make a Hippopotamus Smile?**<br>**The Goat**                **When Sammy Put the Paper on the Wall**<br>**The Snapdragon Song** | | |
| SING | melody<br>pitch<br>rhythm | **8.** *I See Something.* Teacher selects a simple tune and sings a brief description of something in the room. Example: | A,<br>V | |

*Teacher:* I see some-thing that is big and round. ___
*Child:* The clock is some-thing that is big and round. ___

| SING | pitch rhythm beat | **1.** Learn call-and-response songs in games in which the response is one or two words. | A | |
|------|------|------|------|------|
| | | **The Ants Go Marching** **John the Rabbit** **The Good Morning Song** **Train Is A-Coming** **Hello!** | | |
| SING | pitch melody rhythm beat | **2.** Learn call-and-response style songs in which the response is a phrase. | A | |
| | | **False Face** **The Roll Call Song** **The Goat** **Two Little Hands** **I Like You** **Valentine** **Put On a Happy Face** *Tah-boo* ⊙ | | |
| SING | pitch melody rhythm beat | **3.** Select songs for beginning experiences that are short and have very simple or repetitive language. | A, V | For an example of a suitable song to learn using sign language, see "My Father's House." |
| | | **Down, Down** **Put Your Finger in the Air** **Hello!** **Train Is A-Coming** **I Will Clap My Hands** **We're Going Round the Mountain** **Let's Go Walking** **When the Train Comes Along** **My Father's House** | | |

The child uses
**LANGUAGE TO COMMUNICATE IDEAS MUSICALLY**

**EXPRESSIVE LANGUAGE**

| SING/ CREATE | melody rhythm beat | **1.** Sing songs for which children can create new verses by supplying one or two appropriate words (i.e., nouns or verbs). | A, M | If used as a movement activity, rhythm must be changed appropriately for running, skipping, etc.* |
|------|------|------|------|------|
| | | **The Angel Band** **My Farm** **The Good Morning Song** **Train Is A-Coming** *Let's Go Walking** **When the Train Comes Along** | | |
| SING/ CREATE | melody rhythm beat phrase | **2.** Sing songs in which children are required to supply a complete sentence to create new verses. | A | |
| | | **Five Angels** **Put Your Finger in the Air** **Miss Mary Mack** **What Shall We Do?** | | |
| SING/ CREATE | melody rhythm beat phrase form | **3.** Help children create new verses by supplying the first statement and asking them to supply an appropriate response. Example ("Joe Turner Blues"): **Statement:** They tell me it will not rain today. (teacher)                    *(repeat)* **Response:** The sun is out and it is going to stay. (child) | A | When children become proficient in providing responses, they can create both statement and response. |

| SING/<br>CREATE | melody<br>rhythm<br>beat<br>phrase | **4.** Sing songs in which children are required to supply *rhyming* words to create new verses. | A | |

| | | **Hush, Little Baby**    **New River Train**<br>**Miss Mary Mack**    **Put Your Hand on Your Shoe** | | |

| SING/<br>CREATE | melody<br>rhythm | **5.** Help children create new verses for "When the Train Comes Along" by supplying *synonyms* (like words) or *antonyms* (opposite words). Example:<br>. . . freezing . . . cold<br>. . . freezing . . . hot<br>. . . windy . . . cool<br>. . . raining . . . dry | A | Vocabulary possibilities can be increased by changing subject to "I" (e.g., "I may be tired, . . . late . . ."). |

| | | **When the Train Comes Along** | | |

| SING/<br>MOVE | melody<br>rhythm | **6.** Discuss the use of *homonyms* (words that are spelled the same but have different meanings) in "The Snapdragon Song." Point out those that are interpreted as verbs when adding suggested movements (e.g., snap/*snap*dragon; cigar *box*). | A | |

| | | **The Snapdragon Song** | | |

## The child demonstrates
## ABILITY TO USE ACCURATE RHYTHMS AND PITCH INFLECTIONS IN SPEECH

## SPEECH RHYTHM AND INFLECTION

| PLAY | rhythm<br>pitch | **1.** Using either drums or melody instruments, help children play the rhythm of their first names as they say them. The higher pitched instrument is played on accented syllables. Example:<br><br>Pau-*line*  ♪│♪  *Mi*-chael  ♫ | A,<br>M | Full names can be attempted when ready. |

| | | *two drums of contrasting pitch; or bass xylophone; or bells with pitches a third apart* | | |

| PLAY/<br>CHANT/<br>CREATE | rhythm<br>meter<br>pitch | **2.** *Play a talking drum game.* Choose a topic that is limited in scope. After topic is decided and announced to the class, one child (or the teacher) beats the rhythm of a statement about the topic on the drum. Class tries to guess the exact sentence. When the sentence is discovered, the drum is passed to another child for another statement on the same topic.<br><br>Example: (topic—Mary's dress)<br><br>1st child: Mary's dress is green.  ♩ ♫ ♫ ♪ ‿<br><br>2nd child: It has a belt.  ♩ ♫ ♪ ─<br><br>3rd child: It has buttons.  ♩ ♩ ♩ ♫ ‿ | A,<br>M | As children gain proficiency in recognizing speech patterns, topics can be broadened to include more abstract subjects (e.g., weather, current events).<br><br>*Note:* The triplet is a common rhythm in the English language. Children must understand and be able to perform triplets before this activity can be successful. |

| PLAY/<br>CHANT/<br>CREATE | rhythm<br>meter<br>pitch | 3. Children suggest favorite kinds of ice cream or candy. Each suggestion is played and *notated* in either standard or graphic notation. Indicate strong beats or accents and inflections. Example: | V | See *Note* above.<br><br>Suggestions can be combined and sequenced to create a speech chant. |
|---|---|---|---|---|

*low drum or bongo drum*

| PLAY | rhythm<br>beat<br>repetition/<br>contrast | 4. Children select appropriate instruments to accompany each verse of "The Twelve Days of Christmas." The *melodic rhythm* of each verse and each repetition is played on chosen instrument. Example: | A,<br>M | |
|---|---|---|---|---|

**The Twelve Days of Christmas**
*assorted classroom instruments*

| CHANT/<br>CREATE | rhythm<br>beat | 5. Help children compose a Haiku verse to be used as a speech ostinato with "Japanese Rain Song." | M | Practice each line separately as an ostinato before attempting to combine.<br><br>Be sure rhythms are those of natural speech.<br><br>Don't forget expressive touches, such as pitch, dynamics, and accents. |
|---|---|---|---|---|

**Japanese Rain Song**

| SING | tempo<br>rhythm<br>melody<br>timbre | 1. Learn songs that include repetitious consonants. | A | |
|---|---|---|---|---|

| **The Best of Buddies**<br>**Breezes Are Blowing**<br>**Chicka Hanka**<br>**Five Fat Turkeys**<br>**John Jacob Jingelheimer Schmidt**<br>**Miss Mary Mack**<br>**My White Mouse** | **Rig-a-jig-jig**<br>Speech Fugue<br>**Ticky Ticky Tambo**<br>**Tra La La La**<br>**The Twelve Days of Christmas**<br>**When Sammy Put the Paper on the Wall**<br>**Zippers** |
|---|---|

| SING | tempo<br>rhythm<br>melody | 2. Learn songs with repetitious foreign language or nonsense words. | A | |
|---|---|---|---|---|

| | | | | |
|---|---|---|---|---|
| | **Chumbara**<br>**Japanese Rain Song**<br>**Ticky Ticky Tambo**<br>**Walrus Hunt** | *Tah-boo* ⊙ | | |
| **SING** | rhythm<br>melody<br>timbre | **3.** Select melodies that can be sung with scat syllables (e.g., doot, bop) that could be appropriately substituted for lyrics. | A | Select syllables for speech value. |
| | **The Best of Buddies**<br>**Put On a Happy Face** | *Alley Cat* ⊙<br>*I've Got Two* ⊙<br>*One of These Things* ⊙ | | |
| **SING** | timbre | **4.** Learn songs with rhyming words. Point out the words that rhyme, or let children discover them. | A | |
| | **The Ants Go Marching**<br>**Hush, Little Baby**<br>**Joe Turner Blues**<br>**Miss Mary Mack** | **New River Train**<br>**Oh, My Aunt Came Back**<br>**Put Your Hand on Your Shoe** | | |
| **SING/ CREATE** | beat<br>tempo<br>rhythm<br>timbre<br>dynamics | **5.** Help children create a vocal piece using vowels and consonant sounds (e.g., *sh, th, z, p, f, v*). | A, V | Notate.<br><br>To reinforce letter association, have children find pictures or draw objects with names that begin with the letters used.<br><br>Don't forget to vary dynamics and rhythm. |
| **CHANT** | beat<br>tempo<br>rhythm<br>timbre<br>dynamics<br>pitch | **6.** Select poems with interesting and beneficial speech sounds for choral speaking or interpretation. | A | When performing as a choral speaking piece, don't forget dynamics, pitch, rhythm, and voice timbre.<br><br>Use as a basis for a sound piece, adding instruments if desired. |
| | | | V | To reinforce word association, have children find pictures that illustrate each word in the poem, "Sound of Water." |
| | Sound of Water (poem) | | | |
| **SING/ CHANT** | rhythm | **7.** Learn songs and chants that challenge articulation. | A | |
| | **Miss Mary Mack**<br>Speech Fugue | **Throw It Out the Window**<br>**Ticky Ticky Tambo** | | |

# SOCIAL SKILLS

Human beings are naturally social. All children need appropriate social skills, particularly when working or playing with others. Sharing, cooperation, judgment, independence, patience, tolerance, and sensitivity to others are all attributes of the socially mature individual. All these belong to that part of intelligence known as the *affective domain*. Since music is basically a social activity, music education activities inherently include affective goals. Social skills can be emphasized when an activity is designed to foster ego strength, interaction skills, judgment, and responsibility. We must keep in mind the importance of social competence to both ego and educational development. Young children are still developing control systems that will help them deal with frustration and disappointment as adults. Some of our more seriously disturbed individuals have failed to develop those controls that would enable them to cope more successfully with frustration, failure, unsatisfactory environmental influences, or poor self-concept.

Children who lack appropriate social skills exhibit *some* of the following characteristic behaviors.
Reluctance to
- participate in music activities, especially in group settings
- share materials, skills, or ideas
- assume or relinquish leadership roles

Unwillingness to
- respect rules of the learning environment

Inability to
- accept and learn from constructive criticism
- realistically appraise personal strengths and weaknesses
- appreciate strengths and tolerate weaknesses in others
- foresee consequences of behavior
- be aware of their effect on others
- recognize antisocial behaviors or attitudes
- work with others in small- or large-group activities
- adapt easily to new situations
- accept responsibility
- work independently
- control behavior, especially in stimulating or unstructured situations

Children who lack social competence often have a poor overall perception of themselves and their worth. Some may fear failure to such an extent that they give up trying altogether. Activities for these children should be success-oriented in that a degree of success is ensured. However, it would be unrealistic to continually present experiences in which total success is guaranteed. The child must learn to cope with failure by learning from it and, ideally, learning how to turn it into success.

Problem behavior is generally the result of failure to develop certain social skills. Children who exhibit acting-out behaviors in school are likely to be restless, to be easily distracted, and to find it difficult to finish what they begin. Learning problems often go untreated because the smoke screen created by disordered behavior prevents teachers from recognizing them. (See Behavior Disabilities, p. 257.) Usually, these youngsters are unable to foresee the consequences of unproductive and uncooperative behavior. They may lack inner controls and coping strategies, thus succumbing to temper outbursts, impulsiveness, or defiant behavior. Because of their disruptive behavior, apathy, or aggressiveness, problem children are usually rejected by their peers, which compounds their difficulties.

Some children fail to develop social skills because of lack of opportunity. Children with other handicaps frequently have limited contact with peers (especially nonhandicapped peers) during the developmental years. The nature of some conditions (e.g., hearing impairment, physical disabilities) limits social interaction and opportunities to develop independence, responsibility, and personal strengths. This is one reason that the Education for All Handicapped Children Act has placed a high priority on programs for preschool (age three and up) handicapped youngsters. Operation Headstart has already been instrumental in mainstreaming children with handicaps, thereby giving them a head start in developing social skills that might otherwise be inadequate for public school success.

Music is a social activity. It is most often performed and enjoyed in groups. The noncompetitive nature and inherent structure of music activities provide a highly suitable environment in which to foster social skill growth. Participation in music activities unobtrusively demands cooperation and conformity (e.g., "Results are more pleasing if we sing or play in the same key . . . tempo."). Also, someone must assume the responsibility of leader, although occasionally this role can and should change among members of the group. While some children are cooperative when they are in leadership roles, they become behavior problems when asked to follow someone else's direction. Frequent opportunities for each child to experience both the role of leader and the role of follower are characteristic of many music activities presented in this chapter. Activities of this type can help prepare children for the reality of shifting roles in real-life situations. Although some children may need to spend time in individual music sessions before they are ready to cooperate with structure and successfully interact with other children, the group setting is unquestionably the best vehicle for achieving social competence.

Since social skills are affective, they directly relate to how an individual feels about self and environment.

These skills, or lack of them, are obvious whenever the child interacts with others. Social skills should be considered when planning how specific activities will be organized. Affective goal progress is less easily measured than cognitive areas in which facts and performance skills can be objectively assessed. Teachers must constantly be alert to notice individual behaviors that may indicate gains or losses in developing social competence. Timing is of great importance when introducing a new social challenge. One must be certain that the child is ready to accept it, as failure could result in serious setbacks to achieving social maturity.

To summarize, every individual needs to develop social skills in order to realize personal fulfillment and acceptance as a valued member of society. The socially mature individual has a good self-concept, gets along well with others, accepts responsibility, and uses good judgment. Music is a social activity and has its greatest value in group settings. All music activities provide experiences that foster social skill growth.

## The child willingly responds
## TO CHARACTERISTICS OF OWN IDENTITY

| SING/ MOVE | melody rhythm | 1. Sing songs in which children respond with, or to, their names. | A, V, L | A mirror or photograph is a good visual reinforcement for children who have yet to develop a concept of themselves. |
|---|---|---|---|---|
| | | **Charlie Knows How to Beat That Drum** **Charlie Over the Water** **Letters and Names** | **Marty** **The Roll Call Song** **Somebody's Knocking at Your Door** | |
| SING/ MOVE | melody rhythm | 2. Sing songs in which children respond appropriately to personal pronouns, such as "you," "me," "I." | A, V, L | Use a mirror or photograph, as above. |
| | | **False Face** **The Good Morning Song** **I Like You** **I See You** **I Will Clap My Hands** | **Jack-in-the-Box** **Put Your Hand on Your Shoe** **Stretching Song** **Two Little Hands** **Valentine** | |
| SING/ MOVE | melody rhythm | 3. Sing songs that emphasize personal worth. | A, L | |
| | | **The Best of Buddies** **False Face** **I Like to Ride the Elevator** **I Like You** **Jack-in-the-Box** | **Letters and Names** **Stop! Look! Listen!** **What Shall We Do?** **Valentine** *I've Got Two* ⊙ | |
| SING | melody rhythm | 4. Sing songs that reflect a specific mood. | A, M, L | Dramatize those that are appropriate. |
| | | **For Health and Strength** **My Father's house** | **Put On a Happy Face** | Chart: 25 |

**SEE ALSO**

Auditory Activities
  *Perform Rhythm: #5 (p. 36)*
  *Perform Melody: #4 (p. 44)*

Visual Activities
  *Awareness: #1 (p. 57)*

| SING/ MOVE | melody rhythm beat form | 1. Learn partner singing games and dances. | A, M, L | Beginning activities are more successful for some children if they are not required to hold hands. Hoops, scarves, or ropes can be used to join partners. |
|---|---|---|---|---|
| | | **Bingo** (*dance*)     **Rig-a-jig-jig**<br>**I Roll the Ball**     **The Shoemaker** (*dance*)<br>**Miss Mary Mack**     **Step in Time**<br>**My White Mouse** (*dance*)     **Valentine**<br>**Pat-a-Cake**     **Way Down Yonder in the Brickyard**<br>**Polynesian Stick Game** | | |
| SING/ MOVE/ CREATE | melody rhythm beat | 2. Create movement or dramatizations to appropriate songs or other sources. | A, M | See Appendix, p. 276, for suggested body movements. |
| | | **The Best of Buddies**     **Two Little Blackbirds**<br>**The Giant's Shoes**<br>**The Goat**     The Moose and the Goose (poem)<br>**Japanese Rain Song** | | |
| SING/ MOVE | melody rhythm form | 3. Select appropriate echo or call-and-response activities for partners. | A, M, L | |
| | | **The Good Morning Song**<br>**I Like You**<br>**Valentine**     *I See Something*<br>      (see Language/Receptive Language, #8, p. 100) | | |
| SING/ MOVE | rhythm beat form | 4. Learn musical ball games for partners. | A, M | |
| | | **I Roll the Ball**     *Alley Cat (ball dance)* ⊙ | | |

**SEE ALSO**

Auditory Activities
    *Perform Meter:* #6 (p. 33)
    *Create Timbre:* #1 (p. 49)

Gross Motor Activities
    *Locomotor:* #8 (p. 79) (with partner)
    *Nonlocomotor:* #2 (p. 82)
    *Body Awareness:* #10 (p. 84)
    *Balance:* #1 (p. 85)

The child successfully interacts
## IN SMALL GROUP MUSIC ACTIVITIES

(PEER RELATIONS) SMALL GROUP

| PLAY | beat rhythm form melody pitch | 1. Plan instrumental activities for small ensembles. | A, V, FM | |
|---|---|---|---|---|
| | | **Breezes Are Blowing**     **Woodstock's Samba**<br>**Japanese Rain Song**<br>*classroom instruments* | | |

| | | | | |
|---|---|---|---|---|
| SING/ MOVE | beat rhythm form | **2.** Plan singing games and dances suitable for up to eight children. | A, V, M | For samba dance, see Appendix, p. 275. |

| | | |
|---|---|---|
| **Button, You Must Wander** | **Tinikling** | |
| **Charlie Over the Water** | **Woodstock's Samba** | |
| **Polynesian Stick Game** | | |

| | | | | |
|---|---|---|---|---|
| SING/ MOVE/ CREATE | beat rhythm form | **3.** Plan creative movement and dramatization activities suitable for up to eight children. | A, M | |

| | | |
|---|---|---|
| **Breezes Are Blowing** | **Five Fat Turkeys** | |
| **Elephant Song** | **The Old Gray Cat** | |
| **Five Angels** | **Three Little Ducks** | |

### SEE ALSO

Auditory Activities
   *Perform Tempo: #7 (p. 31)*
   *Create Rhythm: #7 (p. 38)*
   *Create Timbre: #1, #5 (pp. 49–50)*
   *Figure-Ground: #6 (p. 52)*

Visual Activities
   *Perform Quantity: #1 (p. 67)*

Gross Motor Activities
   *Motor Integration: #1, #5, #6 (pp. 91–92)*

## The child successfully interacts IN LARGE GROUP MUSIC ACTIVITIES

### (PEER RELATIONS) LARGE GROUP

| | | | | |
|---|---|---|---|---|
| SING/ MOVE | melody rhythm | **1.** Learn action songs and chants in which individuals are chosen to be central figures or leaders. | A, V, M, L | |

| | | |
|---|---|---|
| Bear Hunt | **Oh, My Aunt Came Back** | |
| **Cabin in the Wood** | **Open, Shut Them** | |
| **Letters and Names** | Speech Fugue | |

| | | | | |
|---|---|---|---|---|
| SING/ MOVE | beat rhythm form | **2.** Learn singing games and dances suitable for large groups. | A, V, M, L | For samba dance, see Appendix, p. 275. |

| | | |
|---|---|---|
| **Button, You Must Wander** | | |
| **Rig-a-jig-jig** | | |
| **Woodstock's Samba** | *Step Lively* ⊙ | |

| | | | | |
|---|---|---|---|---|
| SING/ MOVE/ CREATE | beat rhythm form timbre | **3.** Plan creative movement and dramatization activities suitable for large groups. | A, M | |

| | | |
|---|---|---|
| **The Ants Go Marching** | **Lots of Worms** | |
| **Down, Down** | **Singing Top** | |
| **Let's Go Walking** | **Snowflakes** | |
| **A Little Flight Music** | **What Shall We Do?** | |

| | | | | |
|---|---|---|---|---|
| SING/ PLAY | beat rhythm form timbre | **4.** Arrange instrumental activities for large groups. | A, V, FM | |

| | | | |
|---|---|---|---|
| | Japanese Rain Song<br>The Twelve Days of Christmas<br>*classroom instruments* | Woodstock's Samba | |

SEE ALSO

Auditory Activities<br>*Perform Tempo: #7 (p. 31)*

Visual Activities<br>*Tracking: #4 (p. 60)*<br>*Create Distance: #1, #2 (p. 71)*

## The child functions independently<br>IN APPROPRIATE MUSIC ACTIVITIES

INDEPENDENCE

| | | | |
|---|---|---|---|
| **SING/<br>PLAY** | melody<br>rhythm<br>beat<br>form<br>timbre | **1.** Select instrumental activities in which the degree of independent participation is commensurate with individual abilities. | A,<br>V,<br>FM |
| | | **Breezes Are Blowing**<br>**Charlie Knows How to Beat That Drum**<br>**Joe Turner Blues**<br>*classroom instruments* | **Skippin' and Steppin'**<br>**The Twelve Days of Christmas**<br>**Woodstock's Samba** |
| **SING/<br>MOVE** | melody<br>rhythm<br>form | **2.** Select singing games and dances in which the degree of independent participation is commensurate with individual abilities. | A,<br>V,<br>M,<br>L |
| | | **Charlie Over the Water**     **Put Your Hand on Your Shoe**<br>**I Will Clap My Hands**     **Rig-a-jig-jig**<br>**Jack-in-the-Box**     **Somebody's Knocking at Your Door**<br>**Oh, My Aunt Came Back**     **Way Down Yonder in the Brickyard** | |
| **SING/<br>MOVE<br>CREATE** | melody<br>rhythm<br>beat<br>form<br>timbre | **3.** Select activities utilizing creative movement and song dramatizations in which the degree of independent participation is commensurate with individual abilities. | A,<br>M |
| | | **The Angel Band**     **Rolling Along**<br>**Breezes Are Blowing**     **Snowflakes**<br>**Five Angels**     **Three Little Ducks**<br>**Five Fat Turkeys**     **Two Little Blackbirds**<br>**Man on the Flying Trapeze** | |
| **SING** | melody<br>rhythm | **4.** Plan activities in which an independent singing response is commensurate with individual language abilities. | A,<br>L |
| | | **False Face**     **The Roll Call Song**<br>**The Good Morning Song**     **The Twelve Days of Christmas**<br>**Hello!** | |

SEE ALSO

Auditory Activities<br>*Perform Melody: #4 (p. 44)*

## The child demonstrates
# ABILITY TO INTERCHANGE ROLES OF LEADER AND FOLLOWER SOCIAL ROLES

| SING/ MOVE | melody rhythm form | 1. Select singing games and dances in which central figures or leaders change frequently. | A, M, L |
|---|---|---|---|

| | | |
|---|---|---|
| **Button, You Must Wander** **Charlie Knows How to Beat That Drum** **Elephant Song** **False Face** | | **Rig-a-jig-jig** **Way Down Yonder in the Brickyard** **We're Going Round the Mountain** |

**SEE ALSO**

Auditory Activities
  *Perform Melody: #4 (p. 44)*

Visual Activities
  *Awareness: #2, #5 (p. 57)*
  *Tracking: #2, #5 (pp. 59–60)*

Gross Motor Activities
  *Locomotor: #1 (p. 78)*

## The child demonstrates
# RECOGNITION OF RESPONSIBILITY AND GOOD JUDGMENT
# RESPONSIBILITY/JUDGMENT

| SING | 1. Select songs or poems that challenge children to explain the consequences of behaviors involved, emphasizing those that demonstrate good judgment and responsible behavior. | A, L |
|---|---|---|

| **Five Fat Turkeys** | **Three Little Ducks** |
|---|---|
| **The Goat** | **What Shall We do?** |
| **John the Rabbit** | **When Sammy Put the Paper on the Wall** |
| **Marty** | **When the Train Comes Along** |

| SING | 2. Select songs about pets to emphasize kindness and responsibility for care. | A, L |
|---|---|---|

| **The Goat** | **My Farm** |
|---|---|
| **I Had a Little Turtle** | **My White Mouse** |
| **Lots of Worms** | |

| SING | 3. Select songs with environmental themes. | A, L |
|---|---|---|

| **Breezes Are Blowing** | **The Tree in the Valley** |
|---|---|
| **Lots of Worms** | **The Wind Blew East** |

| SING | 4. Select songs with health, safety, and law enforcement themes. | A, L |
|---|---|---|

| **The Man in Blue** | **Upstairs, Downstairs** |
|---|---|
| **Stop! Look! Listen!** | |

| | 5. Listen to story records and program music describing situations in which individuals are faced with making a decision. Stop the record at appropriate places to discuss possible outcomes. | A, L |
|---|---|---|

| *Dukas: Sorcerer's Apprentice* ⊙ *MacDowell: Of a Tailor and a Bear* ⊙ | Charts: 26 27 28 29 |
|---|---|

# Songs, Poems, Stories, and Additional Activities

# THE ANGEL BAND

Folk Song from South Carolina
Arranged by Albert DeVito

There was one, there were two, there were three lit-tle an-gels,
There were four, there were five, there were six lit-tle an-gels,
There were seven, there were eight, there were nine lit-tle an-gels,

Ten lit-tle an-gels in the band.

**Refrain**

Oh, was-n't that a band, Sun - day morn - ing, Sun - day

morn - ing, Sun - day morn - ing! Was-n't that a band,

Sun - day morn - ing, Sun - day morn - ing soon!

# THE ANTS GO MARCHING

*March tempo*

The ants go march-ing one by one, (two by two,) hur-rah, hoo-ray! The ants go march-ing one by one, (two by two,) hur-rah, hoo-ray! The ants go march-ing one by one, the (two by two, the) last one stopped to have some fun, (tie his shoe,) The ants go march-ing 'round and a-round, and in-to the ground, and out in the rain.

The ants go marching three by three . . .
. . . the last one stopped to climb a tree,

The ants go marching four by four . . .
. . . the last one stopped to shut the door,

The ants go marching five by five . . .
. . . the last one stopped to take a dive,

The ants go marching six by six . . .
. . . the last one stopped to pick up sticks,

The ants go marching seven by seven . . .
. . . the last one stopped to gaze at heaven,

The ants go marching eight by eight . . .
. . . the last one stopped to lock the gate,

The ants go marching nine by nine . . .
. . . the last one stopped to give a sign,

The ants go marching ten by ten . . .
. . . the last one stopped to shout "THE END!"

Music of *What Has Become of Hinky Dinky Parlez-vous?* by A. Dubin, I. Mills, J. McHugh, and I. Dash. Copyright © 1924 Mills Music, Inc. Copyright renewed. All Rights Reserved. Words from SALLY GO ROUND THE SUN by Edith Fowke. Copyright © 1969 by McClelland and Stewart Limited. Used by permission of Doubleday & Company, Inc. and McClelland Stewart Limited, Toronto.

The ants go marching one by one, *(hold up finger(s))*
Hurrah, *(fist horizontally across body)*
Hooray, *(fist straight up in air)*
   *(repeat as necessary)*
. . . The last one stopped to *(pantomime action)* . . .
. . . round and around, *(roll fists around each other)*

and into the ground, *(point down)*
and out in the rain. *(point thumb out)*
Last verse: . . . stopped to shout "THE END!"
   *(shout, and end song there)*

# THE BEST OF BUDDIES

Words and music by Richard M. Sherman and Robert B. Sherman

Har - mon -y is where____ it's at, ____ and where it's at for

you is where it's at for me;      Share and share a like____ is
                at for us;      Share and share a like____ is

what it's all a - bout,____ and what it's all a - bout is un - an -
what it's all a - bout,____ and what it's all a - bout just makes us

im - i - ty;                Part-ners!____   Pals!
rap - tur-ous;              Part-ners!____   Pals!

Com-rades!__  Chums!   Bud - dies to the end what-ev - er comes!
Com-rades!__  Chums!   Bud - dies to the end what-ev - er comes!

Me and you,___ a two man crew;
We and you,___ a hap - py crew;

Ev - en if the go - ing's grue - some we can make it as a two-some!
Side by side we're un - i - fied and we will nev - er be di - vi - ded,

Lose or win, sink or swim! We're the best of
lose or win, sink or swim! We're the best of

bud - dies, bud - dy, we're the best of bud - dies, we're the best of
bud - dies, Snoo - py, we're the best of bud - dies, we're the best of

To Coda

bud - dies, me and you.___
bud - dies, we and

D. S. % al Coda

Coda

you.___   ff

# BINGO

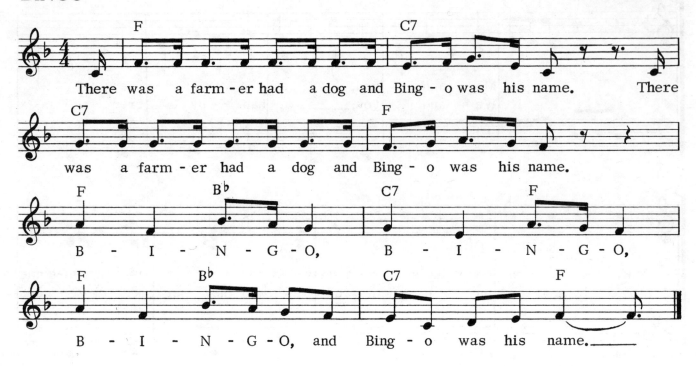

This song is traditionally sung with clapping on B-I-N-G-O. With each repetition one letter (and clap) are left out (i.e., I-N-G-O, N-G-O).

## *Gross Motor Activity*

### Dance—first version

Formation:   Partners, facing each other
1st phrase:   Partners join hands, slide 8 steps right.
2nd phrase:   Slide 8 steps left.
3rd phrase:   Clap melodic rhythm 3 times.

*Ad lib* an interlude of sustained chords: F B♭ F C₇ F. Spell out B I N G O, jumping high on each letter.

### Dance—second version

Formation:   Circle, with partners side by side holding
               inside hands
1st phrase:   Skip around circle.
2nd phrase:   Skip around circle.
3rd phrase:   Join hands, twirl around in place; on
               BINGO, partners face each other, shake
               right hands on B (once), left hands on I,
               right hands on N, left hand on G, throw
               both arms overhead on O.

### Variation

When children can do above well, introduce the grand right and left in the BINGO interlude section. The person facing them on O becomes the new partner. This is a real challenge in laterality and directionality. Point out to children that they

(1) must end their twirling at the end of the second phrase facing each other *on the perimeter of the circle;*
(2) must continue walking in the same direction (partner will go in the opposite direction).

# BONES

*Lively*

Folk Song from
Southern United States
Arranged by W. W. Schmidt

**Refrain**

2. Oh, the leg bone connected to the knee bone,
   And the knee bone connected to the thigh bone,
   And the thigh bone connected to the hip bone,

3. Oh, the hip bone connected to the back bone,
   And the back bone connected to the neck bone,
   And the neck bone connected to the head bone,

4. Oh, the finger bone connected to the hand bone,
   And the hand bone connected to the elbow bone,
   And the elbow bone connected to the shoulder bone,

5. Oh, the shoulder bone connected to the back bone,
   And the back bone connected to the neck bone,
   And the neck bone connected to the head bone.

# BREEZES ARE BLOWING

Luiseno Indian Rain Chant

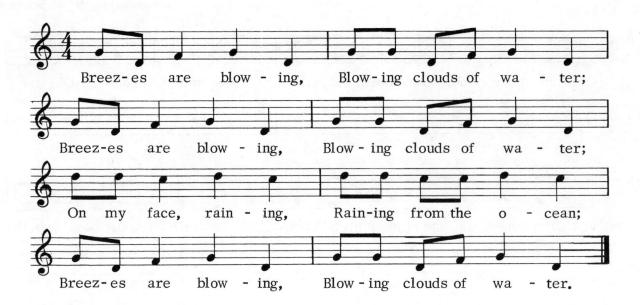

Breez-es are blow - ing, Blow-ing clouds of wa - ter;

Breez-es are blow - ing, Blow-ing clouds of wa - ter;

On my face, rain - ing, Rain-ing from the o - cean;

Breez-es are blow - ing, Blow-ing clouds of wa - ter.

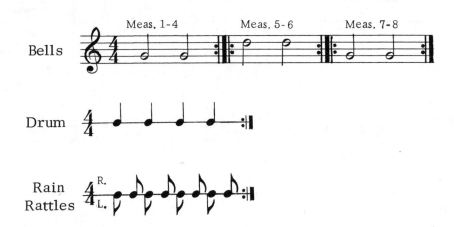

See suggestions in Appendix, p. 275, for dance steps.

# BUTTON, YOU MUST WANDER

Traditional American Game Song

But - ton, you must wan - der, wan - der, wan - der,

But - ton, you must wan - der ev - 'ry - where.

Bright eyes will find you, sharp eyes will find you,

But - ton, you must wan - der ev - 'ry - where.

*Fine and Gross Motor Activity*
*Visual Activity (visual tracking)*

**Materials: button or other flat, round object with some weight, such as a coin or stone**

**Standing version:** Circle formation. One child or teacher goes into the center with the button. Each child, including the leader, holds hands in front of them with palms flat together. A small opening is left between the thumbs just big enough for the button to drop through. As the children sing the song, the leader progresses around the circle extending her or his hand with the concealed button over the outstretched hands of each child. The button is dropped into someone's hands enroute and at the end of the song the class tries to guess who received the button. That individual becomes the new leader. If a receiver is not an ambulatory child, he or she can choose someone to be the next leader.

**Seated version:** Circle formation. All must be seated at the same height and spaced so that outstretched arms will easily reach neighbors on each side. In this version everyone makes a loose fist with each hand. As the song is sung, hands are outstretched to touch those of neighbors on each side on one beat and returned together on the next beat. The button can be passed into a neighbor's hand or can be held. At the end of the song the class tries to guess who has the button. Successfully passing the button without being noticed requires more developed fine motor skills than in the standing version.

# CABIN IN THE WOOD

Traditional

G       D7

In a cab - in in the wood,

Make a roof.

G

Lit - tle old man at the win - dow stood,

Shade eyes.

Am

Saw a rab - bit hop - ping by,

Make rabbit ears and hop.

D7      G

Knock - ing at the door.

Knock.

D7

*"Help me! Help me! Sir," he said,

Raise hands twice.

G

"Or the hunt-er will shoot me dead."

Make gun with two hands. Click it.

Am

"Lit - tle rab - bit, come in - side,

Beckon.

D7 *rit.*     G

Safe - ly to a - bide."

Stroke back of one hand with the other.

From RHYTHMS TODAY by Edna Doll and Mary Jarman Nelson. © 1965 Silver Burdett Company.

* Can be spoken dramatically.
As song is repeated several times, one line at a time is sung silently with the motions until the entire song is performed with just the motions.

# CANDLES OF HANNUKAH

Adapted by Lucille Wood and
Roberta McLaughlin

*Moderately*

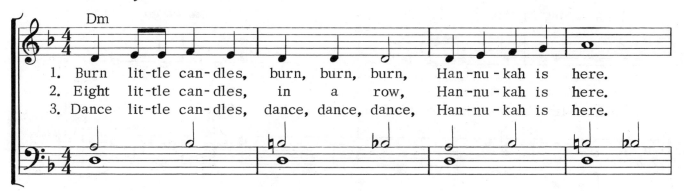

1. Burn lit-tle can-dles, burn, burn, burn, Han-nu-kah is here.
2. Eight lit-tle can-dles, in a row, Han-nu-kah is here.
3. Dance lit-tle can-dles, dance, dance, dance, Han-nu-kah is here.

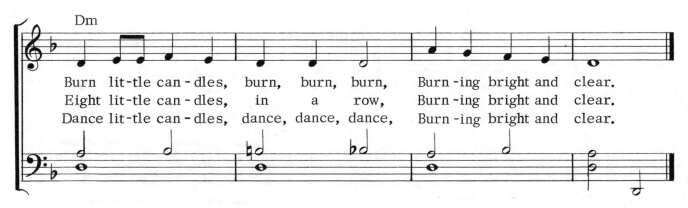

Burn lit-tle can-dles, burn, burn, burn, Burn-ing bright and clear.
Eight lit-tle can-dles, in a row, Burn-ing bright and clear.
Dance lit-tle can-dles, dance, dance, dance, Burn-ing bright and clear.

# CANOE ROUND

Words and music by Margaret B. McGee

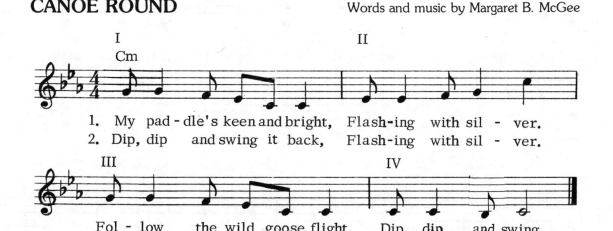

1. My pad-dle's keen and bright, Flash-ing with sil - ver.
2. Dip, dip and swing it back, Flash-ing with sil - ver.

Fol - low the wild goose flight, Dip, dip and swing.
Fol - low the wild goose track, Dip, dip and swing.

**Auditory Activity (tempo, meter, phrase)**
**Motor Activity (laterality)**

Children can feel the duple meter of the song by pretend-ing to paddle canoes. They can paddle individually, in pairs, or in groups of four. Arranging chairs or pillows one behind the other can simulate the feeling of being in a canoe. Show children how to paddle on *each* side, being careful to show how the top hand becomes the bottom when changing sides. Children should practice paddling on the strong beats (1 and 3) changing sides with each new phrase.

When children are comfortable paddling two to a mea-sure, they can try paddling every beat. Point out that the tempo does not increase when paddling every beat, however.

For a more difficult visual and laterality task, paddlers in the rear can be asked to paddle on the *opposite side* from the leader (front paddler) and to change sides when the lead paddler does.

# CHARLIE KNOWS HOW TO BEAT THAT DRUM

Words by Clive Robbins
Music by Paul Nordoff

# CHARLIE OVER THE WATER

Singing Game
Arranged by
Osbourne William McConathy

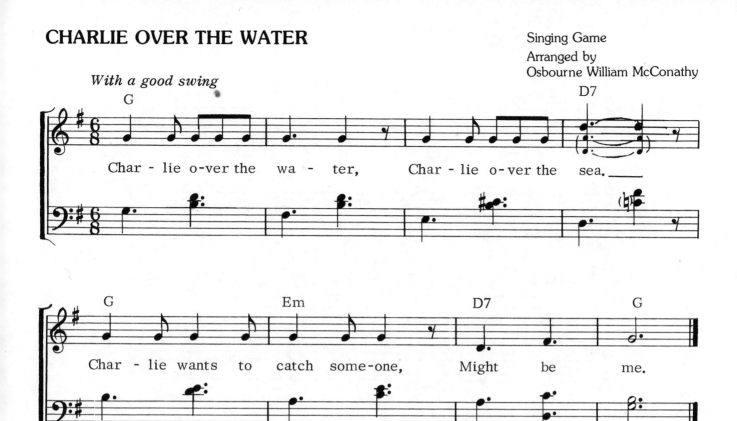

*With a good swing*

Char - lie o-ver the wa - ter, Char - lie o-ver the sea.____

Char - lie wants to catch some-one, Might be me.

From THIS WAY AND THAT, edited by Edna Potter Divine.

## Motor Activity (agility, reaction speed)

Circle, or scatter, formation, standing. "Charlie" stands in the center. Everyone stands still while singing the song. On the last word ("me") all squat down quickly. "Charlie" tries to catch someone before they are in squat position. A nonambulatory "Charlie" can "catch" children *verbally* by calling their names. The game can be adapted for children who cannot stand by deciding on a movement that all will do on the cue word "me" at the end of the song (e.g., close eyes, raise hand).

**Variation:** Tag game. Children run on the last word to a predetermined "safe zone."

## Auditory Activity (pitch)

As above, this can be played in either seated or standing position. "Charlie" or the teacher sings the first line of the song alone, singing either high D or low D on the word "sea." If high, children stand and stretch; if low, they sit on the floor. Physically disabled children unable to stand or to sit on the floor can raise arms up for high; bend over from the waist (or other suitable movement) for low.

## CHICKA HANKA

American Folk Song

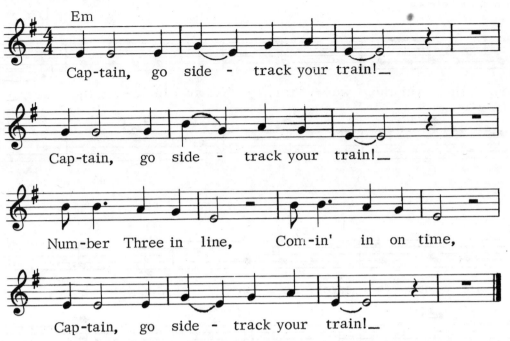

Cap-tain, go side - track your train!

Cap-tain, go side - track your train!

Num-ber Three in line, Com-in' in on time,

Cap-tain, go side - track your train!

Have a small group add a whispered ostinato pattern the last two measures of lines 1, 2, and 4.

chick-a hank-a chick-a hank-a chick-a hank-a

E-minor guitar chord throughout

## CHUMBARA

French-Canadian Folk Song

*Lively*

Chum-ba - ra,___ chum-ba - ra chum-ba - ra,___ chum-ba - ra chum-ba - ra,___

___ chum -ba - ra chum chum chum chum chum chum chum chum, Chum - ba - ra,___

___ chum-ba -ra chum ba-ra,___ chum-ba -ra chum-ba - ra,___ chum-ba - ra chum, chum!

126

# CROCODILE SONG

Traditional

*Happily*

She sailed a - way on a bright and sun - ny day,
On the back of a croc - o - dile. "You see," said she,
"He's as tame as tame can be. I'll ride him down the
Nile." The Croc winked his eye as she waved them all good-bye,
Wear-ing a hap -py smile. At the end of the ride, the
la - dy was in-side, And the smile was on the croc - o - dile.

# DOWN AT THE STATION

Traditional Round

Down at the sta - tion, ear - ly in the morn - ing,

See the lit - tle puf - fer - bil - lies lined up in a row.

See the en - gine driv - er pull the lit - tle throt - tle.

Chug! Chug! Poof! Poof! Off we go.

## DOWN, DOWN

Words by Eleanor Farjeon
Music by Fay Ellis

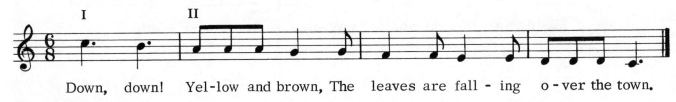

Down, down! Yel-low and brown, The leaves are fall - ing o - ver the town.

Another way to end the song is ". . . falling to the ground."

# ELEPHANT SONG

Folk Song, words adapted
Arranged by Norman Lloyd

*Humorously*

One el - e - phant was bal - anc - ing Step by step on a piece of string. It was such a fun - ny stunt {He She} called for an - oth - er lit - tle el - e - phant.

## Gross Motor Activity (balance)

Place a length of thick string or rope on the floor in either a straight line or a curved pattern. One child is selected to stand with both feet on the string while the class sings the song. With each repetition, the last "elephant" cho another child to join them. ("Two elephants were b ing . . . , Three . . .") Encourage children to kee feet on the string and to stand as still as possible phants" who are good at keeping their balance on string with both feet can try balancing on one foot.

## Visual Activity (quantity)

Number concepts can be reinforced by counting the number of elephants after each addition.

129

# FALSE FACE

Words by Susan Rupert
Music by David Russell

From MUSIC FOR YOUNG AMERICANS, K. © 1966 American Book Company. Reprinted by permission.

"False face" is an easy call-and-response activity, alternating phrases with class (or teacher) and one child. However, the words of this song indicate that the child would respond with phrases 4, 5, and 6. Since this may be long and difficult for some children, change the words so the class sings the longer phrases. When needed, adapt words, such as the following, to suit your group and the activity.

Class:  Who's behind this false face?
Child:  Nobody knows but me!
Class:  Who's behind this false face?
Child:  Nobody knows but me!
Class:  Don't you tell us, We will have to guess; If our guess is right, you must answer "Yes!"
(Repeat first four lines)

## Auditory Activity (timbre, melody, memory)

**Materials: Halloween or pupil-made mask**

While class closes eyes, one child is chosen to stand before the group wearing the mask. As the class sings the song, the masked individual responds "Nobody knows but me." At the end of the song, the class guesses who is wearing the mask. This is a good activity to practice remembering and performing a specific melodic pattern (memory).

## Language Activity

Do the activity as described above. Individuals with serious language deficiencies may be challenged to respond "yes" when the class guesses their identity.

## Social Activity (identity)

Do the activity as described above. Even though most children will recognize the masked individual from other clues such as clothing, it is valuable for both the masked child and the class to associate each individual with their voice and name.

# FIVE ANGELS

English words by Adina Williamson
German Folk Song
Arranged by Lynn Freeman Olson

# FIVE FAT TURKEYS

Traditional

Five fat tur-keys are we, _____ We slept all night in a tree. _____ When the cook came a-round we could-n't be found, So that's why we're here, you see.

# FOR HEALTH AND STRENGTH

Old English Round

*Quietly*

For health and strength and dai-ly food We praise Thy name, O Lord.

# THE GIANT'S SHOES

Words by Edwina Fallis
Music by David Eddleman

**Motions for spoken refrain:** Show left hand, show right hand, roll hands and make tying motion. **135**

# THE GOAT

1. One day my goat (one day my goat) was feel-ing fine, (was feel-ing, etc.)
2. But when the train_____ came in-to sight, _____

Ate three red shirts_____ right off the line!_____
My goat was scared_____ and pale with fright._____

I took a stick,_____ gave him a whack_____
He gave a yell,_____ as if in pain,_____

And tied him to_____ the rail-road track._____
Coughed up my shirts_____ and flagged the train._____

## Auditory Activity (melody, memory)

This is a good echo song as there are only three different phrases and all are very short. When the song is familiar, the class can be divided into two groups with a leader for each.

## Language Activity (verbalization)

Because the phrases are short and the vocabulary simple, this is a good song to elicit repeated language from children. The words "pale" and "flagged" may need some explanation.

# THE GOOD MORNING SONG

Words by Elizabeth S. Lamb
Music by Ellen Bateman

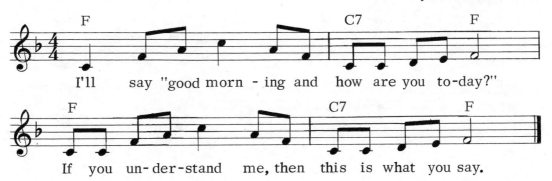

I'll say "good morn - ing and how are you to-day?"

If you un-der-stand me, then this is what you say.

## Auditory Activity (pitch)

Use this song as an echo activity having the child echo your "good morning" at various pitch levels.

TEACHER — Good morn - ing    CHILD — Good morn - ing    TEACHER — Good morn-ing    CHILD — Good morn - ing    TEACHER — Good morn-ing    CHILD — Good morn- ing

## Language Activity (expressive)

Extend the "good morning" phrase into a musical conversation. Use both questions and statements that will motivate the child to respond with original as well as cliché phrases. Examples:

Teacher: Good morning!    Child: Good morning!
Teacher: How are you?    Child: I'm fine.
Teacher: I like your shirt.    Child: It's my brother's.

Note: Beginning activities with children from non-English speaking homes may be more successful if the greeting is in a more familiar language.

Buenos días! (Spanish)
Buon giorno! (Italian)
Bonjour! (French)

# HALLOWEEN NIGHT

Words by Lou Ann Hatcher
Music by Mary Riccio

Witch - es and gob - lins, Jack - o'-lan-terns and fun - ny fac - es!

Black cats and fly - ing bats Come on Hal-low-een night! Boo!

# HEAD, SHOULDERS

Traditional

Head, shoul - ders, knees and toes, knees and toes,

Head, shoul-ders, knees and toes, knees and toes,____ Eyes and ears and

mouth_ and_ nose, Head, shoul - ders, knees and toes, knees and toes.

# HELLO!

Words by Clive Robbins
Music by Paul Nordoff

*Briskly*

Hel - lo!___ Hel - lo!___ Hel - lo, hel-lo, hel-lo! What shall we

do to-day? What shall we do to-day? Hel- do to-day?

*molto ritard.*

# HERE'S THE BEEHIVE

Traditional words
Music by Maria Castillo

*Freely*

Here's the bee-hive, where are the bees? Hid-den a - way where

no-bod - y sees; Watch and you'll see them come out of the hive,

One, two, three, four, five. Bzzz!___

*Fine Motor Activity*
*Visual Activity (quantity)*

**Finger play:** Make a fist with the thumb tucked inside fingers. The fist is held up during the first three phrases, pointed to by other hand during second and third phrases. On last phrase, extend fingers one at a time: thumb, first, second, third, fourth fingers. (The last phrase can be sung *ad lib* instead of exactly on the beat.)

For deaf children who understand sign language, you can use number signs.

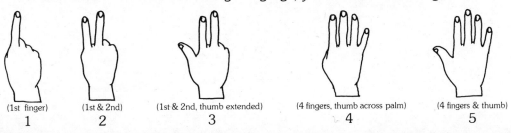

(1st finger)  (1st & 2nd)  (1st & 2nd, thumb extended)  (4 fingers, thumb across palm)  (4 fingers & thumb)

1     2     3     4     5

139

# HUSH, LITTLE BABY

Southern Folk Song
Arranged by Arthur Frackenpohl

*Calmly*

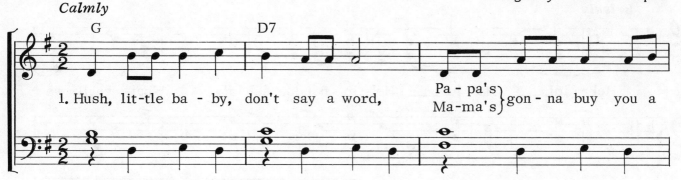

2. If that mockingbird won't sing,
   Papa's (Mama's) gonna buy you a di'mond ring.

3. If that di'mond ring turns brass, . . . a looking glass.

4. If that looking glass gets broke, . . . a billy goat.

5. If that billy goat won't pull, . . . a cart and bull.

6. If that cart and bull turn over, . . . a dog named Rover.

7. If that dog named Rover won't bark, . . . a horse and cart.

8. If that horse and cart fall down,
   You'll be the sweetest baby in town.

# I HAD A LITTLE OVERCOAT

Translated by Teddi Schwartz and Arthur Kevess
Yiddish Folk Tune
Arranged by Albert DeVito

*With spirit*

1. I had a lit-tle o-ver-coat, as
2. I had a lit-tle jack-et, it was old as could be,
3. I had a lit-tle vest,__ it was

Tra la la la la la la la la la la.

What I'd ev-er do with it I just could-n't see,

Tra la la la la la la la la la la.

So I thought a lit-tle while and

made my-self a vest___ (jack-et / tie___) in the ver-y lat-est style,

Tra la la la la la la Tra la la la la la la,

1.–5.

6.

Made my-self a vest___ (jack-et / tie___) in the ver-y lat-est style. ver-y lat-est style.

4. I had a little tie . . .          5. I had a little button . . .
   . . . and made myself a button . . .          . . . and made myself a nothing . . .

6. I had a little nothing . . .
   . . . and made myself a song . . .

142

# I HAD A LITTLE TURTLE

Words by Vachel Lindsay
Music by Satis N. Coleman

*Freely*

There was a lit-tle tur-tle Who lived in a box;

He swam in a pud-dle, He climbed on the rocks.

He snapped at a mos-qui-to, He snapped at a flea,

He snapped at a min-now, He snapped at me.

He caught the mos-qui-to, He caught the flea,

He caught the min-now, But he did-n't catch me!

## Fine Motor Activity

There was a little turtle . . . *(pantomime box shape with hand)*
He swam . . . *(swimming motions, both arms)*
He climbed . . . *(fingers climb up)*
He snapped . . . *(fingers and thumb together, one hand: snapping motion)*
He snapped at me. *(turn hand around, snap at nose)*
He caught the mosquito, *(pantomime catching in air with grasping movement, one hand)*
He caught the minnow, *(grasping movement down low)*
But he didn't catch me! *(shake finger)*

# I KNOW AN OLD LADY

Music by Alan Mills
Words by Rose Bonne

*Lively — not fast*

1. I know an old la-dy who swal-lowed a fly; I don't know why she swal-lowed a fly! I guess she'll die!_____ 2. I know an old la-dy who swal-lowed a spi-der that wrig-gled and wrig-gled and

tick-led in-side her; She swal-lowed a spi-der to catch the fly, But

I don't know why she swal-lowed the fly. I guess she'l die!___

I know an old la-dy who swal-lowed a dog! My, what a hog, to

bird! Now, how ab-surd, to
cat! Im - ag - ine that, to
goat! Just opened her throat, and
cow! I don't know how she

*No repeat first time*

swal-low a bird! 3. She swal-lowed the bird to catch the spi-der that
swal-low a cat! 4. She swal-lowed the cat to catch the bird, She (To 3)
swal-low a dog! 5. She swal-lowed the dog to catch the cat, She (To 4)
swal-lowed a goat! 6. She swal-lowed the goat to catch the dog, She (To 5)
swal-lowed a cow! 7. She swal-lowed the cow to catch the goat, She (To 6)

145

wrig-gled and wrig-gled and tick-led in-side her, She swal-lowed the spi-der to

catch the fly, But I don't know why she swal-lowed the fly;

I guess she'll die! __ I die! __ I die! __ 8. I

know an old la-dy who swal-lowed a horse; She's dead, of course!

# I LIKE TO RIDE THE ELEVATOR

Words and music by Alfred Balkin
Arranged by Lynn Freeman Olson

*With spirit*

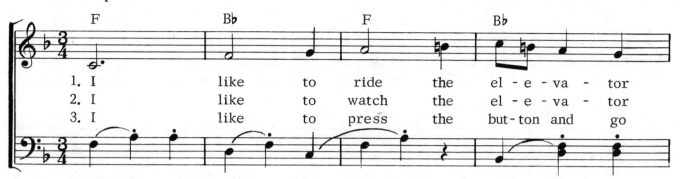

1. I like to ride the el - e - va - tor
2. I like to watch the el - e - va - tor
3. I like to press the but - ton and go

up, up, up, up, up, up! I
stop, stop, on ev - 'ry floor! I
up, up, up, up, up, up! I

like to ride the el - e - va - tor down, _____
like to see the el - e - va - tor o - pen-ing the door,
like to press the but - ton and go down, _____

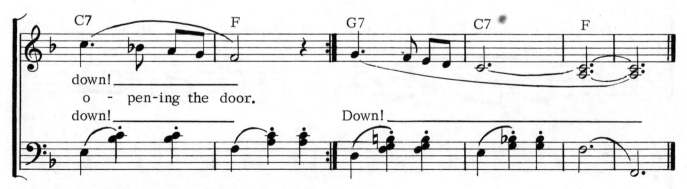

down! _____
o - pen-ing the door.
down! _____ Down! _____

# I LIKE YOU

Words and melody by Barbara Andress

*Freely*

I like you, I like you, You're my spe-cial friend now, I like you,

I like you, Here's where we be - gin now. Shake my hand, shake my hand,

I'm so glad I found you, 'cause deep in-side says "I like you!"___

# I ROLL THE BALL

Words and music by Ray Abrashkin
Arranged by Lynn Freeman Olson

*With a strong beat*

1.)
2.)  I roll the ball to { teach - er, she (he) } rolls the ball to me.___
3.)                    { Dad - dy, he }
                       { _____,* he (she) }

I roll the ball to { teach er, she (he) } rolls the ball to me.___
                   { Dad - dy, he }
                   { _____,* he (she) }

*D. C. al Fine*

Roll the ball, roll the ball, roll the ball, roll the ball.

148

* Name of another child

# I SEE YOU

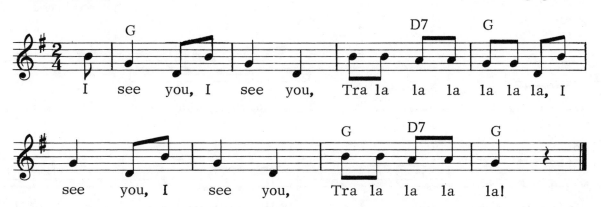

I see you, I see you, Tra la la la la la la, I

see you, I see you, Tra la la la la!

A leader can make up a movement to be mirrored on the "Tra la la's."

# I WILL CLAP MY HANDS

Words and melody by Frances Cole
Arranged by Lynn Freeman Olson

*Freely*

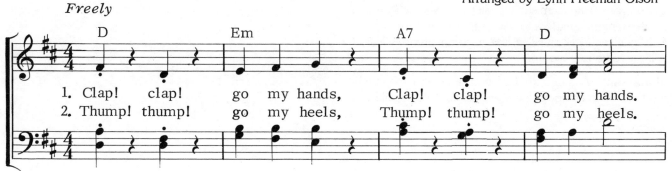

1. Clap! clap! go my hands, Clap! clap! go my hands.
2. Thump! thump! go my heels, Thump! thump! go my heels.

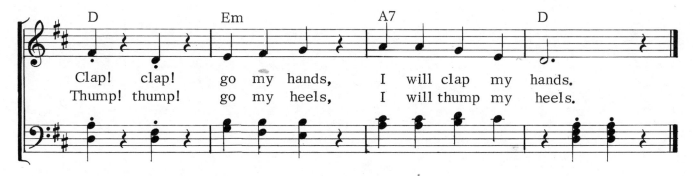

Clap! clap! go my hands, I will clap my hands.
Thump! thump! go my heels, I will thump my heels.

# JACK-IN-THE-BOX

Words by Louise B. Scott
Music by Lucille F. Wood

Jack-in-the box,  still as  a  mouse,  Deep down in-side your lit-tle dark house.

Jack-in - the box,  qui-et and still,  Will  you come out?  Yes,  I  will!

***Gross Motor Activity***
***Fine Motor Activity***

Children can start from squat position, or start in standing position, bending knees slowly until reaching squat position at the end of the first line. On the phrase "Yes, I will!" everyone pops up.

**Variation:** A fine motor variation can be done by tucking thumbs in fist, popping them up on "Yes, I will!"

# JAPANESE RAIN SONG

Japanese Folk Song
Contributed by
Elizabeth Clure and Helen Rumsey
English words by Roberta McLaughlin
Arranged by Albert DeVito

1. Pit - ter-pat - ter, fall - ing, fall - ing, rain is fall - ing down.

Moth - er comes to bring um - brel - la, Rain is fall - ing down.

**Refrain**

Pi chi, pi chi, cha pu, cha pu, ran, ran, ran.

*Pedal*

2. Underneath the drooping willow stands a little child.
   No umbrella, child is weeping, Rain is falling down.

## Auditory Activity (melody, timbre, tempo, dynamics)

The song is appropriately sung softly and at a slow tempo. Help children select instruments with timbres that suggest the sound of rain. Melodic ostinatos played on resonator bells or other suitable melodic instruments can be extracted from the melody or the accompaniment.

Since this song is pentatonic and uses only the pitches C D E G A, children can create their own ostinatos by arranging these pitches in various melodic patterns.

## Language Activity (articulation, verbalization)

There are many good speech sounds in this song (*p, ch, f*). Children with severe articulation problems may be encouraged to join in the last line of the song. English words can be substituted for *pichi, chapu* if desired: "pitter, patter, pitter, patter, plop, plop, plop."

Some children may find it helpful to chant a word pattern as they play their ostinato parts. Example: Pitter, patter, rain. When composing speech chants be sure that the rhythms are those of natural speech.

Children could compose a Haiku verse to be used as a speech ostinato. Instruments may be added later. (See Language, p. 103, #5.)

# JOE TURNER BLUES

American Blues
Arranged by Richard Shadroui

Section Ⓐ is a basic blues setting.

Section Ⓑ is a contemporary blues setting.

✳ . . . ✳ R. H. may be played an octave lower.

152

**Auditory Activity (melody)**

Arrange resonator bells or other appropriate instrument in a basic blues scale: C D E♭ F G A B♭ C. One child is selected to improvise melodies during the interlude measures after each phrase and at the end of the song. Indi-

viduals who are capable of improvising longer melodies can be accompanied with chords (guitar or autoharp) or the contemporary setting of the piano accompaniment (Section B).

# JOHN JACOB JINGELHEIMER SCHMIDT

Traditional
Arranged by J. E. Pool

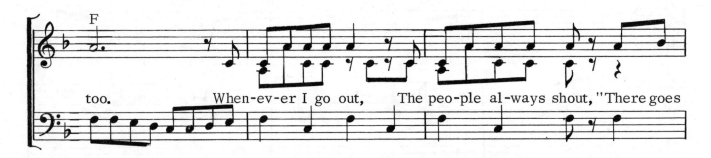

**Auditory Activity (dynamics, articulation)**
**Language Activity**

Traditionally, each repetition is sung a little softer until only mouthing words.
The "tra la la" phrase is always sung *loudly*.

154

# JOHN THE RABBIT

American Folk Game Song
Collected by John W. Work
Arranged by Darrell Peter

# LET'S GO WALKING

Words and music by
Satis N. Coleman and Alice G. Thorn

*Lightly*

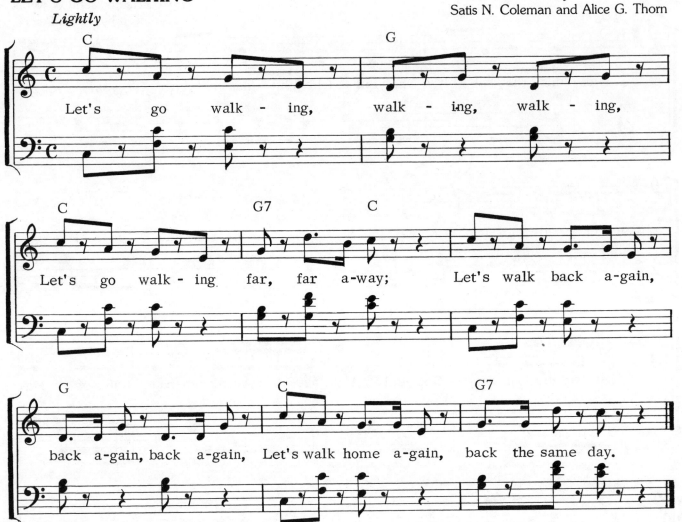

From ANOTHER SINGING TIME: Songs for Nursery & School, by Satis N. Coleman and Alice G. Thorn. Copyright 1937 by Satis N. Coleman and Alice G. Thorn. Renewed, 1965, by Walter B. Coleman, Dr. Charles H. Coleman, and Linton S. Thorn. Published by John Day. Reprinted with the permission of Thomas Y. Crowell.

## LETTERS AND NAMES

Words and music by Hansi Chambers

*Brightly*

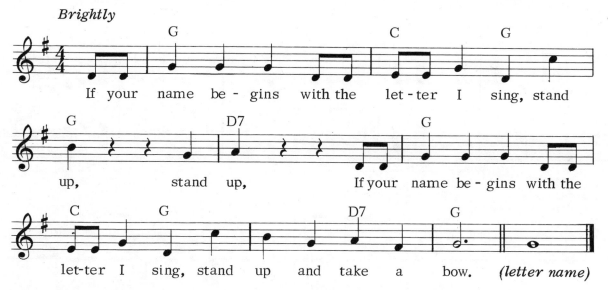

If your name be-gins with the let-ter I sing, stand up, stand up, If your name be-gins with the let-ter I sing, stand up and take a bow. *(letter name)*

### Language Activity

For an *ad lib* ending, letters can be chosen (1) by the teacher; (2) one child writes a letter on the board; or (3) a letter is chosen from a grab bag. Children whose first names begin with the chosen letter stand when it is sung (or raise their hand). Each in turn sing their name. (Teacher can sing for non-verbal children.) The class echoes each name. Names can be accompanied with chords ending with $D_7$. For example:

*ad lib.*

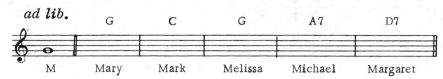

M   Mary   Mark   Melissa   Michael   Margaret

## A LITTLE FLIGHT MUSIC

David Eddleman

*Fast rock tempo*

*For a "stop" version, substitute rests for beats 2, 3, and 4 of these measures.

# LOTS OF WORMS

*Jazzy, but not fast*

Words and melody by Patty Zeitlin
Arranged by Lynn Freeman Olson

*L.H. 8va lower throughout*

2. (I dug the) biggest hole I ever did dig,
   The biggest hole. It sure was big!
   And when I got to the bottom, you know what I found
   'Way under the ground?

3. I found a worm to go on a fishing pole
   Down in the bottom of that deep, dark hole.
   But I left him alone 'cause he liked his home
   'Way under the ground.

4. I found a bumpety bug with big black dots,
   Thirty-three legs and twenty-two spots.
   But I left him alone 'cause he liked his home
   'Way under the ground.

5. I found an old sow bug curled up like a ball.
   He didn't move from there at all.
   So I left him alone 'cause he liked his home
   'Way under the ground.

6. *(Repeat verse one)*

The melodic rhythm will need to
be adjusted to fit the rhythm of the
underscored words in verses 2–5.

159

# THE MAN IN BLUE

Words and music by Alfred Balkin

*Rock it*

There goes the man in blue.

He has a job to do.

Walk-ing up and down the street,__ pa - trol-ling the neigh-bor-hood

beat.　　　　　　　He vis-its all the stores.＿

At　night　he　checks the　　doors.＿

Does the things po-lice-men should,＿　　And goes to know the neigh-bor-

simile

hood.　　　　His job's law and or - der,　Does-n't want a

ri - ot, Tries the ver- y best he can to keep peace \_\_ and

*cresc.*

qui - et. \_\_

*ff*    *f*

*Repeat ad lib. to fade out end.*

There goes the man in blue. \_\_

He has a job to do. \_\_

# MAN ON THE FLYING TRAPEZE

Traditional American Song
Arranged by Norman Lloyd

*With a swing*

He flies through the air with the great-est of ease, This dar-ing young

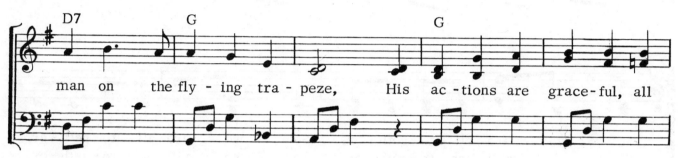

man on the fly-ing tra-peze, His ac-tions are grace-ful, all

girls he does please, And my love he has stol-en a-way.

# MARCHING TO PRETORIA

English words by Josef Marais
Dutch Folk Song from South Africa
Arranged by Darrell Peter

*Brisk march*

1. I'm with you and you're with me, And so we are all to-geth-er,
2. We have food, the food is good, And so we will eat to-geth-er,

*simile*

So we are all to-geth-er, So we are all to-geth-er.
So we will eat to-geth-er, So we will eat to-geth-er.

Sing with me, I'll sing with you, And so we will sing to-geth-er,
When we eat, 'twill be a treat, And so let us sing to-geth-er,

As we march a - long.

## MARTY

Words and music by Malvina Reynolds

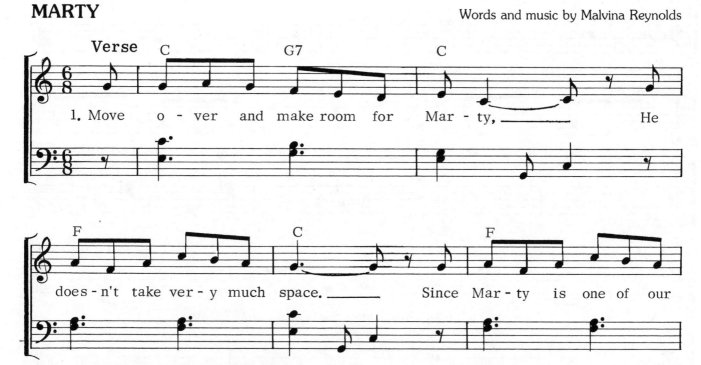

ver - y best friends, We sure - ly can find him a place._____

**Refrain**

Move o-ver,___ move o-ver,___ And quick like a rig-ge-dy jig.____

We'll al-ways move o-ver for Mar-ty,___ For Mar-ty is not ver-y big.____

**Verse**

2. Our lit - tle friend Mar - ty is tar - dy,_____ He

must have got lost on the way._____ We real-ly can't start with-out

*To Refrain*

Mar-ty,_____ We need him at re-cess to play._____

# MISS MARY MACK

American Play-party Song
Arranged by Elsie Plant

*Rhythmically*

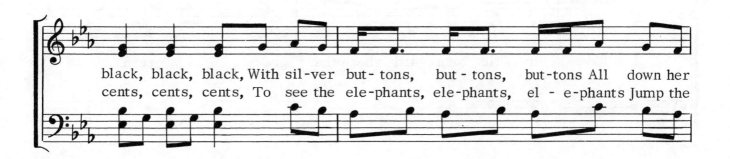

1. Miss Mar - y Mack, Mack, Mack, All dressed in
2. She asked her mother, mother, mother For fif - teen

black, black, black, With sil - ver but - tons, but - tons, but-tons All down her
cents, cents, cents, To see the ele-phants, ele-phants, el - e-phants Jump the

back, back, back.
fence, fence, fence.

3. They jumped so high, high, high
   They reached the sky, sky, sky,
   They didn't come back, back, back
   'Til the fourth of July, -ly, -ly.

4. Miss Linda Light, Light, Light
   All dressed in white, white, white,
   She shined her shoes, shoes, shoes
   'Til they fit too tight, tight, tight.

5. Miss Dinah Dean, Dean, Dean
   All dressed in green, green, green,
   She washed her clothes, clothes, clothes
   To keep them clean, clean, clean.

6. Miss Fannie Flew, Flew, Flew
   All dressed in blue, blue, blue,
   The more she ate, ate, ate,
   The more she grew, grew, grew.

**Motor Activity**
**Language Activity (expressive)**

This is a traditional partner hand-clapping game.
The patterns can be varied. (Clap eighth notes,
eight to a measure.)

- A—clap own hands
- B—slap thighs
- C—partners clap right hands
- D—partners clap left hands
- E—clap partner's hands

For example:

ABAC|ADAE|ABAC|ADAE:‖

BACA|BADA|BAEA|BAEA:‖

(For first verse, begin clapping on beat 1.)

167

# MY FARM

Argentinian Folk Song
Arranged by Darrell Peter

Lively

1.} 2.} I have a lit-tle farm be-side a wind-ing stream,

I have a lit-tle barn-yard where the grass is green.

There the chick-ens go like this: Cluck, cluck, (low) There the chick-ens go like
Ba - by chick-ens go like this: Peep, peep, (high) Ba - by chick-ens go like

this: Cluck, cluck. (low) They run, they run, When I call them to come home, They
this: Peep, peep. (high)

run, they run, When I call them to come home.

1. . . . There the chickens go like this: Cluck, cluck *(low)*
      *(los pollos)*

2. . . . Baby chickens go like this: Peep, peep *(high)*
      *(Los pollitos)*

3. . . . There the big ducks go like this: Quack, quack *(low)*
      *(los patos)*

4. . . . There the ducklings go like this: Quack, quack *(high)*
      *(los patitos)*

5. . . . There the big dog goes like this: Woof, woof *(low)*
      *(el perro)*

6. . . . There the puppy goes like this: Arf, arf *(high)*
      *(el perrito)*

7. . . . There the big cats go like this: Meow, meow *(low)*
      *(los gatos)*

8. . . . There the kittens go like this: Mew, mew *(high)*
      *(los gatitos)*

# MY FATHER'S HOUSE

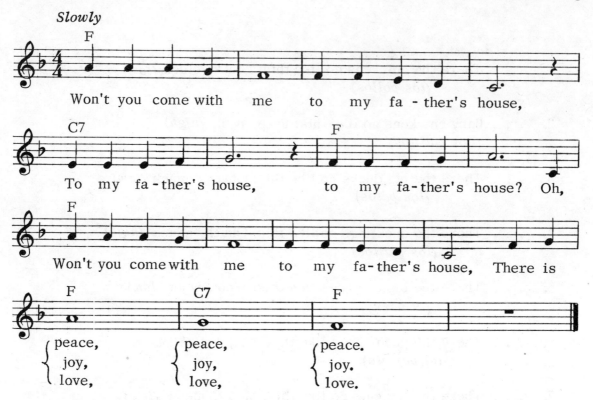

*Slowly*

Won't you come with me to my fa-ther's house,
To my fa-ther's house, to my fa-ther's house? Oh,
Won't you come with me to my fa-ther's house, There is

{ peace,    { peace,    { peace.
  joy,        joy,        joy.
  love,       love,       love.

## Auditory Activity (tempo, dynamics)

The song is slow and soft throughout. The rhythmic structure is even and most of the phrases are the same length. The melody goes both up and down.

## Visual Activity (awareness)

The children can graphically represent the rhythm of the melody. The children can draw graphic illustrations of the direction of each phrase in the music.

The children can learn to sign the song (see the following).

## Language Activity (expressive)

The words of this song are well expressed through sign language. The signs required are simple and many are repeated. The slow tempo and even rhythms help to make this song a good choice for adding signs. All signs are performed one to a beat, including 's, which is made while singing the second syllable of *fa-ther's*. "Oh" is represented by finger spelling the letter *o*. There is no universally recognized sign for the word "joy," but it is an easy word to finger spell. Learning to sign the words of the song while singing is a good way to introduce hearing children to the idea that sign is a language that is fun for all as well as useful and can add an effective visual dimension to singing.

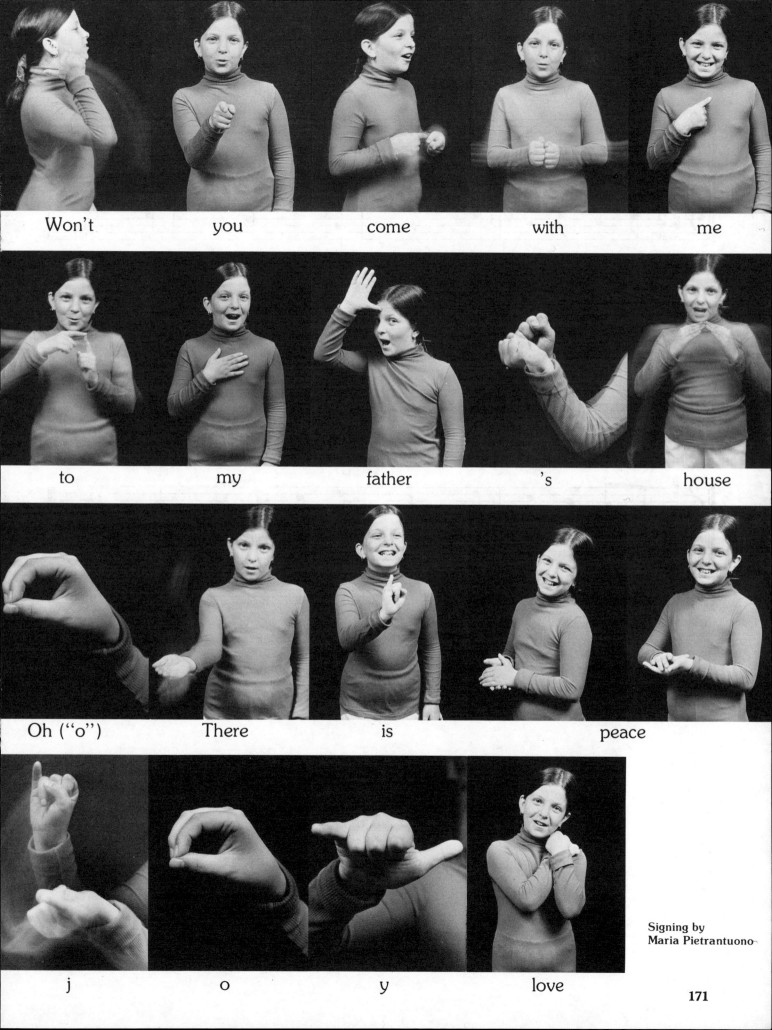

Won't you come with me

to my father 's house

Oh ("o") There is peace

j o y love

Signing by
Maria Pietrantuono

171

# MY LITTLE PONY

Old Folk Song
Arranged by Osbourne McConathy

*Briskly*

1. Trot, trot, trot! Go, and nev - er stop!
2. Jump, jump, jump! Come down with a bump!

Where it's smooth and where it's ston - y, Trot a - long, my lit - tle po - ny;
I can al - ways ride my po - ny, E - ven where the ground is ston - y;

Go, and nev - er stop! Trot, trot, trot, trot, trot!
Come down with a bump! Jump, jump, jump, jump jump!

# MY WHITE MOUSE

English words by Louise Kessler
German Folk Song
Arranged by Elizabeth Rogers

2. One night while I was sleeping, mousie ran away,
   I looked for him, I looked for him.
   One night while I was sleeping, mousie ran away.
   I looked inside a shoe and there was Jim.

3. I found a cracker box and made a nest for Jim,
   A nest for Jim, a nest for Jim.
   I found a cracker box and made a nest for Jim,
   I made a cozy little nest for him.

## *Gross Motor Activity*

A schottische step can be performed to this music. (See Appendix, p. 275.)

# NEW RIVER TRAIN

American Folk Song
Arranged by Cameron McGraw

*Steadily*

## Language Activity

Make up additional verses for "two," "three," "four," and so forth.

# OH, MY AUNT CAME BACK

Traditional

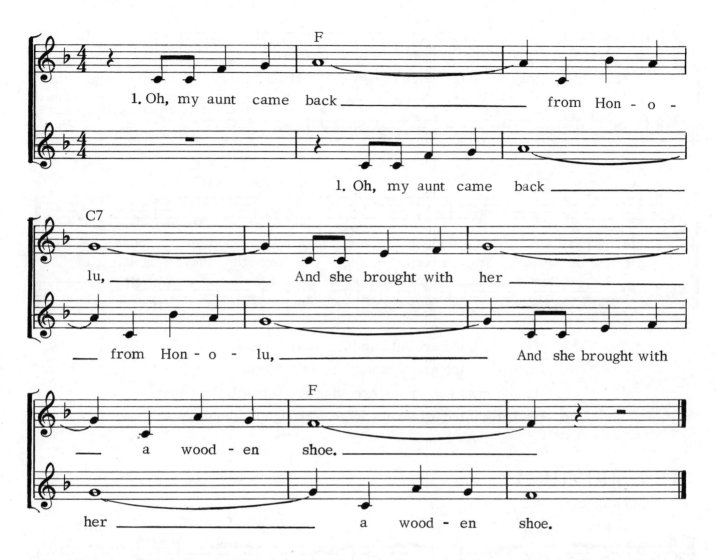

1. Oh, my aunt came back from Honolu,
   And she brought with her a wooden shoe. *(Tap foot on beat.)*

2. . . . from old Japan . . . a waving fan. *(Wave, palm up, on beat.)*

3. . . . from old Algiers . . . a pair of shears. *(Simulate cutting motion, other hand, on beat.)*

4. . . . from Guadalupe . . . a hoola hoop. *(Move body in circular motion.)*

5. . . . from the New York Fair . . . a rocking chair. *(Rock back and forth, on beat.)*

6. . . . from the City Zoo . . . a monkey like you!

Note: Motions can be done cumulatively.

# THE OLD GRAY CAT

Traditional American Song
Arranged by Cameron McGraw

*Freely*

1. The old gray cat is sleep - ing, sleep - ing, sleep - ing. The
2. The lit - tle mice are creep - ing, creep - ing, creep - ing. The

old gray cat is sleep - ing in the house. ____
lit - tle mice are creep - ing through the house. ____

3. The little mice are nibbling ... in the house.

4. The little mice are sleeping ... in the house.

5. The old gray cat comes creeping ... through the house.

6. The little mice all scamper ... through the house.

# OPEN, SHUT THEM

Words and music by Laura P. MacCartenay

*Moderately*

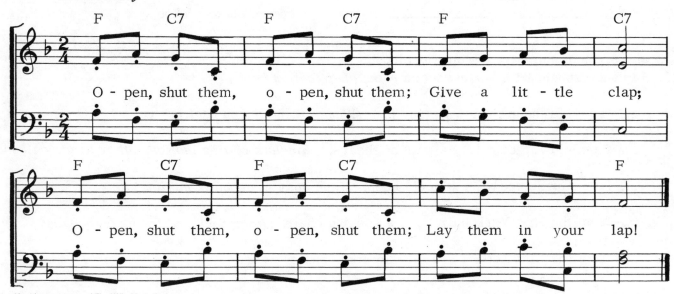

O - pen, shut them, o - pen, shut them; Give a lit - tle clap;

O - pen, shut them, o - pen, shut them; Lay them in your lap!

For slower reacting children, insert a quarter rest after each "open" and each "shut them."

For a version using eyes only, sing the following.
Open, shut them, open, shut them;
Give a little blink!
Open, shut them, open, shut them;
Here's a little wink!

# PAT-A-CAKE

Words anonymous
Music by Tom Glazer

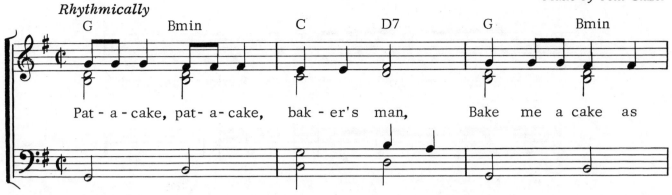

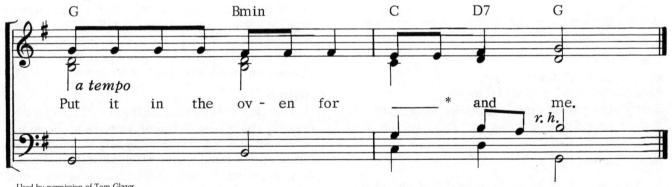

Used by permission of Tom Glazer.

* Initial can be that of a child's name
("T" . . . for Tommy and me.)

# POLYNESIAN STICK GAME

Traditional

Mah ko way ko tay oh way koo-ee tah nah,

Mah ko way ko tay oh way koo -ee tah nah.

**Note: Lightweight stick-like objects made out of compressed paper or stiff plastic tubing may be more suitable than sticks made of wood for use by children lacking good motor control or reflexes. The size should be approximately 3/4″ in diameter and 12″ long.**

Partners sit on the floor facing each other. Practice each pattern and its variations *without* sticks first. Hold each stick with the tips of four fingers in front and tip of thumb behind.

## Basic pattern   (3 beats)
Beat 1—tap floor once with clenched fists (with bottom of sticks)

Beats 2 & 3—tap fists (sticks) together on each beat in front of body

## Pattern 1
Beat 1—tap fists (sticks) on floor

Beat 2—clap hands (tap sticks) together

Beat 3—one partner extends right hand (stick), palm up, while second partner slaps it (taps stick) with left hand (stick), palm down

Repeat pattern

**Variations:**  Beat 1 can be varied by tapping fists (sticks) to the sides or crossing in front of body. Beat 3 can be varied by slapping both hands (tapping both sticks) with both hands (sticks) of partner, or cross slapping (tapping).

## Pattern 2
Beat 1—tap outstretched fingers (tops of sticks) on the floor in front of body

Beat 2—clap hands (tap sticks) together

Beat 3—with hands (sticks) held upright, clap partner's left hand (tap left stick) with right hand (right stick)

Repeat pattern

Note: See variations above for Beats 1 and 3.

**Advanced patterns**   (*only* for very good stick handlers)

## Pattern 3
Beats 1 & 2—basic pattern

Beat 3—sticks can be *tossed* to partner. Practice by beginning with a hand-to-hand exchange of sticks on the same side (i.e., right to partner's left, then left to right). It may be easier for some if tapping the sticks together on Beat 2 is eliminated, taking both Beats 2 and 3 to accomplish the exchange. Later, some children may be able to exchange successfully in one beat. When ready, children can attempt tossing a short distance.

## Pattern 4
Beat 3—sticks can be *flipped,* with each child *catching the opposite end of own stick in the same hand.* Begin by using Beats 2 and 3 to practice flipping. When children become proficient, they can try flipping sticks on Beat 3 only, and eventually flipping to each other on the same side, or cross laterally.

## Patterns for four players
The game can be played by two couples seated in a square, with each pair sitting diagonally across from each other. In this situation, one couple begins to play on the first beat. The other couple must begin to play *on the third beat*—to prevent hands and sticks from colliding. All movements between partners (i.e., tossing, flipping, and hitting) must be executed only on their own third beat, unless the basic pattern is altered.

# PUPPETS

Words adapted
French Folk Song
Arranged by W. W. Schmidt

*Gaily*

See them dance, so, so! All the lit-tle danc-ing pup-pets,

See them dance, so, so! Three lit-tle turns and off they go!

# PUSSY WILLOW

Traditional

*Mysteriously*

I know a lit-tle pus-sy, Her coat is sil-ver gray,___ She

lives down in the mead-ow, Not ver-y far a-way.___ She'll

al-ways be a pus-sy, She'll nev-er be a cat,___ For

she's a pus-sy wil-low, now what d'you think of that!

Meow meow meow meow meow meow meow meow, scat! *(spoken)*

For a variation, sing the following.

I have a little puppy, he has a stubby tail. He isn't very chubby, he's skinny as a rail.
He'll always be a puppy, he'll never be a hound, They sell him at the market for ninety cents a pound.
Bow wow wow wow wow wow wow wow, *hot dog!*

179

# PUT ON A HAPPY FACE

Words by Lee Adams
Music by Charles Strouse
Arranged by James Rooker

*Rhythmically*

Gray skies are gon - na clear up, ___ Put on a hap-py face;

Brush off the clouds and cheer up, ___ Put on a hap-py face.

Take off the gloom - y mask of trag - e - dy, It's not your style;

You'll look so good that you'll be glad ya' de - cid - ed to smile!

*f* Pick out a pleas-ant out-look, __ Stick out that no - ble chin;

Wipe off that "full of doubt" look, __ Slap on a hap-py grin! And

spread sun-shine all o - ver the place, Just put on a

1. hap - py face!

2. face! _____

*Motor Activity (balance)*

**Place strips of tape 4″ apart and 6′ to 12′ in length to simulate a balance beam.**

**Balance Beam Dance:**   Stand sideways, feet together, on one end of the beam. ——————————————————

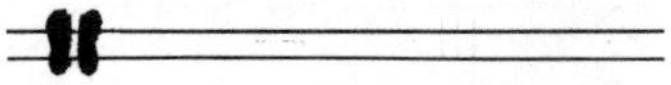

Each pattern is for two measures of music. Since the meter signature is *alla breve*, there are 2 beats to a measure (4 beats to a pattern).

RF—right foot
LF—left foot

## Pattern   (Meas. 1–16)

1   Beginning with RF, take three side steps right (close LF). On beat 4, make a 180° turn to the right, facing in the opposite direction but still standing sideways on the beam.

2   Beginning with LF, continue with four side steps left, close RF.

3   Facing same direction, take four side jumps right, using a full beat for each jump. On the fourth jump, make a 90° turn to the right, facing forward on the beam.

4   Beginning with LF, take six steps forward (3 beats), turning 180° to the left on beat 4 (end facing opposite direction).

5   Beginning with RF, take four steps forward, using one beat for each step.

6   Beginning with RF, take seven quick steps backward, making a 90° turn left on last half of beat 4.

7   Beginning with RF (moving right, one beat each step), step right, LF crosses behind RF, step right, LF crosses in front of right.

8   Same as pattern 1.

Dancer is now at opposite end of beam.

Meas. 17–32: Repeat above 8 patterns.

# PUT YOUR FINGER IN THE AIR

Words and music by Woody Guthrie
Arranged by Osbourne William McConathy

*Crisply*

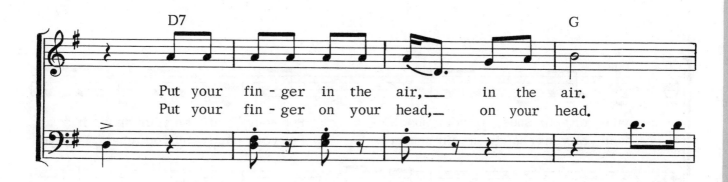

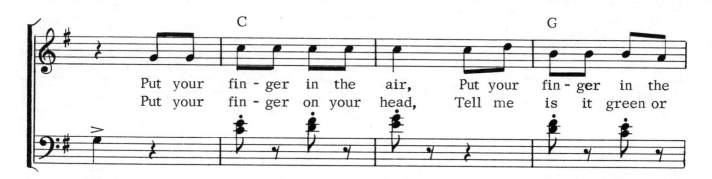

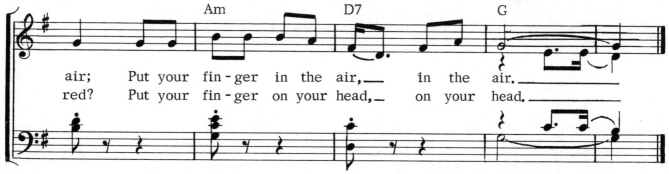

1. Put your fin-ger in the air,__ in the air;
   Put your fin-ger in the air,__ in the air.
   Put your fin-ger in the air, Put your fin-ger in the air; Put your fin-ger in the air,__ in the air.

2. Put your fin-ger on your head,__ on your head;
   Put your fin-ger on your head,__ on your head.
   Put your fin-ger on your head, Tell me is it green or red? Put your fin-ger on your head,__ on your head.

3. Put your finger on your nose,
   And feel how the cold wind blows,

4. Put your finger on your shoe,
   And leave it a day or two,

5. Put your finger on your finger,
   And your finger on your finger,

6. Put your finger on your chin,
   That's where the food slips in,

7. Put your finger on your cheek,
   And leave it about a week,

# PUT YOUR HAND ON YOUR SHOE

Words and melody by Frances Cole
Arranged by Lynn Freeman Olson

*Freely*

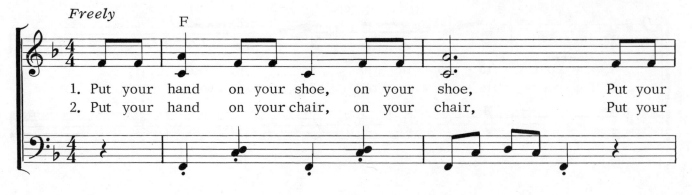

1. Put your hand   on your shoe,   on your   shoe,                        Put your
2. Put your hand   on your chair,   on your   chair,                       Put your

hand   on your shoe,  on your shoe;        Put your hand    on your shoe, It's an
hand   on your chair, on your chair;       Put your hand    on your chair, Then you

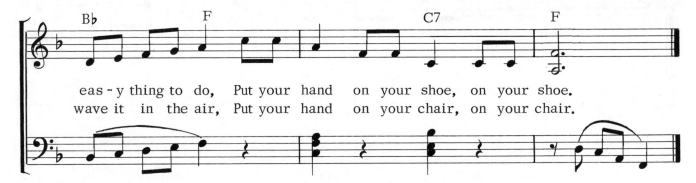

eas - y thing to do,  Put your hand   on your shoe,   on your shoe.
wave it   in  the air, Put your hand   on your chair,  on your chair.

# RIG-A-JIG-JIG

*Briskly*

English Folk Song
Arranged by Darrell Peter

**Gross Motor Activity (locomotor)**

One child walks around the room (or circle) in the $\frac{2}{4}$ section (first two lines) until he or she finds a partner. Both skip throughout the $\frac{6}{8}$ section (last two lines). The first child rejoins the class as the partner becomes the new leader.

# THE ROLL CALL SONG

Words by Clive Robbins
Music by Paul Nordoff

\* Substitute name of child.

# ROLL OVER

American Folk Song

There were ten in the bed, And the lit-tle one said, "Roll
nine,
eight, etc.

o - ver, roll o - ver.". So they all rolled o-ver and

*Last time*

one fell out. There were one fell out. There was

one in the bed, And the lit-tle one said, "Good-night!"

***Visual Activity (quantity)***
***Gross Motor Activity***

Each number, beginning with ten, can be indicated by
holding up appropriate fingers. The song can be
dramatized if floor space and abilities permit. A variation
can be sung by using an addition concept (i.e., "hopped
in" instead of "fell out").

# ROLLING ALONG

French-Canadian Song
Arranged by Marshall Bartholomew

*With a swing*

Roll - ing, roll - ing, roll-ing a-long, See my ball a - roll - ing on.

Appropriate verses can be created to accommodate children rolling to a target (e.g.,
"Here comes Jimmy, rolling along,").

## THE SHOEMAKER

Words adapted
Danish Ring Game

Wind and wind the thread and wind and wind the thread and

Pull, pull, stamp, stamp, stamp. Shoe-man, can you fix my shoe?

Stitch it up so it's like new.

### Gross Motor Activity (laterality, memory/sequencing)

**Dance:** Partners face each other with a large hoop held between them (parallel to the floor).

**Meas. 1–2 (4 beats):** Partners turn hoop in winding motion with right hand crossing over left.

**Meas. 3–4 (4 beats):** Both partners pull hoop sharply on words "pull, pull." Stamp three times on "stamp, stamp, stamp," alternating feet.

Repeat measures 1–4; hoop can be wound in opposite direction, left hand crossing over right.

**Meas. 5–8 (8 beats):** Partners hold hoop with right hands, hold left hands in air as they walk in a circle with the hoop. (Be sure both are facing the same direction.)

Repeat measures 5–8, changing hands and direction.

**Seated version:** This version uses only upper extremities and is useful for non-ambulatory children.

**Meas. 1–2:** Make a fist with each hand and rotate fists around each other at chest level.

**Meas. 3–4:** Pull elbows back sharply on "pull, pull." Clap hands three times to substitute for stamps.

Repeat measures 1–4, rotating fists in the opposite direction.

**Meas. 5–6:** Make fists again, pounding the right on top of the left to the beat (4 times).

**Meas. 7–8:** Same as above, but with left fist on top.

Repeat measures 5–8.

## SINGING TOP

Words and music by Josephine Wolverton

*Gaily*

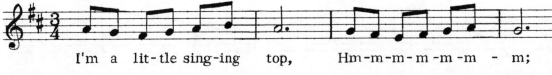

I'm a lit-tle sing-ing top, Hm-m-m-m-m-m - m;

When I'm tired I have to stop, Hm-m-m-m-m-m - m.

# SKIPPIN' AND STEPPIN'

Mary J. Sabol

*Rock style*

# THE SNAPDRAGON SONG

Words and music by
Elizabeth Deutsch (ASCAP)
Arranged by Lynn Freeman Olson

I can see the leaves when they're turn-ing, ___ (turn)

I can hear the thun-der clap, (clap) I can put a stamp on a let-ter, ___ (stamp) But I can't hear the snap-drag-on snap. (snap fingers) I can hear the tea-ket-tle whis-tle, ___ (whistle)

I can make a flap-jack flap, (palms together; flip over)

# SNOWFLAKES

Words by Marian Kennedy
Music by David Eddleman

*Swirlingly*

1. Whirl-ing, swirl-ing, rush-ing, twirl-ing, Sift - ing through the air;
2. Gent-ly slid - ing, float-ing, glid-ing, Mak - ing not a sound;
3. Whirl-ing, swirl-ing, rush-ing, twirl-ing, 'Gainst the win - dow pane;

Snow-flakes scur-ry-ing, scamp-er-ing, hur-ry-ing, Fall - ing ev-'ry-where.
Light-ly danc - ing, skip - ping, pranc - ing, Flut-ter-ing to the ground.
Snow-flakes scur-ry-ing, scamp-er-ing, hur-ry-ing, Win - ter's here a - gain.

# SO LONG

Words and music by Woody Guthrie

*Rhythmically*

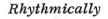
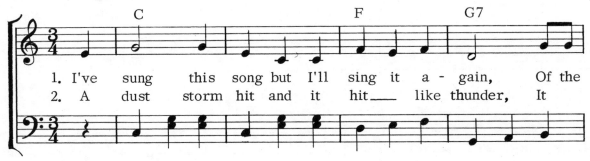

1. I've sung this song but I'll sing it a - gain, Of the
2. A dust storm hit and it hit___ like thunder, It

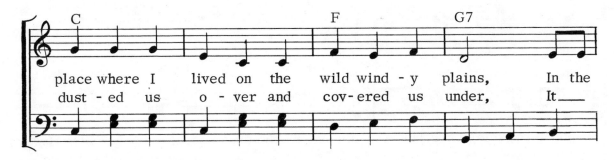

place where I lived on the wild wind - y plains, In the
dust - ed us o - ver and cov - ered us under, It___

month   called   A - pril,   the   coun - ty   called   Gray,   And
blocked   out the   traf - fic   and   blocked   out   the   sun,   And

here's   what   all   of   the   peo - ple   there   say:
straight   for   home   all   the   peo - ple   did   run,   sing - ing:

**Refrain**

"So   long,   it's   been good   to   know you,   So

long,   it's   been good   to   know you,   So   long,   it's

been good   to   know you, This   dust - y   old dust   is   a - get -ting   my

home,   I've   got   to   be   mov - ing   a - long."

# SOMEBODY'S KNOCKING AT YOUR DOOR

Black Spiritual
Arranged by Elsie Plant

## Auditory Activity (rhythm)

This is a fun song for individual echo clapping. Instruments can be used but are not necessary and may hinder the performance of some children. Rhythm patterns should be appropriate to both the auditory and motor skills of individuals. Although most children love to be surprised when hearing their name in the song, some children may need to be warned when their turn is next in order to assure their best listening effort. Children who have serious difficulties repeating patterns accurately may be helped by tapping the rhythm pattern on the back of their chair for an added sensory input (i.e., tactile). Very capable individuals can be challenged by patterns given to them from a location in the room where they cannot see your hands.

# SPEECH FUGUE

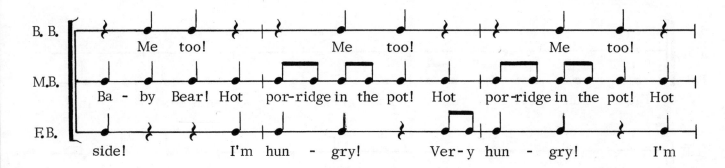

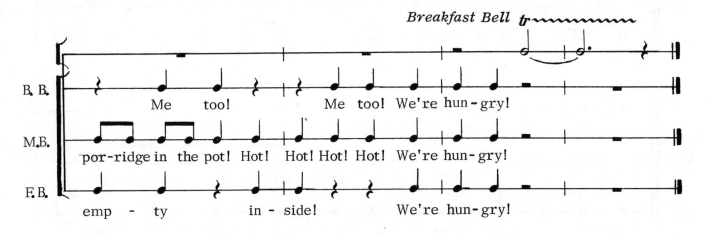

Breakfast Bell

*Auditory Activity (figure-ground)*
*Language Activity (articulation)*

First voice: Baby Bear (B.B.)
Second voice: Mother Bear (M.B.)
Third voice: Father Bear (F.B.)

**Suggested procedure:** Teach first and third voices together. ("Me too!" can be a small group.) When these two voices are learned well, add the second voice.

# STEP IN TIME

Words and music by
Richard M. and Robert B. Sherman
Arranged by Elsie Plant

*Spiritedly*

1. Kick your knees up, step in time!
2. Spin a - bout and step in time!

Kick your knees up, step in time!
Spin a - bout and step in time! Nev-er need a rea - son

nev-er need a rhyme, Kick your knees up, step in time!
Spin a - bout and step in time!

3. Link your elbows, step in time! ...

4. 'Round the circle, step in time! ...

5. Flap like a birdie, step in time! ...

6. Step in time, __ step in time! __...

## Gross Motor Activity (balance, nonlocomotor, strength and energy, reaction/agility, memory/sequencing)

**Dance:** Partners, facing each other

*Verse*

1. Join hands. Step-kick 8 times, starting with the right foot. (Kick gently to avoid partner's leg.)

Step-kick for two measures:

| R | L | L | R |
|---|---|---|---|
| step | kick | step | kick |

2. With hands still joined, partners skip around each other in a circle.

3. Link right elbows; step-kick in a circle.

4. Change arms and step-kick in a circle in the opposite direction. (The stepping and kicking will be reversed.)

5. Drop hands. Tuck hands under arms; flap elbows while stepping (or hopping) the beat.

6. Partners improvise movements to the beat, either individually or together.

**Simplified version**

1. Partners stand *side by side* with inside hands joined. Step-kick 8 times, beginning with right foot.

2. Partners join both hands and skip around each other in a circle.

3.–6. As above.

## STOP! LOOK! LISTEN!

Traditional words
Melody by John S. Murray
Arranged by Elsie Plant

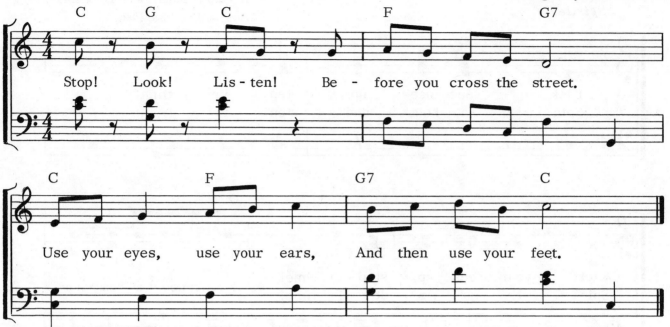

Stop! Look! Lis-ten! Be - fore you cross the street.

Use your eyes, use your ears, And then use your feet.

Used by permission of John S. Murray.

## STRETCHING SONG

Words and music by Eunice Boardman

*Freely*

1. I'm stretch-ing ver - y tall, And now I'm ver - y small.
2. My hands I stretch out wide, Be - hind me they will hide.

Now tall! Now small! Now I'm a ti - ny ball.
Now wide! Now hide! I put them at my side.

### *Fine Motor Activity (grasp and release)*

For another version, sing the following.

> My fingers can be straight,
> Or they can bend like this,
> Now straight! Now bend!
> Now watch me make a fist.

> My fingers can spread wide,
> And now they're tucked inside   (*make a fist*)
> Now wide! Inside!
> Now they are side by side.   (*fingers together*)

## THERE WAS A CROOKED MAN

Mother Goose
Traditional

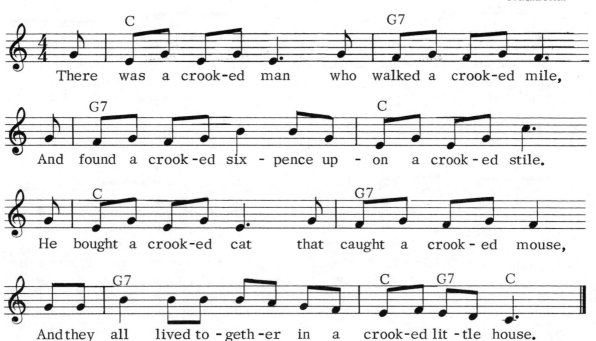

There was a crook-ed man who walked a crook-ed mile,

And found a crook-ed six - pence up - on a crook-ed stile.

He bought a crook-ed cat that caught a crook-ed mouse,

And they all lived to -geth -er in a crook-ed lit -tle house.

## THREE LITTLE DUCKS

Folk Song

*Lively*

1. Three lit-tle ducks went out to play, O - ver the hills and
ACTIONS: *(walk fingers up opposite arm)* *(walk fingers over shoulder)*

far a - way. When the moth-er duck said, "quack, quack, quack, quack,"
*(sing softly)*

Two lit - tle ducks came wad - dling back.
*(walk fingers quickly back down arm)*

2. Two little ducks went out to play, Over the hills and far away.
   When the mother duck said, "quack, quack, quack, quack,"
   One little duck came waddling back.

3. One little duck . . .
   . . . No little duck came waddling back.

4. No little ducks went out to play, . . .
   When the father duck said, "quack, quack, quack, quack," *(spoken loudly)*
   Three little ducks came running back. *(quickly)*

199

# THROW IT OUT THE WINDOW

Nonsense Song, Adapted
Arranged by Elsie Plant

1. Old Moth-er Hub-bard, she went to the cup-board To fetch her poor dog a bone, But when she got there, the cup-board was bare, So she threw it out the win-dow.
2. Lit-tle Miss Muf-fet sat on a tuf-fet Eat-ing her curds and whey, A-long came a spider and sat down be-side her, So she threw it out the win-dow.
3. Lit-tle Jack Hor-ner sat in the cor-ner Eat-ing a Christ-mas pie, He put in his thumb and pulled out a plumb, And she threw it out the win-dow.

The win-dow, the win-dow, the sec-ond sto-ry win-dow,

For additional verses, adapt familiar Mother Goose and nursery rhymes.

# TICKY TICKY TAMBO

Unknown

*Lively*

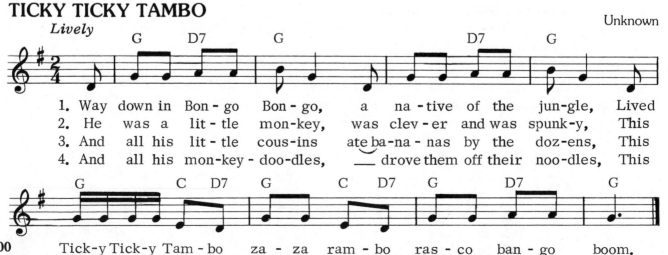

1. Way down in Bon-go Bon-go, a na-tive of the jun-gle, Lived
2. He was a lit-tle mon-key, was clev-er and was spunk-y, This
3. And all his lit-tle cous-ins ate ba-na-nas by the doz-ens, This
4. And all his mon-key-doo-dles, __ drove them off their noo-dles, This

Tick-y Tick-y Tam-bo za-za ram-bo ras-co ban-go boom.

200

# TINIKLING

English words by Margaret Marks
Philippine Dance Song
Collected by Francisca Reyes Aquino
Arranged by James Harris

*Introduction*

Ev-'ry-bod-y dance like the bird Tin - i - kling.
fast - er and fast - er,_ don't stop!

As_ he_ jumps in and out, out_ and in,
Left,_ right,_ left, right, you step and_ you hop.

Hop-ping o - ver
Bet - ter keep the

branch-es so grace-ful and_ light,
pace up, jump in and jump_ out,

Keep_ in_ step and you'll
Or_ the_ bam - boo will

1.
dance this dance_ right.
get you, watch_

Now the dance goes

2.
out.

201

## Gross Motor Activity (agility/reaction; memory/sequencing)

POLER

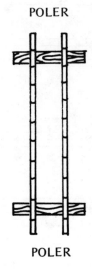

Materials:   masking tape
2 bamboo poles 6′ to 9′
2 boards 2″ × 4″, about 30″ in length

**Pole rhythm:**   (All children should practice the pole rhythm.) Seated, and pretending to grasp poles, bring hands together at the midline on beat 1. Spread hands apart, defining beats 2 and 3. Practice at a slow tempo until ready for a faster one.

When the pattern has been mastered, children can practice with the poles and the music. Lift and strike poles together once on beat 1. Open the poles about a foot apart and hit them on the boards on beats 2 and 3.

Polers should have plenty of practice before accompanying a dancer. Only children who can sustain both rhythm and tempo for the entire song will be successful polers.

POLER

**Dance:**   (All children should practice the dance steps.)

**1.**   *Without* poles, walk through the steps in sequence.

Meas.  1:    beat 1—step on LF *in place* (outside poles)
beat 2—step *to the right* with RF (inside poles)
beat 3—step LF *next to* RF (inside poles)

Meas.  2:    beat 1—step *to the right* on RF (outside poles)
beat 2—step *to the left* on LF (inside poles)
beat 3—step RF *next to* LF (inside poles)

Meas.  3:    beat 1—step *to the left* on LF (outside poles)

(repeat, continuing from measure 1, beat 2)

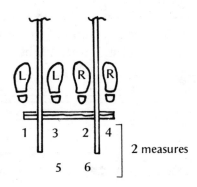

2 measures

**2.**   Add music in slow tempo.

**3.**   When children have mastered the alternating foot pattern, place two strips of masking tape 12″ to 18″ (or more) on the floor to simulate the poles. They need not be long; several pairs can be placed around the room for practice. Footprints with letter, number, or color codes can be used, as illustrated. Continue to practice, stepping in and out of the strips. Children should practice individually.

**4.**   Replace masking tape strips with poles placed 18″ or more apart on the boards. While poles remain stationary, have children practice the steps in and out. They will need to lift their feet higher in order to step over the poles, which are 2″ off the floor.

Add the pole rhythm only for those individuals who can be assured of some degree of success. Begin with a slow tempo. As children become more agile, the tempo can be increased and the children will automatically substitute hopping for stepping.

Some children may eventually be able to do the dance in pairs and/or improvise turns and postures while doing the steps. To do the dance with a partner, each stands to the left of the poles at opposite ends facing each other. Since space inside the poles is cramped, they will need to have good balance and control of hopping movements as well as good agility.

# TRA LA LA LA

Swiss Folk Song
Arranged by Lynn Freeman Olson

*Rhythmically*

Tra  la  la  la  la  la  la  la  la,  Tra

la  la  la  la  la  la  la  la,  Tra  la  la  la  la  la

la  la  la,  Tra  la  la  la  la  la. _____

# TRAIN IS A-COMING

Black Spiritual
Arranged by Albert DeVito

## Language Activity

New verses can be created by asking children to supply parts or cars on a train
(e.g., engine, dining car, freight car).

# THE TREE IN THE VALLEY

Folk Song

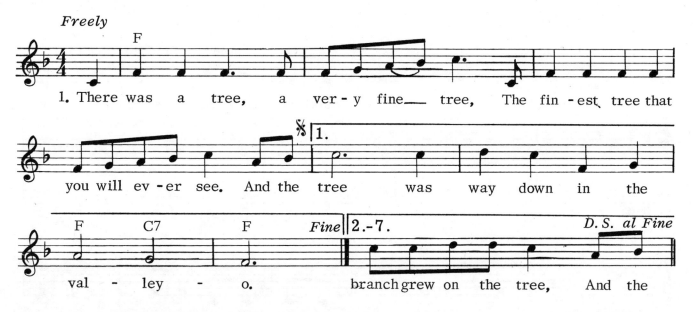

1. There was a tree, a ver-y fine___ tree, The fin-est tree that you will ev-er see. And the tree was way down in the val-ley-o.

branch grew on the tree, And the

2. And on that tree there was a branch,
   The finest branch that you will ever see.
   And the branch grew on the tree,
   And the tree was way down in the valley-o.

3. And on that branch there was a nest, . . .
   . . . nest was on the branch . . . branch grew on the tree, . . .

4. And in that nest there was an egg, . . .

5. And in that egg there was a bird, . . .

6. And on that bird there was a wing, . . .

7. And on that wing there was a feather, . . .

## Motor Activity (sequencing)

*Verse*
1. Meas. 1–4:  Make tree by extending both arms overhead.
   Meas. 5–8:  Sway trunk and arms side to side.
2. branch:  Extend one arm to the side, shoulder high.
3. nest:  Cup hands together, palms up.
4. egg:  Make egg shape with thumb and index finger.
5. bird:  Link thumbs together, flutter fingers.
6. wing:  Flutter fingers of one hand.
7. feather:  Extend index finger and blow on it.

With each new verse, repeat previous verses and motions.

# THE TWELVE DAYS OF CHRISTMAS

Folk Song from England
Arranged by Theron Haithwaite

# TWO LITTLE BLACKBIRDS

Traditional words
Melody by Esther L. Nelson
Arranged by Lynn Freeman Olson

*Happily*

### Fine Motor Activity

Meas. 1–8:    Hold fists together in front of body with knuckles on top.

Meas. 9–12:    Flutter fingers on right hand, moving behind back.

Meas. 12–16:    Flutter fingers on left hand, moving behind back.

Meas. 17–20:    Bring right hand back to fist position.

Meas. 21–24:    Bring left hand back to fist position.

### Locomotor Activity

Seated position. Two children (or groups) are designated "Jack" and "Jill." The song is dramatized with each group "flying away" and "coming back" at the appropriate time.

208

# TWO LITTLE HANDS

Music by David Eddleman

Two lit - tle hands so soft and bright. *(show hands)*

This is the left; *(indicate left hand)* this is the right. *(indicate right hand)*

Five lit-tle fin-gers stand-ing on each, *(show fingers)*

So I can hold a plum or a peach. *(grasp)* But

when I get as big as you, *(raise hands high)*   I'll

show you what these hands can do.   *(hands to the front)*   *(and back)*

### Auditory Activity (memory)

This song can be taught in echo style with the class echoing each phrase after it is sung by the teacher. Appropriate motions can be added.

## UPSTAIRS, DOWNSTAIRS

Words and music by Sona D. Nocera

*Rhythmically*

Climb, climb, climb up the stairs. We won't stop 'til we reach the top.

Down, down, low-er we get, care-ful to watch for the ver-y last step.

### Gross Motor Activity (locomotor)

To use as an accompaniment for going up the stairs or down the stairs, repeat the appropriate line as needed. One *or* two steps can be taken to each measure.

# VALENTINE

Words by Aden G. Lewis
German Folk Melody
Arranged by Lynn Freeman Olson

*With a swing*

1. Val - en -tine, Val - en -tine, Won't you be my Val - en -tine?
2. Dance with me, dance with me, Swing - ing, swing-ing to and fro.

Val - en -tine, Val - en - tine, Yes, I'll be your Val - en - tine.
Dance with me, dance with me, Round and round and round we go.

## Gross Motor Activity (locomotor, memory/ sequencing)

**Dance:** Partners face each other and decide who will be the first person to move in the first version.

Meas. 1–2: Partners join hands and swing arms to the beat.

Meas. 3–4: The first partner walks in a circle around the other.

Meas. 5–6: Same as Meas. 1–2.

Meas. 7–8: The second partner walks in a circle around the first.

**Variations:** There are many ways to make the dance more difficult.

Meas. 1–2: Partners shake right hands on the beat (twice), then shake left hands (twice).

Meas. 3–4: Partners link right elbows and swing around.

Meas. 5–6: Same as Meas. 1–2.

Meas. 7–8: Partners link left elbows and swing around.

(Note: This version changes movement with each new phrase and therefore reinforces the form of the song.)

## Language Activity (receptive, verbalization)

The song has both short and long phrases. New verses can use names of children. For example: "Kevin Black, Kevin Black, Won't you come and dance with me? Yes I will, . . ."

New words can also describe new movements, such as "Touch your toe, touch your toe, Round our partners, here we go . . ."

Non-seasonal: "Be my friend, be my friend, Won't you be a friend of mine? Yes I will, yes I will, We'll be friends a long, long time."

Sing as a call-and-response song: Meas. 1–4, call; Meas. 5–8, response.

# WALRUS HUNT

*Quickly*

**Refrain**

Hock-y tock-y oom-bah, hock-y tock-y oom-bah, Hey did-dle, hi did-dle,

*Slowly and freely*

**Verse**

ho did-dle ay. Ah ta kol-a mish-a wock - y,

Ah ta kol-a mish-a wock - y, Ah ta kol-a mish-a

*a tempo*

wock - y, Hey did-dle, hi did-dle, ho did-dle ay.

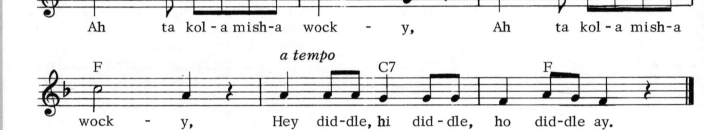

*Refrain:* Paddle kayaks by bringing hands to center and moving elbows up and down.

*Verse (sing four times):*

1st   Hunters shield eyes with hands while looking for walrus; look alternately left and right on each phrase.

2nd   Draw hunting bow, release arrow on last note of phrase.

3rd   Haul walrus into boat a little on each phrase until all in on last.

4th   Hunters wave to families on shore.

# WAY DOWN YONDER IN THE BRICKYARD

**With strong off-beat clapping** ♩ = 168-184

Way down yon - der in the brick-yard, Re-mem - ber me.

Way down yon - der in the brick-yard,__ Re-mem - ber me. Oh,

step it, step it, step it down, Re-mem - ber me, Oh,

step it, step it, step it down, Re-mem - ber me, Oh,

swing your love and turn a - round, Re-mem - ber me.__ Re-mem - ber me.

Written and adapted by Bessie Jones; collected and edited by Alan Lomax. TRO—© copyright 1972 Ludlow Music, Inc., New York, N.Y. Used by permission.

The class can sing the *entire* song, or the teacher (leader) can sing the *call* with the class singing the *response* (i.e., "Remember me"). Start the off-beat clapping before beginning the song.

**Dance:** Circle formation, standing; one child in the center

Meas. 1–8:  Center child walks around the inside of the circle and chooses a partner by standing in front of one child.

Meas. 9–16:  Class continues to clap and sing as center child and partner "step it down"* (the *dance* step) eight times. (Partner remains in place in the circle.)

Meas. 17–20:  Partners link elbows and swing around until center child is in partner's place in the circle. Partner becomes new center child as game repeats. Sing the second ending to end the game.

\* "step it down":

1st beat—extend right foot foward, toe touching floor
2nd beat—return right foot to starting position and step on it (The clap occurs on the stepping beat.)
3rd and 4th beats—repeat above with left foot

Clap:

touch step touch step | touch step touch step
R    R    L    L   |  R    R    L    L

**Variation:** For a child physically unable to "step it down," a clapping pattern can be substituted in this section, or the "step it down" can be done seated.

Adapted from p. 115 in STEP IT DOWN by Bessie Jones and Bess Lomax Hawes. Copyright © 1972 by Bess Lomax Hawes and Bessie Jones. Reprinted by permission of Harper & Row, Publishers, Inc.

# WE'RE GOING ROUND THE MOUNTAIN

Folk Song from Mississippi

1. We're go - ing round the moun - tain,
2. Oh, show us___ a mo - tion, la, la, la, la,
3. That's a might-y fine___ mo - tion,

We're go - ing round the moun - tain,
Oh, show us___ a mo - tion, la, la, la, la,
That's a might - y fine___ mo - tion,

We're go - ing round the moun - tain,
Oh, show us___ a mo - tion, la, la, la, la,
That's a might-y fine___ mo - tion,

So rise, (Sal - ly), rise.

**Gross Motor Activity (reaction/agility)**
**Visual Activity**

Circle formation, standing. One child is chosen to go into the center.

*Verse*

1. Child in center crouches down as children in the circle walk in clockwise direction. On words "So rise (Sally) rise" (substitute child's name), child stands in preparation for performing a motion on the second verse.
2. Children stand still as child in center makes up a motion and repeats it throughout the verse.
3. Class joins the center child in performing the motion. A new leader is chosen by child or teacher at the end of the song.

For nonambulatory children, the circle can be stationary and/or seated; center child need not crouch down on first verse.

# WHAT CAN MAKE A HIPPOPOTAMUS SMILE?

Unknown
Arranged by Lynn Freeman Olson

3. Not a zoom down a slippery slide, or going for a bicycle ride,
   That's not what hippos do. *Refrain.*

4. Not some brand new words to spell, or collecting whistles or marbles or shells,
That's not what hippos do. *Refrain.*

5. Not a movie or an Irish jig, or Halloweening in a funny wig,
That's not what hippos do. *Refrain.*

## WHAT SHALL WE DO?

Words adapted
Game Song
Arranged by Alice Firgau

*With a bounce*

TEACHER: What shall we do on a rain-y day, rain-y day, rain-y day?
CLASS: Jump in the puddles on a rain-y day, rain-y day, rain-y day.

What shall we do on a rain-y day, When we go out to play?
Jump in the puddles on a rain-y day, When we go out to play.

### Language Activity (expressive)

This song offers many possibilities for language experiences in addition to reinforcing weather concepts. Children can supply appropriate verses to complement those introduced by the teacher. Children's verses can be dramatized; nonverbal children may contribute their ideas for verses by acting them out.

### Suggestions:

Teacher:  What shall we do on a snowy day . . .
      . . . When we go out to play?
  Class:  Slide on our sleds on a snowy day . . .
  Class:  We'll build a snowman . . .
Teacher:  . . . windy day . . .
  Class:  We could go sailing . . .
  Class:  Fly our kites . . .
Teacher:  . . . sunny day . . .
Teacher:  . . . very cold day . . .

# WHEN SAMMY PUT THE PAPER ON THE WALL

Traditional

*Brightly*

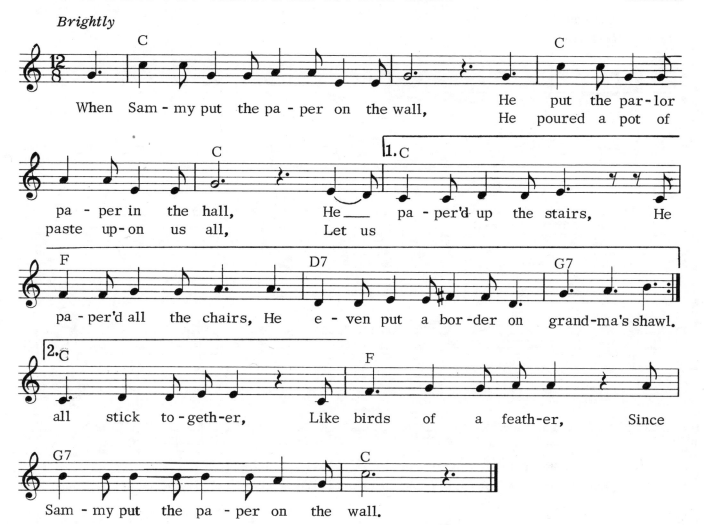

When Sam-my put the pa-per on the wall, He put the par-lor
He poured a pot of

pa-per in the hall, He \_\_ pa-per'd up the stairs, He
paste up-on us all, Let us

pa-per'd all the chairs, He e-ven put a bor-der on grand-ma's shawl.

all stick to-geth-er, Like birds of a feath-er, Since

Sam - my put the pa-per on the wall.

# WHEN THE TRAIN COMES ALONG

American Folk Song
Arranged by W. W. Schmidt

*With a swing*

**Refrain**

When the train comes a-long,__ when the train comes a-long,__ I'll

meet you at the sta-tion when the train comes a-long.

**Verse**

1. It may be snow-ing, It
2. It may be rain-ing, It

may be cold, But I'll meet you at the sta-tion when the train comes a-long.
may be wet, But I'll meet you at the sta-tion when the train comes a-long.

# THE WIND BLEW EAST

Folk Song from the Bahamas
Arranged by James Rooker

Transcribed and adapted from The Library of Congress Field Recording AFS 485.

# WOODSTOCK'S SAMBA
## (Instrumental based on "The Best of Buddies")

Music by Richard M. Sherman
and Robert B. Sherman
Arranged by David Eddleman

I    PIANICAS, MELODICAS, or REED HORNS -- 4 players

C       G       A       F

PIANICAS, or MELODICAS -- 2 players

C       G       A       F

II    BELLS, XYLOPHONE, PIANICAS, or MELODICAS -- 2 to 4 players (for fewer players, combine parts)

F    A      D    B      C    G      D

III   SLIDE WHISTLE (or glissando on XYLOPHONE or PIANO) -- 1 player

IV   KAZOO (melody -- any number of players)

**Suggested procedure**

Teach all parts through the first three endings only, beginning with I. Teach III next by cueing. When I and III are learned, teach II. When these parts are learned well, IV (melody) can be added. When all parts are secure, teach fourth ending in the same instrumental sequence.

Teach rhythm parts one at a time by having the entire class clap one of the patterns until a player is secure enough to play and hold a part while others clap a second rhythm. Continue to add instruments in this fashion until several children can clap, then play each pattern with piano accompaniment. (It doesn't matter whether you begin with melody or rhythm parts, and you can use a combination of any two or more.)

For dance directions, see Appendix, p. 275.

# ZIPPERS

Words and music by J. Lilian Vandevere

*Rhythmically*

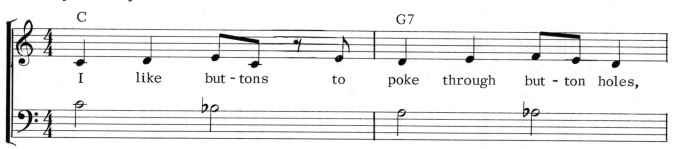

I like but-tons to poke through but-ton holes,

I like snaps that pop! But best of all

I like zip-pers, they go zip-ping to the ver - y top! *(spoken)* Zip!

## THE BUGLE-BILLED BAZOO

*The noisiest bird that ever grew
Is the Bugle-Billed Bazoo
(He's even noisier than YOU.)*

*He starts his YAMMERING as soon
As he's awake, then SHOUTS till noon.*

*Then SCREAMS from noon till six or so,
And then he YELLS an hour or two.*

*He's not like other birds who sing
Because the flowers are out for Spring.*

*He SHRIEKS and SCOLDS the whole day through
Just to be heard. If you do, too,
YOU'RE a Bugle-Billed Bazoo.*

                              —John Ciardi

## CAT

*The black cat yawns.
Opens her jaws,
Stretches her legs,
And shows her claws.*

*Then she gets up
And stands on four
Long stiff legs
And yawns some more.*

*She shows her sharp teeth,
She stretches her lip,
Her slice of a tongue
Turns up at the tip.*

*Lifting herself
On her delicate toes,
She arches her back
As high as it goes.*

*She lets herself down
With particular care,
And pads away
With her tail in the air.*

                    —Mary Britton Miller

## THE MOOSE AND THE GOOSE

*There once was a moose
Who was this tall.
He walked with a goose
Who was this small.
But the moose felt bad
Because he was tall
And the goose was sad
Because he was small.
Whenever they'd go
On a friendly walk
The distance between
Made it hard to talk.
So the goose stretched up
And the moose crouched down
And they walked and talked
All over town!*

                    —Vernon Howard

## RAIN SIZES

*Rain comes in various sizes.*
*Some rain is as small as a mist.*
*It tickles your face with surprises,*
*And tingles as if you'd been kissed.*

*Some rain is the size of a sprinkle*
*And doesn't put out all the sun.*
*You can see the drops sparkle and twinkle*
*And a rainbow comes out when it's done.*

*Some rain is as big as a nickle*
*And comes with a crash and a hiss.*
*It comes down too heavy to tickle*
*It's more like a splash than a kiss.*

*When it rains the right size and you're wrapped in*
*Your rainclothes, it's fun out of doors.*
*But run home before you get trapped in*
*The big rain that rattles and roars.*

—John Ciardi

From THE REASON FOR THE PELICAN by John Ciardi.
Copyright © 1959 by John Ciardi. Reprinted by
permission of J. B. Lippincott Company.

## SOUND OF WATER

The sound of water is:

*Rain,*
*Lap,*
*Fold,*
*Slap,*
*Gurgle,*
*Splash,*
*Churn,*
*Crash,*
*Murmur,*
*Pour,*
*Ripple,*
*Roar,*
*Plunge,*
*Drip,*
*Spout,*
*Slip,*
*Sprinkle,*
*Flow,*
*Ice,*
*Snow.*

—Mary O'Neill

Text copyright © 1966 by Mary O'Neill
From WHAT IS THAT SOUND!
Used by permission of Atheneum Publishers.

## SALVADOR SQUEAK

*Salvador Squeak*
*Was the funniest mouse*
*Who ever lived*
*In anyone's house!*

*He stood on one leg*          (stand on one leg)
*Every morning at three,*       (hold up three fingers)
*And slept with his arms*
*Wrapped around a tree!*       (wrap arms)

*He ate nothing but grass*     (pretend to eat)
*And drank nothing but ink,*    (pretend to drink)
*And he soaked his head*       (bow head)
*In the kitchen sink!*

*He could swim under water*    (make swimming motions)
*For thirty-three miles,*
*And often played catch*        (pretend to toss ball)
*With fierce crocodiles!*

*He told wild stories*
*While perched on a shelf*      (hold hand up high)
*And if no one would listen,*   (cup ear)
*He'd talk to himself!*         (point to self)

*He always wore roses*
*On top of his head,*           (touch top of head)
*And chained a gorilla*
*To the foot of his bed!*        (make low gesture)

*Yes, Salvador Squeak*
*Was the funniest mouse*
*Who ever lived*
*In anyone's house!*

—Vernon Howard

From the book MONOLOGUES FOR BOYS AND GIRLS by Vernon Howard © 1957 by Sterling Publishing Co., Inc., New York. Reprinted by permission.

## BEAR HUNT

*After introducing the activity, narrate the adventure one line at a time. The children repeat each line. The narration is accompanied by a steady "walking" pattern (patting each thigh alternately).   Between the sections of narration, time is allowed to act out in rhythm the motion indicated. When the "bear" is seen, the actions are reversed double-quick, with a very fast "walking" pattern, as if running away from the "bear."*

Let's go on a bear hunt. Repeat after me everything I say, and do all the movements I do.

| | |
|---|---|
| I see a wheat field. | (Walking pattern) |
| Can't go over. | |
| Can't go under. | |
| Let's go through. | (Brush palms together back and forth several times.) |

| | |
|---|---|
| I see a bridge. | (Walking pattern) |
| Can't go around. | |
| Can't go under. | |
| Let's go over. | (Thump chest with fists.) |

Scared?
Not much.

| | |
|---|---|
| I see some mud. | (Walking pattern) |
| Can't go over. | |
| Can't go under. | |
| Let's go through. | (Hand-walk through sticky mud, making "shloo, shloo" sound with mouth.) |

| | |
|---|---|
| I see a lake. | (Walking pattern) |
| Can't go over. | |
| Can't go under. | |
| Let's go through. | (Imitate overarm swim stroke. Shake self as if wet.) |

| | |
|---|---|
| I see a tree. | (Walking pattern) |
| Can't go over. | |
| Can't go under. | |
| Let's go up. | (Imitate climbing a tree. Shade eyes with one hand, looking all around.) |

| | |
|---|---|
| I don't see any bears! | (Imitate coming down a tree.) |

| | |
|---|---|
| I see a cave. | (Walking pattern begins to slow up.) |
| Can't go over. | (Voice becomes quieter.) |
| Can't go under. | (Voice becomes almost a whisper.) |
| Let's go in. | (Whisper) |
| I see two eyes. | (A real whisper) |
| I see a nose. | (Reach out one hand, feeling fur.) |
| It's a bear! | (Voice shouts.) |

*Now reverse all movements—climbing a tree, swimming a lake, walking through sticky mud, crossing the bridge, going through the wheat field—using the "running" pattern instead of a "walking" pattern.*

*At the very end, thrust hand forward as if slamming a door with a loud BANG. Sit back and heave a sigh of relief.*

From RHYTHMS TODAY by Edna Doll and Mary Jarman Nelson. © 1965 Silver Burdett Company.

## THE SORCERER'S APPRENTICE                    (Paul Dukas)

Once there was a young man who was apprenticed to a sorcerer (magician). In return for the opportunity to learn the sorcerer's craft, the apprentice did many chores for his master. One of these was filling the sorcerer's bath by carrying buckets of water from a well outside. It was very tiring work. One day when he was all alone, the apprentice put on a magic cap, picked up a magic wand, and recited some magic words that he had heard his master use to make a broom come to life. To his surprise it worked! He commanded the broom to get water for the bath. Slowly arms and legs appeared on the broom and off it went to begin carrying buckets of water from the well to the bath. The apprentice was very pleased with himself—until the bath was full; then he suddenly realized that he didn't know any magic words to make the broom stop!

   The apprentice didn't know what to do. The bath was already overflowing and water was everywhere. And still the broom hurried back and forth from the well with more water! Hoping to stop it, the apprentice took an axe and split the broom in two. For a moment it seemed that he had succeeded. But then each part of the broken broom began to move and soon both were carrying buckets of water from the well as fast as they could. The water rose higher and the apprentice knew he could not stop the brooms. At that moment, the sorcerer returned home. He spoke some magic words that stopped the brooms and made the water disappear. He was very angry with the young apprentice and scolded him. The apprentice was ashamed that he had acted so foolishly.

## OF A TAILOR AND A BEAR                    (Edward MacDowell)

One day a tailor was busy sewing in his shop. As he worked he whistled a happy tune. Suddenly, a big bear appeared in the doorway. The tailor was frightened, but then he saw the bear was wearing a collar around his neck. "He is probably from the circus," thought the tailor, "and I bet he likes music." So he carefully picked up his violin, tuned it, and began to play. At first the bear just growled. But the tailor kept playing and soon the bear began to dance. Because he was so big and heavy, the bear danced and turned slowly. Then a man came into the shop. He was the bear's trainer and he had been looking everywhere for his bear. When he heard the tailor's violin he knew he would find his bear there. The bear did not want to stop dancing and growled one last time as the trainer led him away. The tailor went back to his sewing, whistling his happy tune. But he couldn't forget the sight of that bear dancing or the sound of his growl!

227

# ADDITIONAL ACTIVITIES

Dances that can be used with the recording of "Alley Cat."

## Gross Motor Activity (locomotor)

**Ball dance:** Partners face each other, 8″ to 12″ apart.

**Suggested procedure:** Learn bounce/catch sequence of Section A first without music. Add music in slow tempo, counting bounces and passes out loud. When secure, proceed in same fashion with Section B.

### Section A

| | |
|---|---|
| Meas. 1—3 (6 beats) | Partner A bounces the ball on beat 1, catches on beat 2 (three times). |
| Meas. 4 (2 beats) | Partner A bounces the ball to Partner B. |
| Meas. 5—7 (6 beats) | Partner B bounce/catches three times (as in Meas. 1—3). |
| Meas. 8 (2 beats) | Partner B bounces ball back to Partner A. |

*Repeat Meas. 1—8.*

### Section B

| | |
|---|---|
| Meas. 9—11 (6 beats) | Partner A bounce/catches the ball while taking three side steps to the right; Partner B sidesteps *left* without a ball. |
| Meas. 12 (2 beats) | Partner A stoops and *rolls* the ball to Partner B. |
| Meas. 13—15 (6 beats) | Partner B bounce/catches the ball as above while side-stepping *right* (three bounce/catches); Partner A sidesteps *left* (back to starting place) without a ball. |
| Meas. 16 (2 beats) | Partner B stoops and *rolls* the ball back to Partner A. |

*Repeat Section A once.*

### Coda

| | |
|---|---|
| Meas. 17—20 (8 beats) | Beginning with Partner A, ball is bounced back and forth between partners every other beat, four times in all. |

### Variations

**1.** Partners can sit on floor with legs extended or crossed; small bounces can be made on either side of the body.

**2.** Vary direction or kinds of steps in Section B. Example: walk forward, backward, on tiptoes, with knees bent.
**3.** Some children, with practice or advanced skills, may be able to bounce and catch on every beat, thus bouncing seven times and passing to partner on the eighth beat in Section A.
**4.** Substitute balloons, hoops, or scarves and adapt accordingly.

**Mirror dance:** Movements can be taught by having children mirror yours. See Appendix, p. 276, for additional movement suggestions.

### Section A

| | |
|---|---|
| Meas. 1—4 (8 beats) | Slap thighs/clap hands in front of body (eight times). |
| Meas. 5—8 (8 beats) | Same, but alternating clapping to left and right sides of body. |

*Repeat Section A, adding left and right side steps.*

### Section B

| | |
|---|---|
| Meas. 9—12 (8 beats) | Swing arms side to side (eight times). |
| Meas. 13—14 (4 beats) | Add side steps to arm swinging (four times). |
| Meas. 15—16 (4 beats) | Touch head, shoulders, hips, knees (each twice). |

*Repeat Section A once*

### Coda

| | |
|---|---|
| Meas. 17 (2 beats) | Extend right arm forward and wave hand up/down from the wrist; same with left arm/hand. |
| Meas. 18 (2 beats) | Point the right elbow twice; left elbow twice. |
| Meas. 19—20 (4 beats) | Left hand on left hip, right arm extended out, make a full turn, counterclockwise, bringing right arm to right hip, ending with both hands on hips. |

Verse 2, seated, for "Ballin' the Jack" (for nonambulatory children)

*First you put your arms way out in space,*
*You bring them right__back, then you cover your__face,*
*Stretch away up high then you bend down low,*
*Then you shake your hands and shake your hands and go,__go, go.*
*Slap your two__ hands upon your knees,*
*Point your elbows out and you flap them in the breeze,*
*Now put both hands up and bring them down,*
*Now roll those hands around and around,*
*Around and around, around and around.*

Sona D. Nocera

Dances that can be used with the recording of "Hornpipe Dance."

For both versions, slower reacting children may slap, clap, or hop only once each measure in Section A, Meas. 1—4. They may use two beats instead of one for motions and hopping in Section B.

**Seated version:** Sitting on the floor in scatter, circle, or line formation.

### Section A

| | |
|---|---|
| Meas. 1 | Slap thighs on first three eighth notes. |
| Meas. 2 | Clap hands on first three eighth notes. |
| Meas. 3—4 | Repeat Meas. 1—2. |
| Meas. 5—8 | Extend arms overhead bringing each down alternately as if pulling down a rope, using left arm on beat 1 and right arm on beat 2 (8 times). |

### Section B

| | |
|---|---|
| Meas. 1—8 | Rock from side to side, putting weight on left hand on beat 1, and right hand on beat 2 (8 times). |

*Repeat Section A*

**Standing version:** Line or scatter formation.

### Section A

| | |
|---|---|
| Meas. 1 | Hop on right foot three times while shielding eyes with right hand, left hand on left hip. |
| Meas. 2 | Hop on left foot three times while shielding eyes with left hand, right hand on right hip. |
| Meas. 3—4 | Repeat Meas. 1—2. |
| Meas. 5—8 | Extend arms overhead and haul in rope (as in seated version). |

### Section B

| | |
|---|---|
| Meas. 9—12 | Beginning with right foot, stop hop in place on each beat, alternating feet and extending opposite arm upward, placing other hand on hip (8 times). |
| Meas. 13—16 | With hands on hips, walk forward on the beat 4 steps, bending knee on beat 4. Walk backward 4 steps. |

*Repeat Section A*

Dances that can be used with the recording of "Step Lively."

**Standing version:**   Circle formation, hands joined.

### Section A

Meas. 1          Step RF forward into circle, beat 1; step LF in place, beat 2.

Meas. 2          Step RF backward out of circle, beat 1; step LF in place, beat 2.

Meas. 3—8      Repeat Meas. 1—2 three times.
(Note: Cue words "forward" and "back" or "in" and "out" may be used.)

### Section B

Meas. 9          Kick RF forward, step RF in place.

Meas. 10        Kick LF forward, step LF in place.

Meas. 11—16   Repeat Meas. 9—10 three times.

*Repeat Section A.*
*Repeat Section B, but kick foot backward.*

### Variations

Section A   When children are comfortable with the in-and-out stepping, teach them to turn their bodies into the circle and bend knee on stepping foot, then turn out with the backward step. This will create a slow clockwise movement of the circle.

**Section B**   Experiment with different kick-step patterns.

**Seated version:**   Circle or scatter formation.

### Section A

Meas. 1—8   Extend arms forward into circle; in place; backward out of the circle; in place (four times).

### Section B

Meas. 9—12   Make up appropriate hand jive. Example:

Slap both hands on knees once; clap hands together once.
Slap right hand on left knee; clap hands together.
Slap left hand on right knee; clap hands together.
Slap both hands on both knees; clap hands together.

Meas. 13—16   Repeat Meas. 9—12.

Additional activities to use with the recording of "Stop and Go."

**Auditory Activities**
**Motor Activities**

Have children learn the song by singing and clapping first. They can emphasize "stop." Substitute instruments or body sounds to accompany the song.

**1.** Have children walk to the song, stopping at the ends of phrases. Incorporate the game *Statues,* having each child assume a freeze position and hold a pose at the end of the phrase.

**2.** Substitute ball bouncing on the beat.

**3.** Vary the tempo by singing the song slower or faster than usual.

# Accommodating Special Learners the in Music Environment

(Characteristics, Learning Style, Learning Needs)

# Accommodating Special Learners in the Music Environment

## MENTAL RETARDATION

### Characteristics

Retarded individuals have been labeled by the terms *developmentally disabled, educable mentally retarded, trainable mentally retarded, educable mentally handicapped, trainable mentally handicapped, mongoloid (Down's syndrome), brain-injured, brain-damaged, neurologically impaired, slow learner, hyperactive,* and many others. Some labels are descriptive of behaviors that may or may not be symptomatic of the condition (e.g., hyperactive) and, hence, are inappropriately used to describe the retarded population as a whole.

*Mental retardation,* according to the definition adopted by the American Association of Mental Deficiency in 1973, *is general subaverage intellectual functioning existing concurrently with deficits in adaptive behavior and is manifested during the developmental period.* Individuals who are retarded usually perform below average in all areas of learning (cognitive, psychomotor, and affective). This means that retarded children can be expected to function on levels characteristic of younger children in gross and fine motor, language, and social skills as well as concept development.

Retardation can apparently be caused by both organic and environmental factors. Children labeled as brain-damaged, brain-injured, or neurologically impaired may be retarded because of organic causes, such as genetic defect, or as a result of infection or injury that can occur before, during, or after birth. Learning problems associated with children retarded because of organic factors may include perceptual and thinking disorders, motor problems, and behavior disorders. Difficulties associated with retardation due to nonorganic causes (e.g., familial-cultural factors) are poor self-concept, lack of motivation, poor health and nutrition, family disorganization, perceptual and thinking disorders, and inadequate language development. Psychologists do not agree to what extent intelligence is inherited or can be influenced by adverse environmental factors. Recent brain research indicates that normally healthy brain cells that receive insufficient stimulation during the developmental preschool years may never fully mature. Nutrition and health are also factors in brain cell development. It is probable that in a significant number of cases both organic and environmental factors contribute to the condition.

The majority of retarded individuals who fall below the mildly retarded range are of the organic type. Many have neurological impairment (or central-nervous-system damage) and may have multiple problems including motor involvement, developmental aphasia (failure to develop language), physical impairments (such as poor vision or hearing), seizures, and bizarre behaviors. Some may be *hyperactive* while others are *hypoactive.* It is a rewarding experience to work with children who must put forth such monumental effort to achieve what the normal individual does naturally at a much younger age. It is in working with these children that a teacher's most creative ideas and energies are challenged. It is the children from this group who are so misunderstood, feared, and neglected in public education, who must constantly struggle to find ways to express intelligence, communicate needs, and demonstrate skills. Sometimes the struggle is too great—some children will give up and begin to function as they think others want or expect, which, all too often, is way below potential. A large number of children in this group are those diagnosed as cerebral palsied. It should be emphasized, however, that not all individuals with neurological impairments are retarded as well. Approximately half of those with central-nervous-system damage have intellectual abilities *above* the retarded demarcation line. There are some who have specific learning disabilities due mainly to perceptual problems, but they do not have the other learning problems associated with retardation. Severe cognitive deficiencies may limit the intellectual development of some, but there is an increasing number of others who have overcome learning difficulties well enough to earn college degrees.

In most school systems, retarded children are still traditionally divided into two groups: educable (mildly) mentally retarded and trainable (moderately) mentally retarded. A child is generally assigned to one of these groups based on an IQ score that, at best, gives a quantitative evaluation of the child's functioning level *at the time of testing.* Intelligence tests are both culturally and language biased, which means that unless appropriate norms are used they discriminate against children with language difficulties, children with language differences (i.e., children from non-English-speaking families and children who speak black-English vernacular), and all children from homes other than white urban middle-class. It is therefore unwise for a teacher to consider the IQ score as an *absolute* measure of a child's ability or potential. The idea that intelligence is fixed is now obsolete. A classic study, still in progress, has shown preliminary data in which the IQ scores of mildly retarded infants were raised 30 points in four years as a result of educational experiences (Heber, et al, 1972).[1] Testing that specifically identifies deficient skill areas is far more valuable to the educator than an IQ score.

Individuals with *mild retardation* constitute 75 percent of the retarded population. The majority of these individuals will become independent adults, attaining basic literacy and computation skills by the time they leave public school. However, the failure of the mildly retarded to achieve academically at even the level of their mental age has led the profession to question the validity of the self-contained special class and has given rise to the practice of mainstreaming. Research findings are mixed but clearly indicate that more social than academic gains are made in special classes. Some of the special class failures prior to the 1970s may be attributed to the fact that, until that time, there were few teachers or supervisors specially trained to work with the retarded. Today, college programs that begin training teachers of the handicapped as undergraduates have the chance to influence the development of attitudes as well as techniques and skills. Many new college graduates have benefited from courses of study that include extensive field experiences with both normal and handicapped populations. It is not surprising that they begin their teaching careers with a confidence that was not enjoyed by the retooled classroom teachers of the 1950s and 1960s. Today, teachers of special learners are less likely to embrace entertainment and recreation as the chief goals for their charges. The development of new materials and more effective teaching techniques have unquestionably helped as well.

Many *moderately retarded* adults are able to function semi-independently, working in sheltered-workshop centers and living in supervised hostels or private homes in the community. Their academic achievements in reading and computation seldom extend beyond the primary level, even if they remain in school until the age of twenty-one or later.

*Severely and profoundly retarded* individuals represent the smallest percentage of the retarded population. Most often they live in residential schools or institutions. A renewed interest in the challenge of developing the intellect to its fullest potential in these individuals has brought about a change in philosophy in an increasing number of institutions. More institutions now view themselves as "developmental centers" rather than "custodial care facilities." This shift in emphasis has been largely due to increasing concern for human rights as well as improved methods and materials for teaching low-functioning individuals. As a result, institutional staffs have been greatly upgraded by the addition of certified teachers. Even teachers in areas such as the arts and physical education are often required to demonstrate teaching competencies in the special approaches that have been found to be effective with this group. *Severely retarded* individuals cared for at home may attend a community day care center where staff and facilities are specially equipped to accommodate their problems, which are often multiple. The *profoundly retarded* require total care and frequently are bedridden. Yet we are seeing an increase in programs in which music has been effectively employed to stimulate their sensory awareness.

## Learning Style

Although the mildly retarded develop most concepts in the same order and stages as normal children, they achieve them later. Their learning styles are characterized by slower rates, smaller quantities, and frequent and exact repetition. They are slower to master language skills, have difficulty generalizing, and show only limited ability to abstract. Social problems arise when they attempt, or are expected, to function commensurate with their chronological peers in this area.

Learning experiences for both the mildly and moderately retarded are most successful when they are concrete. The use of visual aids and manipulative materials is very helpful. Difficulties with language and abstractions make seatwork that requires reading and writing skills a questionable music activity for the retarded. Shorter attention spans are common, so that tolerance for lecture-type presentations is negligible. Surprisingly, attention spans seem to increase when the retarded are actively involved in music making. Although memory functions are reportedly inadequate in the retarded, this is another area in which disparities frequently occur in the music class. Perhaps the music experience is retained longer because it is internalized through multisensory involvement. The retarded enjoy singing, playing instruments, and moving to music. Through rote learning they are capable of performances that are very musical. Generally they will learn at about one-half to three-fourths the rate of normal children. Highly structured, slow-moving, sequential approaches to elementary music reading have been used successfully with the mildly retarded.

Beginning efforts to provide music experiences for low-functioning children often focus on having the children respond, either vocally or instrumentally, to a physical cue, such as gesture or touch. This technique is a step above imitation or mimicking, which even the severely retarded can be taught to do. But the music educator must persist toward a goal of independent response if the child is to grow musically as well as developmentally. Music learning progresses beyond imitative responses to independent playing (or singing or moving) with musical sensitivity, that is, with good tone, phrasing, and vitality, rather than mechanically. Responding musically develops eventually into sensing when to respond, and finally into a completely independent and musical response. The difference between responding on cue and independent response is the essence of musical understanding and, hence, music education. The child who is cued when and how to play can be said to have a musical "experience" because he or she contributes to the ensemble. But the child who responds accurately without cues is demonstrating musicianship—an understanding of one's part as it relates to the musical whole. Even though a youngster may not be able to verbalize specifically about the elements of music or how they are combined in composition, carefully designed activities provide the opportunity to demonstrate understanding of them through performance.

Too often, more attention is given to nonmusic skills with the result that the child's musical potential is never challenged at all. Or, if it is, music teachers expect verbal responses. Since handicapped children so often do not have the verbal skills to say what they mean, this places them at an immediate disadvantage. It is a mistake to believe retardation precludes the existence of innate musical talent. Like normally intelligent individuals, the retarded possess varying degrees of musical talent and ability. Although cognitive limitations will prevent the complete development of musicianship, these talents can be nurtured and expressed in a number of ways—rote learning, playing by ear, and so forth—to provide both enjoyment and a sense of achievement for the retarded.

## Learning Needs

The needs of the retarded include the development of all basic skill areas, concept formation, and reasoning abilities. General education curriculum goals emphasize language development, cognitive skills, self-help skills, and social skills. Curriculums for older groups usually focus on practical skills for living and working in modern-day society (e.g., health and nutrition, managing money, job orientation, and leisure-time activities) that provide many opportunities for music correlation.

The retarded need music experiences that are activity-based. Because of their cognitive deficiencies, they will usually comprehend only the most elementary music concepts. The mental age should be considered when planning for them. For example, a thirteen-year-old with an IQ of 70 will have a mental age of approximately nine years. Thus one can expect academic functioning between a third- and a fourth-grade level. As an individual grows older, the grade gap widens, so that at age sixteen, when compared with normal peers, there may be more than six years difference in grade-level comprehension. Similarly, social and emotional development are likely to be slower as well.

Following are some general suggestions for teaching the retarded. (See Appendix, pp. 278–281, for suggestions regarding specific behaviors.)

**1.** Plan less material, some of which is repeated at least three or four times during the lesson.

**2.** Keep the mental age in mind when planning goals and objectives.

**3.** Keep the level of social development in mind when selecting materials. Older retarded children should not be subjected to primary level songs.

**4.** Speak in short, simple sentences. It is possible to keep the level of language simple without "talking down."

**5.** Plan music activities that encourage independence, making choices, flexibility, and creativity.

**6.** Formulate music goals and objectives that challenge the intellect of the pupils. A continuous diet of success-oriented activities doesn't promote growth.

**7.** Discourage inappropriate behavior by demonstrating while explaining the appropriate behavior. For example, "Good friends say hello by shaking hands. I would like you to shake my hand like this when you want to show me that you are glad to see me."

**8.** Retarded children often need to be reassured of personal worth. This usually motivates their extreme efforts to please and their constant badgering for confirmation of success. For example, "Did I do good? Do you like me?" Always praise good work, but never use praise indiscriminately or dishonestly. When there is room for improvement, don't be afraid to say so and *be specific.*

**9.** Use concrete experiences and manipulative materials to aid in teaching abstract concepts.

**10.** Be satisfied with ministep progressions toward goals and objectives. Other than occasional setbacks and plateaus, which are common, learning should always be moving in a forward direction, albeit inch by inch.

## Summary

Retarded individuals are characterized by general subaverage functioning. Although the mildly retarded will achieve literacy and independence by adulthood, the moderately retarded will be semi-independent and require some supervision in adult life. The severely and profoundly retarded will require care and supervision throughout their lives. Not only do the retarded enjoy music activities, but many show varying degrees of music aptitude and talent.

Music activities for the retarded should be simple, concrete, repetitious, and geared to both social and mental ages. The retarded deserve music education programs that have music goals and instructional value in addition to providing recreation and entertainment.

### *References/Recommended Reading*

Bruininks, R., Rynders, J., and Gross, J. 1974 (Jan.) Social Acceptance of Mildly Retarded Pupils in Resource Rooms and Regular Classes. *American Journal of Mental Deficiency,* Vol. 78, No. 4, pp. 377–383.

Buker, Guy. 1967 (Jan.). A Study of the Ability of the Educable Mentally Retarded to Learn Basic Music Rhythm Reading Through the Use of a Specific Structured Classroom Procedure. *Dissertation Abstracts,* Vol. 27, No. 7, p. 2168-A.

Cruickshank, William. *A Teaching Method for Brain-Injured and Hyperactive Children.* Syracuse, NY: Syracuse University Press, 1961.

Dobbs, J. B. *Music and the Slow Learner.* 4th ed. London: Oxford University Press, 1972.

Erickson, Marion. *The Mentally Retarded Child in the Classroom.* New York: Macmillan, 1965.

Fairchild, Thomas, ed. *Mainstreaming the Mentally Retarded Child.* Austin, TX: Learning Concepts, 1977.

Heber, Rick. 1961 (Sept.). A Manual on Terminology and Classification in Mental Retardation. *American Journal of Mental Deficiency,* Monograph Supplement 64.

[1]Heber, R., Garber H., Harrington, S., Hoffman, C., and Falender, C. *December 1972 Progress Report: Rehabilitation of Families at Risk for Mental Retardation.* Madison, WI: Rehabilitation Research and Training Center in Mental Retardation, University of Wisconsin, 1972.

Kirk, S., and Johnson, G. O. *Educating the Retarded Child.* Boston: Houghton Mifflin, 1967.

Kolstoe, Oliver. *Teaching Educable Mentally Retarded Children.* New York: Holt, Rinehart and Winston, 1976.

Pirtle, M., and Seaton, K. 1973 (Winter). The Use of Music Training to Actuate Conceptual Growth in Neurologically Handicapped Children. *Journal of Research in Music Education,* Vol. 21, No. 4, pp. 292–301.

### Additional Resources

American Association of Mental Deficiency, 5201 Connecticut Avenue, N.W., Washington, D.C., 20012. Journal: *American Journal of Mental Deficiency.*

National Association for Retarded Citizens, 386 Park Avenue South, New York, New York 10016.

# SPECIFIC LEARNING DISABILITIES

## Characteristics

According to the final regulations of Public Law 94–142; Fed. Reg. (1977): 121a. 5(b) (9), *specific learning disability* means "a disorder in one or more of the basic psychological processes involved in understanding or in using language, spoken or written, which may manifest itself in an imperfect ability to listen, think, speak, read, write, spell, or to do mathematical calculations. The term includes such conditions as perceptual handicaps, brain injury, minimal brain dysfunction, dyslexia, and developmental aphasia. The term does not include children who have learning problems which are primarily the result of visual, hearing, or motor handicaps, of mental retardation, of emotional disturbance, or of environmental, cultural, or economic disadvantage."

Although this condition (learning disability) is usually characterized by perceptual deficiencies of some kind, the diversity of problems and manifestations defies generalization and, hence, a characteristic syndrome. The definition is so general, however, that *learning disabilities* has become a wastebasket term for labeling children whom teachers fail to reach in any academic area. It is estimated that many children currently being labeled as *learning disabled* are failing in school because of poor teaching rather than as the result of brain dysfunction. This is a serious problem, as all children occasionally experience learning difficulties in some area of the curriculum. The damage that can be done by labeling a child *slow learner* or a *learning problem* is often irreparable. Also, many children with learning problems due to environmental factors are being identified for programs meant to serve children unable to learn because of diagnosed organic brain dysfunction. Delayed development of perceptual skills, due to impoverished or ineffectual learning environments at home *or* school, probably accounts for a large majority of the children with learning problems in the public schools.

In an effort to curtail mislabeling, the United States Office of Education has tried various approaches to regulating funding, including limiting the number of learning-disabled children that can be counted and redefining the condition. Efforts to come up with a formula for identifying children with learning disabilities have met with strong opposition from professionals in the field. The most recent revision of regulations requires a multidisciplinary team approach to diagnosis and emphasizes that in order to be considered learning disabled, a child must show a severe discrepancy between intellectual ability and achievement.

In the past, children with perceptual handicaps were often placed in classes for mentally retarded, brain-damaged, or even emotionally disturbed, because they may have exhibited *some* of the behaviors characteristic of those conditions. (See Appendix, p. 278.) Even today, it is difficult for some individuals to understand that retardation is not necessarily a factor in perceptual dysfunction, although retarded children may be perceptually handicapped as well. The fact is that this condition can exist in a child with potential for normal or above-normal achievement. It can be significantly improved if diagnosis is early and effective remedial programs are available.

Children with perceptual problems have difficulty processing raw sensory data coming into the brain. Improper or inefficient reception, interpretation, or integration of information brought to the brain through the five senses results in learning problems that are most evident in the academic areas of reading, writing, and speaking (i.e., language) as well as computation and logic.

The following are some general characteristics of children with perceptual problems.

- It takes them longer to get meaning from looking, listening, touching, or moving.
- It takes them longer to learn to integrate information from two or more senses.
- It takes them longer to learn to remember what they've seen, heard, felt, or done.
- Many are slow and inefficient at visual judgments.
- Some get distorted information from listening and/or seeing.
- Some have imprecise control over body movements.

Perceptual difficulties tend to fall into three distinct areas. These are *spatial relations, quantity,* and *time concepts.* Some of the more specific problems and their manifestations in the music class or lesson follow. It is important to keep in mind that not all perceptually handicapped children have all these difficulties.

**Space** Children with problems in spatial relations have difficulties judging size, distance, or direction. However, they may be able to handle very abstract ideas that do not require too much visualization. Dealing with space is obviously closely related to visual perception. In body-movement activities a child with faulty spatial relations will be noticeably clumsy, often bumping into things (including other children) and knocking over objects. Sometimes children feign being the "class clown" in order to cover up their ineptness, and the teacher is led to believe the problem is an "acting out" one. Also noticeable in movement activities is the inability to remember the direction and sequence of movements, as in a dance. Directions in general often impose limitations on a child's performance. Words or phrases such as *behind, next to, in front of,* and *back to back* are often meaningless to this child.

Manipulating objects in space will often be a frustrating and unsuccessful activity for a child with spatial problems. This is most evident when children are given balls, balloons, hoops, scarves, and so forth. Children who cannot throw a ball where they want it to go or catch one coming at them are at a definite disadvantage in many childhood games. Cratty[1] has called attention to the importance of ball-handling skills to the "social success" of young children in the American culture.

Balance and agility are additional skills that can be observed in body-movement activities. Difficulties commonly encountered are the inabilities to balance or hop on one foot (with eyes closed and with eyes open), to hop or jump forward and backward, to go over and under things, and activities that require crossing the midline, such as crossing arms or legs.

Since perceiving space and one's relationship to it is a problem, organizing space is often a monumental task for a perceptually handicapped child. Keeping lockers neat, giving instruments good care and maintenance, and keeping music in good repair is not characteristic of this child. On the other hand, some may go to the opposite extreme and be so fastidious about these things that the slightest disturbance of their "everything-in-its-place" regime is extremely upsetting to them. When one appreciates the difficulty involved in bringing about some external order to things, it is easier to comprehend the emotional outbursts that may result when this order is disturbed.

One other obvious sign of faulty spatial relations is handwriting. In addition to writing letters and numbers backward, some children also make their letters noticeably irregular in size and spacing. The potential problems in teaching music reading and theory are readily seen, since size, position, and quantity are important in music symbolization.

It has been previously stated that reading is often an area of academic difficulty with the perceptually handicapped. Spatial relations are involved here, too, as a left-to-right eye movement across the page, back, and down to the next line is difficult for the individual lacking spatial clues. The music score is even more demanding in the area of spatial judgment. The child may experience difficulty with the basic discrimination of line from space, line from line, space from space. In addition, the look-alike characteristics of various symbols ( ♩ ♪; ♯ ♮ ) and the directional importance of others ( ⌐ ⌐ ) could be overwhelming.

**Quantity**   It is often difficult for some children to do two things at once: look and listen, sing and play, look and play, and so forth. Activities in which we ask children to perform two perceptual motor tasks simultaneously may undo the perceptually handicapped child. For example, sing and clap, clap and walk, or sing and play. Similarly, children may struggle with the mechanics of reading music to the extent that they don't recognize what they've played, even if it is a familiar tune. Consider the rehearsal where we expect musicians to read, play, listen, and look at the conductor! It is simply impossible for some children to do or remember two things at once. If these youngsters remember to bring their horn or trombone on lesson day, they often leave lunch or homework at home! Because of this inability to give attention to more than one thing at a time, they are often described as being inattentive, scatterbrained, and so forth.

**Time**   Some perceptually handicapped children seem to learn more slowly than others. Demonstrations often go by them too quickly. Thus, by the time their turn to perform comes, they are unable to remember the new fingering, the ostinato pattern, or the proper way to hold an instrument. Comprehending the spoken word involves concepts of time, as discrimination of letter sounds is time-related. The difference between the sound of *p* and *b,* for example, is temporal. In spoken language when the words go by too fast, the child tries to fill in what was missed, often with disastrous results. "Put the drum away" may be heard as "Take the drum and play." Obviously, giving multiple directions is not recommended. Perhaps one of the reasons that singing is so successful with language-handicapped children is that syllables, and hence words, are sustained longer in song.

The concept of time is intricately involved with seriation and sequencing skills. One must be able to remember the order of a series of events to master these skills. In language development, the sequence of sounds within a word, of words in a phrase, and of phrases in a sentence is basic to literacy. Mathematical processes are also dependent on these skills. And children who seem to lack a sense of rhythm may have a more general problem with judging time intervals.

Time (rhythm) is a basic element in music. Many music educators will agree that in music, time concepts are the most difficult for children to grasp. Zimmerman[2] reports that, for elementary and junior high students, maintaining the identity of a specific meter or rhythm pattern was more difficult than conserving a tonal pattern. Rhythm discrimination improves "with the increasing attention span and the improvement of the memory function."

## Learning Style

Just as we are unable to generalize regarding deficiencies or behavior, so also the learning style of each child must be considered unique. It generally will be true, however, that the child will show a preference for a particular sensory modality (i.e., seeing, hearing, feeling, or touching). This doesn't mean that we should work through that mode exclusively, but we can pair that mode with a weaker one to assure a degree of success for the child. Prescriptive teaching involves identifying weak skills, then planning activities to strengthen them. (See p. 11.) Every music class should include a variety of perceptual motor tasks such as singing, movement, and playing. A child's endurance level for any one area (e.g., listening) should be constantly monitored. Most activities will need to be very short. Continuing an activity past the point where it has interest and meaning for the child or class will only result in diminishing returns in both attitude and skill development.

Activities should be kept simple in the quantity and dimension of sensory areas utilized. Only when the child consistently handles one arrangement should there be an attempt to make an activity more complex by adding another modality, or more of the same modality. For example, sing a song (without accompaniment, clapping, instruments) until it is learned thoroughly. When the song is secure (i.e., when the child can sing it without help), one more thing can be added (e.g., clapping, one instrument). Gradually add new variations as each preceding one becomes automatic. This will take several sessions. Simultaneously singing, playing instruments, and moving is far too complex to achieve in a few lessons with perceptually handicapped individuals.

Exact repetition, although an effective technique in teaching mentally retarded children, is not always helpful to a child with a learning disability. Drilling note values, key signatures, or even words to a song may result in a response as if the material was new each time. One solution is to try a different type of sensory input. For example, if the first approach was through the auditory mode, switch to a visual, tactile, or kinesthetic one. *Shaping* and *prompting* are techniques that have been successful with all children and can be used to good advantage with the learning-disabled child. Both of these techniques are related to *behavior modification* and involve changing and eventually phasing out the reinforcing stimulus.

## Learning Needs

A good attitude, motivation, self-control, and ego strength are prerequisites to benefiting from remedial academic programs. Music can be the preliminary experience that develops these fundamental requirements for learning. Music is fun, has intrinsic rewards, and is intrapersonal, noncompetitive, and ego-building. Some children with perceptual handicaps must be taught to become sensitive to sensory stimuli, while others must learn to integrate stimuli coming in through the various modes without becoming overwhelmed. Learning-disabled children need highly structured activities if they are to be successful learners. Clear objectives and step-by-step directions, given slowly, and then repeated by the target child, are essential as well.

Although many learning-disabled children tend to be quite verbal, their language is often fraught with mixed-up syntax, inaccurate grammar, and inappropriate word tense. These language problems reflect a lack of development in the more basic areas of discrimination, memory, and sequencing. Although they know what they want to communicate, their language is often not a reliable method of doing so. For this reason, it is advisable to offer the child alternative forms of response (e.g., "Show me.") or to ask for further explanation of an inappropriate verbal response.

Many learning-disabled children are easily distracted by irrelevant auditory or visual stimuli and are sometimes referred to as *hyperirritable*. Keeping the learning environment as free of distractions as possible will help them focus attention on the task at hand. An ideal facility is a soundproof room with cabinets in which instruments and sound equipment can be kept out of sight when not in use. Sometimes the use of earphones is effective in blocking out external sounds when listening to recorded music.

All children with learning problems benefit from teachers with patience who

- allow them to progress at their own rate
- regularly give ego support
- help them specifically evaluate their successful efforts
- offer ideas on how to improve less successful efforts

All children need reliable feedback to reinforce their self-concept of strengths and weaknesses.

The following are some techniques that may be helpful in teaching children who have specific learning disabilities. (See Appendix, p. 278, for suggestions regarding specific behaviors.)

1. Speak in short sentences.
2. When giving directions,
   a. be specific;
   b. give one direction at a time;
   c. speak slowly,
   d. review directions exactly the same way each time; and
   e. ask target child to review directions as he or she understood them or have the child answer Yes or No to your questions reviewing directions.
3. Use nonverbal cues, such as gestures.
4. Make extensive use of simple visual, tactile, and manipulative materials to reinforce concepts.
5. Prepare children for important information (e.g., "Listen carefully." "Eyes here.").
6. Wait longer for a response; don't pressure a child to give a response before ready.
7. Discourage impulsive responses by preceding your question or direction with confirmation that you will wait (e.g., "Now be careful; think for a minute . . .").
8. Use voice inflection and dynamics to dramatize, get attention, peak interest, motivate.
9. Keep procedures consistent (e.g., working with materials, equipment, passing out and collecting music).
10. Structure independent and small-group work.
    a. Confine to clearly delineated work area.
    b. Limit choices and have materials prepared and at hand when group arrives.

**c.** Avoid distracting or irrelevant verbal interaction while child is at work (e.g., conversation with another individual; asking child irrelevant questions).

**11.** In individualized learning situations, make use of audio aids, such as tape recorders and record players.

**12.** Simplify approaches that may be too "busy" or stimulating for the perceptually handicapped child.

    **a.** Limit number of instruments used.

    **b.** Reduce number of ostinatos or accompanying rhythm patterns.

    **c.** Provide extra time for response in call-and-response or echo-type activities (e.g., measure rest after the *call*) to enable slow processing child to respond.

    **d.** Simplify language and articulation in songs or chants to a level that target child can handle.

**13.** Select visual materials with care.

    **a.** Use visuals that are large and uncluttered.

    **b.** Frame (with colored paper, pen, or chalk borders) visual materials that child is to direct attention to.

    **c.** Mask out (with white paper or cardboard) everything on a page except the line the child is to read. (Note: Many instrumental method books have too many exercises on one page. A child with a visual-perception problem finds it difficult to focus on the appropriate line and/or is distracted by the proximity of other exercises.)

**14.** When playing instruments or moving to music, children with faulty kinesthetic perception may need to watch themselves in a mirror to get a more accurate feedback of what body parts are doing.

## Summary

*Specific learning disability* is the term used to describe a condition in which there is a large discrepancy between an individual's intellectual potential and actual achievement and one that is not attributable to causal factors associated with retardation or any physical impairment. The condition is frequently characterized by a dysfunction in sensory processing resulting in faulty perceptions, particularly concerning space, quantity, and time. Although faulty perception may be one of many other handicaps in some children, a child of average or above-average intelligence can be singularly handicapped in processing sensory information. Difficulties are usually encountered in the academic areas that deal with language and computation. The only generalization that can safely be made regarding children with specific learning disabilities is that developmental patterns and subsequent behaviors are unique to each individual. A typical profile of the normally intelligent child with a specific learning disability shows a scattering of scores on standardized tests. The prognosis for those in whom the condition is diagnosed and treated early is very good. Determining the child's perferred learning mode and strengthening the weaker ones through that mode are among the most effective approaches in teaching the child with learning disabilities. Simplifying the learning environment is another. Highly structured activities with clear-cut objectives and individual alternative responses should all be considered.

## *References/Recommended Reading*

Blackwell, Robert B., and Joynt, Robert R. *Learning Disabilities Handbook for Teachers*. Springfield, IL: Charles C Thomas, 1976.

[1]Cratty, Bryant. *Developmental Sequences of Perceptual-Motor Tasks*. Baldwin, NY: Activity Records, Inc., 1967.

Fairchild, Thomas, ed. *Mainstreaming Children with Learning Disabilities*. Austin, TX: Learning Concepts, 1977.

Gearhart, Bill R. *Learning Disabilities: Educational Strategies*. 2nd ed. St. Louis, MO: C. V. Mosby, 1977.

Hallahan, D., and Kauffman, J. *Introduction to Learning Disabilities*. Englewood Cliffs, NJ: Prentice-Hall, 1976.

Kephart, Newell. *The Slow Learner in the Classroom*. Columbus, OH: Charles Merrill, 1971.

Lerner, Janet. *Children with Learning Disabilities*. Boston: Houghton Mifflin, 1971.

Murphy, John. *Listening, Language, and Learning Disabilities*. Cambridge, MA: Educators Publishing Service, 1970.

Rejto, Alice. 1973 (May). "Music as an Aid in the Remediation of Learning Disabilities." *Journal of Learning Disabilities,* Vol. 6, No. 3, pp. 286–295.

[2]Zimmerman, Marilyn. *Musical Characteristics of Children*. Reston, VA: MENC, 1971.

## *Additional Resources*

Association for Children with Learning Disabilities (ACLD), 4156 Library Road, Pittsburgh, Pennsylvania 15234. Information and publications.

## *Professional Publications*

Academic Therapy Publications, 1543 Fifth Avenue, San Rafael, California 94901.

*Journal of Learning Disabilities,* 101 East Ontario, Chicago, Illinois 60611.

# HEARING IMPAIRMENTS

## Characteristics

*Hearing impaired* is a generic term and it could apply to the perceptually handicapped child as well as to a child with a physical hearing loss, although it seldom is. For the deaf and hard of hearing, training in listening and interpreting sound is crucial not only to success in school but also to adjustment to life in a hearing world. The manifestations of faulty hearing, whether due to a malfunction of physical apparatus or of perceptual processing, are amazingly similar. Both types of problems result in inadequate assimilation of auditory information, and hence difficulties in language and speech. In fact, many young perceptually handicapped children have been thought to have hearing losses, and undetected hard-of-hearing children are often suspected of being learning disabled once they start school.

Many people are not aware that there are two dimensions to the sense of hearing. First, the intensity, or loudness, with which sound is received (measured in *decibels*); and second, the quality, or clarity, with which sound is received (measured in *frequencies* or *hertz*). Difficulties concerning only the loudness factor are due to *conductive* losses and can usually be helped, if not corrected, with the use of hearing aids. Difficulties with clarity, however, are due to *sensori-neural* losses. Such losses are usually caused by damage to nerve fibers in the inner ear. The result is faulty or no hearing at specific frequency levels, and at the present time this is not correctable. It is important to keep in mind that many deaf and hard-of-hearing children have *both* conductive and sensori-neural losses. In addition, the condition of *tinnitus* (head noises, like ringing or buzzing) is common in both types of losses. Head colds further reduce hearing, so that a child's hearing level often varies throughout the school year.

Not all hearing-impaired individuals use sign language. Those who cannot communicate without it usually have profound hearing losses of greater than 90 decibels (db). Individuals with losses of 60 decibels or less are considered *hard of hearing* rather than *deaf,* but most still require special education and hearing aids to learn to speak and understand language. Individuals vary in their ability to lip-read (sometimes called speechreading). Some are quite competent even as young children, while others never seem to be successful. Children who have vision problems as well as hearing impairment will be unable to benefit from lip reading. Nearly all hearing-impaired individuals have some residual hearing. Stone-deafness is very rare.

There are many approaches to educating deaf children, but basically they all stem from one of two philosophies—*manual* versus *oral* communication. Obviously, lack of communication is the most serious handicap of the deaf when considering education. Understandably, educators have been totally concerned with seeking the most effective and efficient method of developing both expressive and receptive language in the deaf. In the past all methods have focused on some kind of substitute for the impaired sense of hearing (e.g., lipreading, signing, fingerspelling). Improvements in hearing-aid technology and teaching techniques have given rise to the *auditory-oral* method, which has been well received in England, America, and Scandinavia. The thrust of this approach focuses on developing whatever residual hearing an individual has. Emphasis is on early detection and the use of proper hearing aids, parent education, and *continuous auditory training* for the youngster. Even children with profound hearing losses have been successfully trained in this method, which does not use manual communication in any form. These children are most easily mainstreamed into classes of hearing children. Music education can play a large part in both the pre- and post-lingual auditory training of deaf children.

**Hearing aids** Recent theory and treatment tend to favor the early use of *binaural* (both ears) aids if a hearing aid is deemed appropriate. There are two basic styles of personal aids: (1) body and (2) ear level, usually worn behind the ear. Eyeglass aids may be worn by children with both vision and hearing impairments. Body aids are more often recommended for young children, and the unit that contains the microphone and amplifier is worn in a carrier on the chest. Occasionally, two of these units will be worn in specially sewn breast pockets, resulting in something like stereophonic reception as a separate signal is received in each ear. These units are connected by a thin wire to ear pieces that contain the receiver. Some facts about the performance of hearing aids that are important to the music teacher are the following.

**1.** The average personal aid, like the telephone, amplifies best within a frequency range of 300–3000 hertz (Hz). This is approximately middle C to three octaves above on the piano keyboard. Although most speech sounds fall within this range, it should be pointed out that some speech sounds, such as *s, t,* and *sh,* are produced by higher frequencies. Some children may not respond as well to sounds above or below the normal hearing-aid range unless their aids are specifically designed to give more amplification to upper or lower frequencies.

**2.** Like all microphones, the hearing-aid microphone picks up best what is nearest to it. It also picks up *all* sounds indiscriminately.

**3.** Hearing aids amplify sound and are effective in correcting conductive losses only. Children who have sensori-neural losses will probably be hearing sounds better (i.e., louder) with an aid, but the sounds will continue to be distorted. It is often difficult to tell just what young children do hear in this respect.

4. Once a qualified specialist has determined the optimum volume control setting, the child is usually cautioned against readjusting it. This is important, as the hearing aid should be selected with the appropriate amount of amplification (called *gain*) relative to the individual's specific loss. The volume of a hearing aid is set to provide the optimum gain for *speech* sounds. When the volume is turned lower, speech comprehension may suffer. Similarly, as you increase the distance between you and the child, you decrease the volume at which she or he hears you speaking when the aid is at normal setting.

**Accommodating the child who wears an aid**   Even children with severe to profound hearing losses are commonly being mainstreamed in public schools today. Music teachers are often at a loss to know what a hearing-handicapped child's potential is in music because so little information is available to them. What is available is often not particularly relevant to the music experience. For example, assessment of hearing is a quantitative score based on how loud an individual can hear at three basic frequency levels (i.e., 500, 1000, and 2000 hertz). These frequencies are chosen because they represent the frequency levels for most *speech* sounds. Therefore an assessment of a hearing loss of 85 decibels represents the average decibel loss of these three frequencies. Musically speaking, the quality of sound perception is at least as important as the quantity (decibel level), but the only way a music teacher has of assessing it for individual children is by trial and error. What would be more helpful for a music teacher to know is what the child's hearing ability is *with the aid*. With proper amplification some children can hear sounds at certain frequency levels as loud as individuals without impairment. Other frequency levels may always be too soft to perceive even with amplification. Fortunately for the music educator, the vast majority of hearing-impaired individuals do perceive sounds well within the frequency range of classroom music activities, though perhaps in a distorted fashion. As with many other disciplines, the profession of audiology has traditionally been medically oriented, and testing techniques are geared to provide information that would most benefit the attending physician. Only recently has this profession begun to move in directions that might ultimately be more beneficial to professional educators who serve hearing-handicapped children.

If a child wears an aid, it would be wise to find out specifically to what extent it improves hearing. Unfortunately this is often a fuzzy area with parents, unless one is an electronics buff. A knowledgeable parent or professional should be able to explain how close to normal an aid brings up the child's hearing at the various frequency levels (i.e., 500, 1000, and 2000 hertz). If a child has a mild to moderate loss (i.e., 20–60 decibels), chances are good that the aid will bring him or her at least close

to a normal level of hearing. Audiograms show this information graphically. However, audiometer tests are not normally given while children are wearing their aids. Therefore, they reflect only what a child does *not* hear. Also, these tests cannot evaluate how well the child hears what he or she does hear (clarity), nor do they evaluate how efficiently an individual uses residual hearing. Individuals with greater losses sometimes hear more than those with mild losses because they have learned to use their hearing better.

There are times when the music environment may create some problems for either the hearing-aid wearer or the teacher. Generally these are quite minor and do not interfere with music participation to any great extent. Following are some of the more common situations and some suggested solutions.

1. Most aids have an automatic gain cutoff at the pain threshold. In other words, the aid will amplify only as much as is needed. If an aid does not have this feature, or is malfunctioning, a child could experience discomfort or pain when exposed to loud sounds if the aid continues to amplify at the same rate as for speech sounds. This is sometimes a problem in music, as sensori-neural impairment is often characterized by a phenomenon called the *recruitment factor*. In this condition, once an individual's threshold of hearing has been reached, there is a rapid increase in the sensation of loudness, so that the pain threshold is reached abnormally quickly. You should be suspicious if a child refuses to beat a drum or cymbal, or makes facial grimaces when playing them. If you determine this as the problem, your only immediate alternative is to have the child turn down the volume on the aid, but it should be returned to its normal setting once the activity is completed.

2. Occasionally a child's aid will give off a high-pitched squeal or whistling sound. This could be an indication that the aid is malfunctioning, but it is more likely that the ear mold has partially slipped out. This is a common occurrence with young children, when ear molds may not fit tightly. Inexperienced wearers or young children engrossed in a lively activity may need to be made aware of this problem.

3. Aids frequently give off feedback noise (buzzing, static) during music activities. Usually this is only audible to hearing individuals within the proximity of the child wearing the aid. The wearer is usually unaware of it, so we can assume that it neither interferes with sound perception nor creates discomfort.

4. Auxiliary amplification systems, such as loop induction, Phonic Ear, and Auditory Trainers, are more effective than personal aids and are sometimes provided for hearing-impaired children for use during school hours. If your school is equipped with any of the auxiliary systems available, the hearing resource teacher can best explain what you need to know. While some systems substitute a different unit for the child's personal aid, others require that the child's personal aid be set at the microphone-

telephone (MT) setting. Occasionally, when a child has been using auxiliary amplification in one classroom, he or she forgets to reset the aid back to the microphone position on arrival at the music class. If the aid appears to be "dead," this is the first thing you can check. Next, check for dead batteries. If it still isn't working and everything looks connected, call for help!

Acoustic technology and research in deaf education have encouraged the use of hearing aids with very young children, even infants. Just as the teacher is in a good position to first detect a hearing problem, she or he is also likely to be the first to recognize when an aid is malfunctioning. Young children are naturally active, and the durability limits of an electronic device as delicate as a hearing aid are understandably stretched to the breaking point at times. New wearers or very young children often will not be aware that the aid is not performing as it should. Parents will welcome a note or call if you suspect that the hearing aid needs to be checked.

## Learning Style

The importance of the mental age in relation to the chronological age has been stressed elsewhere in this book. When teaching the hearing impaired, there are two additional "ages" to consider.

**1.** *Listening age*—often dated from the time the child began wearing a hearing aid

**2.** *Linguistic age*—the level of language expression and comprehension

It is important to bear in mind that although a hearing-impaired child may be far behind hearing peers in these later two ages, this is not an indication of inferior intelligence. Since IQ tests rely heavily on language, they are not accurate indicators of the intelligence of hearing-impaired individuals either.

The child with a hearing handicap often lags behind chronological peers in academic achievement because of slower acquisition of language skills. One unique characteristic of Piagetian theory is the belief that thought precedes verbalization. Piaget contends that normal individuals really don't have adequate verbal skills to explain thoughts until they have reached formal operations, the last stage of intellectual development. Lacking verbal skills to explain even one's most basic thoughts, needs, and fears is a constant source of frustration to the hearing-impaired child. Slower language development also affects social growth and maturity. Hearing-impaired children often are less attentive, find it difficult to concentrate, and can't sit still for very long. Language difficulties make common slang or vernacular expressions confusing to them, since their vocabulary comprehension is quite literal. "Don't get uptight" or "Hit it" may not convey what you intended to a child with a hearing loss.

Just as the sense of hearing is developed by necessity in the blind, children with a serious hearing loss tend to be very visual in their learning style. If they depend on lip-reading for receptive language, they will watch your mouth intently when you are speaking and singing. If you are showing a visual (e.g., picture or instrument) at the same time, try to hold it in the vicinity of your mouth so that both may be viewed together. Remember that when the children cannot see your face, they probably can't hear what you are saying. You should not, however, attempt to overenunciate speech or raise your voice when speaking to them. Speechreading is not the most efficient way to understand speech. Less than 50 percent of speech sounds are visible. In addition, beards, moustaches, and nervous habits that bring the hands into the facial area all obscure speech for the lip-reader. Whenever possible, explanations are best made graphically to the hearing impaired.

The hearing-impaired child who has highly developed visual skills usually learns very quickly from visual demonstrations. Techniques in playing an instrument, movement activities, and reading scores are often memorized after one or two experiences. A hearing-impaired child will depend on visual clues if possible. After an activity has become familiar, every effort should be made to remove visual clues in order to encourage more effective use of hearing.

Some deaf individuals are extremely sensitive to *tactile* clues in the environment, such as the movement of air currents. Move vibrating instruments, like drums, far enough away so that you are sure the child is using residual hearing when responding in an echo-type activity where audition is the goal. Drums and piano provide a handy tactile clue for other sounds as well, because of sympathetic vibration properties. Hands off when discrimination is the objective!

Children with hearing impairments are often quite expressive in body movement. If given the opportunity, many excel in creative movement and dance. Body movement offers many opportunities to strengthen and expand auditory skills, and many music concepts can be taught through this medium as well.

## Learning Needs

It is absolutely necessary to provide some nonverbal situations in which a child may demonstrate achievement of instructional objectives. For the music teacher, this should pose no problem. Music is first and foremost nonverbal communication, and if there exists any area in the school curriculum where lack of verbal skills is not a barrier, it should be music education. Music goals for the hearing impaired, particularly in beginning activities, should relate to auditory perception and language development. The entire range of music experiences should be used in developing specific skills related to these areas (i.e., singing, playing instruments, listening, moving).

The hearing impaired need constant practice in auditory skills. Although visual clues should be included to ensure success in beginning experiences, the goal should be to have the child perceive auditory information without being dependent on visual confirmation. A considerable amount of time may have to be spent in developing auditory awareness and localization before going on to specific discrimination skills. Research over the past sixty years has consistently shown that hearing-impaired children have very poor memories for even short auditory sequences. Songs, body movement, and instrumental and listening activities can all be planned with this important skill as the objective. (See Auditory Perception Activities, pp. 24ff.)

Speech and language are the biggest hurdles for the hearing impaired. Unintelligible speech often brands them as different, at best, or unintelligent, at worst. Hearing-impaired children in mainstreamed programs are often more motivated to speak intelligibly and may have better speech because they are surrounded with more models of good speech than are children in special programs for the deaf. Patience and support are what these children need in order to be encouraged to persist in the eternal struggle to understand and to be understood.

Every teacher of a deaf child must be a language teacher. Not only does the child need activities for developing vocabulary, syntax, and grammar, but he or she also needs to consciously learn the pitches and rhythms of normal speech. Deaf children can learn them no other way except deliberately. In addition to songs and speech chants, you will find that rhymes and rounds are valuable resources. Care should be taken to select only material that reflects the *natural* pitches and rhythms of speech. In some songs, words may not be set in their natural speaking rhythm because the melody reflects rhythms characteristic of a specific style of music or folk culture. When working with children who have difficulty producing intelligible speech, it would seem wise to avoid songs with unnatural speech rhythms. It is always a good idea to ask children to explain the meaning of a word you suspect they don't understand, even if they say they do. Consider the similarity in "giraffe" (said quickly) and "graph"; or "ice" and "eyes," which are impossible to differentiate when lip-reading. In teaching language-handicapped children, one quickly learns to read their faces, as their expressions will soon indicate when you have lost them.

Singing is an important activity for hearing-handicapped children. Even profoundly deaf children can learn to sing. The earlier they begin to experiment with the singing voice, the better the chances are for developing a speaking voice with a normal pitch range. The pitch range for speech in deaf children is often found to be between [musical notation] B-flat and E. If a singing voice is already established, it is generally within this same low, limited range. Frequently very young children, or children who have had no previous singing experiences, will have to be taught the difference between a singing and a speaking voice. Even very young deaf children will normally begin making sounds that are low in pitch, and one expert advises teaching the child to make high sounds immediately (e.g., the high-pitched sounds of animals such as mice, kittens, puppies).[1] The feeling is that if this ability isn't developed from the outset, the child may never progress above the low register vocally. Singing activities will generally be most successful when confined within the octave above middle C. However, as with hearing children at the primary level, every effort should be made to extend the vocal range both up and down. Wind instruments such as kazoos, Melodicas, and Pianicas are also helpful in extending the vocal pitch range. (See Language, pp. 96ff.)

## The Use of Musical Instruments With Hearing-Impaired Children

Just about any classroom instrument is suitable for use with the hearing impaired if one takes into consideration the acoustic properties of the instrument as related to the hearing abilities of the child who will play it. For example, a child with no hearing in the upper frequencies can hardly get much of a music experience in playing a triangle if he or she can't hear it. Some instruments are naturally softer (e.g., resonator bells, finger cymbals) or more resonant (e.g., wooden sources) than others. Often, the child is the best judge as to which instruments are the most musically satisfying.

Many hearing-impaired children are capable of learning to play band and orchestral instruments. This is an area of the music education curriculum that is only now beginning to receive attention. Instruments with fixed pitches (e.g., keyboards) are generally recommended. However, there are reports of many competent string and wind players who have hearing losses. Among wind instruments, clarinets and saxophones have been very successfully taught to the deaf. Brass instruments are understandably more difficult for the deaf because of the overtone structure. The slide trombone and orchestral strings would seem to present overwhelming intonation problems, but little has been reported relative to teaching these instruments to the hearing impaired. The harp and guitar are not unrealistic choices, since the playing position brings the sound close to the ear (or aid), and body contact with the instrument provides tactile reinforcement through vibration. Both have been successfully taught to children with hearing impairments. In selecting an instrument for a hearing-impaired child, the degree and type of loss, the ability of the individual child to perceive sound, and the motivation of the child to learn a specific instrument should be the special considerations in addition to the traditional guidelines of natural embouchure, physical size, and so forth. Supervised practice is often necessary for success, particularly in the beginning stages. Usually, parents are willing to assume this responsibility if they feel they are capable. Recording the child's lesson on a cassette tape is one way of providing guidance for parents when they supervise practice time.

## Miscellaneous Hints

Hearing-impaired children are challenging to work with, especially in a subject area in which comprehension depends on auditory perception. Some teachers may find the following general techniques helpful in working with the hearing impaired.

**1.** Avoid startling a child by approaching from behind. Since approaching footsteps are usually inaudible to the child, it is more considerate to approach within the line of direct or peripheral vision.

**2.** When speaking with small children, get down to their level physically, so that they are not trying to lip-read at an upward angle. Your mouth should be in a direct line of vision with their eyes.

**3.** Be patient when a child is trying to explain something to you. Have faith that you will become accustomed to that child's speech eventually.

**4.** Don't be afraid to correct a child's speech or to say that you cannot understand, but do it in a supporting rather than critical manner.

**5.** Praise a child for good listening and/or good speech whenever it is earned.

**6.** When teaching groups of hearing-impaired children, it is helpful to establish a visual signal to get everyone's attention. Classroom teachers often flick the light switch a few times.

**7.** Check the amount of gesturing you do when giving directions. Hearing-impaired children should be given every opportunity to respond to verbal directions before being given visual clues.

**8.** Remember that hearing-impaired children, like all handicapped children, expend much more energy in routine tasks than nonafflicted peers. There are times, particularly later in the day, when energy reserves become exhausted and they have reached their saturation point for auditory concentration. Be sensitive to this problem and have an alternative activity planned.

Music educators are obliged to develop curriculums for the deaf and hard of hearing that will enable them to participate in the cultural mainstream of a hearing world. They need to have the same kinds of music experiences as their hearing peers. These experiences include learning the traditional folk, patriotic, and popular music of their own and other cultures, as well as the same basic music concepts taught to all children through the music education curriculum. There is a danger in believing there are special music materials for the deaf or any handicapped population. Children who reside in special schools have an even greater need for a music education that will give them some common ground on which to musically interact with hearing peers. Music educators should also be cautioned that it is relatively easy to teach deaf individuals to achieve the motor precision necessary to play instruments successfully. However, it is very difficult, but possible, to teach them to understand and appreciate what they are playing. Although some social benefits may accrue from the former, only the latter can be considered music education.

Hearing-impaired children enjoy the participation aspect of music experiences—playing, singing, moving to music. It is debatable whether some will ever covet listening to complex orchestral music as an enjoyable pastime. Given the realities of the distorted way most of them hear music, we must accept the fact that music appreciation takes on a different dimension for them and is no doubt unique for each individual. The important thing to remember is that hearing-impaired children do enjoy music activities and through these experiences can learn aesthetic concepts just as other children do. Since the practice of teaching music skills including singing, listening, and playing instruments is so new in the education of the deaf, there is no significant research yet to indicate whether this more comprehensive music education will enhance music listening as a pastime in their adult life.

### References/Recommended Reading

Allen, Miriam. 1975 (Sept.). "Teacher's Forum: Education Through Music—An Innovative Program for Hearing-Impaired Children." *Volta Review,* Vol. 77, No. 6, pp. 381–383.

Barr, David F. *Auditory Perceptual Disorders.* Springfield, IL: Charles C Thomas, 1976.

Birkenshaw, Lois. 1975 (Oct.). "Consider the Lowly Kazoo." *Volta Review,* Vol. 77, No. 7, pp. 440–444.

———. 1965 (May). "Teaching Music to Deaf Children." *Volta Review,* Vol. 67, No. 5, pp. 352–58, 387.

Fairchild, Thomas, ed. *Mainstreaming the Hearing-Impaired Child.* Austin, TX: Learning Concepts, 1977.

Furth, Hans. *Thinking Without Language: Psychological Implications of Deafness.* New York: Free Press, 1966.

[1]Grammatico, Leahea. 1975 (May). "The Development of Listening Skills." *Volta Review,* Vol. 77, No. 5, pp. 303–308.

Kennedy, P., and Bruininks, R. 1974 (Feb.). "Social Status of Hearing-Impaired Children in Regular Classrooms." *Exceptional Children,* Vol. 40, No. 5, pp. 336–342.

Ling, Daniel. *Speech and the Hearing-Impaired Child.* Washington, DC: A. G. Bell Association for the Deaf, 1976.

Lowell, E., and Stoner, M. *Play It by Ear.* Los Angeles: John Tracy Clinic, 1960.

Nix, Gary. *Mainstream Education for Hearing-Impaired Children and Youth.* New York: Grune and Stratton, 1976.

Northcott, W. H., ed. *The Hearing-Impaired Child in a Regular Classroom.* Washington, DC: A. G. Bell Association for the Deaf, 1973.

Piaget, Jean. *Language and Thought of the Child.* 4th ed. Atlantic Highlands, NJ: Humanities, Inc., 1971.

Stern, Virginia. 1975 (Nov.). "They Shall Have Music." *Volta Review,* Vol. 77, No. 8, pp. 495–500.

### Additional Resources

Alexander Graham Bell Association for the Deaf, Inc., 1537 35th Street, N.W., Washington, D.C. 20007. Information and publications. Journal: *The Volta Review.*

American Speech and Hearing Association, 9030 Old Georgetown Road, Washington, D.C. 20014. Professional organization for those who work with the deaf. Journals: *Journal of Speech and Hearing Disorders; Journal of Speech and Hearing Research; ASHA.*

National Association of the Deaf, 814 Thayer Avenue, Silver Springs, Maryland 20910. Information.

# SIGHT IMPAIRMENTS

## Characteristics

Teachers who have classes including children diagnosed as legally blind (20/200 or less in the better eye *after* correction) or partially sighted (20/70) may benefit from some general information regarding their education. For educational purposes, blind children are described as those who read and write in Braille, while partially sighted or low vision children are those with enough sight to read standard or enlarged print.

It is not unusual for a child with poor sight to go undetected until reaching school age. Alert teachers who notice behaviors such as excessive eye rubbing, awkward positioning of reading materials, irritability, or lack of simple visual skills are often responsible for the first thorough eye examination that reveals a physical disability. In some cases, no physical defect is found and the problem is then treated as a perceptual impairment.

Every teacher concerned with the development of sight-impaired children has a right and a need to know some basic information regarding their condition. Children with handicaps are best served when all those working with them are familiar with all factors that may have a bearing on their ability to learn. The following information should be included in a medical report and should be made available by the school nurse or resource teacher to all teachers concerned. Parents are usually willing to have this information shared with teaching professionals, and their help in understanding a child's condition should be solicited by the appropriate professionals. Wise teachers listen carefully to how parents describe their handicapped child's behaviors because it will help them understand how the child learns.

**Diagnosis** (Identification of the condition) This will help a teacher understand behavior such as irritability, the inability to effectively use vision, or emotional lability. Certain conditions are characterized by increasingly deteriorating sight (e.g., acute myopia, retinitis pigmentosa) and might be accompanied by emotional trauma.

**Etiology** (Cause) Knowing the cause can keep educators alert to signs of other disabilities, both organic and emotional, that may surface at a later date. For example, conditions caused by infections resulting in brain damage (e.g., rubella) may be accompanied by perceptual disabilities in other areas as well. In other words, a child who is totally blind could have the same kinds of perceptual difficulties that some sighted children have (i.e., reversals, directionality problems, discriminations).

**Age of onset** The child born without sight is usually well adjusted to the condition by the time he or she enters school. Emotional and social adjustment will, to a large extent, reflect family attitude and adjustment to the condition. If a child has been without sight since birth or shortly after, he or she obviously has had no opportunity to experience certain visual concepts, such as color. Children who had sight at one time tend to retain some visual memory for these concepts.

**Prognosis** (Probable result or future of the condition) Teachers need to be aware of progressive conditions so they can be prepared to give emotional support when needed and be alert to signs of deterioration in order to modify the learning environment appropriately.

**Degree and kind of loss** As with hearing losses, it is important for teachers to know as much as possible about just how and what a child sees. Evaluations are given for each eye and, in the case of young children particularly, are often given in descriptive terms (e.g., "counts fingers," "sees shadows"). The report should give an evaluation of sight both with and without correction (i.e., glasses), if appropriate. A near vision measure should be requested by the school if it is not included in the medical report. Near vision evaluations are usually given in terms of print size that can be read at specific distances and are extremely important in educational planning for the child.

Children with partial vision are by no means a homogeneous group. For some, sight is nearly normal when objects are within close range. Others may have problems seeing clearly or bringing visual objects into focus. Still others have a limited field of vision, seeing only what is directly in front of them, or sometimes only peripherally. Color loss and distortion can accompany some of these conditions as well. A teacher must be aware of each child's visual limitations and ability to efficiently use whatever vision remains.

The problems of the partially sighted child are frequently underestimated. Because the child looks like and functions like other children in most classroom activities, it is sometimes difficult for peers to tolerate limitations on the playground, where the child's vision is more obviously inadequate. In chorus, band, or orchestra, the child may be able to read the music but most likely will not be able to see the conductor. However, even totally blind musicians are capable of successful participation in all types of performing groups.

## Learning Style

Children with loss of sight are among the easiest to mainstream into regular music classes as they require little in the way of special teaching methodology. Our most difficult task is providing suitable materials for them.

Normally intelligent children with sight impairment tend to be extremely verbal. They especially enjoy word games and are often able to appreciate verbal brain teasers and silly songs before other children do. Sneaking in ridiculous verses when singing familiar action songs is also a good way of keeping them mentally alert and attentive to the ongoing activity. (Example: "If you're happy and you know it, Stand on your ear.")

Most blind youngsters have excellent fine motor skills because of their constant manipulation of things. Activities that utilize hand-mouth movement (blowing instruments, mouth sounds made with the hands, and so forth) as well as tongue movements are very useful for young children especially. (See Language, pp. 97–98.)

Because blind children lack visual stimulation, they tend to be egocentric. Young children often must find ways to entertain themselves, especially if there are no siblings near their age and no opportunity to play with sighted peers. There is a limit to how much time even the most devoted parents can spend with a child. Peculiar mannerisms such as rocking, head-rolling, and eye-poking are the result of compensating for the lack of visual stimulation that bombards the sighted individual during every waking moment. The child who is kept actively involved and participating will have less need for self-stimulating behaviors.

When beginning school, a sight-impaired youngster may have some initial difficulty in adjusting to things like partner and group activities that usually demand following a structure, sharing, and carrying out an assigned task. With the increased willingness of nursery and preschool programs to accept handicapped children, and the advent of mandatory inclusion of the handicapped in Head Start programs, these social inadequacies will, hopefully, be significantly diminished.

The child with impaired sight needs to develop the same basic learning skills as all children. The following describes some of the unique ways in which individuals lacking sight use these skills, and it points up their importance for learning and for living a normal life.

**Auditory perception** Nearly everyone admires the extremely acute auditory sense demonstrated by the majority of blind individuals. Congenitally blind persons are not born with this ability as a compensatory device, although that idea is commonly held by the layperson. The auditory sense develops the same way in the blind as in sighted individuals. It is developed to a greater degree by the individual who learns how to maximally utilize this sense to acquire information that is ordinarily brought to others through sight.

It is important that young children with sight loss have many experiences and opportunities to develop auditory skills to their fullest potential. Young, partially sighted children often have a natural tendency to rely on their sight, no matter how poor. They are sometimes at a greater disadvantage than the totally blind child, since they may have just enough sight to get by with, but not enough to be functional for independent learning. Therefore, they especially must be encouraged to develop efficient auditory skills early. Although intelligent blind individuals will develop excellent auditory skills on their own, we can help young children become better oriented, mobile, and independent earlier by helping them develop and use auditory skills in their formative years. Certainly music education programs can make a significant contribution in the development of these essential skills.

**Tactile perception** The tactile sense is used as a substitute for acquiring visual concepts. Blind children "look at" something by exploring it with their hands. They can also disassemble things with lightning speed, so you may want to guide their exploration of certain objects—unless you are prepared to have your violin returned to you with pegs, bridge, and soundpost on the side!

**Texture** Texture is a characteristic that the blind also use to greater advantage than sighted people. A child will often associate characteristics such as the degree of roughness or smoothness, temperature, and patterns he or she feels, as part of the concept of an item that is explored tactually.

## Learning Needs

The auditory sense is the one through which learning is most easily facilitated in the sight impaired. Most information gathering will unquestionably come through this sense. Discrimination skills are obviously important, but other auditory skills play a larger part in making the blind more independent and mobile than most teachers realize.

**Sound localization** (See p. 26.) This is a very important skill for individuals with loss of sight. In addition to being able to locate the source of sound, they need to develop accuracy in determining their distance from the sound source. This ability will be invaluable when traveling independently and entering unfamiliar buildings. Sighted people are often amazed at the ability of a blind individual to determine the physical characteristics of an unfamiliar room by creating or paying attention to echoes. Blind children often begin to experiment with developing this skill as young as nine or ten years old. They may be observed using mouth sounds or finger snaps as they walk down the hall, into the lavatory, and so forth.

**Auditory memory** (*See* p. 52.)  Auditory memory is another skill that the sight impaired must often rely on, since it is difficult, or impossible, for them to look up information in directories, dictionaries, textbooks, and so forth. Regularly challenging children to supply missing words or phrases in songs is a common way of practicing and sharpening memory skills.

**Auditory figure-ground** (*See* p. 51.)  The ability to concentrate on one sound among others is another essential skill for the sight impaired. Since the auditory mode is often the one that is the most accessible, they must rely on it for information, conversation, and danger warnings.

The choice of materials is often crucial when teaching the child with impaired sight, and every effort should be made to provide suitable materials. Pictures and diagrams should be large and close enough for the partially sighted to see, or in raised form to be read tactually by the blind. Duplicated materials in colors other than black and white are generally useless to the partially sighted, as the contrasts of the ink on paper are not great enough to enable them to see, even if written in large form. Partially sighted children may require large-print music materials, although some are able to read standard print and others can successfully use special aids such as magnifiers.

Blind children will require Braille reading and writing materials, though not necessarily music Braille. Braille is an international system of reading in which embossed dots are read tactually with the fingertips. Three Braille codes, *literary, music,* and *mathematics,* use the same 63 characters that can be derived by varying the combination of dots within the Braille cell ( ⠿ ). Braille music is a very complicated system. An individual must have proficiency in reading literary Braille before being ready to tackle the music code. Even when the music code is mastered, reading each music score is somewhat similar to working a jigsaw puzzle, particularly in the case of keyboard instruments. Keyboard players must be able to analyze rhythmically and harmonically, since Braille characters are read singly, rather than in groups like letters. In addition, music Braille characters have more than one interpretation *within the music code* (e.g., ⠗ [C] = ○ or ♪ ), so that each measure must be read and studied to see if everything "adds up" (e.g., the right number of beats, appropriate chord tones, logical voicing). Music teachers need not be discouraged by the preceding information, however. Although correspondence courses are available through the Library of Congress (there are less than 100 certified Braille music transcribers in all of the United States), music teachers do not need formal training in order to guide students who read Braille

music. Since Braille is always read visually by sighted people anyway, a good Braille resource book (inkprint edition) and a print copy of the score is usually all that is needed.

If a child who needs Braille materials is able to distinguish music from words (i.e., recognize that they are different codes), the psychological value of having his or her own book in the general music class is tremendous. Although unable to read the music, like most primary children, blind children enjoy being able to follow the words of songs. In the beginning they may be slow in both reading and finding where music leaves off and words begin as they start each new line. The teacher who teaches Braille reading to the child should be consulted as to a child's readiness to cope with a Braille music book so that the child will not be frustrated by what is not understood. This teacher can also help in securing a music book for the child to use. Braille and large-print volumes require extra storage space because of their quantity and size. For example, the brailled edition of *Making Music Your Own, Book 3,* requires three volumes, each about twice the size and thickness of the pupil's printed book. The large-print edition is in two volumes that are even larger in size.

Concept development is an area that needs special thought on the part of the teacher. All verbal learning must be backed up with concrete experiences for the sight impaired. For example, it is usually recommended that the congenitally blind child become familiar with numbers and letters as they appear in print. This is also true for music symbols. Tactile aids in which these symbols are in raised form will give the child a mental image of what they look like in print. Although the Braille code does not use music symbols as such, the blind musician is at a disadvantage when interacting with sighted musicians if he or she has no concept of traditional printed music symbols.

Familiarity with print symbols is becoming increasingly important as technological advancements in aids for the blind are developed. One instrument, the Optacon, enables the blind to read print by translating visual images into tactile impressions on the fingertips. Obviously, the reader must be familiar with the printed alphabet to use it. Although not yet practical for reading music, it seems likely that as further improvements are made in such devices, music may someday be read by the blind in similar fashion.

Certain visual concepts, such as size and proportion, cannot always be explored tactually. If the blind could explore all the instrument families, we could be sure of their understanding the difference in size but the similarity in shape (e.g., violin and string bass). The harp, on the other hand, obviously could be felt to be both larger than and dissimilar in shape to the rest of the string family. Lacking the opportunities to provide these experiences will be inevitable for many teachers. Consequently it is extremely important to verbally describe and especially to make comparisons in size and dimension (e.g., "The string bass is as tall as your Daddy" "I use the endpin to rest the cello on the floor because it is just a bit too big to hold up while playing it"). Every effort should be made to explain visual concepts in ways that are analogous to the child's experiences. Call attention to songs and musical stories that emphasize size (e.g., *Three Bears, Three Little Pigs, The Giant's Shoes*), as well as classroom instruments that are graduated in size, such as resonator bells, xylophones, and drums. The concept of big-low, little-high can be explained this way also.

Textured materials make marvelous teaching aids for all children and especially for the sight impaired. Use pieces of fabric, grains, stones, string, and so forth, to make graphic scores or a chart describing characteristics of timbre, dynamics, or even rhythm. Texture paints can also be used. A child with impaired sight also needs to experience the difference in the feel of handcrafted instruments made from natural materials (e.g., gourd rattles, bamboo flutes, squeeze drums) as compared with the feel of manufactured ones.

Independent travel is the biggest hurdle facing the majority of blind individuals. Since it is only through movement that a sight-impaired person can perceive space, gross motor activities are especially important. Children are naturally physically active and adventuresome. It seems logical that a child's early years are the best time to develop a sense of security in moving about independently, regardless of handicap.

Sight-impaired youngsters enjoy running, jumping, and skipping as much as sighted children. Unless their mobility has been stifled by other handicaps or an overprotective environment, there will be few body movement activities the child will reject if they have been carefully explained, and if he or she is familiar with the spatial dimensions in which the activity is to take place. Once fixed obstacles have been located in the room (e.g., a post, piano, teacher's desk), the child will avoid them, especially if gently reminded. Occasionally, memory of these things is not quite permanent until the child falls over them once. Moveable obstacles will probably be cleared away to increase space for movement activities, but the child should be told of any new equipment, especially of a temporary nature. Many blind students have been needlessly embarrassed (and sometimes injured) by bumping into film projectors and the like because thoughtless instructors have neglected to warn them in advance. In locomotor activities, sighted children may have to be reminded that they must be the compromising party if a collision seems likely. Should a sight-impaired child be reluctant to engage in a locomotor activity, encourage her or him to ask another child to be a partner. Sometimes a guide rope that is strung waist high along the length of the room will provide enough security to entice reluctant children to participate independently. Attach a clothespin on the rope well out from each wall so the children literally know when they have reached the

end of their rope and must turn around! A child who lacks sufficient security to participate independently in locomotor activities can be met at his or her level by a number of movement activities designed to explore space within the immediate vicinity of the body. Hoops and ropes can establish boundaries in which to feel safe. Scarves and streamers are good aids for exploring space around the body as well. Since the free play of children with impaired sight is often noticeably less creative than that of the sighted, creative movement should be a constant goal.

In addition to developing spatial relations and independent movement, the sight-impaired child needs to develop body image and awareness. Action songs, singing games, and dances in which the child locates or moves a body part are good practice. Locating body parts on a doll or another person is also recommended.

Children who have been overprotected from fear and guilt are often more egocentric than their age mates, more demanding, and more dependent than even total blindness would warrant. It is sometimes necessary to give special attention to improving the social level of such children if they are to grow in maturity to match their peers. Dressing and undressing, caring for their own possessions, and assuming their share of classroom chores should be expected of them—just as of every other child. Independence in mobility should be expected once they have become familiar with the physical layout of the room and, eventually, the entire school building. Keeping furniture arrangements consistent will promote confidence for moving about independently. Later, however, they should be able to adapt to new arrangements once they are described.

## The Use of Musical Instruments With Sight-Impaired Children

It is difficult to identify any instrument, conventional or classroom, that would be beyond the capabilities of the sight impaired. The reason that children with sight loss are discriminated against in public school instrumental programs is that teachers do not understand how to meet the needs of the child who does not read conventional printed music. We tend to place an undue amount of emphasis on reading in these programs, particularly in the beginning stages when children might better be free to learn about their instrument kinesthetically and aurally. Certainly the approaches of Suzuki, Orff, and Jaques-Dalcroze have vividly pointed this out, but many music teachers still find security in the method book. With teaching methodology and aids available to music educators today, there is no reason for discrimination to persist. As mentioned, sight-impaired individuals often develop superior auditory skills. Absolute pitch and excellent auditory memory are not uncommon among them. The teacher who takes on a child with impaired sight must be creative, flexible, and empathetic to the special problems of the blind musician (e.g., difficulty in obtaining music, inability to see a conductor). The child can learn a good deal about music aurally. In fact, his or her performance ability may become proficient through this medium alone. It would seem that such an individual would have little need for music reading. However, one must ultimately face the fact that a blind musician without the ability to read and write the language of music will never be a completely independent musician.

The sight-impaired child requires little, other than materials, in the way of special attention. The following suggestions are but small considerations. Some will require the help of the resource teacher or other person familiar with Braille and special teaching aids for sight-impaired individuals.

**1.** Label Autoharp, resonator bells, Orff bars, and/or piano keyboard with Braille letters. The children usually enjoy making the labels for you.

**2.** A raised-line drawing board provides a writing surface on which impressions are raised and can be used to tactually teach printed music symbols.

**3.** A Thermoform Brailon Duplicator machine can make copies of raised visuals, such as graphic scores, diagrams, the staff, and music symbols. Most programs for the sight impaired have access to one.

**4.** Flash cards, such as those used to teach music notation, can be brailled in the bottom corner so that the blind child may participate in the activities for which they are used.

**5.** The tape recorder can be an invaluable teaching aid, especially for teaching instrumental lessons. Prepare a tape during the lesson that includes practice reminders as well as the next assignment. Pre-recorded accompaniments and individual ensemble parts allow the blind child to practice more independently.

**6.** When teaching a partially sighted child (or a perceptually handicapped one), it is sometimes easier for the child to focus on the line to be read if everything else on the page is masked out. This is easily done by cutting out a piece of white paper so only the line to be played shows.

**7.** Sight-impaired children can participate in ball activities if an audible ball is purchased or a way is found to attach a bell to a regular ball (e.g., beachball).

**8.** When instrument lockers are assigned, a sight-impaired child will find one on the end of the row easier to locate.

## Miscellaneous Hints

**1.** When calling on a sight-impaired child in a group situation, always address the child by name.

**2.** When meeting a blind individual outside of the environment in which you normally both interact (e.g., on the street, at a party), always identify yourself first when speaking.

**3.** Half-open doors are very hazardous for the sight impaired. They should be fully closed or fully open, never in between.

**4.** When walking with a blind student, encourage him or her to use you properly as a human guide. This will also set a good example for sighted students. Never lead an older student by the arm. Instead, walk slightly ahead and to the side, allowing the student to grasp your arm above the elbow. It should not be necessary to give any verbal explanations regarding direction or obstacles. Never lead a blind individual by pushing him or her in front of you. Young children rarely use mobility aids such as canes or dogs. As students approach junior high school, they will have need for more formal mobility training in order to become independent travelers. They should be encouraged to use proper mobility techniques at all times.

### References/Recommended Reading

Cratty, Bryant. *Movement and Spatial Awareness in Blind Children and Youth.* Springfield, IL: Charles C Thomas, 1971.

Cutsforth, T. D. *The Blind in School and Society.* New York: American Foundation for the Blind, 1951.

Fairchild, Thomas, ed. *Mainstreaming Visually Impaired: Blind and Partially Sighted Students in the Regular Classroom.* Austin, TX: Learning Concepts, 1977.

Harley, R., and Lawrence, G. A. *Visual Impairment in the Schools.* Springfield, IL: Charles Thomas, 1977.

Jaques-Dalcroze, Emile. "Eurhythmics and the Blind." In *Eurhythmics, Arts, and Education.* 1930. New York: Arno Press, 1976.

Jenkins. *Primer of Braille Music.* 1st rev. ed. Louisville, KY: American Printing House, 1960. Available in Braille and inkprint. Based on decisions reached at the International Conference on Braille Music, Paris, 1954 as set forth in rev. *Manual of Braille Music Notation,* comp. H. P. Spanner. Louisville, KY: American Printing House, 1956.

Pelone, A. J. *Helping the Visually Handicapped Child in the Regular Classroom.* New York: Columbia Teachers College, 1957.

### Additional Resources

The American Printing House for the Blind, 1893 Frankfort Avenue, Louisville, Kentucky 40206. Braille, large-print, and recorded music materials.

Recording for the Blind, 205 East 58th Street, New York, New York 10022. Recording service for educational books.

The Library of Congress, Division for the Blind and Physically Handicapped, Music Division, Washington, D.C. 20542. Braille, large-print, and recorded music materials on loan; volunteer Braille transcription service.

The Association for Education of the Visually Handicapped, 711 14th Street, N.W., Washington, D.C. 20005.

Professional organization of teachers of sight-impaired children. Journal: *Education of the Visually Handicapped.*

American Foundation for the Blind, 15 West 16th Street, New York, New York 10011. Information, aids, and service.

# PHYSICAL DISABILITIES

## Characteristics

Physical disabilities include conditions such as cerebral palsy, muscular dystrophy, spina bifida, rheumatoid arthritis, skeletal deformities, and amputations. Chronic health conditions that tend to restrict physical activity, such as heart disease, leukemia, and cystic fibrosis, can also be considered physically disabling. This is by no means an all-inclusive list, but it represents the more common conditions found among children who attend public school.

The majority of physically disabled children have problems that are exclusively medical and do not interfere with their intellectual abilities. For some, academic progress may be retarded because of excessive absences from school. In the past, architectural barriers prevented many physically disabled individuals from attending public schools. They either attended special schools or were taught through homebound programs. Modern architectural and vehicular design, together with new legislation addressing the problems of accessibility to public buildings (Section 504 of the Rehabilitation Act of 1973) and the education of handicapped children in isolated environments (Education for All Handicapped Children Act, P.L. 94–142), has triggered a growing enrollment in public schools of children with physical disabilities.

If a child has no learning problems, accommodation in regular classes mainly involves adapting the physical environment. Wider doorways, ramps, hand rails, and nonskid floor surfaces should be provided in appropriate locations throughout the school building. The classroom (or music room) should have a flexible room arrangement in order that wheelchairs, which take up more space, can be easily accommodated. Furniture in which seat and desk are all-in-one units is not comfortable or easily managed by the child who wears hip braces. Chairs must be well anchored on a nonskid surface or rug so they will securely support a child's weight when getting in or out of them. The only other consideration for the music room might be the addition of a standing table for the child who needs support while standing. Although commercially available, a standing table can easily be made from any small, sturdy table that is approximately waist high on the child. A semicircular piece is cut from the top front. The child leans into the table, leaving hands free for playing instruments such as Autoharp or resonator bells.

The teacher will need to be familiar with the potential mobility and limitations of each child. The best source for this information is the child's physical therapist. Activities most likely to be affected will be those that utilize gross and fine motor skills. Children with limb impairment should always be included in body movement activities. Even those who come to class in wheelchairs but wear support braces can often stand for short periods of time to participate in a game or dance that requires limited ambulation, such as the Hokey Pokey. Some will also need human support. Braces are sometimes worn to *restrict* movement rather than support it, and in these cases the range and direction of movement may be limited. Children who regularly walk with the aid of crutches, canes, or a walker can be expected to participate in walking, marching, and simple dance activities, although tempos may need to be slower or the number and complexity of movements reduced. Children who have difficulty in walking often develop undesirable locomotion postures or patterns. If not corrected, these can result in serious deformities. One of the most common is walking on the toes, characteristic of many children who walk with crutches, as well as those in whom one leg tends to drag. Toe walking results in a tightening of the heel cord and eventually it becomes impossible for the heel to make contact with the floor. Correction is ultimately required and is achieved either through braces or by surgical lengthening of the cord. Movement activities that discourage poor posture or locomotion patterns should be constantly utilized. (See Gross Motor Activities, p. 78.)

For children lacking mobility, understanding spatial relations is a major goal of movement activities. Small children confined to litters or wheelchairs should be taken out and carried for locomotor activities such as walking or marching, and physically manipulated for activities like swinging and rocking. Research indicates that it is likely a child will never understand that which has not been experienced. Even the child whose body must be moved by someone else will learn through experiencing movement. Obviously a heavier child must have some degree of muscle tone to support body weight. Whenever there is a question as to the advisability of removing a child from a wheelchair, it is wise to seek the advice of someone familiar with the physical condition of the child (e.g., school nurse, physical therapist, parent). The size of the child and the support help available may also determine when it is unwise to remove a nonambulatory child from a chair.

Children who are unable to leave wheelchairs can still participate in a good many movement activities. (See Appendix for Nonlocomotor Movement suggestions, p. 276.) Also, it really is not as difficult to include wheelchairs in singing games and dances as it may first seem. Other than plenty of space, the most common need is someone to push the chair. The children themselves often have ingenious ideas for adapting the activity to enable the child in a wheelchair to participate. In locomotor activities like running, skipping, and galloping, the child confined to a chair can provide the drumbeat, operate the record player, give auditory signals on an instrument when appropriate, and so forth. "Walking" fingers, a puppet, or other suitable object is another way to participate. All children learn from watching people move, and the child in a wheelchair, like the others, needs some opportunity to observe the movements of other people. Most often, however, nonambulatory individuals will be participating in some way.

Some considerations may have to be made for children in wheelchairs when playing classroom instruments. Lap boards, or tables that are high enough to allow the child to pull the chair up close for playing, will be necessary. However, certain instruments (e.g., larger Orff types) are difficult for a child in a wheelchair to get close enough to at a height that is comfortable for playing. One can often find a solution by positioning and supporting these instruments in different ways.

While music activities alone cannot correct physical disabilities, these experiences can help maintain the level of functioning that is achieved through other therapies. Muscles need to be kept functioning as long as possible, even in the dystrophic child. Many activities in music can motivate children to use impaired muscles. Instruments can be positioned so that a child must reach and stretch for them. Music has frequently been the catalyst that motivates a child to use a nonfunctioning extremity. While the physical therapist must often struggle and plead for cooperation, the child often participates enthusiastically in music activities in which the same muscle group is exercised. Singing is very good exercise, too. Many physically handicapped children are susceptible to respiratory ailments, such as pneumonia. Exercising the lungs could be vital for them.

Due to the heterogeneity of physically handicapping conditions, a brief description will be given for those most frequently accommodated in public schools. The purpose is to dispel some commonly accepted beliefs that may be erroneous and to clarify implications for teaching music to individuals with physical disabilities.

**Cerebral palsy**   Cerebral palsy accounts for the largest percentage of physically disabled children in public schools today. It is a condition resulting from central nervous system damage often caused by a lack of oxygen (anoxia) before, during, or after birth. There are several types (e.g., spastic, athetoid, ataxic), each having its own distinguishing features, but mixed types in one individual are not uncommon.

Cerebral palsy is *not* paralysis. Muscles lose movement and function because of the inability of the central nervous system to integrate fixed muscle patterns with brain signals. When only part of the signal gets through, abnormal coordination of muscle activity results. Some neurological effects of cerebral palsy are

- delay or arrest in general motor development
- poor head control
- poor balance
- lack of rotation within the body axis
- primary walking patterns
- abnormal coordination patterns
- poor posture control, especially in sitting, standing, and walking
- inability to bring arms forward or overhead
- inability to bring hands together at the midline
- inability to reach, grasp, and manipulate objects
- inability to use arms and hands for support
- tendency of the body to go rigid when voluntary muscle function is attempted

Not all individuals will demonstrate all the above effects, but seriously involved children will have several. Cerebral palsy affects an entire side of the body (i.e., hemiplegia). Therefore, if a leg is affected, the upper torso on the same side of the body will also be affected, although perhaps to a lesser degree. It is possible for both sides of the body to be involved (i.e., quadriplegia), but usually to different degrees. Cerebral palsy is a multiply handicapping condition because motor functions are always impaired and are basic to so many other functioning areas. Speech and language are commonly affected. Additional problems may include vision, hearing, perception, cognitive functioning, and seizures. (For information regarding characteristic learning style and needs of those impairments, refer to the discussions on pp. 234, 238, 243, 247, and 260.) It should be noted that in some individuals, these handicaps are very slight and may not even be noticeable unless pointed out.

A large percentage of cerebral palsied individuals do have difficulties with language development and speech. Often, it is the impaired neurological process in producing and coordinating the speech sounds rather than a cognitive problem that hinders speech. One can never be quite sure just what a cerebral palsied child takes in receptively. It is wise to talk *to* them constantly; talk *about* them only positively when within earshot. Never assume that any individual who doesn't speak also doesn't understand. There is nothing more dehumanizing than having people talk about you as if you weren't even there! Even if speech itself is incomprehensible, the individual can ascertain much about the conversation from body language. The child with cerebral palsy needs activities that will encourage speaking and singing together with movement. Speech chants with rhythmic ostinatos, in addition to songs accompanied by simple instrumental parts or body movement, should be a constant goal. Each motor response should be patterned before introducing objects for manipulation (e.g., instruments, balls, hoops). When neurological processing is impaired, activities that involve combined singing or chanting, playing, and movement must be *layered gradually* to avoid sensory overload. In other words, each additional component is introduced only when the previous ones are fully assimilated.

Difficulties with grasp, eye-hand coordination, and balance will be particularly noticeable in music. When a spastic child uses a functional hand (e.g., to play a resonator bell), the affected side of the body tends to stiffen and the head turns involuntarily to the side. This, of course, makes it impossible for the child to look directly at where the hand is aimed. Abnormal muscle coordination also interferes with the child's ability to maintain balance and shift position, even while sitting.

Teachers need to be aware of additional problems that can be the result of improper attention to the physical disabilities of the child. Respiration and skin problems, muscle contractions, and brittle bones can result from immobility. Also, when mobility is restricted, environmental interaction is limited, resulting in inadequate sensory development. To lessen the possibilities of these conditions, every teacher needs to learn how to physically handle a cerebral palsied child in order for that child to receive full benefit from the learning experiences. Being assured that the child will not break at the slightest touch is often necessary for the uninitiated. However, because muscles work in groups, it is easy to activate the wrong ones, which makes handling the cerebral palsied child a bit tricky. (Suggested basic techniques for positioning, relaxing, and carrying are given in the Appendix, p. 282.) Most importantly, since the type of cerebral palsy (i.e., spastic, athetoid, and so forth) characterizes the type of abnormal muscle functions, proper procedures should be demonstrated by a physical therapist or other person qualified to supervise proper handling of individual children.

**Muscular dystrophy**   Although there are many types of this disease, the most common one is characterized by slow deterioration of the voluntary muscles. Muscular dystrophy usually occurs within the first ten years of life and is more common among boys, but there are types that affect females as well. Falling, clumsiness in walking and climbing, and difficulty in rising from the floor, are early symptoms of the disease. There is a progressive

decline in ambulation, during which the child usually walks with the assistance of crutches and braces before being confined to a wheelchair. As the disease progresses, it will also be more noticeably difficult for the child to raise the arms, sit erect, and hold the head up. The individual also fatigues easily.

There is no indication that mental retardation is associated with muscular dystrophy. Poor school achievement is more likely to be due to excessive absences from school and fewer demands made upon children to achieve, because of the terminal course of the disease. As in many terminal diseases, there are periods of remission. It is important that muscles be kept functioning as long as possible. Therefore, motor activities that involve the use of both large and small muscles *must* be a priority as long as the child is capable of executing them. Singing is also healthy for the dystrophic child, since it can help to maintain lung strength and functioning. Children with muscular dystrophy are very susceptible to respiratory ailments, and lack of lung strength could be fatal. As a matter of fact, when muscle deterioration spreads to those muscles necessary to keep heart and respiratory systems functioning, the terminal stage has been reached. In addition, the child will undoubtedly need a good deal of ego support as loss of function increases. It should be mentioned that muscular dystrophy is not always an early death sentence. Advancements in medical science are helping to extend the life span of many dystrophic individuals well into adulthood.

Dealing with any handicapped child can be a strain on the emotions if one is unable to keep the performance of professional duty and compassion in proper perspective. Dealing with a terminally ill child, however, is often overwhelming emotionally, especially to those finding themselves in this situation for the first time. It is understandable that parents and teachers frequently overindulge such a child, looking the other way when academic or social standards are not met. However, one should consider the fact that individuals who never have any demands made upon them seldom achieve anything, either personally or academically. Such an individual cannot possibly have a positive self-concept either. A healthy self-image is possible for the handicapped only when they are expected to do as much as possible for themselves and to put forth appropriate effort in all tasks. Even though life on earth may be brief for some, let us do whatever we can to develop a sense of personal worth and dignity in each individual during the time spent under our influence. Any teacher who finds this philosophy difficult to live with would be well advised to seek counsel from a professional with experience in this area. An old adage expresses this philosophy rather well:

> "What you think of *me*
> I will think of *me*.
> What I think of *me*
> Will be me!"

**Spina bifida** Spina bifida is a birth defect in which the bones of the spine fail to form completely and cover the spinal cord. Although this condition is frequently accompanied by *hydrocephalus,* the surgical shunt procedure, when used, now considerably reduces the incidence of retardation that formerly was the inevitable result of that complication.

Physical disability among spina bifida children varies from slight to severe paralysis and loss of feeling in the lower body. Incontinence is common and presents both a medical problem and a social one. Urinary infections are a constant threat. Skin or pressure sores resulting from braces or sitting too long are also common because of the lack of feeling in the lower body. Feeling and function in the upper body are usually normal.

If there is no hydrocephalus or complications resulting from the shunt procedure, the child with spina bifida will generally have no other learning difficulties that can be associated with this condition. Gross motor activities that take into account the poor ambulation skills of the child should be encouraged. Although ambulation is often laborious, it is important for the child to maintain both motivation and physical energy to become conditioned to it. Without this, independence, and hence individual potential, is doomed. Lack of mobility tends to limit experiences outside the home and with other children. Some children may need extra attention in developing social skills once they enter school.

**Arthritis** Some forms of arthritis are temporary and last only weeks or months. However, chronic and progressively debilitating rheumatoid arthritis is more common in children than many people realize. This type of arthritis attacks the joints of the body but can also involve organs such as the heart, lungs, liver, and spleen. Swelling and stiffening of affected joints is the most common symptom, but inflammation of eyes, skin rash, and stunted growth are sometimes evident, too. Drugs, heat, physical therapy, and aspirin are used to treat the disorder. Splints, braces, and casts are sometimes necessary to retard inflammation and keep joints from becoming frozen.

There are problems with gross motor skills because the limbs are commonly affected. Fine motor skills will also be poor if joints in the fingers and wrists are affected as well. The range of motion of arms and legs depends upon individual involvement. Visual skills must be continuously monitored, since eye disease is commonly associated with this condition. Every effort should be made to determine if there are physical restrictions placed on the child by the attending physician. Again, it is desirable to keep the joints moving whenever possible. However, a child should never be forced to participate in any motor activities on days when swelling and discomfort are obvious.

**Epilepsy** A great deal of confusion exists about this condition that is caused by an excess of electrical discharge of nerve cells in the brain. Because of the nature of neurological impairments, epilepsy is prevalent among children with brain damage. However, children without neurological dysfunction may also experience epileptic seizures. Often the condition is successfully controlled through medication, and seizures occur infrequently.

There are three basic types of seizures. *Grand mal* is characterized by loss of consciousness, falling, convulsive movements, labored breathing, and drooling. It usually lasts up to several minutes. The child may be confused or drowsy afterward and should be given an opportunity to rest. In contrast, *petit mal* seizures last only a few seconds, and may not even be recognized by the uninitiated. It may look as if the child is daydreaming or staring off into space. The alert teacher may notice that there is a tendency for the eyes to roll back and the eyelids to twitch or jerk. Some children may have a hundred or more seizures of this type in a day. The child is usually unaware of them and will continue with an activity at the point it was left when the seizure began. Teachers should bear in mind that the child who experiences several of these seizures during a class will likely miss important information and directions. *Psychomotor* seizures affect both motor and mental functioning. They can last from a few minutes to hours. The child may chew or smack lips, be confused, engage in purposeless activity such as rubbing arms and legs or taking off clothing. They may also experience fear, anger, or rage. Rest afterward is recommended.

Many teachers are anxious about having an epileptic child in the class because they fear they will not know what to do in case of a seizure. For those people it may be reassuring to know that there really isn't much you can do, since the seizure must run its course naturally. The important thing is to keep calm and routinely check the following.

**1.** Clear the area around the child of people and objects.

**2.** If the child's mouth is open, place a soft object, like a handkerchief, between the side teeth, but do not try to force the mouth open.

**3.** Do not restrain the child's movements in any way.

If this is the first seizure the class has witnessed, it will be necessary to explain to them what epilepsy is, making sure to emphasize that the child isn't in pain, that seizures aren't contagious, and that it is a medical problem that occasionally causes a mild inconvenience (like diabetes or an allergy). If this is not the first seizure the child has had in the presence of the class, the children will probably be able to direct you in the above procedures.

**Allergies** Once the allergen is determined, the condition is generally corrected or controlled by diet, medication, and avoiding the allergen. Most allergic children are not restricted from physical activity in any way, but they may fatigue more easily than other children. Allergy reactions cause sneezing, watering eyes, runny nose, and itching. Asthma has been described as a severe allergy resulting in labored breathing, wheezing, excessive perspiration, and skin pallor during an attack. While asthma attacks are often triggered by allergens, there is some evidence that emotional stress and anxiety can aggravate the condition as well. Most asthmatic children fully participate in all school activities, including those that tend to be physically exerting. A child who is experiencing a period of difficult breathing should not be encouraged to participate in music activities requiring physical exertion (e.g., locomotor rhythms) or to play a wind instrument until breathing becomes more natural.

**Diabetes**  Diabetes is a condition in which the body is unable to utilize or store sugar. It is treated through diet and insulin. Usually the diabetic child is not obvious to the teacher because restrictions in activity are seldom necessary. However, there may be an occasional problem with insulin reaction, which is characterized by extreme hunger, excessive perspiration, trembling, and dizziness. Giving the child a carbohydrate (e.g., candy, sugar cube, raisin) will usually clear up the condition in ten to fifteen minutes. Since reactions are more likely to occur immediately before meals, it is a good idea to monitor very strenuous activity during this time. More rare is the diabetic coma. Symptoms are nausea, vomiting, extreme thirst, and labored breathing. This condition requires that the school nurse be summoned immediately, as an insulin injection is required as soon as possible.

**Nonfunctional limbs and extremities**  Some children have limited or loss of function in limbs and extremities as a result of paralysis or neurological impairment. Others are born without limbs or extremities, or have lost them as a result of injury, infection, or disease. Young children are often fitted with prostheses (e.g., artificial arm, hand, foot) during the developmental years and adapt to them quite easily. Yearly adjustments are routine in order to accommodate increasing growth and function.

Whenever possible, music experiences should include motor activities that make use of bilateral function in order to prevent the habitual use of the unaffected side of the body. Most classroom instruments are easily adapted for players with one functioning hand. Although some children will use their teeth for holding objects, the child can be offered the assistance of the teacher or classmate for those instruments in which two functioning hands are necessary (e.g., Autoharp). Help should always be offered first and accepted by a handicapped individual, rather than routinely given. Although independent functioning is encouraged whenever possible, handicapped children need to accept the limitations imposed by their disability and feel comfortable about accepting assistance when it is really needed.

Accommodating individuals with nonfunctioning hands and fingers may present some challenges for instrumental music teachers. Appendages (i.e., stumps) are sometimes functional and can do the work of fingers and hands. The best approach is to be "up front" with the child about the disability. If the individual's choice of instrument seems unrealistic, demonstrate how it is played and then allow the child to experiment with it. Conventional playing position and techniques may have to be compromised. If the child's heart is set on a specific instrument that appears to be beyond the physical capabilities of the individual, allow the child to try it for a few weeks with the understanding that this is a trial period in which to find out if this instrument is a good choice. If the choice is indeed unrealistic, the child will soon come to realize this and will then be more receptive to alternative suggestions. Meanwhile, seeking solutions, making compromises, and accepting limitations have all served to help the child learn to live with the disability.

Many instruments are possible for players with one functioning hand. The piano is one, although published literature for one hand is limited and difficult. Most of this music was written by keyboard composers who wrote etude-type pieces to develop strength and agility in the left hand, which is usually the weakest. They can, of course, be re-fingered for the right hand. Less proficient pianists may find it fun and challenging to arrange simple pieces for one hand themselves.

The brass family (i.e., valve instruments) appear to be the best suited to players with fewer than five fingers. The larger instruments can be supported by chair or floor stands for a player with one arm. The slide trombone might be a possibility for an individual lacking enough appendage to push down valves but able to manipulate the slide.

The bowed instruments of the string family, as well as folk instruments such as guitar, usually require two functional arms, but they could be handled by an individual with fingers on one hand only. If fingers are only functional on the right hand, the instrument can be strung in reverse (plus adjustment of bridge and soundpost for bowed instruments). The other hand must be able to grasp a bow or strum, however.

Woodwinds will probably be the most difficult instrument for individuals lacking some fingers. Even so, they should not be discounted if the individual has functional appendages.

In addition to assessing the usual physical attributes of prospective instrumentalists (e.g., mouth formation, finger and arm length), music educators will need to consider the implications of physical disabilities such as finger mobility and strength, range of motion of arms, muscle tone, and lung strength. Although many of these can be developed and maintained through playing instruments, teachers must be willing to help and must also know how to adapt materials and technique appropriately. To date, research in this area has been practically nonexistent.

## Multiple Handicaps

Previously, even one handicapping condition created problems so overwhelming to educators that not until recently has attention been focused on meeting the educational needs of the multiply handicapped. The term *multiply handicapped* is used to describe those individuals who have more than one condition that seriously interferes with functioning and learning. (If one considers language as a handicapping condition, it can be argued that the majority of retarded, learning disabled, and hearing impaired are multiply-handicapped individuals.) This population is continually increasing because of advancements in medical science that have saved the lives of seriously injured accident victims as well as infants who would have otherwise been aborted or died at birth. It seems likely that environmental influences that can cause multiple handicaps will continue to increase, so it is imperative that we direct our attention to this segment of the handicapped population.

Facilities for educating the multiply handicapped are still sparse. Ideally, educational placement should be decided on the basis of the most *educationally handicapping* condition. However, many times compromises must be made because of lack of programs, medical priorities, and so forth. For example, a child who is both orthopedically and sight impaired may be placed in a program for the physically disabled even though, educationally speaking, the more serious problem is vision. Justification for the placement may be lack of a program for children with sight losses that can also accommodate a physical disability, a facility suitable for the physically disabled, or accessibility to physical therapy that is available only to children enrolled in the program for the physically handicapped. Both private and state facilities are seriously lacking in their ability to educate a child with combined impairments, such as cerebral palsy-deaf, retarded-blind, deaf-blind. Until recently, only one school in the entire country claimed any expertise in the education of the deaf-blind.

Traditionally, schools for the blind and the deaf were quite selective in their enrollment. Even the vast majority of state-supported schools would not accept children who were below average in intelligence or exhibited any other handicaps. With the advent of mainstreaming and attention given to identifying children with specific learning disabilities, the attitude of these schools is changing rapidly. Most now recognize the fact that even though a group may be homogeneous in handicap (i.e., blind, deaf), they are not in learning style and needs.

At the present time, children with multiple handicaps are the most poorly served of all exceptional children. Programs for them number even fewer than those for the gifted, which clearly places them at the bottom of the priority list. With the implementation of the Education for All Handicapped Children Act, however, special educators will increase their efforts and expertise in meeting the educational needs of multiply handicapped individuals.

The public schools will eventually gain confidence and acquire staffs capable of providing a learning environment that allows the majority of children to attend school with their unafflicted peers. A number of advancements in educational techniques and aids have already been made.

Multiply-handicapped children lack basic skills in numerous and very specific areas. Their needs as well as their learning styles will have to be assessed and planned for individually, as no generalizations could possibly be made concerning such a diverse population.

### References/Recommended Reading

Finnie, Nancie. *Handling the Young Cerebral Palsied Child at Home.* New York: Dutton, 1975.

Haslam, Robert, and Valetutti, Peter. *Medical Problems in the Classroom.* Baltimore, MD: University Park Press, 1975.

Heisler, V. *A Handicapped Child in the Family: A Guide for the Parents.* New York: Grune and Stratton, 1972.

MacDonald, E., and Chance, B. *Cerebral Palsy.* Englewood Cliffs, NJ: Prentice-Hall, 1964.

Somekh, E.N. *Your Allergic Child.* New York: Harper & Row, 1974.

Spock, Benjamin, and Lerrigo, Marion. *Caring for Your Disabled Child.* New York: Macmillan, 1965.

### Additional Resources

American Cancer Society, 219 E. 42nd Street, New York, New York 10017.

American Diabetes Association, 18 E. 48th Street, New York, New York 10017.

American Heart Association, 44 E. 23rd Street, New York, New York 10016.

Arthritis Foundation, 1212 Avenue of the Americas, New York, New York 10036.

Epilepsy Foundation of America, 225 Park Avenue, New York, New York 10003.

Leukemia Society, Inc., 211 E. 43rd Street, New York, New York 10017.

Muscular Dystrophy Association, Inc., 810 7th Avenue, New York, New York 10019.

National Cystic Fibrosis Research Foundation, 3379 Peachtree Road, N.E., Atlanta, Georgia 30326.

National Easter Seal Society for Crippled Children and Adults, 2123 West Ogden Avenue, Chicago, Illinois 60612.

Spina Bifida Association of America, 343 South Dearborn, Suite 319, Chicago, Illinois 60604.

United Cerebral Palsy Association, 66 E. 34th Street, New York, New York 10016.

# BEHAVIOR DISABILITIES

## Characteristics

Some children consistently exhibit behaviors that are considered by educators and others to be personally or socially deviant, thus delaying their adjustment to regular classroom situations. Although behavior disabilities can be due to organic causes, the vast majority of problem children in public schools have unacceptable behaviors that can be attributed to psychological and environmental factors. In some cases, problem behavior is of a transitory nature and will considerably improve, if not disappear altogether, when the conditions that aggravate it become more favorable.

Children with problem behaviors have been described by such medical terms as *mentally ill, psychotic, neurotic, childhood schizophrenic,* and *autistic.* In addition, they have been characterized by such labels as *emotionally disturbed, socially maladjusted, juvenile delinquent,* and *behaviorally disordered.* Special classes for them are often euphemistically called "adjustment" or "transition" classes. As with all labels, these are too often indiscriminately used to describe any child with a problem, and they are of no help to the educator who must deal with specific behaviors and attempt to change those that stand in the way of learning.

Traditional treatment programs for emotional disorders were psychiatric and emphasized therapies that were mostly permissive. The prevailing theory was that the child's problems had to be worked out before education could be useful. Results were usually minimal, and gains were not often sustained. More recently, education has been viewed as therapeutic in itself. Proponents such as Carl Rogers see learning to be self-actualization or fulfillment. An ideal approach to meeting the needs of children with problems would seem to be a public school program concerned not only with education but also with helping the child to work out the underlying problems that motivate unacceptable behavior. Unfortunately, disruptive behavior usually demands quick solutions that too often become standard operating procedure. Whatever the problem, it is generally the behavior manifestation of it that interferes with the child's ability to learn. In the classroom it is the behavior that is most often treated, but it is unrealistic to believe that by controlling behavior (i.e., symptoms) the underlying problem has been solved as well. Problems that manifest themselves in behavior disabilities may have their roots in emotional problems, social problems, or both. It is difficult for child-study professionals to determine the real cause of problem behavior without considerable research including psychological testing results, in-school observations, and knowledge of home conditions. Whenever possible, counseling involves the entire family of the problem child.

Reluctance to identify young children and lack of proven methodology have plagued progress in the field. Recent studies indicate that seriously disturbed adolescents demonstrated symptoms of behavior disorders as early as kindergarten (King)[7]. Other research has shown that teachers can identify potential problem individuals with a good deal of accuracy (Kvaraceus, 1961[8]; Harth and Glavin, 1971[5]). Yet no acceptable screening procedure has been found for identifying such children *before* they have made a career of failure. Since minority and poor populations are disproportionately represented in programs for problem children, it is obvious that the relationship of sociological factors to behavior disabilities is not clearly understood either.

**Emotional problems**   Among the most common factors that affect emotional stability are chronic fears and anxieties. All children have fears and experience periods of anxiety, but the disturbed child is so totally consumed by these that adequate functioning is impossible. Problems at home or in school are the most frequent anxiety-producing agents among children. However, some children are generally anxious about problems that inevitably plague complex societies as well (e.g., pollution, energy, atomic warfare). Or they may have specific fears (e.g., crowds, elevators). When specific fears are intense and apparently without a rational basis, they are called *phobias.* Usually the fear is out of proportion to the real danger, and the child doesn't know what causes it. Phobias can spread to unrelated stimuli, with the result that so much energy is spent being constantly anxious that the child is usually left without reserves to direct toward constructive tasks such as learning. Disorganization, distractibility, emotional lability, and rigidities are just a few of the behaviors that interfere with learning. (See Appendix, p. 278.)

Sometimes children devise their own defense strategies to deal with anxieties and fears. Among these are withdrawal, obsessions, and compulsions. Withdrawal in its most severe form is called *schizophrenia,* and sometimes *autism.* Childhood schizophrenia is often accompanied by disorganization, distorted emotional reactions and the inability to show affection. Other negative coping behaviors include alcohol and drug abuse, regression, fantasy, and pathological aggression. It is understandable that young children with severe disorders are often diagnosed as mentally retarded, since they have developed so few basic skills by the time they reach school age. However, the performance and achievements of children who suffer severe emotional stress should never be taken as a measure of their potential or their capacity for learning. Most research indicates that the majority of emotionally disturbed children have average, or better, intelligence.

Potentially, they represent a waste of human resources shameful to a society as advanced as ours.

When children are unable to cope with failure and frustration, unacceptable behavior patterns in the form of coping strategies can result. The following list represents negative coping behaviors familiar to *every* teacher. One must bear in mind that it is the *frequency* and *intensity* of these behaviors that determine whether a child has a real problem, since most children experiment with all of them on occasion.

Retaliation
Rebellion/defiance
Organizing alliances
Escape (truancy, fantasy, illness)
Withdrawal/dropping out
Vandalism
Aggression
Clowning
Lying/cheating
Stealing
Bullying/bossing
Blaming/tattling
Apple polishing
Submission/conformity (no risk)

Extreme behaviors such as premeditated cruelty, sadism, and repeated fire-setting should signal a warning that a serious problem exists.

**Autism**  Although severe autistics have not been accommodated in the majority of public school programs, a brief discussion of this puzzling condition warrants attention for two reasons. First, the number and kinds of handicapping conditions found among children who attend public school are expanding every day; and second, music has often been effective in initiating treatment for autistic children when nothing else has.

Autistic is the term used to describe a specific group of children who are characterized by extreme withdrawal and self-absorption. The condition was first identified by Leo Kanner[6] in the 1940s. Autistic children display one or several bizarre behaviors (e.g., rocking, twirling, fluttering fingers and hands, head banging) and repeat them incessantly. They seem to be unaware of their surroundings, seldom focusing on anything either visually or auditorily. Although as infants most began to develop normally, they are noncommunicative and often echolalic, resist physical contact with others, and appear to lack emotional sensitivity or response. Treatment approaches have included behavior modification (see Appendix, p. 282), drug therapy (see Appendix, p. 281), and psychotherapy. None have proved very effective.

Until recently, the theory that autism was the result of psychological problems (particularly maternal rejection) was accepted and largely exploited through the work of Bruno Bettelheim[2] during the 1950s and 1960s. However, others (e.g., Rimland,[10] Bender,[1] Schopler) were already beginning to formulate organic cause theories in the 1960s. Today, an increasing amount of research relative to general brain function has seemingly given additional support to the brain dysfunction theories. One of the most interesting proposes that autistic children are either short-changed or over-endowed with sensory perception (Delacato, 1975)[3]. To those who study the behaviors of autistic children from a *pedagogical* point of view, it is fairly obvious that the ability to process sensory information is so severely impaired that the autistic child is totally unable to make sense out of the world at all.

Among descriptions and case studies of autistic children one is sure to find reports of unusually keen responses to music and often extraordinary musical memory. While these children don't ordinarily speak, they will often sing or vocalize, and many learn extensive repertoires from record collections. Gross motor skills may be poor, but fine motor skills are often quite good, probably because of a preoccupation with manipulating things. There is a general fascination with moving objects, especially things that spin (e.g., record players) and shiny objects or lights (e.g., silver and brass instruments). Rigidities are common.

Music sessions with severely autistic children are most effective when conducted one to one. It is advisable to give the child a choice of response modes (e.g., singing, playing an instrument, movement). The goal is to engage the child in musical communication, usually beginning with echo and improvisational activities. Since relating to people is so difficult for the autistic child, it may be several sessions before a response is attempted and several more before any meaningful musical interaction takes place. Once communication is established, further growth and development depend upon the skills and concerted efforts of all who are working with the child. Music in this case has provided an alternative channel of communication that has been understood and accepted by the child. It is unrealistic, however, to hope for increasingly normal behavior based solely on the music experience.

We are beginning to see an increasing number of children in public schools who have some *autistic-like* behaviors. Although a characteristic syndrome has been accepted by the medical profession for more than twenty-five years, it is becoming more and more obvious that even this group of special children cannot be generalized. As more children with *some* of these behaviors enter the public school, educators are wisely becoming more reluctant to accept unquestionably the traditional diagnosis of infantile autism. These children exhibit behaviors that cover a broad range of functioning levels and often the most serious problem is language dysfunction. Usually they are nonverbal, but not necessarily noncommunicative if one is alert to other forms of communication, such as body language, and if alternative response modes are provided. Group music situations may elicit responses that are often misinterpreted as disruptive. Yet if one analyzes them, it is not unusual to find that the child is vocalizing (or screaming) at a pitch approximating, or relating to, the pitch of the music being heard. Sometimes it is possible to discern related rhythm patterns and melodic contours in these responses. Repetitive rocking and head banging often conform to the tempo and meter of the music in the environment.

For autistic children who have reached a developmental level where some basic skills are established, successful teaching techniques are similar to those described for children with specific learning disabilities, neurological impairment, hearing and visual impairments. Skill areas particularly relevant are those dealing with gross motor, language, auditory, visual, and social skills. (Also refer to Appendix, p. 278, for suggestions relating to specific behaviors.)

**Social disorders** Children with serious social disorders are characterized by their disregard for rules and authority. To them, many aspects of school are unfamiliar and irrelevant, since they are characteristically lacking in their home environment. Among these are organization, self-denial, responsibility, focus on future goals, social virtues, and academic excellence. Youngsters with severe social disorders are essentially narcissistic and unwilling to delay pleasure or rewards. Their egocentric view of life renders them incapable of adhering to rules or cooperating when no immediate personal benefits are obvious. They often lack a work ethic; they regard fair play and cleanliness of speech and dress as human weaknesses. Some no doubt arrived at these values as a result of growing up in an environment in which they were surrounded by failure, hostility, and aggression. Others may have been subjected to physical and/or emotional abuse and deprivation during the childhood years. School, social, and medical agencies have only recently come to admit that the problem of child abuse is widespread and increasing in all socio-economic and cultural groups.

Value differences often stand in the way of a teacher's ability to relate to, and deal effectively with, problem children. Obscene language, bizarre dress codes, attitudes toward stealing, lying, violence, sex, and drugs are often directly in contrast to the moral codes of teachers. Some teachers have thought the way to win over these pupils was to pretend to accept the same value system. The hypocrisy in this approach is accurately perceived for what it is in a very short while, often with resentment by the pupils. Teachers should know and understand what their own values are and be prepared to explain them to their pupils if asked to do so. Although not likely to embrace their teachers' values, pupils can respect the individual's commitment to them.

Not all children adopt the values of their family. Although many people believe certain ethnic or minority groups subscribe to value codes that are out of step with the rest of society, this is simply not true. Most competent parents have similar aspirations for their offspring, and these are usually rooted in middle-class values. If children

are reflecting values not learned at home, where do they learn them? Many aspects of modern American society have come under attack, including television and movies, laws that are too lenient toward youthful offenders, liberal education, lack of parental supervision, and so forth. Although these factors may contribute to the problem, the influence of the peer group, especially during the pre-teen and teen-age years, cannot be underestimated. Peer group models are far more influential than adult models. Adults have a tendency to say one thing and do another, but the peer group achieves credibility through behavior. Parents from all socio-economic levels have proved to be poor models of the values they want their children to embrace.

An apathetic or even hostile attitude toward school creates a challenge for teachers of problem children. Behaviors that interfere with learning are impulsivity, distractibility, emotional lability, and short attention spans. Parents and educators often become impatient waiting for social programs and counseling to effect change. However, when one considers the length of time required to establish unacceptable behaviors and values, the task seems formidable indeed.

Although drug therapy (See Appendix, p. 281) is used extensively to treat certain behavior disabilities, drug abuse itself is considered a behavior disorder. Alcohol abuse, too, is a more serious problem among school-age children than many people realize. Drugs and alcohol are part of the social scene at most schools, and indulgence often begins as early as the elementary grades. Both are easily available to children, although acquiring the money to purchase them becomes more difficult as habits increase.

The effects of alcohol on behavior are easily recognized. Signs of drug abuse may not be so familiar to the average teacher, however. In addition to the obvious indications, such as puncture marks on arms and wearing long-sleeved clothing even in hot weather, there may also be drowsiness, nodding, and changes in mood or behavior that are not typical of the individual (e.g., garrulousness, upbeat). Helping a youngster who has a drug problem is difficult for teachers. Since drug abuse is illegal, it is a police problem and treatment must be handled by agencies outside the school. Every school should have a procedure for dealing with suspected drug and alcohol abusers that is thoroughly understood and adhered to by all staff.

Even though most dedicated teachers are reluctant to do so, we must acknowledge the bitter fact that some youngsters are beyond our help and need a more intense program than the typical school can offer. The goal of any program should be to restore the youngster to the mainstream of society as quickly as possible. Schools must be ready and willing to accept these individuals when the time comes for them to be placed alongside peers in the educational mainstream. Even those who have undergone intensive treatment programs will need a tremendous amount of support, acceptance, and individual attention from their teachers.

Teachers need to view the child with behavior disabilities as a child with *learning* problems. Too often, disruptive behavior overshadows the educational problems that teachers should be equipped to do something about. If the child can experience success in one phase of life, the other phases have a better chance for improvement. It is probably true that the majority of schools do not have adequate or effective support services to assist teachers in this task. Suspension from class or school is not the answer. Bringing a child's behavior under control or, rather, helping the child control behavior must be a team effort on the part of all who work with the child. When each of these persons is allowed to handle problems their own way, the child is just further confused. A consistent procedure for dealing with the individual child's problem behavior should be agreed upon in a meeting with all individuals who interact with the child, and this should be done at the first sign of chronic problem behavior. When schools take the attitude that disruptive behavior is the child's handicap (rather than the teacher's problem), a giant step toward educating children with behavior disabilities will have been taken.

## Learning Style

Children with behavior disabilities run the gamut from good learners to those who have learning disabilities. Therefore, individual learning style must be assessed. Often, we may find the child is a "physical" learner requiring many motor activities that lead to abstract thinking. If the home environment has influenced an anti-intellectual or anti-artistic attitude, such a child is more readily reached by emphasizing the practical and more relevant aspects of music. Beginning with the familiar (e.g., soul, rock, country) is most often the way to get started. The vast majority of all children are motivated by the use of instruments, even simple classroom instruments. Activities that include the use and exploration of instruments will generally encourage the cooperation and involvement of many children who are ordinarily apathetic toward learning. Many teachers have experienced this when it has been necessary to take away the privilege of using instruments for a time because ground rules have been abused. When given a second chance, children will usually try extra hard to control behavior.

Some children with behavior disorders have been found to be susceptible to sensory overload, reacting somewhat like children who have neurological dysfunction. Since the music room is generally a very stimulating environment, it may be desirable to simplify it for some classes. Both behavior and learning might be dramatically improved for some children by following suggestions given for managing sensory stimulation. (See Learning Needs, Specific Learning Disabilities, p. 239, and suggestions regarding specific behaviors, Appendix, p. 278.)

Extra care should also be taken to ensure that activities are appropriate to both interests and abilities.

Experiential learning has been far more successful than "academic" approaches that involve lecture, reading, writing, and so forth. In other words, the child with behavior problems, like all children, learns music by making music. Although many children would prefer nondirective teaching methods, direct teaching is sometimes necessary and is more effective when done one to one. This also satisfies the need for individual attention. As with all special learners, we should use strengths to improve weaknesses. The independent learner, on the other hand, is capable of functioning very well in the use of individualized approaches such as programmed materials, learning centers, and contract learning. Behavior modification procedures have also been used effectively to improve work habits. Since social skills are generally in need of improvement, individualized approaches should be used with discretion in order to capitalize on the social advantages of group participation in music.

Music is often an area of the curriculum in which a child with behavior disabilities can function adequately—if it provides the type of learning environment in which the child is known to function best. Music is, by nature, highly structured, as are most of the activities in music classes. Good music programs are experiential and require a minimum of verbal interaction among the group. Goals are generally clearcut, attainable, and immediate. Music is noncompetitive and nonthreatening. In addition, development of talents and skills is proof of one's achievements and personal worth.

## Learning Needs

In a classification of behavior disorders (Quay, 1969)[9], *conduct disorders* of the attention-seeking variety are considered the most common. They include acting-out behaviors such as rudeness, boisterousness, physical and/or verbal aggression, and hyperactivity. The *anxious-withdrawn* child (who has a more serious condition but one that is far less frequently recognized) is characterized by inordinate fears or phobias, lack of confidence, and hypersensitivity, especially to criticism. Fear of failure motivates a "you can't fail if you don't try" attitude. Less serious is the *inadequate-immature* behavior that consists of playing with toys, drawing on desks, frequent daydreaming, and apathy toward learning. This youngster is most often just slow in maturing. *Socialized delinquents* often present problems because of their commitment to an overtly different value system. *Autistic* or *schizophrenic* children and *adjudicated delinquents* present very serious disorders that most schools are not presently equipped to deal with effectively.

Although behaviors can easily be classified, children cannot. Many problem children exhibit a mixture of the above behaviors. Educational management is difficult, as no suitable psychometric or sociometric tests exist that aid in planning educational programs. Tests can confirm that a problem exists, but in and of themselves should not be used as the sole criterion for an intervention procedure. Children function differently at different times, in different environments, and with different individuals. If there was ever a group that needed to be evaluated for mainstreaming on the basis of individual merit, it is children with problem behavior.

There is probably no area in the teacher preparation curriculum more neglected than the one on which effective teaching depends—human interaction. While we systematically present several approaches for teaching everything from Bach to rock, few college courses devote anything more than superficial discussion to classroom management, behavior control, discipline, and so forth. Surely failure among novice teachers is more related to *how* they teach than *what* they teach. Those who survive find, by trial and error, something that works, which is usually some form of teacher power or authority. Unfortunately, this approach is the one least likely to be effective with children who have social and emotional handicaps.

Teachers feel particularly threatened by acting-out children because they view their behavior as a personal attack. Actually, this is seldom the case. Because of a lack of inner controls, the child lashes out at the source of frustration, which in the classroom is most often the teacher or leader of the frustrating activity. Most acting-out children are sending a message that they need attention. All children require some individual attention from the teacher. Fortunately, some require less than others. Since many music teachers see hundreds of children every week, it should be pointed out that individual attention could be thirty seconds while materials are being distributed or collected, a minute or two in the hall or cafeteria, a minute or two before or after school, a minute or two while standing hall or bus duty. Unfortunately, most teachers' individual contact time with children comes by way of reprimand or criticism. Often, when children initiate individual contact by coming to us to relate something that is important to them, we are guilty of brushing them off, or really not listening because we may be preoccupied with getting set up for band rehearsal, selecting materials for the day's classes, or being in a hurry to get to our coffee break! What thirty seconds of undivided attention can communicate to a child is: "I know you, I like you, I'm interested in you because you are YOU." (Not because you are my best alto, the backbone of the first violin section, or a good student.) Perhaps one of the greatest failings of our educational system is that we don't ever seem to have time to help children discover *who they are*. They get their perceptions of themselves partly from our reactions to them, and all too often those reactions reflect only their *relationship to us*. Sadly, some teachers can relate to children only within the context of their classroom. Even children with cognitive handicaps are quite adept at interpreting body language (facial expressions, tenseness, posture). When dealing with children, verbal platitudes are hardly convincing when actions speak louder than words.

Conflict situations are inevitable in human relationships. How they are handled will greatly affect whether they increase or decrease in frequency and intensity. Since the teacher's behavior is crucial, it is wise to be prepared with a consistent procedure that works. Do not feel that all children must be treated the same. This is the day of the individual. Even without explanation, other children accept differential treatment of a child who has a problem if they feel the teacher has everyone's best interests at heart. Other children are all too aware of the problems of the child with behavior disabilities.

Many conflicts can be prevented when teachers take precautions in arranging the learning environment. Lack of good verbal skills is characteristic of many children with behavior disabilities. It is advisable to ensure that the purpose of and procedure for each activity is thoroughly understood by all. (See techniques for Specific Learning Disabilities, p. 239, and Appendix, p. 278.) When children lacking appropriate coping behaviors do not understand why they are doing something, or how they are to do it the resulting frustration will touch off emotional outbursts faster than any other stressful situation.

Children need to know the limits of acceptable behavior in order to manage their own behavior. They must also be aware of the consequences of unacceptable behavior so that it is never a guessing game as to what, if anything, will happen when an infraction occurs. For this reason, some method of establishing rules and limits for those activities that need them is essential. Sharing the responsibility for both educational and social goal-setting is one approach to developing responsibility as well. The goal of programs for behaviorally disabled children is to make the children responsible for their own behaviors and increase their ability to solve their own problems. Problem children often represent one of two extremes in child-rearing: the authoritarian parent either solves the problem for the child or tells the child exactly what to do and how to do it; the permissive parent often doesn't even acknowledge that a problem exists. In both cases, the child is never guided in resolving the problem and hence never learns to avoid behavior that creates problems.

Depending on the level of learning skill development, the child with behavior problems may need to develop skills in one or several basic skill areas. It is a certainty that the area of social skills will be of prime concern. Ego strength, or self-concept, is usually an area of central focus. Success-oriented activities coupled with realistic appraisals of both strengths and weaknesses are essential if the child is to get an accurate perception of individuality. Self-control in dealing with fear and frustration is another common area of difficulty. Positive coping strategies must be deliberately taught. Good peer-group relations and willingness to cooperate can be fostered through carefully planned partner and small-group activities. The ability to predict outcomes, or consequences, and to learn from unsuccessful experiences must also be developed in this child.

All children need to learn alternative behaviors for dealing with disappointment, failure, and frustration. Children who exhibit disruptive behaviors will not be coerced into acceptable ones by threat *or* rewards. Actually, both these approaches tend to reinforce immaturity and dependency, the very characteristics we want to eliminate. (See Behavior Modification, Appendix, p. 282.) There are many good approaches, but all include guiding the child in recognizing and discussing the problem, brainstorming possible solutions, and finally deciding which to try. Frequently, teachers have difficulty in recognizing the real problem underlying disruptive behavior. Children often have difficulty realizing this, too! They may rationalize their desires as their "problems." "I want to sing alto" may be the excuse given by a boy for being rude when asked to sing soprano. The real problem may be his fear of being ridiculed by a peer in the alto section.

It is unfortunate that the majority of children with behavior disabilities are behind their peers in both grade level and achievement, even though average or above in intelligence. Although lacking learning skills, very few are incapable of developing them. Delinquent youth, for example, exhibit two to four years discrepancy between potential and achievement. Many show serious deficiencies in reading and language skills; most are angry at their inability to learn (King)[7]. A significant number of children with problem behavior have also been found to have specific learning disabilities. (See pp. 237ff.) Clearly, the education of children with social and emotional handicaps is a serious problem and one in which significant progress has yet to be demonstrated.

The following are some techniques that have been successfully used in teaching children with behavior disabilities. (See Appendix, p. 278, for suggestions regarding specific behaviors.)

**1. Schedule difficult classes at a time when they are likely to be receptive to learning.** Difficult classes are more difficult at the end of the day, when both teacher and class are at their lowest energy and coping levels. If it is not possible to schedule the music class at a more optimum time, plan activities accordingly, paying particular attention to concentration level demanded, overstimulating activities, and so forth.

**2. Enlist the help of the class to establish classroom rules for those activities that need them.** These are amazingly few. They may or may not include attendance taking, leaving seats or freedom of movement about the room, use of materials and equipment, distribution of materials, and noise level. A list can be made of suggested rules (including the teacher's). Any suggestions that appear unworkable or unfair must be discussed and a compromise approved by all. It is impor-

tant that everyone understand that rules can be added or changed as the situation warrants. A chart can be displayed outlining agreed-upon rules and consequences of infractions. If the music class is held in a room under the supervision of another teacher (e.g., classroom teacher), all rules governing physical aspects should meet with the approval of that teacher as well. In this situation, rules often will have already been established before the music teacher appears on the scene. Some teachers may argue that involving the class in limit setting is too time-consuming. However, when one considers that the average teacher spends 50 to 60 percent of teaching time "disciplining," it may be a time saver in the end.

**3. Stop disruptive behavior *before* it becomes an epidemic.** One method recommended by the TET (Teacher Effectiveness Training) program can be basically implemented in a three-step process.[4]

**a. (1) Define the problem** by stating *your* problem (not your need) created by the disruption. Example: "I can't hear" (not, "There's too much talking"). The statement must also include the specifics of the behavior and circumstances as well as its effects. Example: "When I see someone abusing instruments, it upsets me because I know we do not have money in the budget to buy more."

**(2) Listen** while the child (or class) gives explanations and excuses, and keep listening until the real problem surfaces. The tendency is to comment on first responses with judgmental or reprimanding statements. If you can hold out past the "he or she started it," you have a better chance of discovering the real problem.

**b. Brainstorm for a solution.** Both you and the offender (or class) can suggest and evaluate solutions. Those decided on must be acceptable to all.

**c. Negotiate for a solution and method of implementing it.** Periodic assessment of how effective the solution is may be necessary. (Note the similarity of this procedure to **#2** above.)

**4. Begin and end class with a routine activity** (e.g., special song, choice activity). There is security in being able to predict some things. Most children with behavior problems run into trouble when they are unable to adjust to unexpected situations. They may try to control or take over, to satisfy their need for security.

**5. Alternate high probability activities** (fun, easy things) **with low probability activities** (more difficult, brain-strain things) within the lesson. A series of classes or portion of each class can be devoted to music activities requested or planned by the pupils. (See Behavior Modification, Appendix, p. 282.)

**6. Consider the psychological implications of "social space."** Circle formations convey unity, cooperation, responsibility ("If you leave, you break it"). Line formations provide some security and closeness also, but require relating only to people on either side of you. Partner activities require a child to be able to relate to and cooperate with another child. This can also be a dependency situation or a modeling opportunity. (Pair problem child with one who will "model" appropriate behavior.) Scatter arrangements imply security and independence on the part of each individual, but also require each to respect the space of others. Row arrangements seem to have little social or psychological value.

## Social Space

| | |
|---|---|
| *** * <br> * ⭘ * <br> * * * | Unity, cooperation, responsibility, dependency |
| * * * * * * * | Security, relate to those on each side (except ends) |
| ** ** | Cooperation, dependency, relate to one other |
| * * * <br> * * <br> * | Independence, security, respect for space of others |
| * * * <br> * * * <br> * * * | No social or psychological value |

**7. Consider ways to modify the environment when appropriate.**

• Reduce the number of things to look at around the room.

• Reduce noise by removing shoes for movement activities; carpeting will help a room that is too "live."

• Limit the number of instruments and/or visuals used at one time.

• Mixed media activities are sometimes too stimulating for children lacking behavior controls.

• An assigned place is a symbol of belonging and security. A pillow or piece of carpeting, selected by the child but placed by the teacher, is as good as a chair in establishing "personal space." It is also an excellent control device when children are taught to return to "their place" as soon as the music or activity ends.

• Carefully structure the makeup of groups to work together. Limit to a workable number; spread around aggressive, withdrawn, and easily distracted children; balance each group with competent children who can be depended on to model appropriate behavior.

• Plan occasional treats, such as performing for, or joining with, another class for a group activity (not film viewing). Or bring outside resources into the classroom (e.g., older pupil to demonstrate and perform on an instrument). Perhaps attend a youth concert. Since all these suggestions involve interaction with others in sometimes unfamiliar surroundings, much preparation is necessary so all understand what acceptable behaviors will be for each situation.

• Establish a "time-out" place in the room. A desk or small table can be used; it should be as free from distractions as possible. Set up a learning station that is kept relevant to the material being presented to the group. A record or tape player with earphones would be helpful. Some individualized learning music materials are com-

mercially available (e.g., *On Your Own with Silver Burdett Music*). The time-out place can be used to defuse a potentially volatile situation or to resolve a conflict. A child who has reached the limit of successful group participation before the class is over can be timed-out to work independently until ready to rejoin the group. Time-outing should rarely last longer than ten minutes. It is important that neither teacher nor children view the time-out procedure as a punishment. It is an opportunity for the child to "get it together," after which it is expected that the individual will willingly rejoin the group and function appropriately. Some children time-out themselves when they recognize that their tolerance for the group is low. Usually this is a positive reaction on the part of the pupil. However, the teacher must be careful that the child doesn't use the time-out procedure as an escape mechanism.

**8. Criticize and praise specifically.** For example: "I like the way you remembered to play this measure loud. Now can you play it again and hold out this dotted note its full value, too?" Ambiguous comments such as, "That was pretty good, but you can do better" are frustrating because the child usually doesn't know how to make it "better."

**9. Know the problems of specific children** (health, family, emotional) **that are likely to affect behavior and achievement.** This is a prerequisite to dealing with them in a humane and effective manner.

**10. Know yourself.** If not already aware of them, take note of the times when it is most difficult to cope with noise, changes in routine, petty annoyances. Never attempt to deal with a child when you are angry. Instead, explain that you will discuss the incident later because you are too angry to do it now. When you later handle the problem, remind the child of your behavior that enabled you to be objective in discussing it now. Children need to realize that adults have emotions, too, and they can benefit from observing models of acceptable coping strategies.

## Summary

Behavior disabilities can be the result of organic, emotional, or social problems. Most problem behavior in public school classrooms is the result of attention-seeking/acting-out children. Children who are diagnosed as having chronic emotional or social problems are in need of professional counseling in cooperation with an educational environment judged to be the most beneficial to them and their peers. Classroom conflict situations can often be avoided by preplanning techniques involving scheduling, curriculum planning, and classroom management. Conflicts can most effectively be resolved by methods in which the child in conflict is made responsible for behavior and is further helped to solve problems independently and effectively. Behavior modification techniques are one approach used to change negative behaviors, but they do not deal with the problem as such. The educational needs of children with behavior problems may range from basic skill and language development to the development and reinforcement of appropriate social skills.

Programs for children with severe problems usually are committed to a specific treatment approach with which music programs must cooperate in the interest of the child. To date, landmark legal decisions have mainly focused on the right to education of children with cognitive or physical handicaps. Issues affecting the constitutional rights of children with behavior disabilities are sure to be challenged in the near future, with the result that schools, agencies, and hospitals will be required to be more accountable for the educational treatment afforded these individuals.

## References/Recommended Reading

[1]Bender, Lauretta. *Psychopathology of Children with Organic Brain Disorders.* Springfield, IL: Charles C Thomas, 1956.

[2]Bettelheim, Bruno. *The Empty Fortress.* New York: Free Press, 1967.

[3]Delacato, Carl. *The Ultimate Stranger.* Garden City, NY: Doubleday, 1974.

Fairchild, Thomas, ed. *Behavior Disorders: Helping Children with Behavior Problems.* Austin, TX: Learning Concepts, 1977.

———. *Managing the Hyperactive Child in the Classroom.* Austin, TX: Learning Concepts, 1977.

[4]Gordon, Thomas. *Teacher Effectiveness Training.* New York: Peter H. Wyden, 1974.

Haring, N., and Phillips, L. *Educating Emotionally Disturbed Children.* New York: McGraw-Hill, 1962.

[5]Harth, R., and Glavin, L. 1971 (April). "Validity of Teacher Rating as a Subtest for Screening Emotionally Disturbed Children." *Exceptional Children,* Vol. 37, No. 8, pp. 605–606.

Henry, Jules. *Pathways to Madness.* New York: Random House, 1971.

Hewett, Frank. *The Emotionally Disturbed Child in the Classroom.* Boston: Allyn and Bacon, 1968.

Hirschberg, J. Cotter. 1953 (Oct.). "The Role of Education in the Treatment of Emotionally Disturbed Children Through Planned Ego Development." *American Journal of Orthopsychiatry,* Vol. 23, No. 4, pp. 684–689.

Jenkins, Richard L. *Behavior Disorders of Childhood and Adolescence.* Springfield, IL: Charles Thomas, 1973.

[6]Kanner, Leo. *Child Psychiatry.* Springfield, IL: Charles C Thomas, 1948.

[7]King, Charles. 1975 (Jan.). "The Ego and the Integration of Violence in Homicidal Youth." *American Journal of Orthopsychiatry,* Vol. 45, No. 1, pp. 134–145.

[8]Kvaraceus, William. 1961 (April). "Forecasting Juvenile Delinquency: A Three Year Experiment." *Exceptional Children,* Vol. 27, No. 8, pp. 429–435.

Nordoff, P., and Robbins, C. *Music Therapy with Handicapped Children.* 3rd ed. New York: St. Martin's Press, 1975.

[9]Quay, Herbert. "Dimensions of Problem Behavior and Educational Programming." In *Children Against Schools.* Edited by P. S. Graubard. Chicago: Follett, 1969.

[10]Rimland, B. *Infantile Autism: The Syndrome and Its Implications for a Neurological Theory.* Englewood Cliffs, NJ: Prentice-Hall, 1964.

Wing, Lorna. *Autistic Children.* (cloth), Secaucus, NJ: Citadel Press, 1972; (paperback), New York: Brunner Mazel, 1972.

## Additional Resources

National Institute of Mental Health, 5454 Wisconsin Avenue, Chevy Chase, Maryland 20015. Information and publications.

National Society for Autistic Children, 169 Tampa Avenue, Albany, New York 12208. Information and publications.

## Professional Journals

*Journal of Autism and Childhood Schizophrenia,* Plenum Press, 227 W. 17th Street, New York, New York 10011.

*Journal of Abnormal Child Psychiatry,* Plenum Press, 227 W. 17th Street, New York, New York 10011.

*American Journal of Orthopsychiatry,* American Orthopsychiatric Association, 1775 Broadway, New York, New York 10019.

# THE GIFTED AND TALENTED

Traditionally, children with superior cognitive abilities (gifted) were identified as those who scored very high on intelligence tests (i.e., two standard deviations above the norm) and who performed exceptionally well on achievement measures. Today there is added emphasis on identifying children who may not score high on tests but who show superior talent and creative abilities. Also, there is greater concern for finding more suitable methods to identify those children in whom extraordinary *potential* may be suppressed because of environmental factors and/or lack of opportunity. Contrary to popular belief, gifted and talented children are found in all ethnic, racial, social, and economic groups.

Although giftedness usually implies outstanding performance in a multitude of areas (academic, arts, athletics), while talent is usually understood to be outstanding performance in a specific area, these differences are not evidenced in the following definition from a report given to the United States Congress in 1972 by then Commissioner of Education Sidney Marland.

"Gifted and talented children are those, identified by professionally qualified persons, who by virtue of outstanding abilities are capable of high performance. These are children who require differentiated educational programs and/or services beyond those normally provided by the regular school program in order to realize their contribution to self and society."[3]

"High performance" was further explained as including general intellectual abilities, specific academic aptitude, creative or productive thinking, leadership, ability in visual and performing arts, and psychomotor abilities. Children who meet these criteria are estimated to constitute 3 to 5 percent of the school population.

Specifically, the gifted and talented in music show early evidence of skillful performance, unique creativity, exceptional listening skills (including rapid memorization, analysis, and evaluative abilities), and superior knowledge of facts about music. History has recorded more child prodigies in music than in any other field of endeavor. Some of their biographies give credence to the traditional cognitive criteria for general giftedness; others clearly do not. Probably the earliest known musically gifted child was the biblical David. It appears that he was in his early teens when first summoned to play at King Saul's court to soothe his melancholia. David could also be the first music educator, since in later life he organized music instruction and performance in order to preserve the music traditions of his people.

**Talented special children**    A number of musical prodigies were special children in other ways as well. Some were abused children (e.g., Paganini, Slenczynska) who were beaten and starved while their talents were exploited for profit. Gertrude Mara became crippled as the result of being constantly tied to a chair as a child. The violinist Itzhak Perlman is disabled as a result of polio. The largest group are the sight impaired. Musically talented blind musicians include not only classical but jazz and rock greats, such as Alec Templeton, George Shearing, Art Tatum, Ray Charles, José Feliciano, and Stevie Wonder. All of them were performing professionally before adulthood. Among the most notable disadvantaged children to achieve fame musically were Louis Armstrong and Benny Goodman. Both received early training in music as a result of social programs organized for disadvantaged youth.

Minorities that have been discriminated against are also represented in child prodigy history. A slave child called Blind Tom was dragged around the world by his owner to perform as a freak. Never afforded an education of any kind, he was a self-taught pianist whose musical memory and improvisational skills were extraordinary. Even so, people considered him an "idiot." Traditionally, females have been discouraged from pursuing concert and composition careers. At one time, the Vienna Academy would allow female students to participate only in piano classes. Even the wording of competition prizes during that time discriminated against women, specifying "to the man . . . ," technically disqualifying a woman from collecting the prize money even if she won. We can only speculate as to how differently music history books would read today if Maria Anna Mozart, Fanny Mendelssohn, and Clara Schumann had been allowed to fully develop their potentials in music.

Some prodigies demonstrated behavior problems as children. It is reported that Isaac Albeniz, at the age of six, deliberately smashed a large mirror at the Paris Conservatory following a successful audition. At eight, he began a pattern of running away from home. Unable to control him and tired of chasing after him, his parents finally gave him up as incorrigible. By the age of thirteen, Isaac was his own manager, arranging and performing concerts in North and South America. It is not surprising that many musical prodigies had eccentric behavior as adults. Such behavior might be related to formative years characterized by unhappiness, exploitation, insecurity, unstable home lives, lack of general education, limited peer interaction, and a paucity of recreational activities appropriate to childhood.

The nature-nurture argument rages as strongly among explanations of giftedness and talent as it does in retardation. There is no question that examples of musical ability in families can be found in abundance in the music field. Bachs were on the music scene for seven generations, Couperins for four. The Purcell, Scarlatti, and Strauss families all produced more than one generation of professional musicians. Modern-day examples of multiple talents in a single family can be found as well (e.g., Iturbi, Serkin, Brubeck, Jackson). Heredity no doubt plays an important role in musical talent. Scientists today tend to support a combination gene theory, but no one has yet determined the specific gene combination or statistically predicted its occurrence. At any rate, a favorable environment and good educational management are certainly necessary if an individual is to fully develop innate talent.

## Characteristics

The stereotype of the gifted child as a puny, bespectacled, shy, retiring type has not been confirmed in studies of gifted children. In fact, gifted children tend to be physically superior, outgoing, and well liked by their peers. Although most will not exhibit all the characteristics that follow, many will show evidence of several.

**1.** Gifted children usually have very long attention spans. They can remain absorbed in study much longer than most children. In fact, they may rebel against time limits that characterize most educational design.

**2.** Most seem to learn basic skills faster and with less practice.

**3.** Most possess a large vocabulary. Personal histories usually reveal that, as infants, they began to talk earlier and used complex sentences earlier than the average child.

**4.** They are extremely curious and continually question not only who, what, where, and when, but *why* and *how* at a very early age.

**5.** Their sense of humor favors puns and riddles.

**6.** They often exhibit moral and social concerns (e.g., foreign policy, economics, environment) typical of much older individuals.

**7.** Their ideas are often considered to be "far out."

**8.** They usually show aptitude in one or more areas of artistic endeavor.

**9.** They have a need to work independently on some projects.

**10.** They prefer discovery and creative approaches to learning. Those who are reading oriented often demonstrate almost total recall of information learned through this medium.

**11.** Their leadership abilities tend to surface quite early. They will often dominate ideas and procedures in group projects.

**12.** At a very early age, many have demonstrated empathy for the handicapped and those less fortunate than they.

Identification of the gifted and talented continues to be elusive, but experts agree that the identification process should be one that involves a diverse set of measures including individual testing, achievement, observation, teacher referral, interview, and so forth. Although academic giftedness can frequently be spotted before a child reaches school age, musical talent is more difficult to assess, especially for the untrained observer. Further, musical talent can develop only if there is opportunity for it to do so. Musical talent, therefore, can best be assessed by a music educator who not only is a musician, but understands child development and learning theory as well. The role of the music educator is not only to identify but also to do whatever is necessary to provide the opportunity for talent to develop.

## Learning Style

As with other special children, learning style relates directly to the individual behaviors that are characteristic of the condition. As mentioned above, gifted children usually have very long attention spans. Because of their ability to really delve into material, the half-hour or forty-five-minute music class is most frustrating. Further, the type of environment most suited to their learning style and music education is discovery and creative projects, which tend to hold all children's interest for longer periods of time. Every effort should be made to schedule gifted classes, or regular classes with gifted students, in an open-ended fashion so there will be opportunity to extend music time when appropriate. Before lunch, a free period, or dismissal are some options to consider. The child's schedule should be extremely flexible in order to accommodate this very situation. Even if the music teacher has another class, if only one or two children are involved and the music area offers an out-of-the-way place where they can continue to work, they might be allowed to stay to pursue their project.

Research skills are often learned earlier than in the average child. Most gifted children read at least two to three years above grade level, so they are independent learners earlier. They enjoy doing research reports (library research) and outside assignments, such as reporting on a special television program. They usually prefer to do this type of assignment alone. Once the gifted child is "turned on" to something, it can become a consuming interest until the need to know is satisfied. Whereas other children may read a book or two about a subject that interests them, gifted children will frequently exhaust all available resources before moving on to a new topic.

Gifted students are usually interested in music theory. Biographies of musical prodigies reveal that many of them showed an early interest and ability in composition and improvisation. Even elementary-age pupils will advance quickly through the rudimentary principles of scales, modes, triads, harmonization, rhythm, and meter. They will enjoy analyzing chorales and trying their skills at melody writing and three- and four-part harmonizations. Frequently they are frustrated by their physical inabilities to perform their creative efforts when beyond their vocal range or technical skills. Following music scores, such as string quartets and opera vocal scores, is of great interest to them also.

A large percentage of the gifted population in public schools study a musical instrument if the opportunity to do so is available. Even if they are not involved in the instrumental music program, their interest in musical instruments transcends that of the average child in that they zero in on abstract problems almost immediately. A discussion of instrument characteristics, for example, could easily lead to questions regarding acoustical properties of woods and metals, physical factors affecting intonation, and transposition. They will insist on exploring these aspects until their curiosity has been satisfied.

Creative experiences should really constitute the bulk of activity for the gifted child in music. Original compositions are often elaborated upon, resulting in orchestrated or choreographed versions. Group projects involving several gifted and talented children should be carefully organized. In order to avoid getting in one another's way and rapidly exhausting school and community resources, the more successful group projects will be large in scope and diverse in content. For example, writing and performing an original opera would provide a group with several separate but related aspects to choose from (e.g., vocal music, instrumental music, libretto, drama, choreography, stage production, conducting). Because of the superior abilities of gifted students to analyze, integrate, and synthesize information there are numerous opportunities for correlating music with other subject areas for them. Topics such as acoustics, aesthetics, and non-Western music, can easily be included as part of appropriate units in science, math, humanities, and social studies.

## Learning Needs

Of the special learners in public schools, the gifted and talented have always been discriminated against the most. While there is growing enthusiasm, there are limited funds available at state and local levels. At the national level, support and funding are as yet undetermined. Although no current statistics are available, it would probably be generous to estimate that less than 20 percent of the gifted are being adequately provided for in public schools. A national survey in 1972 revealed that interest in projected programs for gifted and talented students had the lowest priority at all levels of government.

The prevailing attitude that the gifted will make it without help is erroneous. For a number of reasons, some children with potentially superior abilities do not achieve even close to their potential without special programs. Some even have learning problems and, without help, can end up as school dropouts or, at best, underachievers. Gifted children have the same basic needs as all children. When needs are not met, the result is frustration, failure, and, often, behavior disorders. Research shows that programs designed to meet the special needs of the gifted and talented result in better academic performance, better self-concept, better attitude toward others, improved social relations, and fewer behavior problems.

When teachers know students have superior abilities, there is a tendency to assume that teaching them basic skills and concepts is not necessary. Such an assumption should never be made, as potential in any subject area will be swiftly curtailed if there is no foundation on which to build more complex concepts and skills. The gifted child should always be given an opportunity to demonstrate mastery of the basics before going on to a more advanced level.

Program planning for the gifted is a serious problem for public schools. Special schools and classes, although they can best accommodate the special needs and abilities of the gifted, are often criticized for setting the gifted apart as an elitist group. In Russia, gifted and talented children are ferreted out at the earliest possible age and sent to special schools that develop their talents. These schools most often have a single purpose, so their educational program is not broad in scope. This system has produced not only Olympic gold medal winners, but Oistrakh, Rostropovich, Richter, and Ashkenazy. In some American cities there are high schools of music and art in which the development of musical and artistic talent is a primary goal. These are, of course, secondary schools, and they may get some of their students too late to fully develop potential. While acceleration of students with superior abilities has been strongly resisted in American education, most research indicates no negative effects on the children participating in either special classes or acceleration programs. A number of history's gifted children who became eminent scientists, artists, inventors, and so forth, were not public school products. Many were tutored privately, some by their parents. It is obvious that public schools have always had a difficult time meeting the special needs of this group.

The best accepted approach for meeting the needs of the gifted child in elementary school is regular class placement with enrichment opportunities. Enriched content should provide experiences for the gifted student to reach higher levels of competence and understanding. In a general music class, for example, a discussion of electronic music might be enriched for the gifted child by offering the opportunity for further knowledge through an independent project in which an original tape composition is created. Supplementary reading and/or listening would no doubt be included in such a project. Some programs at the elementary level allow a gifted child to study certain subjects at an advanced level (e.g., high school music theory, math, literature). The lock-step arrangement that pervades our educational system (regardless of structures such as open classrooms and multi-age grouping) is a particular hindrance to children with superior abilities. Their *potential* is handicapped if they are forced to sit through sixth-grade arithmetic when they are capable of understanding college calculus. In communities where higher education resources are available, many gifted students, particularly at the high school level, attend college classes appropriate to their abilities, returning to the public school for the remainder of their classes.

Gifted children are exciting to work with. However, a day with them can be quite exhausting. Their energy level is constant and seemingly limitless. In addition, their most expedient technique for information gathering is questioning, which can become tiresome for the teacher who lacks ready explanations (sometimes about very complex topics!) or functional knowledge of available resources to which the learner can be directed. Teacher preparation has been seriously lacking in this field, and evidence of progress is sparse. Apparently, many teachers feel inadequate to deal with the extremely capable child. Presumably, a great deal of in-service training will need to occur if gifted and talented children are to be adequately educated in the regular classroom.

Following are some general suggestions for enriching the music education curriculum for the gifted and talented child.

**1.** When assigned a class with gifted students, familiarize yourself with all available resources at your disposal (i.e., libraries, community musicians and music groups, college music programs, concerts).

**2.** When a gifted child asks a question that is obviously beyond the comprehension of the whole class, make arrangements to meet individually to answer it. This also gives you time to organize your explanation and resources.

**3.** When a child is a more skilled performer than his or her peers, arrange opportunities for that child to play regularly with more advanced musicians (high school ensemble, community group, and so forth).

**4.** Consider and plan for ways to individualize learning for the gifted child.

    **a.** Learning centers

    **b.** Commercially produced programs (e.g., *On Your Own with Silver Burdett Music*)

    **c.** Availability of other programmed resources, such as Computer Assisted Instruction.

    **d.** Enlist help of a more advanced student or parent to play duets with the gifted instrumentalist.

**5.** Allow gifted children to select their own independent study projects and topics. They will anyway, with or without your guidance.

**6.** Familiarize yourself with curriculum approaches that are based on discovery approaches to music learning. (*See* especially Hickok and Smith,[2] Marsh,[4] Schafer,[5] MMCP.[1,6])

**7.** The following verbs are good points of departure for encouraging creative responses: analyze, compare, design, create, criticize, apply, teach, predict, judge. Example: You are a celebrity on this week's "Gong Show." Describe each act and how you would judge it *musically*.

**8.** Present enrichment experiences that are problem-solving approaches. Examples:

    **a.** Think of a favorite selection of music. Listen, sing, or play it several times. Describe it musically (melody, rhythm, meter, form, texture). Use only three of its musical characteristics to create a new piece of your own.

    **b.** All the music composed for your instrument has been lost or destroyed. Find some music composed for another instrument and arrange it for yours.

If other children in a group challenge their right to enrichment projects, let them undertake one. It is unlikely that they will have the independent research skills or the self-motivation to complete the preliminary stages of a project and they will quickly lose interest.

It is not necessary to be gifted in order to be an effective teacher of academically gifted children. What is necessary is the ability to facilitate and guide learning without getting in the way. However, guiding extraordinary talent in music is another matter. Every honest music teacher recognizes when personal skills and talent have reached the limit of effectiveness with an individual student. It is then time to assist the student in locating another teacher—one who can extend the student's skills and talents to an even higher level. To do otherwise is not only unprofessional, but selfish and detrimental to the potential of the student.

## Summary

Musically gifted and talented children are generally characterized by extraordinary listening skills, superior cognitive knowledge, creativity, and skillful performance. Although there have been more child prodigies recorded in music than in any other field, some were clearly skillful instrumental technicians as opposed to gifted musicians. In addition to apparent genetic factors, sound training in music is essential in order for the musically gifted child to realize potential. Gifted children are usually quite verbal, have a distinct sense of humor, are well liked by peers, are extremely curious, and prefer discovery and creative approaches to learning. Identification of the gifted and talented, implementing appropriate programs to meet their needs, and preparing teachers to work with them are the biggest challenges to effective public school education of this group.

### References/Recommended Reading

[1]Biasini, C., and Pogonowksi, L. *MMCP Interaction.* Elnora, NY: Media, Inc., 1971.

Fisher, Renee. *Musical Prodigies.* New York: Association Press, 1973.

Getzels and Jackson. *Creativity and Intelligence.* New York: John Wiley, 1962.

Goertzel, Victor. *Cradles of Eminence.* Boston: Little, Brown & Co., 1962.

[2]Hickok, D., and Smith, J. *Creative Teaching of Music in the Elementary School.* Boston: Allyn and Bacon, 1974.

[3]Marland, Sidney. *Education of the Gifted and Talented.* 2 vols. Washington, DC: U.S. Government Printing Office, 1971.

[4]Marsh, Mary Val. *Explore and Discover Music.* New York: Macmillan, 1970.

Paynter, J., and Aston, P. *Sound and Silence.* New York: Cambridge University Press, 1970.

[5]Schafer, R. Murray. *Creative Music Education.* New York: Schirmer, 1976.

[6]Thomas, Ronald. *MMCP Synthesis.* Elnora, NY: Media, Inc., 1971.

Torrance, E. Paul. *Encouraging Creativity in the Classroom.* Dubuque, IA: W.C. Brown, 1970.

———. *Gifted Child in the Classroom.* New York: Macmillan, 1965.

Torrance, E. Paul, and Myers, R.E. *Creative Learning and Teaching.* New York: Dodd, Mead, 1971.

## Additional Resources

The American Association for Gifted Children, 15 Gramercy Park, New York, New York 10003. Publications.

National Association for Gifted Children, 808 Spring Valley Drive, Cincinnati, Ohio 45236. Journal: *Gifted Child Quarterly.*

Office of the Gifted and Talented, U.S. Office of Education, 400 Maryland Avenue, S.W., Washington, D.C. 20202.

# Appendix

# APPENDIX

## Music Skills

The following music skills are representative of those used to describe behaviors in writing instructional objectives.

| SINGING | PLAYING (instruments) | MOVING | LISTENING |
|---|---|---|---|
| echo patterns | steady beat | steady beat | beat/no beat |
| in tune | on cue | beats in groups of two | tempo |
| on pitch | without cue | beats in groups of three | dynamics |
| accurate rhythm | steady tempo | locomotor rhythms | meter |
| steady tempo | echo rhythm patterns | nonlocomotor rhythms | rhythm |
| with words | echo melodic patterns | changing tempo | melody |
| with accompaniment | with dynamics | specific rhythms | melody with |
| without accompaniment | solo | solo/with partner/in group | accompaniment |
| solo | in group | copy movements | timbre |
| in group | with good tone (wind | patterned movement | texture |
| rounds, part songs | instruments) | interpret melody, rhythm, | repetition and contrast |
| with dynamics | with appropriate technique | dynamics, texture | simple musical form |
| improvise | memorize patterns | interpret simple form | style |
| | (rhythmic and melodic) | improvise | |
| | improvise | | |

## Some Representative Tests Used In Identifying Special Learners

| TITLE | AGE RANGE | WHAT | COMMENTS |
|---|---|---|---|
| Bayley Infant Scale, 1969 | 2–30 months | global intelligence | individual; includes mental, motor, behavior items; sometimes given by visiting nurses or home-care workers |
| Bender-Gestalt Test, 1970 | 4 yrs. and over | visual motor | individual; consists of form copying; sometimes used to screen for brain damage or personality disturbance |
| Caine-Levine Social Competency Scale, 1963 | 5–13 years. (retarded) | social competence | determined through parent interview |
| Cattell Infant Intelligence Scale, 1960 | 3–30 months | global intelligence | individual; nonverbal; downward extension of Stanford-Binet |
| Denver Developmental Screening Test (DDST), 1970 | 2 wks.–6 yrs. | motor skills, language, personality, and social development | individual; gives a mental age |
| Detroit Test of Learning Aptitude (DTLA), 1968 | 3 yrs. and over | global intelligence | individual; gives a mental age; includes auditory, visual, verbal, and social development items |
| Frostig Developmental Test of Visual Perception, 1966 | 4–10 yrs. | visual perception | individual or group; paper and pencil test; can be given by teacher |
| Gesell Developmental Schedules (GDS), 1949 | 4 wks.–6 yrs. | global intelligence | individual; gives a mental age |
| Goodenough-Harris Drawing Test, 1963 | 3–15 yrs. | nonverbal intelligence; body image, personality | gives a mental age; sometimes used to screen for brain damage and personality disturbance |
| Illinois Test of Psycho-linguistics, (ITPA), 1968 | 2–10 yrs. | mental processing | individual; helpful in determining specific sensory weaknesses |
| Iowa Test of Basic Skills (ITBS), 1973 | grades 1–9 | academic achievement | Braille edition available |
| Leitner International Performance Scale (LIPS), 1955 | 2 yrs. and over | global intelligence | nonverbal; often used for preschool evaluations |
| Merrill-Palmer Scale of Mental Tests, 1931 | 24–36 months | global intelligence | individual; nonverbal; often used for preschool evaluations |

| TITLE | AGE RANGE | WHAT | COMMENTS |
|-------|-----------|------|----------|
| Metropolitan Achievement Test (MAT), 1972 | grades 1–9 | academic achievement | group; highly verbal |
| Motor-Free Visual Perception Test (MVPT), 1972 | 4–8 yrs. | visual perception | |
| Nebraska Test of Learning Aptitude, 1966 | 5–10 yrs. | global intelligence | nonverbal; widely used with hearing impaired |
| Peabody Picture Vocabulary Test, (PPVT), 1970 | 2½–18 yrs. | verbal intelligence (receptive language) | individual |
| Pre-School Attainment Record (PAR), 1967 | 6 mo.–7 yrs. | developmental skills | individual; includes tests for ambulation, manipulation, communication, social skills, and creativity |
| Purdue Perceptual Motor Survey, 1966 | 4–10 yrs. | motor development | can be given by teacher |
| Slosson Intelligence Test (SIT), 1963 | 2 wks. and over | global intelligence | individual; quick screening device based on Stanford-Binet and Gesell Developmental Schedule |
| Stanford-Binet, 1973 | 2 yrs. and over | global intelligence | individual; gives a mental age and IQ score |
| Valett Psychoeducational Test of Basic Learning Abilities, 1968 | 5–12 yrs. | basic learning skills | can be given by teacher |
| Vineland Social Maturity Scale (VSMS), 1965 | infant–adult | social competence | determined through parent interview |
| Wepman Auditory Discrimination Test, 1973 | 5–8 yrs. | discrimination for speech sounds (single words) | requires same/different concept; can be given by teacher |
| Wechsler Intelligence Scale for Children (WISC), 1949 | 5–15 yrs. | global intelligence | individual; gives separate verbal and performance scores |
| Wechsler Preschool and Primary Scale of Intelligence, (WPPSI), 1967 | 4–6½ yrs. | global intelligence | individual; gives separate verbal and performance scores; downward extension of WISC |
| Wide Range Achievement Test (WRAT), 1965 | K–college | word recognition, spelling, arithmetic | individual |

## LOCOMOTOR ACTIVITIES

### Locomotor Rhythms

Teachers often avoid locomotor activities because they lack experience in body movement themselves or the criteria with which to select or perform appropriate musical accompaniment. The following guidelines may be of help in alleviating both of these problems. A drum beat, or clapping, is a good starting accompaniment for all locomotor rhythms.

**Walk** In walking, the child steps forward, backward, or sideways, keeping one foot on the ground at all times. When children are allowed to initiate their own walking patterns, there is a fine opportunity to observe general coordination, body rhythm, posture, and lateral dominance (the preferred foot will usually be used to start out). Look also for an even heel-toe movement, no dragging feet, weight evenly distributed, and the forward swinging of the right arm with the left foot (and vice versa). Appropriate musical accompaniment will most often be found in moderate $\frac{4}{4}$ and slow $\frac{2}{4}$ meters with the accented beats more often felt than emphasized. Tempo should be slow enough to be comfortable for all, but ideally not too draggy. Children with poor ambulation skills may find it easier to step to every other beat. If a scatter formation is used, this will not interfere with those children who are able to step to every beat.

**March** Snappy marches are usually written in $\frac{2}{4}$ or *alla breve*, and in lively tempo. Although it is possible to find recordings of this type of march that are slower than the 120 cadence of the marching band, many will need to be investigated before finding some that are suitable. Stepping to every other beat can create a balance problem and therefore may not be a viable alternative. A piano accompaniment is best, but a drumbeat will also make it possible to adjust tempo to children. Be sure the children make a distinction between walking and marching. In marching, knees should be lifted high and arms swung more vigorously. Contact with the floor is made with a toe-heel sequence, although you may prefer not to introduce this technique to children who are chronic toe-walkers. (See Physical Disabilities, p. 251). Slow, stately marches, or promenades, are in slow $\frac{2}{4}$ and $\frac{4}{4}$ meters and will be challenging for children with balance problems.

**Slide** In sliding, one foot moves along the floor; the other foot closes up beside it. This is usually done sideways; it may be even or uneven.

**Trot** In trotting, small steps are taken while lifting knees high. Arms can be extended forward or held up with elbows bent and held close to the body. Quick duple meters are the best sources for trotting music.

**Run** Moderate to fast tempos in duple meters are more suitable. Light, thinly scored instrumental music with contrasting slower sections is ideal. Running steps are executed basically on the balls of the feet with the heels making very light, if any, contact with the floor. Arms are held close to the body for short running, but swing more on long strides.

**Gallop** In galloping, the legs move forward in a combination of a run-walk. Since the same foot always leads, practice should be given in starting out on each foot. The starting foot walks forward; the back foot "tries to catch up" with a run. Usually, the rhythm for galloping is ⁶⁄₈.

**Jump** Jumping is a springing movement executed with *both* feet leaving and returning to the floor *at the same time*. Watch for one-foot landings or uneven weight distribution that will affect balance. The children should land with knees slightly bent. Jumping can be accompanied by any meter, but the rhythm pattern should include space (rests) between even beats to be satisfactory for extended periods.

**Hop** Hopping is unlike jumping in that it is executed on *one* foot at a time. Both feet should get practice, however. A moderate to fast tempo is suitable. Some children may need to build up endurance gradually to sustain a hopping movement for more than four consecutive beats.

**Skip** Skipping is a complex movement and often, in teaching, it must be broken down to its component parts. Basically, it is a walk-hop (or bounce) on the *same* foot. Care must be taken to ensure that the children understand that the hop or bounce is a "traveling" movement to the next step. Targets such as hoops or pillows can be placed on the floor to give the children something to move toward. Feet *alternate* on the strong beats, which particularly makes this a difficult movement for children with laterality problems. They often lapse into a galloping step when they keep the same foot leading. Although it is possible to skip to other duple meters, music in ⁶⁄₈ is usually most suitable. The rhythm pattern is the most important criteria (i.e., the relationship of the step to the hop).

**Roll** Rolling is one way for nonambulatory children to move from one place to another. It is done in reclining position on the floor. Usually, the head turns first; arms, trunk, and legs follow in that order. Duple meter accompaniments probably give a better rolling effect, but some fast triple meters are acceptable. Children should be able to begin a roll starting on either the left or right side. When arms are extended overhead, their use in supporting the turning body is eliminated, therefore presenting a greater physical challenge.

**Crawl** A slow to moderate tempo in duple meter is best. Children should be able to move arms and legs on the same side of the body together, and in opposition (i.e., left arm with right leg).

**Leap** The momentum for a leap is usually begun with a run. Take off is on one foot high into the air. The forward foot is straightened out as much as possible for distance. The melodic contour of good leaping music is as important as the rhythm, which must allow for time spent airborne.

**Lunge** Lunging is a giant step forward with bent knee. Lunging can be executed in place, in which case the lunging foot is returned to the starting position. Melodic contour and dynamics are important in selecting good music to accompany this movement. Tempos should be fairly slow.

## Variations on Locomotor Rhythms

**a.** In place
**b.** Forward
**c.** Backward
**d.** Sideways
**e.** Around obstacle course
**f.** Turn at end of phrase
**g.** On heels
**h.** Cross over step
**i.** With knees bent
**j.** On tiptoe
**k.** Little steps
**l.** Giant steps
**m.** With hands on head, hips
**n.** With arms outstretched to sides, front, overhead
**o.** With head turned side to side
**p.** With eyes closed
**q.** While blindfolded
**r.** While bouncing ball
**s.** While playing an instrument
**t.** While clapping

### Walk
1. See items a–t above.
2. Bride's walk (step forward on one foot; bring other foot up to meet it before stepping forward on opposite foot).
3. Combine items b–h with i–t where appropriate.

### March
1. See a–f, m–q, s–t.
2. With accented left (or right) foot.
3. With "baton" extended forward, overhead, to side.
4. In lines, rows.

### Slide/Gallop
1. See b–f, m–o, s–t.
2. While slapping thighs.

### Trot
1. See a–f, m–q, t.
2. With partner extending arms back as reins.
3. With partner and hoop as rein.

### Run
1. See a–f, j–o, r, t.
2. With scarves, streamers.

### Jump
1. See a–f, k–q.
2. In circle.
3. Into, out of, through a hoop.
4. With a partner.
5. Straddle jump (spread legs apart and raise hands overhead; return to standing position).

### Hop
1. See a–f, k–q.
2. In circle.
3. Into and out of hoop laying on floor.
4. With a partner.
5. On each foot separately, then alternately.

## Skip

1. See b–c, e–f, m–o, r–t.
2. With partner.

## Roll

1. See b–c, f, p.
2. Diagonally.
3. To a target.
4. On various surfaces (i.e., wood, tile, rug, grass).
5. Left to right, right to left.
6. With hands under body, or outstretched overhead.

## Leap/Lunge

1. See b, d, m–o, r, t.
2. With each foot separately, then alternately.
3. With scarves, streamers.

## Simple Dance Steps

**Waltz step** This is done in triple meter. Develop by having children bend knee of the stepping foot on the first beat, and raise up on toes while stepping on the second and third beats. Accompany this rhythm with high- and low-pitched drums or by striking one drum in the center for "one," and on the rim with the stick part of the mallet on "two, three." The bending step will alternate from left to right foot each measure.

**Schottische** Develop by having children first walk to a steady drumbeat, stopping when the beat stops. Play a game of stop-and-go, varying the number of beats between stops. Gradually begin repeating a pattern of three beats walking followed by a one-beat rest. When the children do this easily, add a hop on the rest using the *same* foot.

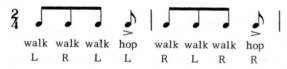

```
 2
 4

walk walk walk hop   walk walk walk hop
 L    R    L   L       R    L    R   R
```

When the step is secure, this dance can be done with partners. In circle formation, partners join hands, facing the same direction. (Both hands can be held crossed—left with left, right with right—if children are capable.) Group proceeds around the circle clockwise. For a greater challenge, some children may want to try facing partners to do the dance. In this situation, formation is scattered and one partner begins by stepping back while the other moves forward. Children should turn on the phrases in order to give each partner the experience of stepping backward. Also, in this position, each partner will begin on a different foot so that forward and backward steps are taken on the same side.

**Polka** Using the gallop step, develop by playing the stop-and-go games to a drumbeat. Vary the number of beats between stops and starts. Gradually repeat a pattern of two beats (gallops) and stop. When gallop is resumed, the lead foot is *changed*. To proceed in the same general direction, children will have to turn their body 180 degrees. Gradually work into a rhythm of two gallops, changing (and turning) after each set of two. As children become comfortable with this and the tempo is increased, they will automatically put in a hop on the turn. When ready, the step can be done with a partner in either circle or scatter formation. Partners hold inside hands and start out on *outside* feet. When outside feet are leading, partners face each other; when inside feet are leading, partners turn away from each other (still holding hands). When children are ready for a greater challenge, have partners face each other holding both hands, turning together, and changing lead feet every two steps.

## Indian Dance Steps

**Toe-heel step** This step is performed to a drumbeat that is alternately loud and soft. On the first (loud) beat, the left foot moves forward and the left toe lightly touches the floor. On the next (soft) beat, the left heel is brought down hard. The step is repeated with each foot alternating.

**Drag step** This step is also performed to a drumbeat that is alternately loud and soft. The first step begins on the *soft* beat by stepping forward and touching the toe to the floor. The same foot is dragged backward on the loud beat and the heel is brought down hard when in place beside the other foot.

## Fancy Stepping

**Brush** Graze the floor with the ball of the foot in a circular pattern.

**Point** Raise leg slightly and point toe to front, side, back.

**Touch** Extend foot to front, side, back; touch floor but do not put weight on foot.

**Pivot** Turn foot without losing contact with floor; pivot in a circle by stepping in place with opposite foot to push pivot foot around.

**Shuffle** Brush leg forward and back.

**Flip** Keeping leg straight, brush it back.

**Knee lift** Point knee to left, to right.

### Dance for "Woodstock's Samba"

(Note: All steps are taken *on the beat*. Include finger snaps beat 4 of Meas. 1—4.)

Meas. 1  Moving left, step LF, close RF; step LF, touch RF
Meas. 2  Moving right, step RF, close LF; step RF, touch LF
Meas. 3  Moving forward, step LF, close RF; step LF, touch RF
Meas. 4  Moving backward, step RF, close LF; step RF, touch LF
    *Repeat Meas. 1—4 for second and third endings.*
*Fourth time (fourth ending)*
Meas. 1–2  Same as above.
Meas. 3  Moving in a circle, step LF, pivot RF (four times)
Meas. 4  Moving in a circle, step RF, pivot LF (four times)
Meas. 5–6  Repeat Meas. 1–2.
Meas. 7–8  Step LF on downbeat;

slap thighs

snap fingers

## Special Walks

**Bear** Both hands and feet touch floor; arm and leg on *same side* of body move together.

**Dog** Both hands and feet touch floor; arm and leg on *opposite* side of body move together. Run on hands and *feet* (not knees). For lame dog, hold one hand up.

**Crab** Squat; place hands flat on floor behind body. Lift hips off floor; extend head and neck down toward floor. Hands and legs on same side move *together sideways*. (This will be too difficult for some children.)

**Rabbit** Crouch, hands touching floor between legs. Jump forward, landing in same position.

**Kangaroo** Crouch with fingers touching floor between knees. Jump *up and forward* with body straight out, landing in crouched position.

**Seal** Lie face down on floor, hands placed beside shoulders. Straighten arms and move forward using *hands only.*

**Duck** Waddle in crouched position, palms together behind back. Spread fingers open for tail.

**Inchworm** Lie face down on floor, hands close to shoulders, and *balls of feet* touching floor. Straighten arms. Walk forward, keeping knees straight until feet reach hands; move hands until trunk of body is again stretched out.

**Elephant** Clasp hands; bend forward at waist. Take heavy steps with arms swinging loosely toward the stepping side.

**Giraffe** Clasp hands together and stretch arms overhead; walk on tiptoe with legs apart and knees stiff. Sway arms and trunk, but maintain upward point.

**Bird** Place feet together. Take little jumps forward keeping knees together. (Holding an object between the knees helps.)

**Horse** Practice galloping, trotting, and running.

**Cat** Get into crawl position, back rounded; stretch.

**Monkey** Take straddle stance, knees slightly bent and arms extended forward. Bounce up and down, moving arms up and down alternately (as in climbing a rope).

**Frog** Squat; spread knees apart, hands touching floor between knees. Jump *forward and up* staying in crouched position.

### Ball, Balloon, and Hoop Activities

**Ball activities** In selecting balls, consider the size, weight, and texture of the ball. Large balls (8–10 inches in diameter) are easier to catch than small tennis-size balls; small ones are easier to throw; heavier balls are sometimes better for kicking than lightweight balls. Experimenting with a variety of types is recommended for children who have difficulty in ball handling.

*Roll*
- To a target or partner; gradually increase distance
- With both hands, one hand
- Catch a rolled ball with two hands, then one hand

*Bounce*
- With both hands; each hand separately; alternately
- In sitting position between knees
- In kneeling position
- To a partner or target (e.g., hoop)
- Catch bounced ball in front, to sides, high, low
- Step forward, then backward, then sideways, while bouncing

*Throw and catch*
- Underhand; overhand; with each hand separately; with both hands
- To a partner or target
- In front, to sides, high, low
- With arms extended overhead; from crouched position
(Substitute a beanbag for children unable to grasp a ball.)

*Kick*
- With each foot separately, then alternately
- From stationary position
- From moving position
- While ball is rolling
- To a partner or target

**Balloon activities**
- Substitute a balloon for ball activities (rolling, throwing, and kicking).

- Keep balloon aloft by hitting it on the beat.
- Hit balloon with each hand separately, then alternately.
- Keep balloon aloft by bouncing it off various body parts (head, knees, elbows, etc.).
- Keep balloon aloft by hitting only on the strong beats of a three-beat accompaniment (e.g., waltz).

**Hoop activities**
- Substitute hoop for rolling ball activities.
- Balance hoop on hand, stick, knee, foot.
- Twirl hoop around with hand or stick.
- Rotate hoop around body by swiveling hips.
- Jump through, into, over hoop.

### Balance Beam Activities

Place strips of tape on the floor 4″ apart and 6′ to 12′ in length to simulate a balance beam. Stepping on the beat, *walk* beam (unless otherwise indicated) forward, backward, then sideways. Use a drumbeat or music.
- With arms held sideways, overhead, on top of head, or hips
- With hands clasped behind back
- On tiptoe
- With knees bent
- With eyes closed
- With same foot leading
- Forward, stepping *over* a small object (stooping *under* a stick) midway and continuing to end without losing beat
- Forward, then backward, with something balanced on head
- Sideways, crossing left foot over right, then right foot over left; left foot behind right, then right foot behind left
- Hop the length of the beam on right foot, then left foot (forward; sideways)
- 6 beats to center of beam; kneel on beats 7 and 8
- 8 beats to end of beam
- To a familiar song, turning on phrases
- To "Stop and Go" or "A Little Flight Music" ("Stop" version), balancing on one foot on pauses
- Sideways 8 beats; turn 180 degrees and continue walking 8 beats to end (with opposite foot leading). Try with same foot leading.
- Backward 8 beats; turn 180 degrees and continue walking 8 beats to end
- Forward 8 beats; backward 8 beats
- Hop to middle of beam; turn; hop back on same foot
- Hop forward 8 beats; turn; hop backward 8 beats
- Hop to middle of beam and balance on one foot for as many beats as balance can be maintained. (Try on both left and right feet.)
- Stand on beam with feet side by side until balance is lost (do the same, standing with one foot in front of the other)
- With eyes closed, balance with feet side by side; in front of one another; on one foot
- Walk on beam like a cat, a dog, a rabbit, a kangaroo, a duck, an inchworm, an elephant, a bird
- Two children (at opposite ends) walk length of beam and pass each other in middle without breaking rhythm or falling off.

## NONLOCOMOTOR ACTIVITIES

### Nonlocomotor (axial) Movement

**Standing rock** Place one foot forward; shift weight from front to back foot. Try with each foot in the forward position, as well as starting the rock from both forward and back feet.

**Sitting rock** Shift weight from hip to hip.

**Standing sway** This is a lesser movement than rocking. Keeping feet flat on the floor, sway from side to side (in standing position). Make sure that weight is never entirely on one foot.

**Sitting sway** Maintain movement in upper trunk with no obvious weight shift.

**Swing** Move body vigorously from side to side in an arc. Swing arms high, low, or in circles.

**Standing bend** Bend from waist down as close to floor as possible. Bend side to side; then bend from knees to squat position and return.

**Sitting bend** Bend head and shoulders as close to knees as possible. Sitting on the floor, bend side to side toward floor, then forward to toes, as close as possible.

**Stretch (standing or sitting)** Extend arms overhead, stretching from waist up.

**Twist (standing or sitting)** Place hands on waist; twist trunk of body to the right so left elbow follows right shoulder, then twist to the left. Try with hands clasped overhead, then with arms folded.

**Twirl** Move feet in circular direction in place as body turns. A hoop may be used to help confine movement to body axis.

## Hand and Arm Movements

Where appropriate, try all hand/arm movements left, right, together, separately and/or alternately, to the left and to the right.
• Touch index fingers to nose.
• Cover eyes with hands.
• Snap fingers.
• Make hand gestures (i.e., "come," "stay," "go away").
• Clench and open fists.
• Touch thumb to each finger on same hand.
• Extend fingers one at a time from clenched fist.
• Clasp hands together with fingers laced; extend forward, overhead, then over each shoulder.
• Fold arms across chest.
• Touch shoulders with hands on same side, on opposite sides.
• Clap hands in front, on each side, in back below knees, overhead, at shoulder level.
• Extend arms forward at shoulder height; to sides at shoulder height.
• Pat palms on table, knees.
• Hold palms up/down; turn in/out; circle each.
• Outline imaginary shape (e.g., triangle, square) in air, showing all points.
• Touch top/bottom of imaginary vertical line, horizontal line.
• With arms extended forward, move up/down/to the sides.
• Swing arms forward/back.
• Slap fist into open palm of opposite hand.
• Tap fists together one on top of the other; side by side; rotate.
• Make circles in the air with arms extended forward, overhead, to the sides.
• Make hitchhiking gesture over each shoulder.
• Wave hand with fingers held straight; twist wrist; do overhead, at waist level, etc.
• Point elbows to side.
• Make circles with elbows.
• Slap thighs with open palms.
• Extend fists forward; move up/down.
• Slap forearms with open palms.
• Swish palms together.

## Seated Feet And Leg Movements

Where appropriate, try all movements left, right, together, separately and/or alternately, to the left and to the right.
• Tap toes, then heels.
• In place: walk, march, tiptoe, heel walk.
• Keep heels together; move toes apart.
• Move feet forward, then back.
• Spread knees apart, then bring together.
• Cross and uncross legs.
• Move feet to the side.
• Cross and uncross ankles.
• Keeping toes together, click heels.

## Partner Activities

• Slap palms held vertically, horizontally, left, right, etc.
• Shake hands.
• Hook elbows.
• Twist a hoop in cross-extension pattern.

## Head And Mouth Movements

• Blink eyes separately, together, alternately.
• Wink each eye, then alternately.
• Wrinkle nose.
• Thrust tongue in and out, side to side.
• Puff cheeks; collapse.
• Smile; frown.
• Nod head up/down, side to side.
• Change facial expression (e.g., surprise, worry, fright).
• Turn head left/right; alternately left/right.
• Open/close mouth.
• Smack lips, buzz, pucker, stretch; curl them up/down.
• Do tongue clicks.
• Hiss.
• Pop cheeks.
• Turn corners of mouth up/down.

## Instrument Specifications

Classroom instruments for use with handicapped children should include both melody and rhythm instruments. Representative playing techniques should utilize a variety of motor skills (i.e., palmar and pincer grasps, wrist movements, finger movement). Wind instruments are also important as they help to develop breath control and facial muscles necessary for speech. Some wind instruments should require very little pressure to produce a sound while others demand good breath support and diaphragm breathing. Instruments that are put into the mouth must be sterilized after each individual's use. Some disinfectants are available in convenient spray containers.

Good tone quality is a principal consideration in selecting instruments. Instruments that have poor resonating or ringing qualities are not suitable for use by children who may have difficulty processing sounds. All instruments must be of durable construction with replacement parts where appropriate (e.g., drumheads). Although deliberate abuse should never be tolerated, instruments played by children who have poor motor control and limited muscle strength do tend to be dropped more often. Instruments that are ordinarily held for playing should be constructed of lightweight materials and easily manipulated by children with small hands and underdeveloped muscles. Finally, instruments should have no sharp edges or protuberances and they should be made of materials unaffected by moisture (i.e., drooling).

# Quick Tricks With Classroom Instruments

**Tape** (masking, adhesive, plastic, etc.)
• Make a holder for instruments such as triangles, cymbals, or gongs by taping a rhythm stick or ruler to the edge of a desk or chalkboard tray to enable player with one hand to play without assistance.
• Tape the handle of a tone block to the edge of a desk or chalkboard tray to enable player with one hand to play without assistance.
• Tape down holes on melody flutes, recorders, to produce appropriate pitch for children unable to cover holes.
• Code keys or bars of instruments to be played with colored tape.
• Tape small mallets or shaking instruments to the palm of a child lacking a pincer grasp. Larger mallets can be supported with a splint.

**Tape** (magnetic)
• Attach to the back of lightweight resonator bells or other small instruments that are struck. Magnetic tape will adhere to steel surfaces (e.g., metal cabinets) or to another piece of tape placed on desk, chalkboard, lapboard, etc. Also useful for attaching visuals to magnetic boards.

**Elastic bandages**
• Fasten maracas and other lightweight shaking instruments to forearms or palms by stapling bandage for a tight fit.

**Velcro**
• Use to attach mallets or small instruments to a player's hand. Available where sewing aids are sold.

**Children's mitten guards** (strip of elastic webbing with fasteners at each end)
• Use to attach triangles, hand drums, and other small instruments to player's clothing to keep from falling to the floor if grasp is lost. May need to attach a length of ribbon or cord to some.

**Styrofoam or rubber balls** (small)
• Insert stick of mallet through the center of ball to enable child lacking pincer grasp to hold with a palmar grasp. Use also as pencil holders.

**Extension mouthpiece for Pianicas and Melodicas**
• Use to enable child to rest the instrument on a desk or table and still see the keyboard.

**Teething rings** (especially pretzel-shape)
• Use as strummers (for Autoharp, Chromaharp) by children lacking a pincer grasp.

**Spray disinfectants**
• Use with tissues or paper towels as a fast, neat way to sterilize mouthpieces, slide whistles, etc. Readily available at drugstores.

---

# Behaviors That Interfere With Learning

| BEHAVIOR | SUGGESTED TEACHING TECHNIQUES |
|---|---|

### A. ABSTRACTING-SYMBOLIZATION
*Inability to understand relationships, especially to relate a symbol to its object*

• Inadequate language development

• Below-average reading skills

• Unable to associate sound with symbol

1. Use concrete and manipulative materials.
2. Give response choices.
   a. Explain verbally.
   b. Show through movement or dramatization.
   c. Draw picture.

### B. CATASTROPHIC REACTION
*Sudden loss of control for no apparent reason (usually passes quickly)*

• Bursts into tears

• Throws things

• Temper tantrums

• Uncontrolled or hysterical laughing

• Low frustration tolerance

• Trembling

1. *Prevention:* reduce the possibility of panic and anxiety in new situations by structuring the activity so that it is less threatening.
   a. Incorporate a familiar element (e.g., a partner the target child works well with, an instrument that has been successfully handled before, a familiar song).
   b. Use multisensory approaches to new musical concepts (visual, tactile, motor).
   c. Use concrete and manipulative materials.
2. *First aid:* remain calm.
   a. Comfort and reassure the child.
   b. Change the activity.
   c. If necessary, direct the child to an individual activity for a brief period to provide time for composure before rejoining the group (e.g., learning center activity, doing a special job for you).

## C. CLASSIFICATION AND SORTING DIFFERENCES
*Groups objects or ideas differently by
using unusual sorting criteria*

• May classify instruments according to color
(i.e., silver, gold, black); size (i.e., small/large,
skinny/fat); those with keys, bell-shaped ends,
holes at top, and so forth

1. Before deciding a response is incorrect (rather than different), consider all possible sorting criteria, or ask child to point out similar features.

## D. CONCRETE BEHAVIOR
*Inability to generalize or perceive different aspects of objects, symbols, or ideas*

• Interprets directions, stories literally

• Tends to be rigid due to highly unreliable feedback from perceptual processing

• Difficulty transferring learning from one situation to a new one

1. Build confidence by using target child's strongest sensory learning mode to support weaker ones (i.e., if child is a visual learner, present concept visually first, then relate the auditory aspect).
2. Plan activities that involve classification and sorting to enable child to perceive similarities.
3. Introduce variations to routine procedures carefully and gradually, pointing out those aspects that will remain the same.
4. Avoid idiomatic and slang expressions that assign new meanings to common words (e.g., "bring out your part," "punch that note," "from the top").
5. Carefully plan step-by-step transfer of concepts and skills to new activities.

## E. DISORGANIZATION
*Inability to carry out a task or pay attention to the material at hand*

• Responses appear random and meaningless

• Personal untidiness; messy desk, locker

• Disarray of work materials

• Inflexible to new situations

1. Establish consistent procedures for routine events (i.e., open and close of class lesson, passing out music, use of instruments).
2. Structure activities tightly.
3. Give step-by-step directions.
4. Limit choices to two or three (i.e., "Shall we accompany this song with a drum or a tambourine?").
5. Reduce distractions (e.g., put away instruments, music as soon as activity is completed).

## F. DISTRACTIBILITY
*Constantly distracted by extraneous stimuli*

• External distractions: room, hall, or outside noises; room temperature; open windows; fly buzzing; jewelry or printed clothing worn by teacher, etc.

• Internal distractions: uncomfortable clothing, hunger pains, headache, etc.

• All stimulus is given equal importance so attention jumps from one thing to another

• Inability to focus on the main activity

• Wants to touch everything

1. Simplify the environment by putting *everything* out of sight except the materials to be attended to.
2. Avoid "sensory overload" by limiting the number and dimension of sensory materials used in one activity (i.e., visuals, instruments, body movements, etc.).
3. Structure activities tightly and keep them short.
4. Use simple, attractive visual aids.
5. Frame blackboard, charts, or flannelboard work with bright colored border.
6. Position target child where you will have proximity control (i.e., arm's length away) without losing eye contact with entire class. A gentle touch is often effective in refocusing lost attention.

## G. FIGURE-GROUND CONFUSION
*Inability to separate background from foreground material; pays too much attention to insignificant details*

*Visual*
• Frequently loses place in music

• Skips notes, measures, lines

• Unable to focus on important things on a crowded page

1. Use large, simple visual aids with few details (e.g., black-and-white line drawings, photographs)
2. Simplify music notation (e.g., two or three line staff; Kodaly system, etc.).
3. Frame parts of visuals or music page to aid in focusing.

*Auditory*

- Unable to identify familiar instruments when disassembled (e.g., clarinet)

- Unable to block out background noise

- Unable to distinguish melody from accompaniment

- Unable to hear separate parts in vocal music, or instruments in ensemble

- May pay too much attention to an accompanying element, such as a rhythmic pattern, while being unaware of melodic theme in listening experiences

4. Mask out *extraneous* visual material when possible (i.e., irrelevant exercises, pictures).
5. Use two-track stereo recordings to highlight melody *or* accompaniment, specific instruments.
6. Have target child use earphones for recorded listening.
7. Demonstrate how instruments are assembled and taken apart.
8. Help child interpret visual and auditory materials through discussion of the main features.
9. Point out categories (e.g., instrument families, vocal classification, instrumental ensembles, etc.) and their similarities.
10. Add instruments to ensemble activities one at a time.

## H. HYPERACTIVITY
*Excessive or uncontrollable movement or activity without purpose*

- Reacts to all stimuli

- Something constantly in motion (e.g., hands, feet, etc.)

- Leaves seat continually

- Unable to control motor responses, especially in slow tempo

1. Simplify environment by reducing the number of things to look at, touch, or hear.
2. Plan many and varied activities of short duration with obvious goals.
3. Alternate quiet activities with physically active ones.
4. Alternate fun, easy activities with difficult ones that require more concentration.
5. Plan most activities with motor involvement that will keep hands busy (e.g., use two mallets, pantomime words to songs, draw melody in air, keep beat, trace or point to pictures or score).
6. Plan generous amounts of gross motor activities.
7. Gradually increase endurance for remaining in one position by developing and extending familiar activities that hold interest for the target child.

## I. IMPULSIVITY
*Acts on impulse due to inability to anticipate or evaluate consequences*

- Runs to window

- Shouts out comments, answers

- Impelled to touch and handle things, especially in unfamiliar surroundings

- Overreacts

1. Exploit motor reactions by planning generous amounts of movement activities to help dispel excess energy.
2. Provide outlet for compulsive actions (e.g., action songs, creative movement).
3. Structure other activities so that those likely to trigger impulsive behavior are tightly controlled.
4. Keep materials (e.g., instruments, record player, etc.) well out of reach of target child and, if possible, out of sight when not in use.

## J. PERSEVERATION
*Unnecessary repetition of movement or speech*

- Continues to sing after class has finished the song

- Continues to play after the activity has ended

- Continues movement after a "stop" signal

- Repeats some words two or three times when expressing ideas, relating stories, etc.

1. Signal the end of one activity and the beginning of another by collecting and putting away materials after each activity before bringing out those for the next.
2. Arrange activities within the lesson in a contrasting order (e.g., singing followed by movement, followed by listening).
3. Physically change positions with a new activity (e.g., stand up to sing a song; move closer to record player, etc.).

## K. REACTION TIME
*Delayed response to sensory stimulus*

- Unable to perform on the beat

- May not react to an activity for several minutes, hours, or days

1. Give the child longer than usual to make a response. Never prompt or pressure a response.
2. Provide extra time in call-and-response or echo-type activities to enable target child to respond (i.e., measure rest between call and response; sing action songs in free rhythm).

## L. RIGIDITIES
*Inability to adapt to changes in the environment*

- Resists doing things differently (i.e., new instrumentation, new words, etc.)

- Changes in room arrangement or schedule may be disturbing

- Changes in tempo, key, accompaniment style may be disturbing

1. Establish predictable routines for beginning and ending lesson (i.e., greeting, choice of song, etc.).
2. Use consistent management and control techniques.
3. Modify familiar activities only slightly, pointing out the features that will remain the same.

## M. SHORT ATTENTION SPAN
*Inability to concentrate more than a few minutes on one activity, even without distractions*

- Suggests new activity before present one is completed

- Wanders off in the middle of an activity

- Complains of boredom or fatigue

- Watches clock

- Becomes irritable

1. Structure plans, space, and materials so that lesson flows smoothly from one activity to another.
2. Begin with very short, high interest activities, such as action or name songs, that focus on individuals.
3. Keep activities short and varied.
4. Repeat "good" performances frequently, thereby increasing their length.
5. When attention span begins to increase, select some ongoing activities suitable to expansion and development in subsequent lessons (e.g., compose new verses or accompaniments, create dances, musically adapt favorite poem or story).
6. Insist that each activity be completed before moving on to another.

## N. VARIABLE PERFORMANCE LEVEL
*Erratic achievement or behavior*

- Steady improvement may suddenly be followed by stagnation or even regression to a lower level

- Understanding of a difficult concept may be demonstrated even though previous performances have failed to demonstrate understanding of more basic concepts

1. Plateaus are common. Child apparently needs time to assimilate, digest, and transfer new learning.
2. Do not leave an activity too soon because it doesn't seem to be accomplishing the desired goal. It sometimes takes a long time to get the *initial* response. Introducing new material will only confuse the objective.

## Drug Therapy

Drug therapy is widely used to treat children with behavior disorders, particularly those of organic origin. While some children receive drugs to control seizures, more children are given drugs to reduce hyperactivity. Stimulants, which have a tranquilizing effect on preadolescent children, are commonly used. Tranquilizers themselves are usually prescribed only after stimulants have proved to be ineffective for the individual child. Tranquilizers are more commonly used to treat psychosis in adolescents and adults. Antidepressants have not been found to be as effective as stimulants in controlling hyperactivity in children. Although megavitamin therapy appears to hold some promise, there is insufficient research data to draw conclusive results as to its effectiveness. This is also true of diet therapies that restrict the intake of sugar and food additives. Both of these approaches are receiving widespread attention, partly because of increasing concern among all consumers regarding nutrients in packaged foods.

Drugs help to make some children more manageable by controlling hyperactivity and reducing distractibility. However, they are not without disadvantages, some of which are the following.

- All drugs take a long time (often several months) to build up sufficient accumulations in the body before their effects are seen.

- It often takes months of trying various drugs and dosages before a suitable one is found for a specific child. The child's behavior can be erratic during this period.

- Most drugs last only for a brief period (3–4 hours) so medication must be frequent. This is sometimes a problem in public schools, as school nurses or teachers are not always authorized to dispense such medication.

- Most drugs have some unpleasant side effects including insomnia, nausea, irritability, loss of appetite, and lethargy.

The long-range effects of drugs on children are still not known. Those individuals who advocate and participate in drug therapy programs obviously feel that the resultant improvement in the behavior of children who receive drugs outweigh these disadvantages.

## Behavior Modification

Behavior modification programs are based on B. F. Skinner's theory that behavior is directly related to consequences. According to this theory, unacceptable behavior can be changed by arranging an environment in which only acceptable behaviors are rewarded.

Much confusion and misunderstanding surrounds the application of behavior modification theory to education. For example, positive reinforcers (i.e., rewards) do not have to take the form of tangibles, such as candy or trinkets. Indeed, these kinds of rewards represent the lowest level of a hierarchy leading to intrinsic or self-reinforcing rewards. Actually, most teachers have always used behavior modification techniques to some extent by using praise or promising a special treat or activity as a reward for good work or behavior.

Some important elements of behavior modification programs that are too often ignored, even by some advocates, are the following.
- A well-designed and -executed program involves much record keeping before, during, and after intervention.
- Reinforcement is programmed to make rewards progressively more difficult to attain.
- Rewards must be changed periodically to maintain interest.
- The program must provide for phasing out the reward system altogether.

Reinforcers can be either positive or negative, and can motivate both acceptable and problem behavior. Positive reinforcers that promote acceptable behaviors include tokens and tangibles, contingency management, and social and intrinsic rewards. Tokens and tangibles, often referred to as *primary reinforcers*, are frequently used to enlist the initial cooperation of the target child. Sometimes a point system is used in which accumulated points are converted to rewards. A point system is usually too abstract to be effective with low functioning and very insecure children, however. Rewards earned by such children must be dispensed immediately to be effective. *Contingency management* is based on the Premack hypothesis that low probability behavior can be increased when followed by high probability behavior. Contingency rewards are conditional and are commonly used by teachers every day. (Example: "If we can finish our listening activity before music time is over, you may choose songs for the remaining class time.") Since this is a deferred reward, the children must be able to wait for reinforcement. *Social reinforcers* are also frequently used by teachers. They include praise and attention. In using praise as a behavior-shaping device, timing is a vital factor, as the praise must be immediate and, of course, sincere. The ultimate goal in reinforcers is *intrinsic,* achieved when an individual is self-reinforced by pride, satisfaction, and so forth.

*Negative reinforcers* are punitive actions that tend to temporarily curb inappropriate behavior. They include aversive measures such as electric shock and corporal punishment, deprivation (taking away tangibles or privileges), scolding, and removing the child from the learning environment. (Removing the child should not be confused with *time-outing* in which the child is not just removed from the learning environment, but *relocated* in a different learning environment that is more conducive to work.) Ironically, punitive measures often reinforce the behaviors they are meant to discourage because they may be providing a "payoff" of some kind, such as attention, peer status, or control over the teacher's emotions. *Extinction,* or ignoring the child and his or her behavior, is the negative reinforcer advocated by behaviorists. Extinction can work well in one-on-one situations where the child has nowhere else to turn for attention and approval. In group situations, however, it is less likely to produce the desired results before the unacceptable behavior has found an appreciative audience, and may even have reached epidemic proportions. Although it is unrealistic to think we can eliminate negative reinforcers entirely, teachers should use them sparingly. Children who are coerced into acceptable behaviors solely by the threat of punitive consequences have little chance of developing into mentally healthy and secure individuals.

Implementing a behavior modification program involves a good deal of planning and cooperation on the part of *all* who interact with the target child or group. The specific behavior to be changed must be identified, described, observed, and analyzed before an intervention program can be planned. After implementation, continuous monitoring and evaluation are essential. On the surface, behavior modification looks simple. But as one realizes the amount of organization, bookkeeping, and constant evaluation required for success, it is apparent that many programs lack some of these basic components.

Among the most frequent criticisms of behavior modification as an educational technique is that it is dehumanizing since animals are trained in much the same way. Also pointed out is the fact that a child has no opportunity to exert a choice of behavior and therefore is not learning to be responsible for behavior. Finally, the approach treats symptoms (behaviors) only and doesn't deal with the underlying causes of problem behaviors.

---

## Some Recommended Techniques for Physical Handling of a Child With Cerebral Palsy

**Any handling of a child with cerebral palsy should first be demonstrated by a qualified person.**

**Relaxing** All handling must start with the child in a relaxed position. All movement must be done *slowly.*

1. To rotate the trunk, gently push the child's shoulder forward with the *palm* (not fingertips) of your hand. Do both shoulders to bring hands to the midline. This technique can also be used to open a clenched fist.

2. Also, to open a clenched fist, you can gently push down on the top of the child's clenched hand with the *open palm* of your hand.

3. To flex a child's head, gently push forward *from the crown* of the head, never the neck.

**Positioning** Whether in a wheelchair or at a desk, the child should be positioned *symmetrically.* Pillows or bolsters made from rolled up towels or diapers are used to support the trunk and to center the child in the chair. Feet must be supported, never left dangling. Children should be secured in wheelchairs with a standard seat belt. Tying children into chairs restricts mobility of the upper torso, constricts breathing, and poses a safety hazard in the event the child must be removed from the chair quickly (e.g., fire). The position must (a) be comfortable for work and learning, (b) minimize balance difficulties, (c) enable use of the hands to the best advantage, and (d) be the easiest for eye-hand coordination. A lap board not only helps keep the child in position, but provides a working surface on which to place instruments and books.

**Carrying** Small children without braces can be carried most easily in a way that allows arms and legs to be controlled from flinging. Pick up the child from behind, positioning your arm under the hips so that the child's knees can bend over it. Hold the child close to your body so that you can wrap your other arm around the child's shoulders to control arms that are likely to fling outward when the head is turned.

**Lap sitting**   There are two ways to hold a small child in your lap for rocking, swaying, and so forth.

**1.** You can face the child away from you, supporting the back with the trunk of your body.

**2.** You can seat the child facing you with legs on either side of your hips. If sitting on the floor, you can get the child into this position by first laying the child on his or her back on your outstretched legs. Slowly bend your knees, gradually bringing the child to a sitting position, again with legs on either side of your hips. The child's back and head are supported by your thighs. Control arms from the shoulders if needed.

**Motor skill assistance**   When a hemiplegic child uses a good hand to reach out and grasp (e.g., an instrument or beater), the arm on the affected side of the body is likely to react by flinging up or clenching the fist. To relax, turn the *arm out and up at the shoulder,* keeping the *elbow straight* and the *palm up and open.* If the child uses the open palm for support, it will help to maintain this position.

Practice movement patterns that will be required *before* giving the child an object or instrument for manipulation. This helps the child to control muscle function and reduces the tension brought on by the excitement of the activity.

Some children, such as those with athetosis, (i.e., athetoid) have involuntary movements that interfere with motor responses. Chances for success are enhanced by providing stability, such as holding the child's legs together as she or he plays an instrument (e.g., resonator bells). This makes it easier for the child to hold head and arms steady and will improve the ability to grasp and manipulate an instrument.

In handing an instrument or other object to a right-handed child, approach directly in front but just to the left of midline (just to the right, for a left-handed child). It will then be unnecessary for the child to turn his or her head, which can cause extension and involuntary movements.

## VOCABULARY

**a tempo**   Return to the original tempo.

**abstract reasoning**   The process of arriving at conclusions through the use of symbols or generalizations rather than concrete materials.

**accelerando**   Gradually becoming faster.

**acceleration**   The practice of advancing a learner through the educational program more rapidly than is normal, as in "skipping" grades.

**accent**   Emphasis or stress on a note.

**acoustics**   The science of sound.

**acuity**   Sensitivity of perception.

**adaptive behavior**   Behavior that helps the individual interact more effectively with the environment.

**ad lib**   To perform extemporaneously.

**affective**   Having to do with or expressing feelings, attitudes, emotions, as in *affective behavior.*

**agnosia**   Partial or total inability to recognize objects and their meaning.

**alla breve**   A tempo marking indicating $\frac{2}{2}$ time. The half note is the beat note.

**allergen**   Any substance that causes an allergic reaction.

**ambulation**   The act of walking or moving about.

**amusia**   The inability to recognize or reproduce tones.

**anoxia**   Severe oxygen deficiency that can result in brain damage.

**antonyms**   Words having opposite meanings.

**anxiety**   Fearful apprehension.

**aphasia**   The inability to understand or produce spoken or written language as a result of brain damage. *See also* developmental aphasia, expressive aphasia, receptive aphasia.

**aphasic**   Relating to or affected by aphasia.

**apraxia**   The loss or impairment of the ability to perform complex coordinated movements, such as driving a car, dressing oneself, or playing baseball.

**arthritis**   Inflammation of the joints due to infectious, metabolic, or genetic causes. *See also* rheumatoid arthritis.

**asthma**   An allergic condition characterized by wheezing, coughing, difficulty in breathing; sometimes triggered by emotional stress.

**ataxia**   A type of cerebral palsy characterized by staggering and by loss of balance, coordination, and distance perception.

**ataxic**   Pertaining to or affected by ataxia.

**athetoid**   Pertaining to or affected by athetosis.

**athetosis**   A type of cerebral palsy characterized by continuous extraneous involuntary movements that increase when voluntary muscle function is attempted.

**auding**   The process of hearing, recognizing, and interpreting.

**audiogram**   Graphic representation of auditory acuity as tested by an audiometer.

**audiology**   The study of hearing and hearing disorders.

**audiometer**   An instrument used to measure an individual's auditory acuity.

**auditory**   Relating to experience of hearing.

**aural**   Relating to the ear or to the sense of hearing.

**autism**   A childhood condition characterized by complete withdrawal resulting in an inability to relate to people or situations.

**autistic**   Pertaining to or affected by autism.

**awareness**   Sensitivity to an object, sound, etc.

**beat**   The basic temporal unit in music.

**behavior modification**   Approach in which positive or negative reinforcers are used to affect desired changes in behavior.

**bilateral**   Having two sides.

**binary form**   A basic musical form consisting of two sections: AB.

**blind**   A term used to describe central acuity of 20/200 or less in the better eye after correction (i.e., glasses); or a peripheral field in which the widest diameter takes in an angle of distance no greater than 20 degrees.

**cadence**   A point of arrival, or musical punctuation, used to end a phrase or section.

**call-and-response song**   A song or chant in which a solo voice is answered by a group; the group responds either by imitation or in a set pattern.

**canon**   A composition in which two or more voices have the same melody and rhythm, but enter in succession instead of simultaneously.

**cataract**   An opacity or density of the eye lens that may cause partial or total blindness.

**catastrophic reaction**   Sudden loss of control for no apparent reason.

**central nervous system (CNS)**   The brain and the spinal cord.

**cerebral palsy (CP)**   Muscular incoordination due to brain damage. *See* ataxia, athetosis, hypotonic, rigidity, spasticity.

**chronic**   Characterized by long duration or frequent recurrence.

**chronological age (CA)**   Age in years.

**coda**   Italian word meaning "tail"; the closing section of a composition.

**cognitive**   Pertaining to the act or faculty of knowing or perceiving, as in *cognitive behavior.*

**concept**   A mental image of an action or a thing; a thought, opinion, or idea, as distinguished from a percept.

**conceptual reasoning**   Categorical reasoning; reasoning pertaining to concepts.

**concerto grosso**   Typically baroque concerto for a small group of solo players and full orchestra.

**conductive hearing loss**   Hearing impairment due to dysfunction of outer or middle ear.

**congenital**   Existing at birth.

**convulsive disorders**   Transient episodes usually involving a change in the state of consciousness; also known as convulsions, seizures, fits, epilepsy.

**covert behavior**   Behavior that is not obvious.

**crescendo**   Growing gradually louder.

**cross extension pattern** or **cross lateral pattern** A set of movements in which an extremity crosses the midline of the body (e.g., patsch on left knee with right hand).

**cumulative song** A type of sequencing song in which each verse is longer than the one before it. The verses become longer by repeating portions of the preceding verses in reverse order.

**cystic fibrosis** An inherited childhood disease characterized by functional failure of glands that secrete mucus and digestive ferments; involves lungs, liver, pancreas, and many other organs.

**decibel (db)** A unit for measuring differences in the intensity of sound.

**decoding** The ability to understand written or spoken language. *See also* receptive aphasia.

**decrescendo** Growing gradually softer.

**deficiency** or **deficit** An inadequacy, defect, shortage.

**delayed speech** Below-average speech development due to slower rate of language acquisition; especially associated with retarded, culturally deprived, and hearing-impaired children.

**developmental aphasia** The inability of a child to develop language during the developmental period.

**diatonic scale** Any natural scale consisting of five whole tones and two semitones as produced on the white keys of a keyboard. Diatonic scales may be built on any pitch, using the same patterns of whole tones and semitones.

**diminuendo** *See* decrescendo.

**diplegia** Paralysis of both sides of the body; the lower limbs are usually more involved than the upper.

**directionality** The sense of direction in space (up, down, right, left, etc.).

**discrimination** The ability to comprehend differences or distinctions.

**distractibility** An inability to maintain attention to a stimulus or task presented; the uninhibited response to external stimuli.

**Down's Syndrome** A genetic defect sometimes (but not always) characterized by slanting eyes, flattened skull, stubby fingers, and by retardation ranging from very mild to profound. Also known as mongolism.

**dysarthria** Neuromuscular impairment of articulators, interfering with the production of speech.

**dysfunction** Impaired functioning.

**dyslexia** A neurological dysfunction that causes reading difficulties.

**echo song** A type of song in which words or phrases are imitated exactly.

**echolalia** Automatic reiteration of words or phrases, usually those that have just been heard.

**educable mentally retarded (EMR)** Mildly mentally retarded individuals who are able to acquire functional literacy and social competence through special education.

**emotional instability** Unstable emotional control ranging from apathy and depression to irritability and tantrums.

**encephalitis** Inflammation of the brain or its membranes.

**encoding** The ability to express oneself through written or spoken language. *See also* expressive aphasia.

**enuresis** Incontinence of urine; bedwetting.

**epilepsy** *See* convulsive disorders.

**etiology** The cause of an abnormal condition; the study of such a cause.

**experiential** Relating to, or based upon, direct experiment or experience; empirical.

**expressive aphasia** The inability to express oneself in spoken or written language, or even through gesture. *See* receptive aphasia.

**figure-ground perception** The ability to attend to one aspect of the visual or auditory field while perceiving it in relation to the rest of the field.

**fine motor** Referring to the activity of small muscle groups.

**form** In music, organization or structure.

**found sounds** Sounds found in the environment.

**frustration** The inability to gratify a desire, to satisfy a wish, or to attain a purpose.

**gestalt** A term designating an undivided articulate whole, the nature of whose elements depend on their relationship to the whole.

**gross motor** Referring to the activity of large muscle groups.

**hard of hearing** A term used to describe those in whom the sense of hearing, although defective, is functional with or without a hearing aid.

**hearing** As distinguished from listening, the process of receiving sound.

**hemiplegia** Paralysis of one side of the body.

**hertz (HZ)** A unit of frequency equal to one cycle per second.

**homonyms** Words that are spelled the same but have different meanings.

**hydrocephalic** *See* hydrocephalus.

**hydrocephalus** A condition in which the head becomes enlarged due to accumulation of spinal fluid in the brain. The subsequent pressure may increase to such a point that the cranial organs are damaged, resulting in retardation. *See* shunt.

**hyperactivity** Excessive and uncontrollable movements or activity without purpose.

**hyperirritable** *See* distractibility.

**hyperkinetic** Having excessive and uncontrollable movements; hyperactive.

**hypoactivity** An abnormally low level of activity.

**hypotonic** A term given to a type of cerebral palsy usually associated with very young children. Lack of muscle tone results in floppy or rag-doll movements; child usually matures in athetoid or rigid manner.

**incontinence** Inability to control urination and/or defecation.

**Individualized Educational Program (IEP)** As required of schools by the Education for All Handicapped Children Act (P. L. 94—142), a written statement, drawn up annually for each handicapped child, that describes goals and objectives based on present educational performance and developing needs. The statement must be written with the help and approval of the child's parents and must describe specific services to be provided, as well as evaluation criteria.

**integrative learning** The type of learning in which all modality systems function simultaneously, working together as a unit. Also the process of incorporating input stimuli with previously learned information.

**intelligence** The power or act of understanding.

**interval** The distance in pitch between two tones.

**kinesthetic perception** Muscle sense; the sense stimulated by bodily movement and tension.

**lability** Instability in emotions or behavior.

**lateral dominance** The tendency for one hemisphere of the brain to be dominant over the other for most functions.

**laterality** Preferential use of one side of the body; sidedness.

**legato** Smoothly connected tones.

**leukemia** Malignancy of bone marrow. In children, the condition often results in fatigue, weight loss, joint pains, and excessive bruising.

**listening** As distinguished from hearing, the process of perceiving sound with comprehension.

**low vision** A term used to describe very limited visual acuity, usually less than 5/20.

**mainstreaming** The practice of meeting the special educational needs of the handicapped through class placement in the least restrictive environment.

**megavitamin therapy** The practice of prescribing massive doses of certain vitamins for treatment of disorders such as hyperactivity.

**melodic sequence** Repetition of a melodic idea at a different pitch level.

**meningitis** Inflammation of the membranes of the brain or spinal cord.

**mental age (MA)** The assessed level of mental development in relationship to chronological age norms.

**meter** In music, basic grouping of beats and accents.

**microcephalic** Having an abnormally small head.

**mildly retarded** *See* educable mentally retarded.

**modality** The pathways through which an individual receives information and thereby learns.

**moderately retarded** *See* trainable mentally retarded.

**mongolism** *See* Down's Syndrome.

**monoplegia** Paralysis of only one extremity.

**multiply handicapped** Having more than one condition that seriously interferes with functioning and learning.

**muscular dystrophy** A primary wasting disease of muscles characterized by progressive muscular weakness.

**music therapy** The use of music as remedy or treatment; the functional use of music to achieve non-music goals.

**myopia** Nearsightedness.

**neurological disorder** A condition that is the result of a dysfunction of the central nervous system (e.g., epilepsy, cerebral palsy).

**neurological impairment** A condition that is the result of damage or injury to the central nervous system.

**ostinato** Repeated melodic or rhythmic pattern.

**overt behavior** Behavior that is obvious.

**palmar grasp** A grasp involving the palm of the hand.

**paraplegia** Paralysis of the lower limbs.

**partially sighted** A term used to describe visual acuity between 20/200 and 20/70 in the better eye with the best possible correction.

**patschen (patsch)** Slapping the thighs.

**pentatonic scale** Five-tone scale corresponding to the black keys of a keyboard (F#, G#, A#, C#, D#).

**percept** An impression of an object obtained by direct use of the senses, as distinguished from a concept.

**perception** Awareness or understanding.

**perceptual process** The process of organizing or interpreting the raw data obtained through the senses.

**perceptual disorder** The inability to recognize objects, relations, or qualities, involving the interpretation and integration of sensory stimuli.

**perceptual motor** The simultaneous use of perceptual and motor skills.

**perseveration** Unnecessary repetition of movement or speech.

**phobia** Persistent and irrational fear.

**phonetics** The science of speech sounds; the analysis of words into their constituent sound elements.

**phrase** A melodic idea punctuated by a cadence.

**pincer grasp** A grasp in which the fingers and thumb pick up, hold, or manipulate objects.

**poliomyelitis (polio)** A viral disease that causes inflammation and destruction to areas within the spinal cord that innervate muscles, resulting in chronic paralysis.

**Premack hypothesis** The theory that low probability behaviors can be accelerated and reinforced when high probability behaviors are contingent upon them.

**prescriptive teaching** An educational approach in which goals and teaching strategies are formulated on the basis of the assessment of developing strengths and weaknesses.

**profoundly retarded** Individuals in whom the developmental process is so retarded that educational programs for them must first develop sensory awareness and basic motor functioning before development of specific learning skills can be a realistic goal. These individuals require total care and often have additional handicapping conditions.

**prognosis** Expected outcome or progression of a disease or condition.

**prompting** An educational technique in which answers or behaviors are elicited by cuing the next word or response. See shaping.

**prosthesis** An artificial device that replaces a missing part of the body.

**proximity control** Keeping target child close by.

**psychometric tests** Tests that measure mental functioning.

**psychomotor** Of or relating to voluntary, conscious movements. Development of muscular action and neuromuscular coordination necessary for skilled behavior such as musical performance.

**psychosis** Extreme mental illness.

**psychotherapy** Mental healing; any procedure intended to improve the condition of a patient and directed at a change in mental condition, particularly attitude toward self and environment.

**pulse** See beat.

**quadraplegia** Paralysis of all four limbs.

**receptive aphasia** The inability to understand spoken or written language. See expressive aphasia.

**recruitment factor** Rapid increase in the sensation of loudness once the threshold of hearing has been reached.

**residual** Remaining; that which continues to function, as in hearing and sight impairment.

**resource room** Facility equipped with materials and staff to assist classroom teachers in teaching children with learning problems.

**reticular activating system** A center located in the brain that is believed to regulate the level of consciousness and the selection of incoming perceptual stimuli.

**rheumatoid arthritis** A type of chronic arthritis. In childhood conditions, eye inflammation and involvement of other organs are possible complications. More prevalent in girls.

**rigidity** (1) A type of cerebral palsy characterized by very stiff posture and movements; (2) Inability to adapt behavior to changes.

**retinitis pigmentosa** Inherited disorder of the retina of the eye characterized by color loss and progressive blindness.

**rhythm** Organization of sounds and silences in time.

**ritardando (rit., ritard.)** Gradually becoming slower.

**rondo** A basic musical form consisting of a main theme (A) alternating with contrasting themes: ABACADA, etc.

**rubella (German measles)** A contagious, eruptive disease of short duration and mild character. It is one of the major causes of handicapping conditions in children when contracted by pregnant mothers during the first trimester.

**schizophrenia** General term for psychotic disorders characterized by withdrawal, disordered thinking, and loss of reality reasoning.

**sensori-neural hearing loss** Hearing impairment due to damage along the nerve pathway from the inner ear to the brain stem.

**sensory overload** More sensory stimulation than an individual can successfully process at one time.

**sensory perception** The process of organizing and interpreting raw data coming into the brain through the five senses.

**sequencing song** A song in which the order of the verses is intrinsic to the meaning.

**shaping** An educational technique in which praise or encouragement reinforces successive steps to the ultimate goal. See also prompting.

**shunt** Surgical procedure commonly used to prevent hydrocephalus in children. A plastic tube is inserted in the brain to redirect spinal fluid into the heart to circulate with the blood.

**sociometric tests** Tests that assess an individual's social functioning.

**soft neurological signs** Neurological dysfunctioning that is mild or slight and difficult to detect, as contrasted with gross or obvious neurological impairment.

**spasticity** A type of cerebral palsy characterized by jerky, explosive movements.

**special education music** Field of music education concerned with the dual goals of aesthetic education and basic learning skill development in children, especially those with handicapping conditions.

**spina bifida** Birth defect in which there has been incomplete formation and fusion of the spinal cord, usually resulting in paralysis of the lower body.

**staccato** Short, detached.

**subdivided beat** A beat that has been divided into two or more equal parts.

**subito largo** Suddenly becoming very slow.

**subito presto** Suddenly becoming very fast.

**symbolization** The ability to relate an object to its symbol.

**syncopation** A deliberate upset of the regular metrical accent in music.

**syndrome** The array of symptoms characteristic of a given disease or condition.

**synonyms** Words that have the same meaning.

**synthesis** A whole that has been put together from discrete elements.

**tactile** Using the sense of touch.

**tempo** Rate of speed.

**ternary form** In music, a three-part form in which the first and third sections are alike, and the middle section contrasting: ABA.

**tessitura** The general range of a melody or voice part.

**texture** The relationship of the vertical and horizontal elements in music.

**timbre** The distinguishing qualities of vocal, instrumental, or environmental sounds.

**tone color** See timbre.

**tracking** The ability to visually or aurally follow a path along which something moves or has moved.

**trainable mentally retarded (TMR)** Mentally retarded individuals who are able to acquire rudimentary learning and social skills through special education.

**trauma** (1) An injury or lesion of the skin produced by mechanical causes, such as falling, stabbing, crushing, or bruising; (2) An emotional shock leaving a deep psychological impression. **traumata,** pl.

**triplet** The division of a beat into three equal parts.

**tutti** In orchestral parts, an indication that the whole orchestra is to play.

**unilateral** Pertaining to one side.

**visual-motor coordination** The ability to coordinate vision with the movements of the body or parts of the body.

# INDEX OF SONGS, POEMS, STORIES, ADDITIONAL ACTIVITIES, AND RECORDINGS

*All selections pp. 113-223 are recorded. Selections recorded in two versions are indicated by ***

# LIST OF VISUALS AND STUDENT ACTIVITY PADS

**Visuals are available for use with REACHING THE SPECIAL LEARNER THROUGH MUSIC.**
*In the activities, pp. 24-110, the following charts are referred to by Chart number.*
*(Chart* 19 *is the reverse side of Chart* 1 *, Chart* 28 *is the reverse side of*
*Chart* 10 *, etc.)*

## CHARTS—Package 1

| | | | |
|---|---|---|---|
| 1 | Violin, string bass, clarinet | 19 | High/Low |
| 2 | Bassoon, sousaphone, oboe | 20 | Motor postures (walk, run, hop, jump) |
| 3 | Loud/Soft | 21 | Motor postures (twist, squat, stretch, leap) |
| 4 | Big/Little (steady) | 22 | Melodic contour ("Hill and Dell") |
| 5 | Near/Far | 23 | Melodic contour ("There Was a Crooked Man") |
| 6 | Sounds (street construction) | 24 | Melodic contour ("Skippin' and Steppin' ") |
| 7 | Sounds (street sounds) | 25 | Facial expressions |
| 8 | Up/Slow | 26 | "Sorcerer's Apprentice" (story) |
| 9 | Down/Fast | 27 | "Sorcerer's Apprentice" (story concluded) |

## CHARTS—Package 2

| | | | |
|---|---|---|---|
| 10 | Slow/Fast; Getting slower/Getting faster | 28 | "Of a Tailor and a Bear" (story) |
| 11 | Even/Uneven | 29 | "Of a Tailor and a Bear" (story concluded) |
| 12 | Beat/No beat | 30 | Feet movement |
| 13 | In twos (beats) | 31 | Body percussion |
| 14 | In threes (beats) | 32 | Miró: "Blue II" |
| 15 | Duration: Long/Short | 33 | "Five Fat Turkeys" |
| 16 | Classroom instruments | 34 | Seasons: Weather |
| 17 | Classroom instruments | 35 | At the supermarket (sound story) |
| 18 | Classroom instruments | 36 | At the supermarket (sound story concluded) |

# SET OF SEQUENCING CARDS

*In the activities, pp. 24-110, sequencing cards are referred to by SC numbers. Some*
*cards can be used for more than one song. (* SC 31 *is the reverse side of* SC 1 *, etc.)*

**SC 1-9**

**Environmental sounds**
1  motorcycle
2  church bell
3  running water (rain)
4  typewriter
5  door knocker
6  zipper
7  hammer
8  hand saw
9  telephone

**SC 10-12**

**Instruments**
10  drum
11  trumpet
12  flute

**SC 13-20**

**"My Farm"**
13  chicken
14  baby chicks
15  duck
16  baby ducklings
17  dog
18  puppies
19  cat
20  kittens

**SC 21-25**

**"I Had a Little Overcoat"**
21  overcoat
22  jacket
23  vest
24  tie
25  button

**SC 26-31 & 17, 19**

**"I Know an Old Lady"**
26  fly
27  spider
28  bird
(19)  cat

(17)  dog
29  goat
30  cow
31  horse

**SC 32-37 & 28**

**"The Tree in the Valley"**
32  tree
33  branch
34  nest
35  egg
(28)  bird
36  wing
37  feather

## SET OF STUDENT ACTIVITY PADS

*The set of twenty-four Student Activity Pads is coordinated with activities, pp. 24-110. General and specific teaching suggestions are given inside the front cover of each pad.*

| | | |
| --- | --- | --- |
| 1 | DYNAMICS | Loud |
| 2 | DYNAMICS | Soft |
| 3 | DYNAMICS | Growing Gradually Louder/crescendo |
| | | Growing Gradually Softer/decrescendo |
| 4 | TEMPO | Fast |
| 5 | TEMPO | Slow |
| 6 | TEMPO | Steady Beat |
| 7 | TEMPO | Gradually Becoming Slower/ritardando |
| 8 | TEMPO | Gradually Becoming Faster/accelerando |
| 9 | METER | Beats in Twos/Threes |
| 10 | RHYTHM | Long/Short |
| 11 | RHYTHM | Patterns |
| 12 | RHYTHM | Graphic Score: Shapes |
| 13 | MELODY | Direction: Up/Down/Same |
| 14 | PITCH | Low/High |
| 15 | MELODY | Graphic Score: Contour |
| 16 | MELODY | Graphic Score |
| 17 | MELODY | Phrase/Form |
| 18 | TIMBRE/ | |
| | RHYTHM | Environmental Sounds |
| 19 | TIMBRE | Vocal |
| 20 | TIMBRE | Environmental: Weather |
| 21 | TIMBRE | Instrumental |
| 22 | SEQUENCE | |
| 23 | STYLE | |
| 24 | TEXTURE | |

## LIST OF COMPONENTS

*The following components for use with REACHING THE SPECIAL LEARNER THROUGH MUSIC are available from the publisher.*

| | |
| --- | --- |
| Record set of twelve 12" LP recordings | (77 18P 00) |
| Set of 36 student charts | (77 17P 00) |
| Set of 60 student sequencing cards | (77 12P 51) |
| Set of 24 student activity pads | (77 12P 00) |
| Instruments kit (includes a selection of instruments for use with activities) | (90 186 01) |

# INDEX OF GOALS

## DEVELOPING AUDITORY PERCEPTION

# Index

and sight impaired, 247
and specific learning disabilities, 238
**Letter recognition,** 56, 63, 99, 104, 238, 248
**Leukemia,** 251
**Linguistic age,** 243
**Lipreading,** 241, 245. *See also* Speechreading.
**Listening vs. hearing,** 23
**Listening age,** 243
**Looking vs. seeing,** 55

**Mager, Robert,** 18
**Mainstreaming,** 4-7, 105, 234, 261, 264
   in music, 6-7
   and physically disabled, 4-6, 13, 241, 242, 244, 247, 256
   and P.L. 94-142, 4-5, 11, 237, 256
   and teacher training, 5, 7, 234, 261
**Marland, Sidney,** 265
**Materials**
   for blind students, 247, 248, 250
   charts, 22, 27, 29, 46, 47, 62, 99
   environmental sounds, 28, 29, 35, 38, 41, 49, 50, 51, 54, 73, 98
   found sounds, 27, 34, 39, 50, 62, 73, 98
   graphic, 27, 29, 32, 34, 35, 38-40, 42, 47, 48, 51, 52, 62, 66-69, 99
   instruments. *See* Musical instruments.
   manipulative, 22, 24, 37, 55, 56, 59, 60, 62-66, 77, 83, 86, 234, 235
   radios, 24
   record players, 24
   recordings, 22
   sequencing cards, 22
   sound mobiles, 27, 34, 38
   student activity pads, 22
   tactile, 51, 248
   tape recorders, 24, 48, 49, 250
   textured, 37, 40, 62-65, 69, 72, 249
   visuals, 22, 24, 27-30, 32, 34, 35, 38, 42, 43, 47-49, 51, 52, 54, 56-59, 62, 63, 65-69, 72-75, 80, 84, 85, 99, 106
**Memory**
   auditory, 52-54, 234, 238, 248, 258
   and language development skills, 238
   motor, 90-91, 249
   visual, 73-74, 238
**Mental age,** 234, 235, 243
**Mental illness,** 257
**Mental retardation,** 233-236, 253
   and mainstreaming, 233
**Mentally handicapped**
   educable, 233
   trainable, 233
**Mentally retarded**
   educable, 233
   trainable, 233
**Mongoloid, (Down's Syndrome)** 233
**Montessori, Maria,** 3
**Motor activities**
   and behavior disabilities, 259
   gross, 249, 251, 259
   and hearing impaired, 243
   and laterality, 255

locomotor, 76, 78-81, 249, 251
   and neurologically impaired, 253
   and physically disabled, 251, 255
     arthritis, 254
     cerebral palsy, 253
     spina bifida, 254
   and sight impaired, 247, 249
   and tempo, 76-83, 87, 88
**Motor integration (activities),** 77, 91-92
**Motor skills,** 25, 28-41, 43-95, 233
   agility, 76, 77, 87-88, 238
   axial movement, 76
   and auditory skills, 25, 28-41, 43-54
   balance, 76, 77, 85-86, 238, 253
   body awareness, 76, 83-85, 249
   crossing midline, 77, 88-89, 238
   difficulties, 76-77, 238, 251, 252, 254
   directionality, 76-77, 87, 89-90, 237
   endurance/energy, 76, 86-87
   fine, 27, 34, 38, 55, 58, 77-78, 92-95, 98, 107-109, 247, 251, 254
   gross, 76, 95, 251, 254, 258
   integration, 77, 91-92
   and language skills, 99-103
   lateral dominance, 31, 76-77, 88-89
   laterality, 31, 76, 78, 88-89
   locomotor, 76, 78-81, 249, 251
   memory, 90-91
   and mentally retarded, 233
   mirroring, 85, 228
   muscle strength, 76, 86-87, 253
   nonlocomotor, 82-83, 252
   patterned movement, 87-88, 253
   and physically disabled, 251
   reaction speed, 77, 87-88
   sequencing, 31, 54, 77, 90-91, 237
   and social skills, 106-110
   and visual skills, 57, 59-75
**Muscular dystrophy,** 251, 253
**Music concepts**
   beat, 25, 33, 53, 57, 60, 67, 70, 71, 73, 74, 78-95, 99-104, 107-109
     accent, 23, 33, 72, 81, 82, 88, 103
     divided, 35
     no, 32
     steady, 32
   dynamics, 23, 27-29, 58, 64, 67, 79, 81, 82, 88, 92, 99, 100, 103, 104
     contrasts, 27, 28
     crescendo, 27, 28, 81
     decrescendo, 28, 81
     loud/soft, 23, 27, 28
   form/style, 42, 57, 60, 64-66, 74, 75, 80-83, 86-88, 90, 92, 100, 101, 107-110
   harmony, 23, 62, 75, 93
     texture, 52, 72, 75, 93, 95
   intensity, 23. *See also* music concepts, dynamics.
   legato/staccato, 35, 81, 83
   melody, 42-46, 51-53, 57-70, 73-75, 82, 83, 88-90, 92, 93, 100-104, 106-110
     contour/direction, 42, 44, 45, 68-69, 80, 81, 86
     pattern, 43